Also by
FREDERICK MERK

*Manifest Destiny and Mission
in American History* (1963)

*The Monroe Doctrine and
American Expansionism, 1843–1849* (1966)

*The Oregon Question:
Essays in Anglo-American Diplomacy and Politics*
(1967)

(EDITOR) *Fur Trade and Empire:
George Simpson's Journal, 1824–1825*
(Revised, 1968)

(CO-AUTHOR) *Dissent in Three American Wars*
(1970)

*Fruits of Propaganda
in the Tyler Administration* (1971)

Slavery
and the Annexation of Texas

SLAVERY
and the
ANNEXATION
OF TEXAS

BY

Frederick Merk

WITH THE COLLABORATION OF

LOIS BANNISTER MERK

Alfred A. Knopf: New York

1972

THIS IS A BORZOI BOOK
PUBLISHED BY ALFRED A. KNOPF, INC.

Copyright © 1972 by Frederick Merk
All rights reserved under International and Pan-American Copyright Conventions. Published in the United States by Alfred A. Knopf, Inc., New York, and simultaneously in Canada by Random House of Canada Limited, Toronto. Distributed by Random House, Inc., New York.

Library of Congress Cataloging in Publication Data:

Merk, Frederick, 1887–
Slavery and the annexation of Texas.

Includes bibliographical references.
1. Texas—History—Republic, 1836–1846. 2. United States—Politics and government—1841–1845. 3. United States—Politics and government—1845–1849. I. Title.
F390.M55   976.4'04   72–2229
ISBN 0–394–48104–6

Manufactured in the United States of America

FIRST EDITION

To Lois

Contents

Preface

A STORM TORE ACROSS the United States in the John Tyler Administration over the issue of the annexation of Texas. It opened on March 16, 1844, when the *National Intelligencer,* a widely circulated Washington newspaper, charged the Administration with having carried on for seven months a clandestine negotiation for an annexation treaty. The storm rose to new force six weeks later when the treaty itself, and its supporting documents, appeared in the Senate in executive session, only to be promptly betrayed to the public by an antislavery senator. In the revulsion of feeling that followed, the treaty was overwhelmingly defeated, and the issue entered the turbulent campaign of 1844. After the election it moved into Congress, where it generated a flurry of joint resolutions of annexation. One of the resolutions was maneuvered, by clever legislative tactics, to enactment. The issue was then carried to Texas, where, after further turmoil, the Joint Resolution won approval, and Texas entered the Union.

The prospect of a treaty enormously extending the slave territory of the nation was revolting to antislavery Northerners regardless of party. It also troubled Whigs regardless of section. It confronted the latter with the likelihood of disruption of their party—indeed, of the Union. The journal giving warning of the impending treaty compared it with a foreign invasion, a rebellion at home, a pestilence, or an earthquake. The convulsion it produced proved a turning point in the nation's history.

The background of the treaty lay in the preceding twenty years of Mexican history, particularly in an experiment for obtaining the settlement of the Texan wilderness. In 1823 the Mexican Congress, at the instance of two trusted Americans, Moses Austin and Stephen F. Austin, adopted a colonization law to this end. The law was framed to safeguard the colonizing process by attracting immigrants of mixed nationality—American, European, and native Mexican—

to Texas. But the immigrants who responded to its attractions were principally Americans. This produced alarm in Mexico City. In 1830, after an investigation, the law was repealed; instead a law was enacted forbidding further American colonization and imposing restrictions on settlers already in Texas. The law was not effectively enforced, however, and its only result was friction with the settlers already in Texas or still coming. In 1835 came revolt. The revolt developed into a war for independence; then, after independence had been won, the revolt was transformed into an agitation for annexation to the United States.

Opposition to annexation appeared at once in the United States, especially in the North. It was based primarily on objection to the extension of slavery, but also on a belief that there had been connivance in the revolt, that American neutrality obligations had not been effectively enforced by the Jackson Administration during the war. In view of this feeling, an immediate annexation was not attempted. But a recognition of Texan independence was granted just before Jackson left office. In the Van Buren Administration Texan proposals of annexation were likewise declined, and again in the early years of the Harrison-Tyler Administration.

Then came a complete reversal of policy following the withdrawal of Daniel Webster from the Tyler Cabinet and his replacement in the spring of 1843 by Abel P. Upshur of Virginia. The shift brought into the State Department the driving force of slavery extremism in the South. Annexation of Texas became the passion of the Tyler Administration.

Already at an early stage in the Texan revolt Northern antislavery agitators suspected that the separation of Texas from Mexico and its annexation to the United States had been related parts of an American conspiracy. In Philadelphia a Quaker abolitionist, Benjamin Lundy, persistently developed that theme in a newspaper —the *National Enquirer and Constitutional Advocate of Universal Liberty*—established in August, 1835. In 1838 John Quincy Adams set forth the same theme in a famous filibustering speech in the House of Representatives that defeated a joint resolution of annexation. He was convinced that the failure of Jackson effectively to enforce the neutrality laws of the United States had been part of the conspiracy. He spelled out this thesis in addresses to his Massachusetts constituents and included it in an address to the public signed by himself and twelve other congressmen, which was published by the *National Intelligencer* on May 4, 1843, and which is reproduced in the Documents. The thesis seemed to be confirmed by the subsequent annexation treaty and its documents.

The reply of annexation proponents was denunciation of Adams and insistence that misgovernment, corruption, and tyranny in Mexico had produced the revolt. They pointed out that Texas had maintained its independence as a republic for eight years before the annexation treaty was drawn. They urged that Southern security required annexation, that the British were intent on abolishing slavery in Texas, and that British success would imperil slavery in all the Southern states. Finally, they maintained that in the face of the British threat the safety of the nation was endangered. This thesis was later incorporated in the notable book *The Annexation of Texas* (1911) by Justin Smith. It also colored the views of biographers of the leaders of the Tyler Administration.

On the other hand, historians of strong antislavery convictions incorporated the charges of Lundy and Adams into their writing on the Texas issue. One of them was William Jay, son of John Jay, who in 1849 wrote *Causes and Consequences of the Mexican War.* He saw in the annexation of Texas and its dénouement in the Mexican War the machinations of slaveholders. James Schouler, whose six-volume *History of the United States* was published in 1880, took the same point of view in the volume covering the Tyler-Polk era. Hermann Von Holst, in his eight-volume *Constitutional and Political History of the United States* (1876–1892), devoted much of his second volume to the same theme, as he also did in the pertinent sections of his Calhoun biography (1882).

In the twentieth century these works were overshadowed by more scholarly studies. In 1906 George P. Garrison, of the University of Texas, published a volume, *Westward Extension 1841–1850,* in the American Nation series, chapters VI to X of which were a dispassionate survey of the Texas problem. He followed this with a monumental three-volume series, *Texan Diplomatic Correspondence,* in the *Annual Reports* of the American Historical Association (1907–1908). These established a secure base for further studies of the role of diplomacy in the annexation of Texas. Justin

Smith's volume, based on immense foreign research, was a further development of this trend, but was marred by partiality to American expansionism and nationalism.

In the period of the two world wars the significance of propaganda inspired by government became apparent to historians. This stirred fresh interest in the propaganda spread in earlier crises and suggested applying the new insights to a study of the Texan crisis. The study offered here is of this nature. It departs from the emphasis of older works on the diplomatic aspects of the Texas issue. It proceeds from the postulate that the Texas controversy, at its core, was political rather than diplomatic, and that to understand it an examination is required of the propaganda spread in the course of the controversy. The propaganda used is analyzed here in the text and is reproduced in original form in selected documents. It is presented as it appeared on opposite sides, in diplomatic documents, messages of the President, speeches in Congress and on the hustings, in newspapers, and in pamphlets. Stressed also are the tactics used in the fight: those displayed in presidential messages, and those employed by both sides in Congress in the fight over the treaty and in the maneuvers of the final contest over the Joint Resolution of Annexation.

The propaganda was a mixture of fact and fancy, of truth and falsehood, of humanitarianism and racism. The antislavery propaganda emanating from the North was nearer the truth than that flowing from the Southern circle of slavery extremists urging annexation. Certainly it was more in harmony with international trends for abolition of slavery and the slave trade, better attuned to the humanitarianism found in England and France on these issues.

In the propaganda of the Tyler circle—secret and open—there was an exceptionally high percentage of misconception, misrepresentation, and outright falsehood. Especially was this true of the propaganda of the prolific and influential Duff Green. His report of a plot of the British government to abolitionize Texas, which sparked off the annexation drive, is merely one example. Another is his concept that the British crusade against the slave trade and slavery was motivated by sheer materialism and hypocrisy. Another is his notion of a monarchist alliance between northern antislavery leaders and the British, which might be dismissed as a nightmare except that it persisted throughout his mature life.

Upshur's thesis that Edward Everett was an abolitionist who ought not, for that reason, to be trusted, was of the same quality. So was his concept, which he shared with Calhoun and others in the Tyler circle, that Northerners were rankly materialistic and could, by appeals to their pocketbook, be won to approval of the annexation of Texas. The institution of slavery, on the other hand, was not conceived of in this circle as an evidence of materialism at all, but as a blessing to society and a blessing to the slaves themselves. Northern abhorrence of the concept that black human beings could be treated as chattel property seemed to these Southerners to be evidence of fanaticism.

Northerners of antislavery instincts found it hard to stomach the sophistries contained in the safety-valve thesis of Robert J. Walker, to which Tyler was partial. They found revolting the use made by Upshur, Calhoun, and Walker of notoriously defective census statistics to demonstrate that freedom led emancipated Negroes into insanity, vice, and crime. They were shocked by the intellectual laxity that permitted strict constructionists in Tyler's circle to embrace broad construction as a means of winning congressional annexation. They found the messages of Tyler to Congress filled with misrepresentations and obfuscation. The success of such propaganda in winning Texas tormented the antislavery North. The South, in the process of winning territory and protecting slavery, seemed to have lost its soul. This poisoned the relations between the sections and augured ill for the future.

The documents assembled at the close of the narrative deserve special mention. Evidence in this direct form is essential in a volume that challenges accepted explanations of the success of the annexation cause. It is desirable in other respects. There is a freshness as well as an authority in the thought and language of a period that cannot be recaptured in the cold analysis of a later time. Most of the documents offered here are not easily accessible. Gathered conveniently, they may interest the general reader as well as the scholar. They are faithful copies of the originals, except in a few cases where elisions have been made of materials not strictly germane to the subject.

I am indebted to many institutions, especially to friends in them, for help in preparing this volume. I have received repeated aid from the reference staffs of the Widener and Houghton Libraries of Harvard University; the Massachusetts Historical Society; the Adams Manuscript Trust; the Boston Athenaeum; the Boston Public Library; the New-York Historical Society; the New York Public Library; the Library of Congress; the National Archives; the State Archives in Jackson, Mississippi; the Earl Gregg Swem Library at the College of William and Mary, Williamsburg, Virginia; the Alderman Library, University of Virginia, Charlottesville; the University of West Virginia Library, Morgantown; the University of North Carolina Library, Chapel Hill; and the Robert Muldrow Cooper Library, Clemson University, Clemson, South Carolina. I am grateful to the five libraries last mentioned for permission to publish manuscript letters in their possession in my document section.

My greatest obligation is to my wife, Dr. Lois Bannister Merk, who has broadened my research, deepened its analysis, and clarified my writing. If my wishes had prevailed her name would appear not as a collaborator but as one of the authors of this book.

F.M.

Cambridge, Massachusetts
October, 1971

Slavery
and the Annexation of Texas

CHAPTER I

The Tyler Texas Junto

O<small>N</small> M<small>ARCH</small> 16, 1844, a sensational charge appeared against President John Tyler in a prominent Washington journal. It was that he was concluding a treaty with a foreign state, which would carry the nation into disaster abroad and at home. The treaty, almost ready for signature, was about to be sent to the Senate for "advice and consent" as secret as had been the negotiation. The President was preparing to spring a fait accompli on the nation— the annexation of Texas. What rendered this project the more objectionable was that it reversed a well-established national policy. The journal printing these charges was no irresponsible scare-sheet. It was the widely respected and internationally read Whig daily— the *National Intelligencer*. The editorial in which the charges appeared read in part as follows:

> No longer ago than the 26th of last month, though our suspicions were not altogether laid, we treated the report of a pending negotiation for "annexation," received by way of Texas and New Orleans, as being probably the work of wanton mischief or interested speculation. Little did we even then dream that the influences to which we then alluded, as being employed in agitating the question of annexation, had been seconded by the Executive power of this Government, in the manner and in the extent to which we are forced, by information from different quarters, reluctantly to believe.
>
> Matters have proceeded so far, however, that it is proper we should state to our readers what knowledge we have recently acquired on this subject, from sources to be relied upon, and endeavor to open their eyes to the dark cloud which overhangs the

3

public peace and the national welfare, if not the existence of this Union.

It is now some months ago—probably not long after the retirement of Mr. Webster from the Department of State—that an overture was made, *by this Government,* through the Secretary of State, *inviting,* from the Executive of Texas (Gen. Houston), a proposition for the annexation of Texas to the United States. This overture was, at first, if we understand rightly, rather coolly received by the Chief of the young Republic. But, since the meeting of [its] Congress, the Government of Texas having been again approached— we will not say importuned, though circumstances almost justify the use of that phrase—by the Executive of the United States, Gen. Houston did at length *consent* to negotiate on the subject. The terms of an arrangement between the high contracting parties are already arranged; and, if not already done, they are to be reduced forthwith to the form of a Treaty, through the agency of a special Minister from Texas (Mr. Henderson), who is already on his way to this city for the purpose, if, before this paper goes to press, he have not already arrived.

So far as the President of the United States and the President of Texas are concerned, the Treaty is all but made.

This information has, we confess, filled our minds with humiliation and apprehension. Humiliation at the unauthorized and almost clandestine manner in which, after having heretofore solemnly rejected, for unanswerable reasons, a proposition for annexation, when sought by the Government of Texas, our own Government has gone a-wooing to that of Texas and solicited its favors; and apprehension of the consummation of the Treaty, which the President [Houston] at least has been made to believe will be promptly ratified by a constitutional majority of the Senate of the United States.

The sudden occurrence of this question, we have already intimated, is one of those occasions of engrossing interest, which, like that of a foreign invasion, or a rebellion at home—a pestilence, or an earthquake—ought to suspend for a time all mere party differences and contentions. It is a question of peace or war, of self-preservation, of national existence, in comparison with which the ordinary topics of party controversy dwindle into absolute insignificance.[1]

---

[1] *National Intelligencer,* March 16, 1844. The knowledge that secret Texas negotiations were going on was a shock to Daniel Webster, who had been a member of the Tyler Cabinet until May, 1843. The emotional effect is described by George Ticknor in a reminiscence, printed in George Ticknor Curtis, *Life of Daniel Webster,* 2 vols. (New York, 1870), II, 230–5, which is reprinted in Documents.

In other Whig journals of antislavery views, these accusations were repeated. The New York *American* went so far as to charge that a treaty had already been signed and would go at once to the Senate, where noses had been counted and found sufficient to ensure ratification.[2] A prominent Democratic journal of antislavery views—the New York *Evening Post*—also expressed alarm, though questioning certain assertions in the *American*. The editor of the *Evening Post* wrote:

> We have our doubts in this matter, notwithstanding the positiveness of the *American*. Whatever may be the merits of the question of admitting Texas as a member of the Federal Republic, we can hardly suppose that any Administration would be so rash as to conclude the treaty spoken of, without first taking the proper steps to ascertain the will of the PEOPLE. It would not be sufficient for a conscientious Administration to obtain an expression of assent from the two branches of the present Congress, inasmuch as they were not elected with the most remote view to this question, and therefore cannot be said to represent the opinion of their constituents. It is a measure involving momentous consequences; a measure for the maturest consideration and the most deliberate expression of the will of the nation; and is not to be hurried through the forms of business, like an appropriation for building a lighthouse. It should be long [kept] before the People, fully discussed, considered in all its bearings, and the final decision should be made by a Congress chosen with regard to this great question.
>
> If the treaty have in fact been concluded, the Senate, in ratifying it without further consultation of public opinion, would imitate the rashness and haste of the Executive. A strange guest would then sit down at our table who comes only on the bidding of the cook and the waitress, and without the consent of the company.
>
> We therefore question both branches of the rumor—the existence of the treaty, and the readiness of the Senate to give it an immediate ratification.[3]

What troubled these editors was that, by stealth and without any attempt to ascertain public opinion, the Administration was undertaking to reverse a policy that three preceding Presidents—Andrew Jackson, Martin Van Buren, and W. H. Harrison—had established. Andrew Jackson, though eager for Texas, had refused to approve

[2] New York *American,* March 15, 1844.
[3] New York *Evening Post,* March 16, 1844.

annexation. Indeed, he was unwilling to recognize even Texan independence until the end of his Administration. Van Buren had been positive against annexation, and the Harrison-Tyler Administration had been silent on it prior to the retirement of Webster.

The reason for the earlier prudence varied from administration to administration. One reason was constant: fear of a clash between the sections of the Union over the issue of the extension of slavery. Another was the fact that the Texan army, which had annihilated the Mexican army at San Jacinto and won a de facto independence for Texas, had been composed largely of Americans who had crossed the border in blatant violation of American neutrality. If Texas were to be annexed too soon, world opinion would be outraged. The Mexican government, moreover, threatened a full-scale invasion of Texas if an annexation negotiation were agreed to.

The issue of slavery, resurgent in American politics, had been the most potent among the forces producing caution on the annexation issue. It had polarized public opinion in the sections. The North had been willing for the most part to abide by the compromises of the Constitution, which left existing slavery under the control of the individual states. But it objected to the extension of slavery. The South was uneasy in general about the morality of slavery, but took solace in the thought that the "peculiar institution" had been imposed on it by the British in the colonial period, that it had become rooted in the Southern economy, and that it was virtually impossible to eradicate. A means of eradication—returning the Negroes to Africa—had been tried, and had proved not feasible. Emancipation without expatriation was a cure worse than the disease. However, this resigned view was giving way in some circles during the decade of the 1830s to one more positive. The new view was that slavery was an actual good, was indispensable to the South, and was above all beneficent to the slaves economically, morally, and spiritually. That doctrine was emanating more especially from the intellectual centers of the South—primarily from Virginia and South Carolina.

A polarization still more serious was occurring over the slave trade. No real difference existed regarding the maritime slave trade, which was frowned on in all sections of the Union, as it was in most parts of the Christian world. In American law it was equated with piracy. The British had been active in efforts to suppress it. They had sought international agreements permitting peacetime visit and search at sea of vessels suspected of being slavers. Those efforts had been resisted, however, because in the United States and France they aroused fears that visit and search might be used by the mistress of the seas for purposes other than the suppression of the slave trade. In 1842, however, that obstacle was overcome by a plan, incorporated in the Webster-Ashburton Treaty, for a coordinated Anglo-American surveillance of the slave coast of Africa by cruisers of the two nations; this had won approval in the North and acceptance in the South. It was soon copied by the French.

What chiefly disturbed the relations between North and South in the early 1840s was another aspect of the slave trade: the interstate traffic in slaves. That traffic seemed to Northern radicals to be subject to congressional control, as part of interstate commerce. The spectacle of the trade in the nation's capital, as well as the existence of slavery there, was repulsive to many Northerners, and petitions to forbid both flooded Congress. John Quincy Adams, more than any other congressman, identified himself with the cause of presenting such petitions on the floor of Congress.[4] The Southern response was anger and the adoption of the so-called gag rules of Congress.[5] The gag rules, in turn, were denounced as an unconstitutional interference with the right of petition in the North.

A further force polarizing sectional views was that of Northern commemorative exercises marking a great achievement in the history of freedom. The achievement was the emancipation by the British Parliament of the slaves held in the British West Indies. The act had been adopted on August 1, 1833, and had gone into effect a year later. It entailed initial costs to British taxpayers amounting

---

[4] For the contest over the right of petition in its earlier stages, see Dwight L. Dumond, *Anti-Slavery: The Crusade for Freedom in America* (Ann Arbor: University of Michigan Press, 1961), pp. 237–48, and Gilbert H. Barnes, *Anti-Slavery Impulse 1830–1844* (New York: D. Appleton, 1933), chap. 11–13. The issue dominates the diary of John Quincy Adams in the years 1843–4. See Charles F. Adams, ed., *Memoirs of John Quincy Adams,* 12 vols. (Philadelphia, 1874–7), Index.

[5] For the Southern response, see the *Madisonian,* January 20, 1842. The editor, in common with other Southerners, chose to ignore the fact that the greater part of the petitions to Congress dealt with issues which were proper subjects of congressional control, such as the interstate traffic in slaves, slavery in the District of Columbia, and slave auctioning there.

to $100,000,000 and was pronounced by William Ellery Channing, the humanitarian preacher and reformer, an exhibit of moral sublimity.[6] On August 1, 1842, he delivered an eloquent commemorative address at Lenox, in the Berkshires, in which, after describing the horrors of the slave trade and of slavery, he demanded a change in the American Constitution that would free the Northern states of responsibility for the preservation of the slavery evil. He was no abolitionist, but he believed the Southern states should bear alone the onus of maintaining the evil institution.[7] Among others who commemorated the emancipation of British West Indies slaves was Ralph Waldo Emerson, who in an address at Concord bemoaned Northern indifference to what was happening in Congress.[8]

In just this emotional period there appeared in the expansionist press agitation for the annexation of Texas. It was heralded by a widely noticed letter of Thomas W. Gilmer, a member of Congress and a close friend of Tyler, which appeared on January 23, 1843, in the *Madisonian,* the Tyler organ in Washington.[9] A prominent argument in the letter was that annexation would open an immense market for the manufactures and agricultural surpluses of the non-slaveholding states. Also, it would reaffirm manifest destiny. To the growers of cotton and sugar in the South it would be least beneficial; indeed, it would injure the South from the standpoint of agricultural competition. A demand for annexation would doubtless raise the issue of slavery. But the slaveholding states were ready to leave this issue where the Constitution had left it—with the states. Most people in the nonslaveholding states would probably take the same course. Should they allow themselves to be misled, however, by the

[6] For this discussion see William Ellery Channing, Letter to Henry Clay on the Annexation of Texas [August 1, 1837], in William Ellery Channing, *Works,* 6 vols. (Boston, 1866), II, 181–260. "I know not that history records [another] national act so disinterested, so sublime." *Ibid.,* p. 212.

[7] The address was delivered in Lenox shortly before his death. Its effect on the audience is described in William H. Channing, *Life of William Ellery Channing* (Boston, 1890), pp. 689–91; also in Mary E. Dewey, ed., *Life and Letters of Catharine M. Sedgwick* (New York, 1871), pp. 282–3. The address is published in Channing, *Works,* VI, 379–420.

[8] Ralph W. Emerson, *Complete Works,* 12 vols. (Boston: Houghton Mifflin, 1904), XI, 97–147. For an account of commemorative exercises in Boston on July 29, 1844, with a letter written by John Quincy Adams for the occasion, see New York *Tribune,* August 5, 1844.

[9] The letter was initially published in the Baltimore *Republican and Argus,* January 19, 1843. It was republished in the *Madisonian,* January 23, 1843.

fanatical and criminal spirit of the abolitionists, the Union would be dissolved. As for the constitutionality of acquiring Texas, the issue would not need to arise. The acquisition of Louisiana and Florida had reduced that question to a mere issue of expediency.

This letter drew an echoing one on February 12, 1843, from Andrew Jackson, who vigorously seconded Gilmer's arguments and added others, such as the dangers to the nation of allowing Texas to drift into the arms of the British. In view of the quiet which still prevailed on the Texas issue, the Old Hero's letter was stored for publication until March, 1844, when the climate for its reception had improved.[10] In the meantime a steady flow of editorials urging annexation appeared in the *Madisonian* in the autumn and winter of 1843–4, which contained a suspiciously large amount of inside diplomatic information. Those editorials coincided in time with the appointment of Abel P. Upshur to the secretaryship of state in the Tyler Cabinet.

In February, 1844, another journalistic sensation occurred with the appearance in the expansionist press of a *Letter of Mr. Walker of Mississippi, Relative to the Annexation of Texas.* Mr. Walker was a senator from Mississippi and the most active member in the Senate of the crusade for Texas. His *Letter* was designed to win Northerners to the cause by demonstrating to them that annexation was the surest and most peaceful mode of solving the slavery and race problems. Annexation would draw slaves to Texas from all the worn-out lands in the South. Then, after Texas, too, was worn out, the planters, faced with bankruptcy, would emancipate their slaves, who would simply cross the Rio Grande into Mexico. This was the "safety-valve" argument. Appeals were also made in the *Letter* to Northern concern for the pocketbook and to Northern anti-British prejudice.[11]

The *Letter* ran rampant across the North. It was said to have circulated, in newspapers and pamphlets, by the million. A "Texas Fund," established in Washington by rich Southerners and speculators in Texas lands, facilitated its circulation, and so did an ex-

[10] John S. Bassett, ed., *Correspondence of Andrew Jackson,* 7 vols. (Washington: Carnegie Institution, 1926–35), VI, 201–2.

[11] The *Letter* is reproduced in facsimile in Frederick Merk, *Fruits of Propaganda in the Tyler Administration* (Cambridge: Harvard University Press, 1971), pp. 221–52.

tensive use—not to say abuse—of the Senator's franking privilege in sending out the *Letter* in pamphlet form. The *Letter* was effective with hesitating Northern Democrats.

Proannexation propaganda called out antiannexation replies. One came from John Quincy Adams, "An Address to the People of the Free States," drawn up on March 3, 1843. It had been formulated shortly before as a set of resolutions for the Committee on Foreign Affairs of the House, of which Adams was chairman, but had been rejected. In it Adams described the open violation of American neutrality that had occurred during the Texan war for independence. He acidly cited the spread of the new Southern doctrine that slavery was a positive good, and the argument of Gilmer that the addition of Texas to the Union would not violate the Constitution even in the eyes of a strict constructionist. He declared the purpose of the drive for annexation to be the increase of the slave power in Congress. He pronounced annexation identical with dissolution of the Union. Thirteen members of Congress signed the "Address," and the number was later increased to twenty-one.[12]

Webster joined the ranks of the antiannexationists after his retirement from the Tyler Cabinet. On January 23, 1844, in a letter to the citizens of Worcester, he came out flatly against the thesis that the annexation of Texas was constitutionally permissible. He drew a distinction between acquiring colonial possessions of foreign states, such as Louisiana or Florida, and adding a complete nation to the Union, such as Texas, encumbered with treaty obligations and institutions of its own. He warned against the overextension of the national domain, being urged by crusaders of manifest destiny, and cited the admonition of an ancient Spartan to his countrymen: "You have a Sparta, embellish it!"[13] He refrained from aggressively drawing the slavery question into his letter, but called attention to an address he had made in New York City on March 15, 1837, in which he had expressed himself on the issue of the extension of slave territory in no uncertain terms.[14]

More indicative of grass-roots feeling against annexation in dedi-

[12] Adams, *Memoirs,* XI, 330 (February 28, 1843); also in *Niles' Register,* 64 (1843), 173–5, 284.

[13] Daniel Webster, *Writings and Speeches,* 18 vols. (Boston: Little, Brown, 1903), XVI, 418–26.

[14] *Ibid.,* II, 204–7. This is the Niblo's Saloon speech.

cated antislavery circles was the crescendo of denunciation that greeted the Walker *Letter,* and more particularly, its specious thesis that annexation would establish a "safety valve" drawing slaves and race problems into Mexico in the not-distant future. Examples of resounding replies were those of Theodore Sedgwick in the New York *Evening Post* and Horace Greeley in the New York *Tribune.* Sedgwick pronounced the Walker thesis one of the most extraordinary for boldness ever put forth. He declared that slavery would come to an end only if new lands were kept closed to it, that to open new lands to it would extend its life by affording slavebreeders new markets.[15] Greeley declared the thesis was intended to drug the conscience of those who wanted to believe they could vote for annexation without incurring the guilt of extending human slavery.[16] Northern feeling found vent also in disgust with the *Letter*'s harping on the dangers of a British take-over in Texas unless it were annexed.[17] Had it been suspected that the Tyler Administration was engaged at the time in a negotiation for a treaty of annexation under cover of all this propaganda, the antislavery public would have exhibited sooner than it did the excitement that the *National Intelligencer* betrayed in its warning of March 16, 1844.

But how could the Tyler Administration have brought itself under these conditions to enter into a secret discussion with the Texans, in the summer and autumn of 1843, designed to lead to a treaty of annexation? What crisis required a venture so dangerous? The answer is that the secretary of state, Abel P. Upshur, received from an American agent in London in July, 1843, "authentic" word of a British "plot" to abolitionize Texas, and at about the same time received verbal notice from the Texan minister in Washington that his government was suspending consideration of the question of annexation of Texas to the United States.[18]

[15] The articles were republished in April, 1844, as a pamphlet, *Thoughts on the Proposed Annexation of Texas to the United States* (New York, 1844).

[16] New York *Tribune,* November 27, 1844.

[17] Merk, *Fruits of Propaganda,* pp. 32–3.

[18] For an account of the "authentic" word sent to Upshur, see Upshur to Murphy, August 8, 1843, in *Senate Documents,* 28 Cong., 1 sess. (ser. 435), no. 341, 18–19 (hereafter cited as *Sen. Doc.*). For the notice by the Texan minister to Upshur, see Van Zandt to Jones, September 18, 1843, in George P. Garrison, ed., *Diplomatic Correspondence of the Republic of Texas:* American Historical Association *Report* [hereafter cited as *A.H.A. Report*], 1908 (Washington, 1911),

The British "plot" implicated Lord Aberdeen, the secretary for foreign affairs. He was alleged to have promised a government guarantee of interest on a loan to Texas on condition that the Texan government would abolish slavery. News of the "plot" had come from a letter to Upshur, written by Duff Green in London, of which only an undated fragment in a copy remains. The fragment is as follows:

> I learn, from a source entitled to the fullest confidence, that there is now here a Mr. Andrews, deputed by the abolitionists of Texas, to negotiate with the British Government. That he has seen Lord Aberdeen, and submitted his *projet* for the abolition of slavery in Texas; which is, that there shall be organized a company in England, who shall advance a sum sufficient to pay for the slaves now in Texas, and receive in payment Texas lands; that the sum thus advanced shall be paid over as an indemnity for the abolition of slavery; and I am authorized by the Texan minister [Ashbel Smith] to say to you, that Lord Aberdeen has agreed that the British Government will guaranty the payment of the interest on this loan, upon condition that the Texan Government will abolish slavery.[19]

This exciting news, which Green sent also to the President and to Calhoun,[20] was forwarded by Upshur in haste to W. S. Murphy, the American chargé d'affaires in Texas. He did not disclose the name of his informant, but described him as a private citizen of Maryland:

> He is a man of great intelligence, and well versed in public affairs. Hence I have every reason to confide in the correctness of his conclusions. There is, however, some difficulty in understanding the terms of the proposition as he has given them. If the money to be advanced is to be repaid in Texan lands, it can scarcely be regarded as a loan, and of course there is no necessity for any guarantee on the part of the English Government. I think it probable that alternative propositions have been made: the one for an advance to be

---

II (1), 207–10. Van Zandt reported in this letter that he had verbally informed Upshur of his government's instructions of July 6 suspending consideration of the subject of annexation.

[19] Upshur to Murphy, August 8, 1843, in *Sen. Doc.*, 28 Cong., 1 sess. (ser. 435), no. 341, 18–19.

[20] Green to Calhoun, August 2, 1843, in James F. Jameson, ed., *Correspondence of John C. Calhoun*, in A.H.A. *Report*, 1899, II, 846–9. The letter is misdated in the *Report;* the "1842" should be 1843. Green's letter to President Tyler (July 3, 1843), in transcript form, is in O. P. Chitwood Papers, University of West Virginia Library, Morgantown. See Documents.

repaid in lands, and the other for a loan to be guaranteed by the English Government. But, whatever the precise terms of the proposition may be, there seems to be no doubt as to the object in view, and none that the English Government has offered its co-operation.[21]

Murphy was directed to watch narrowly the development of British relations with Texas. The consequences of the abolition of slavery in Texas upon slavery in the United States were grimly described. "Few calamities can be fal [*sic*] this country more to be deplored than the establishment of a predominant British influence and the abolition of domestic slavery in Texas." Four days after this dispatch had gone off, the Texan agent in Washington, Isaac Van Zandt, who greatly desired annexation, wrote privately to Anson Jones, the Texan secretary of state, of Upshur's zeal on behalf of Texas: "Mr. Upshur, I think, is disposed to act up to my most sanguine expectations in relation to Texas."[22]

Duff Green, the London author of the letter to Upshur, was an intimate of Tyler, whom he had helped to win the nomination to the Harrison-Tyler ticket in 1840. He was no mere private citizen of Maryland in 1843 when he wrote his warning. He had been sent as executive agent by Tyler to arrange, if possible, a negotiation in Washington for a reciprocal lowering of tariffs and other matters. He had made little progress in effecting that project, and his letter to Upshur was the principal fruit of his labors. Earlier, in 1841, he had been sent by Tyler as executive agent on a similar commercial mission to England and France and had remained there for the greater part of a year with similarly disappointing results. He had labored in Paris, in collaboration with Lewis Cass, American minister to France, to defeat ratification of the Quintuple Treaty for suppression of the maritime slave trade, which Guizot, the French premier, had approved. He helped to defeat ratification of that treaty by the French Chamber of Deputies, a principal reward of his European sojourn.

Green was a man of unusual energy and diversity of interests. He was owner and editor of a succession of newspapers in St. Louis, Washington, and New York. He was a land speculator and entre-

---

[21] See n. 19.

[22] Van Zandt to Jones, August 12, 1843, in Anson Jones, *Memoranda and Official Correspondence Relating to the Republic of Texas* (New York, 1859), pp. 243–4.

preneur in mining and transportation ventures. In the years 1841–3 he was in financial straits, and a private object of his 1843 mission to London was to get aid from bankers in London or in Paris in his efforts to stay afloat. He was above all a restless politician and an apostle of Southern slavery. He was caustically described by John Quincy Adams, in public, in the autumn of 1843, as America's "ambassador of slavery" at the court of London.[23] He was a firm believer in the doctrine that slavery is a blessing to the Negro as well as to Southern society. He attributed the opposition of the British public to slavery to misguided philanthropy and religious fanaticism. The efforts of the British government to suppress the slave trade were, he thought, motivated by selfish economic and imperialistic considerations, especially by an ambition to dominate the commerce of the world. The alleged offer of Aberdeen to guarantee the interest payments on a loan to Texas to abolish slavery seemed to him even more clearly to rise from the economic interests of England.

According to Green, the abolition of slavery in the British West Indies had come to be recognized by the British government as a disastrous mistake. Freed Negroes could not be made to produce sugar as cheaply or efficiently as slaves. The abolition experiment had brought the empire under a fatal handicap. In order to restore equality with competitors in the production of tropical staples the government wished, if possible, to abolitionize the competitors, especially Cuba, Brazil, Texas, and the United States. After equality of competition had thus been restored, England would once more achieve supremacy by her control over manufacturing and commerce. The offer to assist Texas in a program of abolition could thus be explained, and abolition in Texas would inevitably produce a like result in the United States.[24]

This thesis was not wholly new in 1843. It had been evolving during the contest over the Quintuple Treaty in 1841–2. It came to flower only in the report to Upshur of Aberdeen's alleged promise and in Green's subsequent private and public correspondence.

Green's relations with Edward Everett, the resident American

[23] *Niles' Register*, 65 (1843–1844), 149–50.
[24] Green to Upshur, October 17, 1843, copy in Calhoun Papers, Robert Muldrow Cooper Library, Clemson University, Clemson, South Carolina. See Documents.

minister at the court in London, were not cordial. He had brought a personal letter from the President to Everett, which would more normally have come from the secretary of state.[25] The date on the letter is meaningful. It was April 27, 1843, while Webster still held this office. Green was received with suspicion by Everett, in consequence of his preceding visit as executive agent to London. Everett suspected Green of having opened and read the President's letter of introduction. An immediate difference arose over Green's desire to have a letter of introduction to Robert Peel, the prime minister. Green wished to be introduced as one connected with the American legation in order that he might ask Peel for a letter to the banking house of Baring Brothers & Company, from which he hoped to receive financial aid for his various American commitments. Everett balked at writing such a letter, at which Green assumed a tone of lofty remonstrance.[26] Later, Green returned and asked for a less official note to Peel, which Everett agreed to write, having previously given Peel private warning of the impending visit. After this episode Everett wrote the President, describing what he had done, and got back word that his caution had been approved.[27]

In the meantime Green was reluctantly received by Peel, who listened to him with civility while he discoursed at length on American fiscal history and policy. The Prime Minister offered no other comment at the end than a request to Green to reduce his ideas to paper. Peel may have had the feeling that Everett expressed to Webster in a letter: "The great difficulty is that General Green's sanguine temperament leads him, after talking a half an hour to a person who listens with silent civility, to think that person assents to all he has said, and reports accordingly." [28]

The confidence of Green in the excellence of the slavery system of the South was matched by his distrust and dislike of Northern abolitionists. Abolitionists were radicals who were disruptive of the Union and had even been traitorous in the past. They were aligned

---

[25] See Documents.

[26] Everett to Webster, May 18, 1843, Everett Papers, Massachusetts Historical Society (hereafter cited as M.H.S.).

[27] Everett to Tyler, May 17, 1843, Everett Letter Books, M.H.S.

[28] Everett to Webster, May 31, 1843, Everett Papers, M.H.S. The substance of the lecture to Peel is reported in Green to Tyler, May 31, 1843, and in Green to Peel, June 27, 1843, copies in Duff Green Papers, Southern Historical Collection, University of North Carolina Library, Chapel Hill. See Documents.

with British monarchists and had at all times been predisposed to British ideals and institutions. A book written by Green in 1866, entitled *Facts and Suggestions,* in which he made a systematic survey of the part played by this element in American history, suggests his views in 1843. In this publication he portrays the leaders of the old Federalist party, especially those of antislavery views in the Northeast, as dedicated monarchists. Among the monarchists Alexander Hamilton, John Adams, and John Quincy Adams were conspicuous. That theme is pursued uninterruptedly from Chapter VI to Chapter X. Chapter VIII is devoted to the archabolitionist: John Quincy Adams. It is entitled "John Q. Adams' Plan of Making the Government a Monarchy." Chapter IX is "The Boston Federalists —A British Disunion Party," and the next chapter is "Further Proof that the Radicals are British Monarchists." Evidence is offered by Green, from Boston newspapers of an early date, that New England Federalists had sought to excite Southern Negroes to rise and massacre their masters. J. Q. Adams is credited with having organized the antislavery party with a view to governing North and South. A subtitle to Chapter X is "Unquestionable Proof That the Boston Monarchists Are Disunionists." It ought to be said on behalf of Green that he wrote the book in his middle seventies. But in its selectivity of evidence, its sweep in defining abolitionists, and its thoroughness in associating abolitionism with other equally unpatriotic ideas, it was as vigorous as the author's correspondence in the 1840s.[29]

The crucial clause in the Green-Upshur letter of July, 1843 was, "I am authorized by the Texan minister [Ashbel Smith] to say to you, that Lord Aberdeen has agreed that the British Government will guaranty the payment of the interest on this loan, upon condition that the Texan Government will abolish slavery." That clause was what induced Upshur at once to warn the representative of the United States in Texas to be on his guard.[30]

It is unlikely that Ashbel Smith's word to Duff Green concerning Aberdeen's alleged promise to guarantee interest on a loan to Texas was as explicit as Green had reported. Smith had not been a mem-

[29] Duff Green, *Facts and Suggestions, Biographical, Historical, Financial, and Political* (New York, 1866).

[30] Upshur to Murphy, August 8, 1843, in *Sen. Doc.,* 28 Cong., 1 sess. (ser. 435), no. 341, 18–19.

16

ber of the group to which Aberdeen made the alleged promise. He had learned of it from an abolitionist, none too reliable, who had been in the party. A month later Smith wrote his government, after a conference with Aberdeen that allayed his suspicions as to British policy in Texas, a more guarded statement about the promise, as will appear. However, on July 2, 1843, he did unquestionably write his government an unguarded letter that could be misinterpreted.[31]

Upshur's immediate acceptance of an unverified report and his hasty course of action on the basis of it seem strange for a secretary of state. Green, after all, was not the minister of the United States in London, and his report was intrinsically of dubious accuracy. An individual member of the British Cabinet does not make to a visiting delegation of abolitionists an offhand promise of a government guarantee of interest on a loan to be made to a foreign state. Such a promise comes necessarily after sanction by the Cabinet as a whole or by Parliament itself, and Upshur, as an historian of constitutional developments, should have known this. What is equally difficult to understand is that Upshur, as secretary of state, did not attempt to verify the Green report before opening discussions with Texas designed to lead to a treaty negotiation. The same questions arise as to the course of President Tyler.

The answer to the first of these questions may be that Upshur considered the annexation of Texas indispensable to the protection of Southern slavery, which in turn was indispensable to the South. He agreed with the view eloquently set forth by Professor Thomas Roderick Dew, of the College of William and Mary, that slavery not only is required by the South but is in itself a beneficent institution. Dew had written in 1831–2 a eulogy of slavery as a historical development in a review of the recent debate in the Virginia legislature on the issue of state emancipation.[32] Upshur also fully agreed with an elaborate defense of slavery written by Chancellor William Harper of South Carolina in 1837: a *Memoir on Slavery*, which is considered by historians one of the most important of the pro-

---

[31] Ashbel Smith to Anson Jones, July 2, 1843, in A.H.A. *Report,* 1908, II (2), 1099–1103.

[32] Thomas R. Dew, *Review of the Debate on the Abolition of Slavery in the Virginia Legislature, 1831–1832* (Richmond, 1832). The essay was republished by Duff Green in his Washington *Political Register,* October 16, 1833.

slavery arguments appearing in that period.[33] An appreciative review and extension of the argument of these two scholars was written by Upshur himself in the *Southern Literary Messenger* of October, 1839.[34] Dew, he thought, had well traced the evolution of slavery to its sources; Harper had considered slavery with reference to its moral influences; and Upshur, in his article, dealt with it in its political bearings. Slavery, Upshur wrote, is the normal state of the black man; it reflects an ordinance of God. Any attempt at emancipation would interfere with the laws of nature. Slavery is essential to the agriculture of the South and is the true foundation of Southern democracy. It has the great political value of giving Southern whites, however poor, a sense of superiority to the blacks. It creates a sense of white equality, dignity, and self-respect necessary to a true democracy. These views were, of course, known to Tyler, who nominated him in June, 1843, as secretary of state to succeed Webster.

Upshur had another reason for taking seriously the "alert" Green had sent him. Green was a Southerner and watchful of Southern interests. Edward Everett was a New Englander, not to be trusted to protect the interests of the South with regard to slavery and Texas. Upshur's opinion of Everett is indicated in a confidential letter critical of Tyler's appointments, written to a close friend, Judge N. Beverley Tucker of Virginia, on August 7, 1841, when Everett was named minister to England:

> The present condition of the country imperiously requires that a Southern man & a slaveholder should represent us at that court. How could a politician [Tyler] reared & living in lower Virginia fail to see this? And yet a Boston man is appointed, half schoolmaster, half priest, & whole abolitionist! I see no excuse for this, it is abominable. Neither can I account for it, unless it be a mere concession to Webster. Let this be as it may, if Tyler has any party at all, it is that party which he treats, on all occasions, with utter neglect. To what can this be owing if it be not to the fact that he *dares* not assert the independence which belongs to his position? . . .[35]

[33] William Harper, *Memoir on Slavery* (Charleston, 1838).
[34] *Southern Literary Messenger,* October, 1839. Upshur was a boyhood friend of Tyler.
[35] Upshur to N. Beverley Tucker, August 7, 1841, Tucker-Coleman Papers, Earl Gregg Swem Library, College of William and Mary. See also Upshur to

Upshur considered the legations in France and in England the most important in the world from the point of view of American external interests. He thought that both, particularly the one in England, should be occupied by Southern men, and he toyed with the idea of seeking appointment himself to either of them after he had completed his labors on the Texas and Oregon negotiations.[36] His feeling that Everett was a "whole abolitionist" was doubtless a factor in his determination to move forward to Texan annexation at once on receiving Duff Green's report, instead of waiting for confirmation of its accuracy by writing to Everett.

But Upshur was also an admirer of Duff Green and of his views, and felt drawn to him by the family connection of Green to Calhoun. A year before the sensational report of the plot to abolitionize Texas, while Green was still in London on his first mission for Tyler and was writing letters to the *Times,* Upshur wrote him cordially that the essays "are much admired" in Washington.[37]

During the flurry of excitement produced by Green's Texas communication, Upshur turned to Calhoun for advice. He did so naturally, for the two saw eye to eye on slavery issues, and also because he owed his appointment to the State Department to Calhoun's influence.[38] In a letter of August 14, he described to Calhoun his apprehensions concerning England's determination to abolish slavery throughout the American continent, and the dire consequences of her success. In Texas an initial consequence would be the erection of an asylum for runaway slaves from Louisiana and Arkansas, then forcible attempts on the part of the owners to recover their property, then war with Texas, followed by a rupture of the Union. Also, Texas would receive decisive import favors from the British and would become a haven for smugglers who wished to send goods into the United States. Also, Texas would be obliged to accept other British favors, which would be disastrous all around.

Upshur continued:

Calhoun, November 8, 1843, Calhoun Papers, Clemson University Library. See Documents.

[36] Upshur to Tucker, October 10, 1843, Tucker-Coleman Papers, William and Mary College Library. See Documents.

[37] Upshur to Duff Green, July 11, 1842. Duff Green Papers, Southern Historical Collection, University of North Carolina Library, microfilm roll no. 4.

[38] As early as March 19, 1843, Upshur was being groomed by Calhoun to

What then ought we to do? Ought we not to move immediately for the admission of Texas into the Union as a slave holding State? Should not the South *demand* it, as indispensable to their security: In my opinion, we have no alternative. To admit Texas as a non-slave holding State, or to permit her to remain an independent and sovereign non-slave holding state, will be fatal to the Union, and ruinous to the whole country. I have no doubt that a proposition to admit her into the Union would be received, at first, with a burst of repugnance at the North; but the more the subject is reflected on, the more clearly will they see that the measure is absolutely necessary. To the South, it is a question of *safety;* to the North, it is one of interest. *We* should introduce rivals of our most productive industry [cotton growing], and should be, so far, losers; they [the North] would profit by that very rivalry. I have never known the North to refuse to do what their interest required, and I think it will not be difficult to convince them that their interest requires the admission of Texas into the Union as a slaveholding State.

Pray favor me with your views upon the subject as much at large as you deem proper. Would it not be well to break the subject to the people of the South through the public prints? Both parties may unite in that, for it is a *Southern* question, and not one of whiggism and democracy. The Southern people are far, far too lethargic upon this vital question. They ought to be roused and made of one mind. The history of the world does not present an example of such insult, contempt, and multiplied wrongs and outrages from one nation to another as we have received and are daily receiving from our Northern *brethren!!* It is a reproach to us that we bear it any longer. We are *twelve States,* and we have a right to be heard and regarded in a matter which concerns not only our rights, but our safety. The present is a proper occasion, and this is a proper subject on which to unite the South as one man. Can nothing be done to produce this result? Are there no idle pens in So. Carolina which would agree to be so employed? I trust that something will be done *among the people;* without their support, the Government is powerless.[39]

In reply to this anxious appeal, Calhoun gave full approval to Upshur's opinion that the crisis should be boldly met. In a letter from Fort Hill, marked "confidential," he wrote:

---

succeed Webster. See Calhoun to Duff Green, February [March] 19, 1843, A.H.A. *Report,* 1899, II, 525–6. The date of Webster's retirement was May 8, 1843.

[39] Upshur to Calhoun, August 14, 1843, in *William and Mary Quarterly,* 2d ser., 16 (1936), 554–7. See also same to same, November 8, 1843, Calhoun Papers, Clemson University Library.

You do not, in my opinion, attach too much importance to the designs of Great Britain in Texas. That she is using all her diplomatick arts and influence to abolish slavery there, with the intention of abolishing it in the United States, there can no longer be a doubt. The proceedings of the abolition meeting recently held in London, & the answer of Lord Aberdeen to the Committee, which, they appointed to call on him in reference to the subject, taken in connection, fully establishes the facts on both points.[40]

That her object is power and monopoly, and abolition but the pretext, I hold to be not less clear. Her conduct affords the most conclusive proof. No nation, in ancient, or modern time, ever pursued dominion & commercial monopoly more perseveringly & vehemently than she has. She unites in herself the ambition of Rome and the avarice of Carthage.

If she can carry out her schemes in Texas, & through them her designs against the Southern States, it would prove the profoundest & most successful stroke of policy she ever made; and would go far towards giving her the exclusive control of the cotton trade, the greatest trade, by far, of modern Commerce. This she sees and is prepared to exert every nerve to accomplish it.

The danger is great & menacing, involving in its consequences the safety of the Union and the very existence of the South; and the question is, what is to be done? On that you desire my views, I shall give them freely and frankly.

In my opinion, the first step ought to be a demand on the British government for explination. There are sufficient facts to warrant it, before the publick, & I presume you have others unknown to it. The demand ought to be accompanied by a forcible statement, explanatory of the danger of the measure to our peace & security, and its certain tendency to involve the two countries in the most deadly conflict.

That ought to be followed by a suitable representation to the Texian government, tracing its hostile and dangerous character, both to them & us, accompanied by the expression of the most friendly feelings & disposition; and a communication to our Minister in Mexico apprizing him of the facts & the course adopted, with instructions to baffle, as far as it may be possible, the attempts of the British government to draw Mexico into her schemes. In addition, an able minister, completely identified with the South, and taken from South of the Potomack out [sic] to be sent to France, and be instructed to make suitable representations, explanatory of

---

[40] Calhoun was relying on Duff Green's letter to him of August 2, 1843, for which see n. 20. For Calhoun's answer to this letter see A.H.A. *Report,* 1899, II, 545–7.

the ambitions & monopolizing sperit [sic] of Great Britain in this movement on Texas, and to show how far it would go to consummate her schemes of universal dominion & monopoly, should she succeed in her design. The like representation should be made to the Prussian Government, through our Minister at Berlin on the subject. The part of Germany under the control & influence of Prussia begins to be jealous of Great Britain, on the subject of commerce. All these papers should be drawn up with the utmost care, & so as to be calculated to make a deep impression on the publick mind generally, & to rouse the South should they be called for at the next Session, as they ought, if Great Britain should not explicitly disavow. In that event, the Message ought to take due notice of the subject.

In the meantime, I am of the impression, with you, that the attention of the people of the South ought to be turned to the subject, but not through the papers of this State. I have taken so prominent a stand on all subjects connected with abolition, that any movement, at this time, in this stte [sic] would be regarded as intended for electioneering & would do more harm, than good. I am decidedly of the opinion, that it ought to commence in Virginia, & through the Columns of the Enquirer, and that the opening & leading articles should be from your Department & pen. No one else, has the whole subject so fully before him, or can do it as full justice. You can have it communicated by some friend. They can be copied & followed up in the Southern papers.

I am of the impression, that the question of annexation ought not to be agitated till discussion has prepared the publick mind to realize the danger; but assurance ought to be given to the Texian government of the hearty cooperation of the Executive towards effecting it, when the proper time arrives.

Connected with this subject, Cuba deserves attention. Great Britain is at work there, as well as in Texas; and both are equally important to our safety. Much can be done in France in reference to each. Would it not be well for our govt. & that of France to enter into a guaranty of its possession to Spain, against the interference of any other power? The overthrow of the British influence there & the establishment of the French, would seem to be favourable to an arrangement of the kind. I throw it out for reflection. Would it not also be well if the West should push the Oregon question, to unite with it the annexation of Texas, in the shape of an amendment of the bill and make them go hand in hand.[41]

Here was a master plan, a blueprint for the Administration, by the master mind of the South. It not only laid out the grand strategy

[41] Calhoun to Upshur, August 27, 1843, State Department Record Group 59, Miscellaneous Letters, 1789–1906, National Archives.

but gave detailed directions for implementation. There should be an initial confrontation with the British government. Suitable warnings of British hostility should be conveyed to the Texan government. A communication should be sent to our minister in Mexico to be on guard and to baffle the attempts of the British government to draw Mexico into the abolition scheme.

In the meantime, according to Calhoun, propaganda should flow from Virginia—not from South Carolina. Leading articles should come from Upshur's own pen, which could then be copied and followed up by Southern papers generally. Formal negotiations with Texas concerning annexation should be withheld until the public had been prepared. The government of Texas should be given the necessary assurances when the time for them had arrived. This was the course Upshur and Tyler followed thereafter, with variations from the plan only in detail.

Additional reports of the malevolent designs of the British government reached the American government soon after the revelation of the loan plot. On August 18, 1843, Lord Aberdeen allowed himself to be drawn into a statement regarding British aspirations in Texas by a question put to him on the floor of the House of Lords by Lord Brougham, a critic of slavery and of the slave trade. The question was prefaced by a brief survey of Texan slavery, of the disgraceful overland flow of slaves there from the United States, and of the never-ending semiwar between Mexico and Texas. What, asked Brougham, was Her Majesty's Government doing to end that state of affairs? Lord Aberdeen chose not to answer the question directly. He did say that the government was using its good offices to produce peace between the belligerents, and he announced that an armistice had been arranged. He added what he thought the world knew—that the British public and government hoped to see the abolition of slavery in Texas and everywhere else, and was willing to continue its good offices in Mexico until an actual peace had been achieved.[42]

This discussion appeared the next day in the London *Morning Chronicle* and from that source came to the attention of President Tyler. It stimulated him to decision on two fronts: the Texan and the British. The decision on the Texan front was to give Upshur

---

[42] *Hansard's Parliamentary Debates*, 3d. ser., 71 (July–August, 1843), 916–18. Hereafter cited as *Hansard's*.

permission, to the latter's unrestrained joy, to offer annexation to Texas in the form of a treaty. Later the President wrote of that electric moment, "I remember how highly gratified he [Upshur] was, when, after receiving voluminous despatches from abroad, mostly bearing on the matter, I announced to him my purpose to offer annexation to Texas in the form of a treaty, and authorized him at once, and without delay to communicate the fact to Mr. Van Zandt, the accomplished minister from that Republic." [43]

On September 18, 1843, the good news was communicated to Van Zandt. It was received by Van Zandt, however, not with joy, but on the contrary with embarrassment. On July 6 his government had written him to inform the American government verbally that it considered it advisable to take no further action for the present concerning annexation, but instead would await the outcome of "events now in progress." The "events now in progress" were negotiations it was carrying on with Mexico for an armistice and ultimate peace, which the British were encouraging. They were likely to be interrupted if Texas would agree to a negotiation for annexation to the United States. Van Zandt had taken care to inform not only Upshur, but the President, of those instructions when they arrived, doing it verbally in each case. [44]

In writing to his government on September 18, Van Zandt noted that the word he had passed to Upshur had served only to fire him with new zeal for annexation. It had produced conferences in which the American secretary of state had returned repeatedly to the merits of annexation and to his hope for a change of heart on the part of the Texan Administration. The only concession Van Zandt had made to the urgings of Upshur was a private and unauthorized suggestion that if the American government would make a definite proposal of annexation, with strong assurances that a treaty of annexation would be ratified by the Senate, a negotiation might be agreed to by Texas. According to Van Zandt, annexation was "the great measure of the administration here," and he [Upshur] "was actively engaged under the instructions of the President, in preparing the minds of the people for it, and in learning the views of

[43] Lyon G. Tyler, *Letters and Times of the Tylers,* 3 vols. (Richmond, 1884–96), II, 389.
[44] Jones to Van Zandt, July 6, 1843, in A.H.A. *Report,* 1908, II (1), 195.

Senators on the subject; and so soon as they conceived it safe, they would renew the proposition on their part." [45]

Upshur pressed Van Zandt to seek from his government, by special courier, authority to act on an annexation proposal that the Tyler government would make and that he confidently believed would receive the approval of the Senate. But the Texan minister discouraged such urgency, and expressed the opinion that the powers would not be given unless a definite American proposal were made in advance. This Upshur felt unable to agree to, and, indeed, did not think it proper to offer unless Van Zandt had the needed authority. On this indecisive note the conferences came to an end. Van Zandt did, however, in concluding his dispatch home, make clear that he personally favored an annexation negotiation. [46]

On October 16, before any word from Texas had arrived, Upshur once again opened the subject. He observed that recent occurrences in Europe had imparted a fresh interest in annexation. Though he could not give a definite assurance that annexation would be acceptable to all branches of the American government, he did give assurance that the Administration would present the issue in the strongest terms. He was ready therefore to enter negotiations as soon as the awaited powers arrived. [47] Evidently, the "recent occurrence in Europe" was the Aberdeen-Brougham exchange in Parliament. From Mexico also were coming protests and threats of hostile action if Texas were annexed.

In spite of all this, the powers for Van Zandt did not come. The alleged imminence of action by the British government regarding abolition in Texas had not frightened Texans. The Texan secretary of state, Anson Jones, who was a warm friend of Charles Elliot, the British representative in Texas, reported that the issue "was never so much as mentioned or alluded to by the British Minister . . . except to disclaim in the most emphatic terms any intention on the part of England ever to interfere with it [slavery] there." [48] The danger taken more to heart in Texas was that Mexico would terminate the armistice or even commence hostilities, if an annexation treaty were concluded, and that the good offices of England

[45] Van Zandt to Jones, September 18, 1843, in *ibid.,* 207–10.
[46] *Ibid.*
[47] Same to same, October 16, 1843, in *ibid.,* 221–4.
[48] Anson Jones, *Memoranda and Official Correspondence,* p. 82.

for peace would be withdrawn. Upshur and Tyler, however, continued to believe that what was called for was more urgent offers. The American government had become the suitor of Texas, as the *National Intelligencer* had put it, in humiliation, in its editorial of March 16, 1844.

Meanwhile, Upshur had been moving also on the British front. On September 28, 1843, after reading the account in the *Morning Chronicle* of the Aberdeen-Brougham exchange in Parliament, he wrote Everett two long dispatches, one official, the other confidential. In both he pressed the view that Lord Aberdeen's statement was a public admission by the British Foreign Office of intention to interfere with slavery in a state bordering the United States, which, if it succeeded, would imperil slavery throughout the Southern states, and would confront the nation with the prospect of disaster. The President, Upshur declared, was reluctant to believe England entertained a design so unfriendly to the American Union, but was compelled to accept this view because Lord Aberdeen's declarations were perfectly consistent with other information, that the British policy in regard to the abolition of slavery was not limited to Texas alone. No foreign government should be permitted to interfere with the established institutions of the United States or of the separate states, and if Lord Aberdeen had not been misunderstood he had strangely mistaken our disposition or ability to counteract him. It was important to discover whether the design of England actually was to procure the abolition of slavery in Texas, whether it contemplated destroying, or injuriously affecting, the institution in the United States, and what measures would be used. Everett was directed to bring this matter to the attention of Lord Aberdeen as soon as possible and to obtain information also from Ashbel Smith, the Texan chargé d'affaires in London.[49]

In his confidential dispatch of the same day Upshur discussed more unreservedly the motives he thought were actuating British policy. Here he relied heavily on the ideas of Duff Green. The British, he wrote, were not moved by mere feelings of philanthropy in their crusade against slavery. They were acting from self-interest —to revive the economy of their East Indies and West Indies, to

[49] Upshur to Everett, September 28, 1843, in *Sen. Doc.*, 28 Cong., 1 sess. (ser. 435), no. 341, 27–31.

destroy the competition of the United States, and to establish themselves in new markets. In Texas they would demand special commercial favors, once slavery had been abolished, and Texas would have no alternative but to yield. British pressure would disastrously affect all sections of the United States. It would eventually force abolition on all the South. A flow of emancipated Negroes would occur into the North, inundating the North and producing intolerable economic and social dislocation. The emancipated Negroes remaining in the South would insist on social and political equality. War would follow and with it, the extermination of the Negroes. War would break out between the North and South also. The British would, in the meantime, come to dominate the Gulf of Mexico, which had been their aim ever since 1830. They would set up in the New World their favorite doctrine of the "balance of power." [50]

In these two dispatches Upshur carried further his implementation of Calhoun's master plan. He instructed Everett to make a demand "on the British government for explination [*sic*]." He was to present "a forcible statement, explanatory of the [British] measure to our peace & security, and its certain tendency to involve the two countries in the most deadly conflict." He was to obtain evidence of British hostility to slavery in the United States that could be used in the diplomatic documents later accompanying an annexation treaty to the Senate. To the Senate such evidence would serve as an inoffensive reminder of its duty to protect the Union by a prompt ratification of an annexation treaty. Representations had already been made to the Texan government regarding the British policy, "tracing its hostile and dangerous character, both to them & us accompanied by the expression [to Texas] of the most friendly feelings & disposition." But one conspicuous omission marked Upshur's two dispatches: reference to Duff Green's discovery of Aberdeen's promise to guarantee interest on a loan to Texas. This was not even mentioned. It had proved unverifiable. No evidence whatsoever of such a guarantee had turned up, and all reference to that evil promise vanished from the dispatches of Upshur or of others in official circles.

The two dispatches reached Everett during Aberdeen's absence from London. Early in November, on Aberdeen's return, Everett

[50] *Ibid.*

obtained an interview. He was on terms of personal friendship with his host, which permitted questioning with entire frankness. Questions were concentrated upon the alleged offer of a guarantee of interest on a loan, though the matter had not been mentioned in Upshur's dispatches. Assurance was given by Aberdeen in reply that his government had never proposed to Texas the abolition of slavery as part of any treaty, that it had never considered a loan to Texas with abolition of slavery as a condition or consequence, and that British connection with the slavery issue in Texas had consisted solely of advice to Mexico to recognize Texas in the hope that the abolition of slavery in Texas might become part of a peace agreement. This reply Everett wrote out and had Aberdeen approve before mailing it to Washington.[51]

Evidence regarding that alleged promise was solicited by Everett from Ashbel Smith also. Smith was in Paris at the time. He had not been at the conference of the abolitionist group to which Aberdeen had made the alleged promise. He had heard of it only from one of the abolitionists in attendance, Stephen Pearl Andrews. Smith had neglected, in reporting the promise to his government on July 2, 1843, to point this out. However, later in the month, after a friendly interview with Aberdeen, he had modified his earlier account and had reported Aberdeen as saying to the group that "he was not prepared to say whether the British government would consent hereafter to make such compensation to Texas as would enable the Slaveholders to abolish slavery; the object is deemed so important perhaps they might, though he could not say with certainty." [52]

Ashbel Smith also wrote Everett that he had heard of Aberdeen's promise only from Andrews. This crucial information Everett passed on to Upshur, adding that as between Aberdeen and Andrews he preferred the word of the former.[53]

Later in life Smith confirmed in his *Reminiscences* the account he had given Everett. He cited Aberdeen as having replied to the question from Andrews that the British government was extremely averse to giving guarantees of the sort in question, but if it were the wish of the *"people of Texas"* he was not prepared to say they

[51] Everett to Upshur, November 3, 1843, in *ibid.,* 38–40.
[52] Same to same, November 16, 1843, in *ibid.,* 40–2.
[53] *Ibid.*

28

would not accede to it. He regretted having received that committee. Smith added that "at no time, in no manner, did the British government attempt to exercise any political influence in the affairs of Texas, or to possess any advantage, obtain any facility, enjoy any privilege that was not equally . . . accorded to every other power in amity with England." Regarding Upshur, Smith wrote that his means of preparing the way for an annexation treaty included "inflaming the public mind [in the United States] still more by charging on the British government the machinations and plots of anti-slavery fanatics for interfering with Southern institutions, and on that government the fixed purpose to secure a firm footing in Texas and control over its policy." Regarding Duff Green, Smith dismissed him as an alarmist, spreading false impressions in the American press.[54]

The Aberdeen-Brougham exchange in Parliament became thenceforth the stock in trade of Upshur. It required a good deal of interpretation of the language used, but Upshur was practiced in interpretation. He succeeded in fastening on Aberdeen's remarks the gloss required, and this was carried over into the diplomatic documents by Upshur's successor in the State Department after his death in February, 1844.

The judgment passed on Everett by Upshur, that he was a "whole abolitionist," was never verified, though proof of it would have been important in ascertaining the minister's usefulness to his government. It appears to have had no firmer basis than had the loan plot charge. Everett was no radical on the slavery issue, as his entire career made evident. Indeed, he was not even antagonistic to the annexation of Texas. On April 16, 1844, he entered this illuminating note in his Diary:

> A great excitement appears to exist on the subject of Texas, growing out of the rumor that a treaty is in progress to effect it. I am inclined to think that the importance of this mission is overrated at the North. I do not think the fortunes of slavery likely to be at all affected by annexation or non-annexation. When abolition comes it will be from the effect of influences which will be equally strong in either event. Meantime, were it not better that Texas should be attached to our Union? [55]

[54] Ashbel Smith, *Reminiscences of the Texas Republic* (Galveston, 1876), pp. 38–60.
[55] Edward Everett Diary, April 16, 1844, Everett Papers, M.H.S. See also entry for July 3, 1844.

Everett was even doubtful of the abolitionist fervor of the Peel-Aberdeen government. On November 3, 1843, he sent Upshur a private letter accompanying the public one in which he had described Aberdeen's and Smith's replies to his inquiries regarding Aberdeen's promise. He wrote:

> I do not know that it is in my power to add anything to the contents of despatch 62 relative to slavery in Texas. As concerns that whole subject, it is well to bear in mind, that though all England is now unanimous in the general principle that the whole influence of the Government & Country is to be used against the slave trade & slavery, there are diversities of opinion and feeling as to the degree to which the end is to be promoted either by legislation or diplomacy. There are those who are willing to go all lengths, but they are not of the party now in power. It was not, as you are well aware, by this party that emancipation was carried in the West Indies.[56]

A letter Duff Green offered the London *Times* in November, 1843, may be quoted at this point as commentary on his communication of the preceding summer to Upshur. The letter was the last of a series of three to the *Times* in which Green discussed American abolitionists, defaulted bonds of American states held by British investors in large amounts (which the sharp-tongued Reverend Sydney Smith had discussed bitterly in the press), the Texas issue, the inflamed Oregon issue, and other controversial subjects. Green also brought British imperial issues into the letter. He observed:

> You will see that Sir Robert Peel places his refusal to repeal the discriminating duty on slave-grown sugar on the ground that it will aid you [British] in abolishing slavery, and is necessary to protect you from the imputation of being influenced by mercantile and pecuniary considerations; whilst Mr. Calhoun (and, I may add, such will soon be the opinion of the continental powers of Europe), looks to the manner in which that question is treated by your government, as conclusive proof that your persevering efforts to abolish slavery in Cuba and Brazil are attributable, not to any benevolent desire to ameliorate the condition of the blacks, but to a

---

[56] Everett to Upshur, November 3, 1844, Everett Papers, M.H.S. The Emancipation Act of 1833 was the legislation of a Whig administration—that of Earl Grey—with E. H. Stanley, the colonial secretary, as its chief sponsor.

conviction that your scheme of emancipation has entirely failed, and that the abolition of slavery elsewhere is indispensable to the prosperity of your colonies.[57]

The London *Times* refused to print this letter. It observed in an editorial on November 14:

The gentleman's impudence amounts to a talent. We stare and are astounded as we stare, at the mode in which this advocate and representative of a confederation of public bankrupts coolly turns the tables, and, without having, or pretending to have a word of valid defence, begins lecturing us, his creditors, on the hypocrisy of our pretensions to philanthropy, and the selfishness of our exertions to abolish slavery and the slave trade.[58]

Everett felt obliged to describe Duff Green's troubles with the London press in a private letter to Upshur accompanying his formal dispatch of November 16, 1843. He mentioned the recently rejected letter of Green to the London *Times,* which had called forth its scorching editorial. Concerning an earlier Green letter, mentioned to Lord Aberdeen in his recent interview, Everett wrote:

In speaking . . . of the uneasiness, which had been excited in the United States, in reference to the measures supposed to be pursued by Great Britain to effect the abolition of Slavery in Texas, I told him there were persons in the United States who firmly believed that Great Britain was pursuing this object . . . with a view to aggrandize herself and Colonies, at the expense of the United States in general and the Slave-holding States in particular; and I sketched to him the . . . policy in this respect, which is ascribed to Great Britain in a letter recently addressed by General Duff Green to the editor of the Boston Post.—Lord Aberdeen treated it as a notion too absurd and unfounded to need serious contradiction. He said, however, that bearing in mind the sensibilities that existed on this subject, he would endeavor hereafter to express himself with great caution, when it became necessary to speak of Slavery.[59]

Everett also informed Upshur in this confidential letter of another situation in which Duff Green had figured, one which was too embarrassing to be reported in his public dispatch. Two London

[57] Printed in the Boston *Post,* December 14, 1843.
[58] London *Times,* November 14, 1843.
[59] Everett to Upshur, November 16, 1843, in W. R. Manning, ed., *Diplomatic Correspondence of the United States: Inter-American Affairs 1831–1860,* 12 vols. (Washington: Carnegie Institution, 1932–9), VII, 251. The letter of Duff Green, referred to here, appears in the Boston *Post,* October 10, 1843. See pp. 231–4.

journals, the London *Times* and the *Morning Post,* representing the views of the Peel Administration, and annoyed with the freedom with which Green was expressing himself in the press, made caustic references to him as a "diplomatic agent of the United States" and as a "gentleman connected with the American embassy," and Everett had been obliged to send a correction to each of them.[60] Neither this report, nor the evidence in Everett's former dispatch of the baselessness of Duff Green's tale concerning Aberdeen's alleged guarantee-of-interest promise, can have been pleasant reading to Upshur.

[60] Everett to Upshur, November 16, 1843. For the full dispatch see Despatches, Great Britain, vol. 51, National Archives. The dates of Green's letters to the press are not given in the dispatch.

CHAPTER II

Upshur
and the Secret Treaty

I F THE TALE of an alleged British promise to help finance abolition measures in Texas was of this doubtful verity, why was it used
so promptly by the Administration to reverse the policy of prudence
of Tyler's predecessors? Why was it then withdrawn to make way
for another bogey just as unsubstantial? Why was Everett's reply to
the belated Upshur inquiries not awaited in Washington before the
annexation issue was raised with Texas? All these questions were
asked later by critics of the Administration, and in the absence of
answers were answered by the critics with explanations of their own.

One explanation was that the President had set his heart on re-
election and was looking for an issue. He had become President as
a consequence of being nominated to second place in 1840 on the
Whig ticket and succeeding to the first on the death of President
Harrison. He had clashed at once with Whig leaders over measures
that they thought essential but that he vetoed. He had been read
out of the party. He had then undertaken to form a party of his
own. He had achieved one triumph in foreign affairs: the Webster-
Ashburton treaty. If he could balance this with a Texas triumph in
the South, he would become a national hero. The temper of the
period was expansionistic. If the Texas and Oregon issues could be
combined, with California somehow added, he might ride this tide
into a term of his own in the White House. Texas, however, was an
explosive issue because of Northern repugnance to extending the
area of slavery. Yet there were many Northerners who were eager
expansionists and others who were attracted by the economic gains

annexation would bring. Those who had qualms concerning the extension of slavery might be soothed by sedatives. They could be induced to support their country if they could be persuaded of the truth of British intervention in the affairs of Texas. Such intervention had been just what Green described to Upshur in the fateful letter of July, 1843.

Another explanation of the eagerness of the Administration to open negotiations with Texas was the alarming negativism of the Texan authorities. The instructions given Van Zandt on July 6, 1843, to notify the American government that President Houston deemed further action regarding annexation inadvisable, and that he had decided to await the issue of events in progress, had frightened the Tyler Administration; the fright had been heightened by the fact that Van Zandt had passed this word both to the President and to the Secretary of State.

Yet another explanation of the ardor of the Administration was its devotion to slavery and to its security. This certainly was a primary consideration in the minds of Upshur, Gilmer, Duff Green, and Calhoun. It was an emotion not likely to be shared by the antislavery elements in the North. Offered as a ground for an annexation negotiation, it was likely to produce the "burst of repugnance at the North" mentioned by Upshur to Calhoun. But Tyler was hopeful that the burst would yield to a more rational attitude.

A mirror of the thoughts and hopes of the Administration in this period is the government newspaper in Washington—the *Madisonian*. This was not a time-honored journal. It dated back only to 1837, had been suspended for a time, and had then made its comeback with Tyler. It took orders from the President, and its editorials closely reflected his thinking. It gave the Texan question little attention until the summer of 1843. On July 27, 1843, it printed a note entitled "Slavery in Texas" on the editorial page. The note was an account of a society organized in England to offer a loan to Texas on condition of abolishing slavery. This comment was added: "It is said that Lord Aberdeen has agreed to recommend the plan to Government." The editor had evidently been in touch with Upshur. What is puzzling, however, is that nothing more incriminating was reported than that a favorable recommendation was to be made to the British government by Aberdeen.[1]

[1] *Madisonian*, July 27, 1843.

From the appearance of this item in the *Madisonian* down to 1845, the editorial columns of the paper were filled with advocacy of annexation. A veritable crusade went forward. Room was found for an unending series of lengthy unsigned articles by the editor and for reprints of editorials in other papers in the nation that were enlisted in the same cause. Surfeit of the reader was avoided by adding denunciations of journals which were so fanatical or obtuse as to hesitate or even to oppose annexation. A parallel course was taken as to the aspirants for the presidency in the coming elections. The one aspirant entitled to support was, of course, the incumbent President. Other aspirants, whether Whig or Democratic, who were opposed to immediate annexation or remained uncommitted were denounced. Clay, Van Buren, and Benton were the chief targets of the *Madisonian*. No other journal in the nation had as high a percentage of its typographical resources committed, it is safe to say, as this one to the causes of annexation and Tyler too.

Upshur was believed to be providing editorials to the *Madisonian*, especially the more belligerent ones, in the Texas cause. An indication that he was doing so is the frequent appearance in the editorials of knowledge and of points of view known only to the State Department.[2] One fact, seemingly unknown to the editor, however, from the autumn of 1843 to the spring of 1844, was that all this agitation for annexation was running parallel with strenuous efforts to get a negotiation started.

The dilatory pace of the Texan government in moving toward a negotiation finally broke down what little reserve Upshur had hitherto shown. As already noted, he formally proposed on October 16, 1843, a union as soon as Van Zandt had obtained the needed powers. And on this occasion Van Zandt did agree to the extent of dispatching the proposal to his government by special messenger.

Even yet the banns could not be proclaimed. The Texan government, on the contrary, sent instructions to Van Zandt on December 13, 1843, to notify the American secretary of state that Texas was not ready for the proposed negotiation, and that to give up hope of a settlement with Mexico, in view of the uncertainty of Senate ratification of a treaty, would be impolitic.[3] This coldness toward

[2] Claude H. Hall, *Abel Parker Upshur* (Madison: State Historical Society of Wisconsin, 1964), chap. 8.

[3] Jones to Van Zandt, December 13, 1843, in A.H.A. *Report,* 1908, II (1), 232–5.

the United States had been made doubly emphatic by President Houston in his message to his Congress on December 12, 1843, and by his maintaining silence on the subject of American negotiations while referring gratefully to the kind offices of foreign governments.[4] Privately he confided to Elliot that if Mexico could be brought to recognize the independence of Texas, he would agree to no treaty of annexation to the United States.[5] He even expressed bitterness in public toward the United States, and, by contrast, friendliness toward England.[6]

Upshur, however, persisted stubbornly in his courting. On January 16, 1844, he sent a long dispatch by special messenger to Murphy, which was to be shown to Houston. He accounted in it for past American failures to respond to Texan overtures. The issue had not been understood, Upshur said, by the American public as it now was. The present chief executive was eager for annexation. Reliance of Texas on England would be fatal. "The policy of England is purely commercial. Her object is to engross the commerce of the world—by diplomacy, if she can; and by force, if she must." She is bent on destroying slavery. War with her is inevitable. The peace of the civilized world, the destinies of millions in Europe and America depend, Upshur maintained, on the decision of Texas. The public of the United States is now favorable to annexation. When that measure had been first suggested few friends for it were found among the statesmen of other sections than the South. *"Now, the North, to a great extent are not only favorable to, but anxious for it, and every day increases the popularity of the measure among those who originally opposed it. Measures have been taken to ascertain the opinions and views of Senators upon the subject, and it is found that a clear constitutional majority of two-thirds are in favor of the measure.* This I learn from sources which do not leave the matter doubtful . . ."[7]

[4] Sam Houston, *Writings,* ed. A. W. Williams and E. C. Barker, 8 vols. (Austin: University of Texas Press, 1938–43), III, 459–75.

[5] E. D. Adams, *British Interests and Activities in Texas, 1838–1846* (Baltimore: Johns Hopkins Press, 1910), pp. 151–2.

[6] Murphy to Upshur, December 5, 1843, in W. R. Manning, ed., *Diplomatic Correspondence of the United States: Inter-American Affairs 1831–1860,* 12 vols. (Washington: Carnegie Institution, 1932–9), XII, 317.

[7] Upshur to Murphy, January 16, 1844, in *Sen. Doc.,* 28 Cong., 1 sess. (ser. 435), no. 341, 43–8.

The source relied on by Upshur for this favorable nosecount was his close friend, Thomas W. Gilmer, whose proannexation letter has been referred to earlier. A member of the House of Representatives and of Tyler's inner circle, he knew the secret of the anticipated treaty negotiation. He was doubtless handicapped in his efforts to ascertain Senate feeling concerning a treaty not yet in the negotiating stage, and which he could not assure anyone would ever get there. Yet he was able to find a clear constitutional majority of the Senate favoring the measure. How this was managed was not explained by Upshur in his letter, and it has remained a puzzle ever since.

In the mind of Houston, a deterrent to entering upon an annexation negotiation was unrelieved anxiety regarding a Mexican attack on Texas, an attack which would be made when the Mexicans learned that a treaty had been signed. If this could be quieted, Van Zandt thought, Houston would more readily agree to a' negotiation. Van Zandt, therefore, on January 17, without instructions from home, posed the question to the American secretary of state whether the United States would agree to station army and navy forces at points along the Texan border and on the Gulf at the request of Texas, as a protection against invasion during the interval between the signing of an annexation treaty and its ratification.[8] This question was sent in writing. It raised an embarrassing issue for the Administration. Under the Constitution, Congress alone has the power to declare war. The President, however, is the commander-in-chief of the army and navy. The question posed was whether the President could set the stage for a war by concentrating menacing army and navy forces along the borders of an area that was still claimed by Mexico.

Upshur was a strict constructionist. He was a keen critic of the broad interpretation of the powers of the federal government under the Constitution. In 1840, under the nom de plume "A Virginian," he had written *A Brief Enquiry into the True Nature and Character of Our Federal Government, Being a Review of Judge Story's Commentaries on the Constitution . . .*[9] He was fearful of what some

[8] Van Zandt to Upshur, January 17, 1844, in *House Documents,* 28 Cong., 1 sess. (ser. 444), no. 271, 88–9 (hereafter cited as *House Doc.*).

[9] [Abel P. Upshur], *A Brief Enquiry into the True Nature and Character of Our Federal Government* (Petersburg, Virginia, 1840), p. 117.

despot in the White House (conceivably Andrew Jackson) might do with the ill-defined powers given the chief executive. At the end of 1843 he was engaged in a heated controversy with the Mexican minister in Washington over the issue whether the annexation of Texas could be rightfully considered a hostile act toward Mexico, a view the Mexican foreign minister had expressed, and that Upshur considered a threat of war.[10] Upshur canvassed these questions with the President.

The answer Upshur gave Van Zandt concerning American military protection against Mexico, in case of an invasion of Texas, was unwritten. But it enabled Van Zandt, on January 20, 1844, to write his government:

> I am authorized by the Secretary of State, who speaks by the authority of the President . . . to say that the moment a treaty of annexation shall be signed, a large naval force will be assembled in the Gulf of Mexico, upon the coast of Texas, and that a sufficient number of the Military force will be ordered to rendezvous upon the borders of Texas ready to act as circumstances may require; and that these assurances will be officially given preliminary to the signing of the treaty, if desired by the Government of Texas; and that this Government will say to Mexico that she must in no wise disturb or molest Texas.[11]

In Texas the sentiment of the public was overwhelmingly favorable to annexation. Throughout the disturbed period following San Jacinto it had been favorable regardless of diplomatic maneuvering. It did not nurse the grandiose ambitions of Houston of expansion westward and northward over Mexican territory to build a power rivaling the United States. It preferred present security, and this had been the strength of Van Zandt in Washington. Its wishes were particularly evident in the Congress that assembled early in December, 1843.

On January 20, 1844, Houston performed an about-face on Texas policy. In a secret message to the Texan Congress he declared that annexation to the United States was very desirable.

---

[10] Upshur to General J. N. Almonte, in *Sen. Doc.*, 28 Cong., 1 sess. (ser. 435), no. 341, 96–103.
[11] Van Zandt to Jones, January 20, 1844, in A.H.A. *Report,* 1908, II (1), 239–43.

However, a treaty of annexation might fail in the Senate, and knowledge of the consent given to it by Texas would injuriously affect the future course of England and France toward her. If annexation should be found out of reach, a treaty of alliance—at least a defensive alliance—should be made with the United States. Too much anxiety should not be evinced for American favor. "The voice of supplication seldom commands great respect." However, an additional agent should be sent to Washington to cooperate with Van Zandt in an annexation negotiation.[12]

While waiting for action by the Texan Congress, Houston took an important interim step. He ordered detailed instructions sent to Van Zandt, including the direction that if Van Zandt should become satisfied that the American Congress would open the door in any manner ensuring the success of annexation, he might proceed immediately to a negotiation. In the negotiation the principal points were to be the status accorded Texas in admission, the Texan debt, and the public domain.

Regarding the first point, a census of the population of Texas was to be immediately taken. If the population proved sufficient to entitle Texas to representation in Congress, she was to become a state, with a guarantee of all the rights of states, including slavery. Otherwise she was to be admitted as a territory with like guarantees and an assurance of statehood as soon as her population justified it.

The public debt of Texas, amounting to some twenty million dollars, was to be assumed by the United States, together with any sum that might be allowed Mexico to liquidate the Texan share of the debt of that country. Regarding the public lands of Texas, all claims upon them were to be adjudicated, and all rights to lands privately held were to remain inviolate. The public domain remaining was to pass to the United States. A full power to conclude a treaty on this basis was to be sent as soon as proper action had been taken by the American government, and a special minister to act in conjunction with Van Zandt was to be ordered to the United States. If doubt appeared that such a treaty would be ratified, an agreement of alliance against Mexico, offensive and defensive, would be very acceptable, with the understanding that Texas would be given time to take action with some other government whose friendly dispo-

[12] Houston, *Writings,* III, 521–3.

39

sition could be relied on.[13] The combination of this instruction and Upshur's oral pledge of military aid to Texas against Mexican attack was enough finally to open negotiations for the desired treaty.

New developments in Texas gave further stimulus to negotiation. One was the approval of Houston's program by the Texan Congress, which its author had anticipated. It came on February 5, 1844, and led to the sending of General J. Pinckney Henderson, a warm advocate of annexation, to Washington to act in conjunction with Van Zandt. Another was the arrival of Van Zandt's dispatch of January 20, which brought word of Upshur's and Tyler's verbal pledge to concentrate army and navy forces on the borders of Texas for the period between the signature of the treaty and its ratification. That dispatch confirmed the wisdom of the decisions already taken and reduced anxieties regarding an adverse vote on the treaty by the Senate.

Nevertheless, the Upshur pledge had not been airtight. It was an oral pledge and might be dismissed if things went wrong in the Senate. It might be deemed a misunderstanding by Van Zandt of what Upshur had said. What was needed was a pledge in writing that could not be repudiated.

Such a pledge was easily obtained from Murphy, the American chargé, who had been "exquisitely pleased" by the progress of his hopes. On February 14, 1844, he informed Anson Jones, the Texan secretary of state, in writing that he had no hesitation in declaring, on the part of his government, that neither Mexico nor any other power would be permitted to invade Texas on account of any negotiation to which Texas had been invited by the United States; the invitation would be a guarantee of honor to Texas that no evil would result from accepting it.

> As far, therefore, as my power and authority may go, I will take care that my Government is speedily apprized of your views and wishes, and that a sufficient naval force shall be placed in the Gulf of Mexico, convenient for the defence of Texas, in case of any invasion which may threaten her seaboard pending such negotiation; also, that measures shall be taken, as required by you, to repel any invasion by land of a like character.

[13] Jones to Van Zandt, January 27, 1844, in A.H.A. *Report,* 1908, II (1), 248–51.

In addition, Murphy emphatically declared to Houston that the naval force of the United States in the Gulf easily overmatched any force possessed by Mexico. He was not fully advised regarding the land forces on the southwestern border, but he gave assurance that no time would be lost in providing Texas ample protection there.[14]

Murphy sent Upshur a report of these pledges on the next day, adding, "I took upon myself a great responsibility, but the cause required it, and you will, I hope, justify me to the President."[15] He sent along, also, a hastily written note marked "confidential," which read:

> The President of Texas begs me to request you, that no time be lost in sending a sufficient fleet into the Gulf, subject to my order, to act in Defence of the Texan Coast in case of a naval descent by Mexico & that an active force of Mounted men, or Cavalry be held ready on the line of U.S. contiguous to Texas, to act in her defence by land—for says the President [Houston]: "I know the Treaty will be made & we must suffer for it if the U. States is not ready to defend us—" Do comply with his wishes immediately.[16]

Taking time by the forelock, Murphy also sent a secret order, at the earnest request of Houston, to Lieutenant J. A. Davis, commanding the U.S. schooner *Flirt,* to proceed to Vera Cruz to ascertain whether hostile action by sea or land was meditated by Mexico. Davis was directed by Murphy also to alert other American war vessels, met on the way, to the desirability of cruising between Vera Cruz and Galveston while awaiting further orders. All this was reported to Upshur in a dispatch of February 22.[17]

Murphy's dispatch arrived in Washington after the death of Upshur. On February 28, Upshur attended a gay reception aboard the steam warship *Princeton,* the pride of the American navy, on an excursion down the Potomac. A distinguished party was in attendance, including the President, Mrs. Tyler, Upshur, Gilmer, and Benton. Part of the festivity was an exhibition of the ship's firing potency. At the third discharge of her great gun, the "Peacemaker," the breech exploded. Upshur and Gilmer and a number of others

[14] Murphy to Jones, February 14, 1844, in *Sen. Doc.,* 28 Cong., 1 sess. (ser. 435), no. 349, 4–6.
[15] Murphy to Upshur, February 15, 1844, in *ibid.,* 6–7.
[16] Manning, *Diplomatic Correspondence,* XII, 329.
[17] Murphy to Upshur, February 22, 1844, in *Sen. Doc.,* 28 Cong., 1 sess. (ser. 435), no. 349, 8–9.

41

were instantly killed, Benton was knocked to the deck senseless, and the commander, Robert F. Stockton, was wounded. The President was below at the time and escaped harm. Murphy's dispatch, written in Texas six days before, reached Upshur's successor, the ad interim secretary of state, John Nelson.

Murphy's dispatch was a shock to Tyler. It revealed that a written assurance had been given the Texan government, which crossed the narrow line between an oral and a written pledge. It put a signature on a pledge. If a Senate opposition—jealous of encroachment by the executive on the right of Congress to declare war and reluctant in any case to sanction an immediate annexation of Texas—were to call on the President for any correspondence concerning American naval or military promises to Texas, an answer could not be refused, and the fat would be in the fire. That was just what the Senate did later, acting under the leadership of Benton.[18]

The President, foreseeing this contingency, took the necessary precautions. On his orders Nelson sent Murphy a reproof. On March 11, 1844, he wrote:

> The President is gratified to perceive, in the course you have pursued in your intercourse with the authorities of Texas, the evidences of a cordial co-operation in this cherished object . . . ; but instructs me to say, that, whilst approving the general tone and tenor of that intercourse, he regrets to perceive, in the pledges given by you in your communication to the Hon. Anson Jones of the 14th of February, that you have suffered your zeal to carry you beyond the line of your instructions, and to commit the President to measures for which he has no constitutional authority to stipulate.
>
> The employment of the army or navy against a foreign power, with which the United States are at peace, is not within the competency of the President; and whilst he is not indisposed, as a measure of prudent precaution, and as preliminary to the proposed negotiation, to concentrate in the Gulf of Mexico, and on the southern borders of the United States, a naval and military force to be directed to the defence of the inhabitants and territory of Texas at a proper time, he cannot permit the authorities of that Government or yourself to labor under the misapprehension that he has power to employ them at the period indicated by your stipulations.
>
> Of these impressions, Mr. Van Zandt, the chargé d'affaires of

[18] For Tyler's message of May 31, 1844, in answer to a May 22 request by the Senate, see *Sen. Doc.*, 28 Cong., 1 sess. (ser. 435), no. 349, 1.

the Texan Government, has been, and General Henderson, who is daily expected here, will be, fully advised. In the mean time, the President desires that you will at once countermand your instructions to Lieutenant Davis, as far as they are in conflict with these views.

In any emergency that may occur, care will be taken that the commanders of the naval and military forces of the United States shall be properly instructed. Your request that they may be placed under your control cannot be gratified.[19]

The negotiations for an annexation treaty, begun by Upshur and Van Zandt, had moved forward amicably and rapidly until Upshur's death. The two negotiators had been eager for a favorable outcome of their discussions. Their progress was described by Van Zandt in a dispatch to his government on March 5, 1844:

> For some days previous to Mr. Upshur's death we had been engaged in discussing the terms of a treaty of annexation and had agreed on all the main points, subject, however, to any changes which might be made necessary upon the receipt of further instructions from your Department. I had given to him for examination an outline of the points which would be required to be included; and he had submitted to me a similar draft, in his own handwriting, embracing his views, which corresponded fully with my own in every main particular. In this situation I was awaiting a reply to my last communication on this subject. Had instructions arrived to authorize me to consumate it, the treaty could have been concluded in half a day. Who may be called to the State Department is yet uncertain. I fear it will not again be so well filled.[20]

This formal report by the Texan minister and its lament for the dead Upshur indicated the close collaboration of the two in the cause of annexation. It revealed that each deemed annexation essential to the future of his own country and that each considered a secret negotiation best suited to accomplish it. Though the matter of assurances of military and naval protection to Texas had not yet been concluded, the treaty had been virtually drawn before disaster struck, and a prompt ratification of it by the Senate seemed likely.

[19] Nelson to Murphy, March 11, 1844, in *Sen. Doc.*, 28 Cong., 1 sess. (ser. 435), no. 349, 10–11.
[20] Van Zandt to Jones, March 5, 1844, in A.H.A. *Report*, 1908, II (1), 261–2.

CHAPTER III

Calhoun, the Treaty, and the Not-So-Secret Executive Session of the Senate

Secrecy in diplomacy is not intrinsically an evil. It can be made a constructive force. It can be used, in a difficult negotiation, to create quiet compromises of conflicting interests not attainable if every move lies open to the public. Secrecy was a valuable and an unquestioned reliance of the American government throughout the first half of the nation's existence in negotiating treaties, and particularly treaties of territorial acquisition. When Tyler sought to persuade the Texan government to agree to a negotiation for annexing Texas to the United States, he relied as a matter of course on secrecy.

This raises the question why the exposé by the *National Intelligencer*, when he was caught in the act, was such a political sensation. Why did it astound his critics? The answer probably is that the negotiation transcended ordinary diplomacy. The annexation of Texas was a problem primarily of sectional and party conflict. It involved, as the *National Intelligencer* pointed out, the very permanence of the Union.

So explosive was the annexation issue that even Andrew Jackson, as President, had been awed by it. At that time the Texan government was eager for annexation. It had applied for annexation as soon as it organized a formal government in the autumn of 1836.[1] But Jackson's reception of the minister sent to obtain it was negative and revealed the obstacles to annexation. Jackson even then was eager for Texas but was aware of a sectional storm that would arise if even recognition of Texas came prematurely. He was deeply interested in the election of Van Buren as his successor and was fearful of injecting the slavery issue into the campaign. He withheld recognition of Texas until the very close of his Administration. And Van Buren, who succeeded him, was equally prudent.

The late summer of 1843 was an especially dangerous time to reopen the Texas issue. Slavery was at a new crisis in the nation; the gag rule in Congress was stirring up intense sectional feeling; a renewal of war between Mexico and Texas impended. What was evident from past history and present clash was that an annexation negotiation would be a political rather than a diplomatic problem. And yet Tyler was impatient with delay. By use of secrecy the dangers of politics could be avoided, and at the same time the great end of diplomacy could be won.

Secrecy would be useful at each stage in a negotiation. It could cover promises made to the Texan government in overcoming reluctance to enter a negotiation and in prevailing on it to sign an annexation treaty despite dangers of a resulting Mexican attack. Promises of military support in case of an attack could be made, and also assurances of prompt Senate ratification of an annexation treaty. Secret promises would lead to no outcry from politicians, who would be none the wiser about a treaty until it had been ratified.

The process of disarming hostile politicians could go forward while a negotiation was in progress. The method would be propaganda broadcast to the public. The propaganda could be manufactured and distributed without any avowal as to its source. During the incubation of the treaty, the public would be prepared to give it a friendly reception.

The propaganda, to be effective, must be attuned to the ears of a

[1] Austin to Wharton, November 18, 1836, in A.H.A. *Report,* 1907, II (1), 127–42.

divided audience. One line of argument would be directed to the Northern audience, another to the Southern. The Northern would listen appreciatively to the pocketbook argument. It would be attracted by visions of Manifest Destiny. Its moralists on the slavery issue would find attractive the thesis that annexation would automatically solve both the slavery and race issues. The timid would take comfort in the thesis that annexation would avert foreign military dangers on the western frontier. The Southern audience would respond to the thesis that annexation would render the South immune to the virus of British abolitionism—also that New Orleans would be forever secure from a British invasion based on a satellite Texas. Politically minded Southerners would be attracted by the prospect that the North-South balance in the Senate would be tilted southward if Texas were annexed. Some of these theses were contradictory to others, which meant that there should be a selective circulation of the propaganda.

A pattern is discernible in the propaganda that friends of the Administration were distributing to the public from the opening of the annexation drive to the signing of the treaty in the spring of 1844. It was all impregnated with Southern concepts. The opening salvo was the famous letter of Thomas W. Gilmer of January 10, 1843, which appeared at first in the *Baltimore Republican and Argus* but was promptly given wider circulation in the *Madisonian* of January 23, 1843. It demonstrated that the chief economic gains of annexation would flow to the North. To the Northeast benefits would flow from the vast commerce that a developed Texas would generate and also from the rich markets it would open for manufactured goods. The Middle West would have an unfailing consumer of its annual farm surpluses. In each case the thrust of the argument was upon economic gain. That was just what Upshur had in mind when he wrote Calhoun, "I have never known the North to refuse to do what their interest required, and I think it will not be difficult to convince them that their interest requires the admission of Texas into the Union as a slaveholding state."

Material inducement was what Duff Green also emphasized in his public letters and what Upshur stressed in his dispatches to Everett that were expected to go before the Senate. It was even more heavily emphasized by Walker in his famous *Letter Relative to the*

Annexation of Texas. The President tactfully set the theme forth later in his message to the Senate urging ratification of the treaty.[2]

Another theme these Southerners urged upon the North in the propaganda was expansionism. The doctrine of Manifest Destiny was believed to be popular in the cities of the northeastern seaboard and in some of the rural communities of the Middle West. Gilmer touched on the theme in his letter in the *Madisonian*. He represented Texas as the road to California and the Pacific. This was an old idea. As early as 1836 it had been confidentially suggested by Andrew Jackson to a Texas agent sent to Washington to obtain annexation to the United States. Jackson explained to him that, owing to sectional objections in the North, annexation was not yet possible, but recommended as a preliminary to it an idea that the agent reported home in ecstasy.

> Genl. Jackson says that Texas must claim the Californias on the Pacific in order to paralyze the opposition of the North and East to Annexation. That the fishing [whaling] interest of the North and East wish a harbour on the Pacific; that this claim of the Californias will give it to them, and will diminish their opposition to annexation. He is very earnest and anxious on this point of claiming the Californias and says we must not consent to less. This is in strict confidence. Glory to God in the highest.[3]

The aspiration to win Oregon was linked to the Texas cause in the propaganda of the group shaping Tyler's policy. The two causes were linked naturally, since both meant territorial gain, and at the same time, defeat of British aggression. In 1843 the process of tying the two in a package was well under way. Green contributed to it in his letters, and Walker did so even more consciously in his epistle of February, 1844. The "reannexation" of Texas and the "reoccupation" of Oregon became the leading plank of the Democratic platform by the spring of 1844.

Gains for the South of an economic nature were minimized in the propaganda. Indeed, the South was shown to be sacrificing its real economic interests in any admission of Texas to the Union. The cotton and sugar planters of the South, Gilmer pointed out, would suffer severe competition from an annexed Texas "for which they

[2] James D. Richardson, *Messages and Papers of the Presidents,* 10 vols. (Washington, 1896–8), IV, 308–9.
[3] Wharton to Rusk, February 16, 1837, in A.H.A. *Report,* 1907, II (1), 193–4.

could find no immediate equivalent except in the vast acquisition of national wealth, prosperity and harmony which would result" provided the people of the two sections would shake themselves free of party trammels. This was a common view in the South.

The overriding compensation to the South from annexation would be security—security from European, especially British, malevolence. If Texas were left unannexed, it would pass under British domination, which would mean exposure to designs of the British to dissolve the Union over the issue of slavery. Protection of slavery was, after all, no sectional concern. It was national, inasmuch as slavery was recognized in the Constitution and was under its protection.

Also emphasized in the propaganda addressed to the Northern public was the dread alternative to annexation. Abolition in Texas under British auspices would be followed by abolition in the Southern states of the Union. The emancipated Negroes would pour in a flood over the cities of the North, which would, for all future time, bear an intolerable burden of pauperism, insanity, crime, and racial disorder. The Negroes remaining in the South would insist upon social equality, which would produce anarchy and race war and the ultimate extermination of the blacks. That theme was stressed by Upshur and Calhoun in the diplomatic documents and by Walker in his *Letter Relative to the Annexation of Texas,* and it was in the mind of Jackson in his later writings.[4]

As for slavery itself, its positive virtues were not advertised much in the published propaganda. The nearest approach to doing so came in the later dispatches of Calhoun. However, even in these the theoretical aspects were not discussed—only the beneficent effects of slavery (as practiced in the South) on the health and morals of the blacks, as compared with evil effects of other labor systems on them and on whites in the North and in England.

Upshur could have had little sympathy with the argument in Walker's *Letter* that the slaves of the South would be siphoned off into an annexed Texas and then would disappear into Mexico after the soils of Texas had become exhausted. Upshur desired the permanence of slavery. But the *Madisonian* of February 7, 1844, did

[4] John S. Bassett, ed., *Correspondence of Andrew Jackson,* 7 vols. (Washington: Carnegie Institution, 1926–35), VI, 271–2.

publish a letter signed "Virginius," enthusiastically applauding Walker's exposition of the rightfulness of annexation, the manifold dangers of allowing the British to make Texas a dependency, and the wisdom of the policy of allowing time to solve the slavery problem. "Mr. Walker," the writer observed, "regards Texas as the natural outlet of the slave population of the United States, and that, by gradually drawing it off from the middle portions of the Union, room will thus be made for that great tide of public sentiment which, starting in the North in the days of the Revolution, has ever since steadily advanced towards the South, and which will ultimately sweep the colored race from the United States into those natural reservoirs of amalgamation, Mexico and the South American Republics." [5]

The safety of the Union and the safety of the "institution" of the South appeared in this propaganda incessantly. They seemed especially menaced by the British. British territories and sea power encircled the United States. At the north lay British North America and its claimed extension in the Oregon Country; on the Pacific lay California, which was included because of British influence in Mexico; at the south lay Mexico itself; at the southeast were the British Islands of the Caribbean; and British sea power faced the eastern seaboard. The whole constituted a noose around the republic. Were Texas to become a British dependency, the noose would be completed and the knot tightened.

British control of the Indians on the frontiers was a phase of this problem. It was especially emphasized after the Oregon issue became intertwined with that of Texas. The Indians of the Northwestern frontier were pictured as a projection of the problem of Indian atrocities in the Old Northwest during the War of the American Revolution and the War of 1812. The Western Indians were said to be waylaying and destroying fur traders and emigrants to the Oregon Country. That theme was especially developed for consumption in the Middle West. [6] Walker dwelt on it at length in his *Letter Relative to the Annexation of Texas.* Regarding the defense of the Southwest against the allied power of the Indians and the

---

[5] *Madisonian,* February 7, 1844.

[6] Frederick Merk, *The Oregon Question: Essays in Anglo-American Diplomacy and Politics* (Cambridge: Harvard University Press, 1967), p. 247.

British, Jackson was the expert. He had won glory in his campaigns against the Indians during the War of 1812 and by his defeat of the British in the Battle of New Orleans. His letters of 1843 and 1844, in which he pointed out the dangers of allowing the British to establish themselves in Texas, were powerful arguments for immediate annexation.

British determination to maintain a "balance of power" in the New World was another danger to American security. According to Upshur's confidential dispatch of September 28, 1843, to Everett, the determination dated back to the 1830s, and its objective was to convert the Gulf of Mexico into a British lake. This meant a violation of the principles set forth by President Monroe in his message to Congress of December, 1823. Such an attack on American security was at first thought of as primarily British. But in a later phase of the issue Polk found that the French monarchy, associated with the British, was also implicated in it. A speech by Guizot, the French premier, to the Chamber of Deputies on June 10, 1845, was cited by Democratic advocates of annexation and was skillfully interpreted to prove this. European monarchy in general was shown to be in league in opposing the republicanism of the United States.[7]

The President eschewed propaganda of the more blatant sort. That was left to the party press and the *Madisonian,* the Administration organ. The inner circle of the President's advisers manufactured propaganda, especially the secretaries of state, Upshur and Calhoun, who introduced it into the diplomatic documents. A more artful type found its way into Tyler's messages to Congress, an approved mode of communicating with the people. In the message submitting the Texas treaty to the Senate the President blandly declared, "No intrigue has been set on foot to accomplish it. Texas herself wills it, and the Executive of the United States, concurring with her, has seen no sufficient reason to avoid the consummation of an act esteemed to be so desirable by both." In the message the President reduced to the vanishing point the fearful sectional clash that, from the outset, had confounded the issue. Such words as "slave" or "slavery" or any of its equivalents were nowhere mentioned. The message emphasized foreign attacks that had been

[7] Frederick Merk, *The Monroe Doctrine and American Expansionism, 1843–1849* (New York: Alfred A. Knopf, 1966), chaps. 3 and 4.

directed against a "feature" in the relations of the states, and that, "although foreign governments might disavow all designs to disturb the relations which exist under the Constitution between these States, yet that one [the British], the most powerful amongst them had not failed to declare its marked and decided hostility to the chief feature in those relations and its purpose on all suitable occasions to urge upon Mexico the adoption of such a course in negotiating with Texas as to produce the obliteration of that feature from her domestic policy as one of the conditions of recognition by Mexico as an independent state." This was the nearest the President came to pronouncing the word "slavery," and it came in association with an appeal to the Senate to prevent British disturbance of "the relations which exist under the Constitution between these states." [8]

After the failure of the treaty, when the President asked Congress to reconsider the issue in his message of June 10, 1844, he once more emphasized the nationwide character of the interests benefited by annexation. He observed how very fortunate it was that "the question involved was in no way sectional or local, but addressed itself to the interests of every part of the country and made its appeal to the glory of the American name." He showed that annexation would be beneficial especially to the North, by "making an addition to the carrying trade to an amount almost incalculable and giving a new impulse of immense importance to the commercial, manufacturing, agricultural, and shipping interests of the Union, and at the same time affording protection to an exposed frontier and placing the whole country in a condition of security and repose."

He emphasized in the message an issue on which all sections of the Union would be agreed: resistance to European interference. He observed, "The Government and people of the United States have never evinced nor do they feel any desire to interfere in public questions not affecting the relations existing between States of the American continent. We leave the European powers exclusive control over matters affecting their continent and the relations of their different States; the United States claim a similar exemption from any such interference on their part." [9] Here again the British were the culprits.

[8] Richardson, *Messages and Papers,* IV, 309, 312.
[9] *Ibid.,* pp. 323–7.

For the day-to-day propaganda of the Administration, the principal medium was the *Madisonian*. It was more particularly Upshur's medium. Its editorials on the Texas issue appear to have been often fresh from the pen of the secretary of state. Yet the editor, J. B. Jones, was unaware of Upshur's pursuit of Texas—or at least so it seemed—and of the actual negotiation of a treaty of annexation. Indeed he steadfastly challenged the authenticity of the information of the *National Intelligencer* after that journal's exposé of March 16, 1844.

The initial reply of Jones to the *Intelligencer*'s charges, printed on the very afternoon of its appearance, was a sarcastic characterization of it as "a long rigamarole of 'State Secrets.' " The editor went on to write:

> Some of the enemies of the Intelligencer have called it "the British Ministerial organ in the United States," and whether or not it has a British spy in the State Department, in a confidential position, may depend upon the justice of the charge, and the accuracy of the "State Secrets" it purports to give.
>
> Others, again, are uncharitable enough to aver that Whig opposition to the annexation of Texas, is one of the stipulations in the "Treaty of Ashland" wherein it was agreed that Messrs. Van Buren and Clay *should* be the candidates and the *only* candidates for the Presidency. That inasmuch as it might be necessary for Mr. Van Buren to tamper with the Abolitionists, to sustain himself in New England, Mr. Clay stipulated to oppose annexation as a set-off in the North, and to hold the South in check.[10]

In the next issue the editor presumed the *Intelligencer* knew nothing of the proceedings of the executive. "If its information comes from no authentic source, of course it is not authentic." If an unauthorized person has been in touch with the *Intelligencer,* "is it not possible, is it not probable, that he has perpetrated an unmerciful hoax on our respected neighbors?" But if the President should send to the Senate a treaty of annexation, "we make bold to say, for the especial benefit of the Intelligencer, that he will be wholly influenced by patriotic motives. He will entertain no sectional or party considerations." [11]

During the weeks following the exposé in the *Intelligencer,* Jones

[10] *Madisonian,* March 16, 1844.
[11] *Ibid.,* March 18, 1844.

alternated between proving that it was idle rumor and demonstrating that secrecy always had been the rule of the State Department in foreign negotiations. He wished to know whether, if Webster had been retained in the Cabinet, he would not have won as much credit from Whigs for having negotiated a Texas treaty as he had for the settlement of the Northeastern Boundary issue.[12]

The editor reprinted a letter from Andrew Jackson urging that "The present *golden moment* to obtain Texas must not be lost, or Texas Must, From Necessity, be thrown into the *arms of England,* and Be Forever Lost to the United States!" The editor showed that annexation would be to the advantage of all the sections, though economically disadvantageous to the South; and also that the objectionable features feared by Henry Clay to be in the treaty were actually not there at all, though the editor still did not know that there was such a treaty.[13]

With the death of Upshur, John C. Calhoun, who had been the inspiration for the initial moves in the negotiation, was summoned to the State Department. He was named secretary a week after the tragedy on board the *Princeton,* after considerable indecision on the part of Tyler. The reasons for the indecision are still a subject of conflicting views among historians. The President was troubled, according to his son, Lyon Gardiner Tyler, by the intense antipathy felt by influential leaders of the Democratic party for Calhoun, and by the fear that this would extend to any treaty he would conclude.[14] The opinion has also been expressed that the President was fearful of being overshadowed by Calhoun in the Cabinet and of losing the credit, in the coming presidential campaign, for the principal achievement of his Administration, to the man who might be his rival.[15] After his retirement the President, it may be interpolated, bemoaned the emphasis Calhoun had placed on slavery, and the constitutional obligation to protect it, in the documents accompanying the treaty. Yet he cannot have been wholly averse to that em-

---

[12] *Ibid.,* March 19, April 5, 6, 11, 30, 1844.

[13] *Ibid.,* April 3, 1844. The italics and capitalization are the editor's.

[14] Lyon G. Tyler, *Letters and Times of the Tylers,* 3 vols. (Richmond, 1884–96), II, 293–4. See also St. G. L. Sioussat, "John Caldwell Calhoun," in S. F. Bemis, ed., *American Secretaries of State,* 10 vols. (New York: Alfred A. Knopf, 1927–9), V, 127–8.

[15] George L. Rives, *The United States and Mexico, 1821–1848,* 2 vols. (New York: Charles Scribner's Sons, 1913), I, 603–4.

phasis, inasmuch as Upshur had been widely known as one of the new school of slavery extremists in the South, and this had been no obstacle to his appointment. Nor had Upshur's emphasis on the defense of slavery in the diplomatic correspondence produced apprehension in the mind of the President.

A tale regarding Calhoun's appointment, told in the 1870s by Henry A. Wise, an intimate of the President, in his lively *Seven Decades of the Union,* should be mentioned in this connection. It is that Wise himself virtually forced the nomination on Tyler. He wrote that he had called on the President the morning following the *Princeton* disaster to urge the appointment. The President quickly and firmly rejected the suggestion. Then Wise made the confession, so he says, that without consulting the President, he had given Senator George McDuffie, Calhoun's South Carolina colleague, the impression that the President wished McDuffie to prevail on Calhoun to accept appointment to the State Department and that the Senator had already done so. This meant that the President had been committed without his knowledge. The President was dumfounded and his embarrassment was increased by Wise's plea, "If you do not sanction what I have done, you will place me where you would be loath to place a foe, much less a friend. I can hardly be your friend any longer unless you sanction my unauthorized act for your sake, not my own." The President capitulated, and at once made the appointment.[16]

This story was written with a surprising fullness of detail, considering that it was told many years after the event, and it seems open to challenge on the score of its timing of the events. But it comported with the reservations the President later expressed as to the wisdom of making the Calhoun appointment; it appeared after the Civil War when it was common to sever Southern heroes from defense of slavery; and it was readily taken over into Lyon Gardiner Tyler's account of his father's presidency. From that source it has spread into many historical works on the annexation of Texas.[17]

[16] Henry A. Wise, *Seven Decades of the Union* (Philadelphia, 1876), pp. 220–5. For Wise's abrasive slavery expansionism see his speech in the House on April 13, 1842, which is reproduced in the Documents.

[17] The tale of Wise is well dissected in Charles M. Wiltse, *John C. Calhoun, Sectionalist 1840–1850* (New York: Bobbs-Merrill, 1951), pp. 161–5, 508–9.

The negotiation of an annexation treaty moved smoothly forward after Calhoun's appointment. One important matter, not previously adjusted with finality, was American aid in the event of a Mexican attack on Texas in the interval between the treaty's conclusion and its ratification. The earlier verbal assurances by Upshur and the President to Van Zandt had been weakened by the Administration's disavowal of the written assurances of Murphy to Jones. The whole matter was reopened by Van Zandt and Henderson in the final stages of the negotiation. At the direction of the President, a formal assurance that seemed unbreakable was given by Calhoun. Calhoun wrote:

> I am directed by the President to say that the Secretary of the Navy has been instructed to order a strong naval force to concentrate in the Gulf of Mexico, to meet any emergency; and that similar orders have been issued by the Secretary of War, to move the disposable military forces on our southwestern frontier for the same purpose. Should the exigency arise to which you refer in your note to Mr. Upshur [January 17, 1844], I am further directed by the President to say, that, during the pendency of the treaty of Annexation, he would deem it his duty to use all the means placed within his power by the constitution to protect Texas from all foreign invasion.[18]

This assurance did contain, however, one wide-open loophole in its concluding sentence: ". . . he would deem it his duty to use all the means placed within his power by the constitution to protect Texas from all foreign invasion." No means was in the possession of the President to protect Texas "from all foreign invasion," except as derived from the war power, which could be exercised only with the consent of Congress. That hole was visible to the Texans, and they wanted something more solid.

Calhoun made detailed oral promises. One of them was that a powerful naval force of ten or twelve vessels would be ordered to the Gulf of Mexico, the commander of which would warn the Mexican commander, if any serious demonstration against Texas were made by water, that such an attack would be considered a hostile act that the President would feel bound to use every means to repel.

[18] Calhoun to Van Zandt and Henderson, April 11, 1844, in *Sen. Doc.,* 28 Cong., 1 sess. (ser. 435), no. 349, 11. Van Zandt's letter to Upshur of January 17, 1844, is in the same document.

Also, Calhoun promised that General Gaines, who commanded the Western Division of the army, with headquarters at Fort Jesup, would have similar orders as to any Mexican attack by land, and he and the chargé d'affaires in Texas would maintain an active correspondence with the Texan President. Should they receive from the latter any communication indicating a serious Mexican intention to invade Texas by land, word would at once be sent to President Tyler, who would request Congress to adopt such measures as might be necessary for the defense of Texas and who would say that in the meantime he considered it his duty to defend Texas against aggression.

The Texan plenipotentiaries took the precaution of writing down Calhoun's words and giving them to Calhoun to read. He read, and agreed to them without dissent. Much more passed in conversation, which the Texans, in their dispatch, wrote they could not report. A part of Calhoun's remarks was, at his request, obliterated, but the rest went to the Texas government to guide it in any future exchange of ratifications after the Senate would have agreed to the treaty.[19]

The treaty framed under these conditions seemed favorable to the Texan plenipotentiaries. It provided that Texas would come into the Union as a territory with a right to statehood as one state or several under the provisions of the federal Constitution. This was what Van Zandt and Henderson desired. The subject of slavery —indeed, even the word—was avoided, but the issue was to be governed by the clause of the treaty "which secures to us [Texas] the right of property etc.," which was understood to include "our right to slaves, as the Constitution of the United States recognizes that species of property." [20]

The problem of the boundary was not dealt with in the treaty, which was a considerable omission, inasmuch as the Texan claim to territory extended to the Rio Grande. The treaty simply provided that Texas cede "all its territories" to the United States. The public lands of Texas were to go to the United States in that cession. They were to become subject to the laws of the United States reg-

[19] Van Zandt and Henderson to Jones, April 12, 1844, in A.H.A. *Report,* 1908, II (1), 269–73.
[20] The words quoted are in *ibid*. For the "right of property" clause in the treaty, see Documents under date April 12, 1844, clause 2.

ulating public lands in other territories. The public debts and liabilities of Texas, however created, were to be assumed by the United States. They were estimated in the treaty to be no greater than ten million dollars.

Taken as a whole, the treaty appeared to Van Zandt and Henderson to be good, though not such a one as they had expected or wished. Had they dealt only with the President and the Cabinet, they wrote, it would have been much more favorable. But account had to be taken of the views of the two leading parties in the United States, which meant avoiding the very liberal terms Southern politicians would have been willing to grant and the restrictions the antislavery North would have wished to impose. Kept constantly in mind was what the Senate would ratify.[21]

The President assured Van Zandt and Henderson that if the treaty were rejected in the Senate, he would at once send a recommendation to Congress in the strongest terms to adopt a measure annexing Texas as a state—under the provision of the Constitution authorizing Congress to admit new states into the Union. The friends of annexation in Congress were confident such a measure would be passed.[22] Heartened by such private assurances, the Texan plenipotentiaries on April 12, 1844, signed the treaty.

On that day the treaty and the dispatch quoted above, containing the full account of the assurances, went to the Texan government. Thus, more inside information concerning the treaty went to the Texan government than came to the Senate.

A delay of ten days occurred between the signing of the treaty and its submission to the Senate. Calhoun needed that time for the copying of earlier dispatches and the preparation of two new ones, important to send to the Senate. One of the new items was a reply to a letter the British minister in Washington, Richard Pakenham, had written on February 26, 1844, to Upshur. Pakenham's letter had not, in itself, been significant. It had merely transmitted a dispatch Aberdeen wished to have recorded in the State Department concerning his answer to Brougham's question in Parliament on August 18, 1843, regarding Texas and the slavery problem—which

---

[21] Van Zandt and Henderson to Jones, April 12, 1844, in A.H.A. *Report,* 1908, II (1), 269.

[22] *Ibid.,* 271.

American expansionists had misrepresented. Pakenham had sent Upshur the dispatch, which had gone unanswered. Aberdeen had said what he thought the world knew, that Great Britain wished slavery to be done away with everywhere, Texas included. He had added that the British government would do nothing secret or underhanded in carrying out this desire. As a mediator in the Texan-Mexican war, England would rejoice to see a recognition of Texas independence, based on a Texan undertaking to abolish slavery eventually, but would merely give counsel. With regard to slavery in the states of the United States it would resort to no measures, secret or open, tending to disturb their tranquility.[23]

Calhoun resurrected Pakenham's dispatch and on April 18, 1844, made it the text for a lengthy reply, to be included among the documents for Senate reading. He first expressed pleasure with the disavowals of Aberdeen, but deep concern with the avowal for the first time that "Great Britain desires and is constantly exerting herself to procure, the general abolition of slavery throughout the world." Calhoun observed that still greater concern was felt by the President over the desire of Great Britain to see slavery abolished in Texas, and "as he infers is endeavouring through her diplomacy to accomplish it, by making the abolition of slavery one of the conditions on which Mexico should acknowledge her independence." Should Great Britain succeed in her endeavors, it would expose the most vulnerable portion of our frontier to inroads, and would place in British power the most efficient means of abolishing slavery in the neighboring American states. This would be so dangerous to the prosperity and safety of the Union that failure to prevent it

[23] *British and Foreign State Papers 1844–1845*, XXXIII, 232. The date of the Aberdeen dispatch is December 26, 1843. The anxiety of Aberdeen concerning the twisted construction that Calhoun and the Tyler government had given, and were giving, to the exchange in Parliament with Brougham in August, 1843, is indicated in a statement Aberdeen made to Everett in the autumn of 1844, which is recorded in Everett's diary: "He [Aberdeen] alluded in terms of indignation to the attempt to inculcate the opinion that they were endeavoring to prevail upon Mexico to make the abolition of slavery in Texas a condition of [Mexico's] recognizing the independence of Texas. He said on the contrary they had attempted no such thing but had said to Mexico: We [Great Britain] acknowledged Texas with slavery and we cannot ask you to make any condition as to its abolition. He added that undoubtedly, they could not be expected to be indifferent to our extension in that quarter and had addressed themselves to France seriously on the subject & France was inclined to take the same view." Everett Diary, October 17, 1844, Everett Papers, M.H.S.

would be an abandonment of the most solemn obligation imposed by the Constitution to protect the states from dangers without or within. In obedience to this obligation, Calhoun wrote, a treaty of annexation had just been concluded.

With regard to the question of slavery, Calhoun continued, the American government concedes to Great Britain the right to adopt whatever policy it deems best in its own possessions. In the United States this right lies with the states. A large number of the states have decided that it is neither wise nor humane to change the relation which has existed between the two races from their first settlement. The undersigned would not regard this as a proper occasion to discuss the subject. "He does not, however, deem it irrelevant to state, that, if the experience of more than half a century is to decide, it would be neither humane nor wise in them to change their policy."

At this point Calhoun demonstrated, from the census and other authentic documents, that "in all instances in which the States have changed the former relations between the 2 races, the condition of the African, instead of being improved, has become worse. They have been invariably sunk into vice and pauperism accompanied by the bodily and mental afflictions incident thereto—deafness, blindness, insanity, and idiocy, to a degree without example; while, in all other States which have retained the ancient relation between them, they have improved greatly in every respect, in number, comfort, intelligence, and morals, as the following facts, taken from such sources, will serve to illustrate."

Here followed a detailed statistical discussion, from which Calhoun drew the conclusion that "what is called slavery is in reality a political institution, essential to the peace, safety, and prosperity of those States of the Union in which it exists." Also, that Great Britain, could she succeed in accomplishing in the United States what she avows to be her desire and object of her constant exertions to effect throughout the world, "would involve in the greatest calamity the whole country [United States] and especially the race which it is the avowed objects of her exertions to benefit." [24]

The second new item sent to the Senate with the treaty was a copy of a recent dispatch Calhoun had written the American chargé

[24] Calhoun to Pakenham, April 18, 1844, in *Sen. Doc.*, 28 Cong., 1 sess. (ser. 435), no. 341, 50–3.

in Mexico City, instructing him to announce the treaty to the Mexican government and to try to reconcile that government to it. This implemented the view he had earlier recommended to Upshur in the far-sighted letter of August 27, 1843, that Mexico be kept informed of British intrigues in the New World with directions to "baffle, as far as may be possible, the attempts of the British Government to draw Mexico into her schemes." Benjamin E. Green was the American chargé in Mexico City to whom the instruction was sent. He was the son of Duff Green, and had been appointed in appreciation of his father's services. He was told by Calhoun to give the Mexican government strong assurances that the American government, in adopting annexation, was actuated by no feelings of

> disrespect or indifference to the honor or dignity of Mexico, and that it would be a subject of great regret if it should be otherwise regarded by its Government. And, in the next place, that the step was forced on the Government of the United States, in self-defence, in consequence of the policy adopted by Great Britain in reference to the abolition of slavery in Texas. It was impossible for the United States to witness with indifference the efforts of Great Britain to abolish slavery there. They could not but see that she had the means in her power, in the actual condition of Texas, to accomplish the objects of her policy, unless prevented by the most efficient measures; and that, if accomplished, it would lead to a state of things dangerous in the extreme to the adjacent States, and the Union itself. Seeing this, this Government had been compelled, by the necessity of the case, and a regard to its constitutional obligations, to take the step it has, as the only certain and effectual means of preventing it. It has taken it in full view of all possible consequences, but not without a desire and hope that a full and fair disclosure of the causes which induced it to do so would prevent the disturbance of the harmony subsisting between the two countries, which the United States is anxious to preserve.

In order to give the Mexican government a just conception of the motives compelling American action, Calhoun enclosed in the dispatch a copy of Aberdeen's letter to Pakenham and the reply he had just made to it. Green was directed to read this to the Mexican secretary of state, but not to leave copies, since it would be part of the documentation for the treaty. He was to assure the Mexican government of the American desire to settle all questions growing out of the treaty on the most liberal terms. The government of the

United States would have been happy to act in concurrence with that of Mexico if circumstances had permitted, but could not allow the safety of the Union to depend on the contingency of obtaining the previous consent of Mexico. However, every precaution had been taken to make the terms of the treaty as unobjectionable to Mexico as possible, and among other matters the boundary of Texas had been left without specification so that the line might be an open question to be fairly and fully discussed and settled according to the rights, mutual interest, and security of the two countries. This dispatch, together with the author's letter to Pakenham, went to the Senate as part of the documentation of the treaty.[25]

In the letter of April 18 to Pakenham, comparing the sound mental health of Southern slaves with the hard lot and frequent insanity of Northern free Negroes, Calhoun relied on statistics from the census of 1840. He had no question as to their accuracy or impartiality. They had been earlier relied on by Upshur in his confidential letter of September 28 to Everett. They showed that, under the kindly paternalism of plantation masters, slaves flourished, and that by contrast, free Negroes in the North, living under an impersonal wage system, disintegrated. Robert J. Walker had leaned heavily on those statistics, also, in developing his thesis that the annexation of Texas would solve both slavery and the race problems of North and South.

But a New Englander—a specialist on insanity and its geographic incidence—had no such reverence for those statistics. Indeed, he questioned their very essence: their accuracy. He was Dr. Edward Jarvis, of Concord, Massachusetts, a Harvard graduate, and a disciple of a distinguished figure in the world of vital statistics, Lemuel Shattuck, of the Massachusetts General Hospital. As a New Englander, Jarvis was not sympathetic to the institution of slavery, and his antagonism to it had hardened as a consequence of five years' residence as a practicing physician in Louisville, Kentucky. On the appearance of the census volume in 1841, he had noticed at once unmistakable errors in their statistics regarding insanity. In the summer of 1842 he wrote an article for the *Boston Medical and Surgical Journal* on "Statistics of Insanity in the United States," which appeared in the September 21 number. In it he used the census figures

[25] Calhoun to Benjamin Green, April 19, 1844, in *ibid.*, 53–4.

rearranged in tables on a sectional basis. The tables disclosed the surprising fact that in the Northern states as a whole, 1 free Negro out of every 162 was insane, which was almost ten times the rate found among Negroes in the slave states of the South. Especially shocking was the insanity rate among free Negroes in the New England states: 1 out of every 14 in Maine, 1 out of 28 in New Hampshire, 1 out of 43 in Massachusetts, and 1 out of 185 in Connecticut. On the other hand, the rate in the South, among Negroes, slave and free, was only 1 out of 1,309 in Virginia, 1 out of 2,447 in South Carolina, 1 out of 2,397 in Mississippi, and 1 out of 4,310 in Louisiana.[26]

Another table of census statistics, rearranged by Jarvis, was limited to the South—the insanity rate of the slaves, cared for at the charge of their masters, compared with that of free Negroes, at public charge. The rate was far lower among slaves than among the free Negroes: only 1 in every 1,807 among slaves, as against 1 in every 659 among free Negroes. In other words, the rate among slaves was only about a third as high as that among free Negroes in the South.

These figures, viewed from every angle, raised problems for an alert and impartial analyst such as Jarvis. In one portion of his article he pointed out that in the Northern states the ratio of insane Negroes to insane whites, as shown by the statistics, was actually 6 to 1, whereas in the Southern states the ratio between insane blacks and insane whites was 3 to 5. Jarvis may have written with tongue in cheek in adding:

> Slavery has a wonderful influence upon the development of moral faculties and the intellectual powers; and refusing man many of the hopes and responsibilities which the free, self-thinking and self-acting enjoy and sustain, of course . . . saves him from some of the liabilities and dangers of active self-direction. If the mental powers and . . . propensities are kept comparatively dormant, certainly they must suffer much less from mis-direction or over-action. So far as this goes, it proves the common notion, that in the highest state of civilization and mental activity there is the greatest danger of mental derangement; for here [the South], where there is the greatest mental torpor, we find the least insanity.[27]

[26] *Boston Medical and Surgical Journal,* 27 (September 21, 1842).
[27] *Ibid.*

The author was confident that statistics of pauper insane, found in local and state sources, were more accurate than those in the federal census. On the other hand, they were more circumscribed and therefore less meaningful. He lamented the fact that defects in the taking of the census had defeated the potentialities of a nationwide survey.

In the South much notice was taken of the insanity statistics among Negroes and of the disproportion between the rates in the Northern and Southern states. Explanations of the disproportion differed. Some commentators thought the climate of the North was an important causative factor in the deterioration of the Africans. Others denied it.

A respected Southern economist and statistician, Professor George Tucker of the University of Virginia, dealt with the problem in a widely read book, dated July 1, 1843, entitled *Progress of the United States in Population and Wealth . . . As Exhibited by the Decennial Census.* He had written it to mark progress in the fifty-year period since the first census was taken in 1790. He published tables showing increases in population, industry, and wealth. As part of his population study, he discussed increases in the number of slaves, and in that connection also the "extraordinary difference among the States, in the proportion of insane of the coloured race." He offered a table of ratios very like the one Jarvis had published. Then he went on:

> It thus appears, that the proportion of insane is greatest among the coloured population of the northern States, and that it considerably decreases as we proceed South; from which we may infer that the rigours of a northern winter, which have no influence on the temperament of the whites, affect the cerebral organs of the African race. There are, however, two other circumstances, which operate to produce the great diversity we see; and these are, emigration and slavery—the slave population seeming to be less liable to this malady than the free coloured population, and the insane very rarely migrating. By a due regard to these three circumstances, of coldness of climate, migration, and the proportion of slaves in the coloured population of a State, we may probably go far to reconcile most of the diversities which are exhibited in the above table. But perhaps it is premature to theorize on this subject; for when we see in some of the States so large a proportion of the coloured population as 1 in 43 [Massachusetts], and in Maine nearly 1 in 14, so

anomalous a fact throws a doubt over the correctness of this part of the census, and at least inclines us to suspend our opinion, until we have further evidence or explanation.[28]

An explanation by an anonymous Virginian, who thought well of slavery, appeared in the June, 1843, issue of the *Southern Literary Messenger*. He attributed the heavy disproportion to moral rather than to climatic factors. He singled out Massachusetts as a state in which free Negroes had deteriorated, with a consequent high crime rate, and compared their record with that of the underprivileged in England and France to fortify his point:

> These statements show that the free negroes of the northern states are the most vicious persons on this continent, perhaps on the earth. In England with its immense mass of starving, homeless, houseless poor, with every temptation that can be offered to human frailty to violate the laws, there was but one convict in 1373 of the population. While in Massachusetts, where the negroes have been free more than half a century, in the land of *steady habits* where they have been caressed, and latterly the males have been the "love of ladies," if not the "theme of song," there is a felon in every 164, and a maniac in every 43 of the population.[29]

Jarvis was impelled by these heresies to return to his crusade for more reliable census statistics. In 1843 he made an exhaustive study of every town and county in the free states listed in the census as containing insane Negroes. He compared in each town the number of reported Negro insane with the town's total Negro population. He found repeated cases of Negro insane more numerous than the total Negro population. In January, 1844, he published in the *American Journal of the Medical Sciences* page after page of such statistical phenomena found in the census in towns from Maine to Iowa. He listed equally egregious errors of other sorts. In the town of Worcester, Massachusetts, for example, he found reported 133 Negro insane. They were actually, as he knew personally, white insane in a state hospital situated in that town. "This single mistake," he observed, "multiplies the coloured lunatics of this state threefold, and if this were corrected it would reduce the proportion

---

[28] George Tucker, *Progress of the United States in Population and Wealth . . . As Exhibited by the Decennial Census* (New York, 1843), p. 79.
[29] *Southern Literary Messenger*, 9 (June, 1843), 346–52.

of coloured insane from one in forty-three to one in one hundred and twenty-nine." [30]

In concluding his article Jarvis expressed his disappointment, and that of other scientists, at the outcome of a government-financed investigation of a grave medical and social problem. He wrote:

> Scientific men and philanthropists looked for the results of this investigation with confident hope; for henceforward the statistics of insanity, of deafness, and of blindness, were to be no more a mere matter of conjecture, but of positive and extensive demonstration. In due time the document came forth, under the sanction of Congress, and "corrected at the Department of State." Such a document as we have described, heavy with its errors and its misstatements, instead of being a messenger of truth to the world, to enlighten its knowledge and guide its opinions . . . is, in respect to human ailment—a bearer of falsehood to confuse and mislead. So far from being an aid to the progress of medical science, as it was the intention of government in ordering these inquiries, it has thrown a stumbling-block in its way, which it will require years to remove.
>
> Where these errors originated, whether with the thousand marshals who counted the people in all the districts of the nation, or with the clerks in the State Department, who analyzed and reduced their returns to tables as now published, we have no means of judging. But so far as they were made at Washington, the case is not without remedy. The original returns may be re-examined, and a new and more accurate set of tables of the numbers of the insane, the deaf, and the blind, may be prepared. We commend this matter to the attention of the next Congress.[31]

Where the initial errors of the census originated was an inquiry to which Jarvis returned later in life in writing his autobiography. The answer lay partly in the complicated forms marshals were given to fill out:

> In the tables of population there were columns for ages, sexes, insane, idiots, blind, etc. The columns of the white insane were next to those of the colored insane. These columns were long and many towns on a page, and it required a very accurate eye and careful discipline to select the proper column for a fact, and to follow it down from the heading. But, for want of this care, the figures rep-

[30] *American Journal of the Medical Sciences* (Philadelphia), new series 7 (January, 1844), 12–13.
[31] *Ibid.*

resenting the white lunatics of many towns were placed in the column of the colored. Consequently towns which had no colored population on one page, were represented on the other as having colored lunatics; and in many others the number of colored lunatics was more than that of the colored living; others were stated to have a large part of their colored people insane.[32]

It should be added that the census of 1840 represented the first nationwide gathering of statistics on insanity.[33]

To check the spread of false conclusions from the manifold errors of the census, Jarvis obtained in the spring of 1844 the assistance of the prestigious American Statistical Association. He induced it to establish a committee of three, with himself as chairman and two others as associates—J. Wingate Thornton, representing the field of education, and William Bingham, representing the field of trade—to prepare the report. However, he wrote the final draft.

As preparation for the section of the report on Negro insanity, Jarvis examined with special care the detailed manuscript originals of the census for Massachusetts. He went to the district clerk's office in Boston for the enumerators' returns for the state; to the consolidated returns of the state marshal; and to the printed edition of Blair & Rives. He found extraordinary variations at every stage. He fortified his earlier essay by citing names. Thus, in the original enumeration of Deputy Marshal James Estabrook, he found the report on one page that there were 133 colored paupers in the family of S. B. Woodward in Worcester, Massachusetts,[34] and on another page that there were no colored persons in the said family. In the consolidated manuscript for the town of Plympton there were reported four colored pauper lunatics and one colored blind person in the family of Jacob Cushman, and on another page that there were no colored persons at all in said family. In comparing the manuscript of the consolidated return at Boston with the printed edition of Blair & Rives, he was forced to the conclusion that a large part

[32] Edward Jarvis [Autobiography], Houghton Library, Harvard. For copies of the forms distributed to marshals, see *Sen. Doc.,* 26 Cong., 1 sess. (ser. 355), no. 13. A "Compendium" of the census was authorized and came out in two rival printings—Blair & Rives, and Thomas Allen. See W. A. Weaver, *Reply to a Pamphlet by Thomas Allen* (Washington, 1842).

[33] For the act laying down directions for the census, see *Statutes at Large,* V, 331–7.

[34] S. B. Woodward was superintendent of the state mental institution at Worcester.

of the printed errors were made by the printer himself, and "that hardly any errors of the original document are left out."

Jarvis tested the returns from all the Northern states of the Union in this systematic fashion, with special attention to the statistics of the colored insane. He dealt also with the statistics of deaf, dumb, and blind Negroes, leaving to his colleagues on the committee, schools, professions, and trades for whites. The committee's conclusion on the census as a whole, embodied in a memorial to be presented to Congress, was

> that such documents ought not to have the sanction of Congress, nor ought they to be regarded as containing true statements relative to the condition of the people, and the resources of the United States. They believe it would have been far better to have had no census at all, than such an one as has been published, and they respectfully request your honorable bodies to take such order thereon, and to adopt such measures for the correction of the same, or if the same cannot be corrected, of discarding and disowning the same, as the good of the country shall require, and as justice and humanity shall demand.[35]

Of the three articles Jarvis had written on the subject, the second, the one in the *American Journal of Medical Science* of January, 1844, was brought to the attention of John Quincy Adams soon after it appeared. It probably came to him directly from the author. It promptly became the basis of a challenging resolution submitted by Adams to the House of Representatives on February 26, 1844. The resolution ran:

> *Resolved,* That the Secretary of State [Upshur] be directed to inform this House whether any gross errors have been discovered in the printed "Sixth Census, or enumeration of the inhabitants of the United States, as corrected at the Department of State in 1841," and, if so, how those errors originated, what they are, and what, if any, measures have been taken to rectify them.[36]

The resolution was sent with House approval to the State Department. A curious error occurred in the transmission, as sometimes happened in the case of requests of troublesome House mem-

---

[35] The report of the committee is published in *Hunt's Merchants Magazine,* 12 (January–June, 1845), 125–39.

[36] *Congressional Globe,* 28 Cong., 1 sess., 323. See also *House Journal,* 28 Cong., 1 sess. (ser. 438), 471.

bers. The date "1841" in the original had become "1843," [37] which changed the bearing of the request. The resolution had been intended for Upshur. He was spared the embarrassment of answering it by the explosion on board the *Princeton* on February 28. The problem fell into the lap of Calhoun, who was too overwhelmed with other matters for several months to be able to attend to it, and it was set aside for a time.

Meanwhile, the treaty and its accompanying documents went automatically on their arrival on April 22 to the Senate Foreign Relations Committee, which was controlled by the Whigs, as was the Senate itself. The chairman of the committee was William S. Archer of Virginia. His two Whig colleagues were John M. Berrien of Georgia and Rufus Choate of Massachusetts. The two minority seats were held by Democrats. The committee deliberated on the treaty for nearly three weeks, then returned it without recommendation to the Senate on May 10. It was accused of having sat on the treaty.

In the meantime, on April 27, five days after the treaty reached the Senate, it was betrayed with all its documents to the New York *Evening Post* by an antislavery senator—a Democrat, Benjamin Tappan, of Ohio. On the same day letters from Henry Clay and Martin Van Buren appeared in the press, declaring their opposition to the immediate annexation of Texas. As a consequence of the betrayal, the Administration's devious underground campaign for annexation was brought into the full light of day. By the Clay and Van Buren pronouncements the public was warned that neither the present nor the near future was a safe time to bring the Texas issue to a decision. These journalistic events were not good auspices for the ratification of the treaty.

On the day of these crowded developments Calhoun was quietly writing Pakenham a second letter in the now-famous exchange on the Texas issue. The first, of April 18,[38] had drawn from Pakenham the next day an acknowledgment of receipt and a statement that it was being forwarded to his government. In addition, Pakenham felt obliged to immediately express regret at Calhoun's attribution of

[37] Charles F. Adams, ed., *Memoirs of John Quincy Adams,* 12 vols. (Philadelphia, 1874–7), XII, 23.
[38] Calhoun to Pakenham, April 18, 1844, in *Sen. Doc.,* 28 Cong., 1 sess. (ser. 435), no. 341, 50–3.

responsibility for the treaty of annexation to the British government and to take notice of Calhoun's statements, "founded on statistical information, in defence of the institution of slavery as now established in a portion of this [American] Republic." [39]

In reply Calhoun, in turn, expressed regret at an error on the part of Pakenham in supposing that his statistical comparison of the condition of Negroes in the Northern and Southern states constituted a defense of slavery in the United States. It merely showed that the condition of the African race was far worse in states that had abolished slavery than it was in states that had not. Calhoun conceded that Aberdeen's dispatch had contained explanations expressed in a spirit of frankness and good faith. If they failed to allay anxiety, it was because they were accompanied by an avowal in reference to the abolition of slavery in general, and in Texas, in particular, calculated to defeat the object of the explanations. "It was not possible for the President to hear with indifference the avowal of a policy so hostile in its character and dangerous in its tendency, to the domestic institutions of so many States of this Union, and to the safety and prosperity of the whole." [40] The letter indicated that the expression of a humane sentiment on the part of the British government was equivalent, in Calhoun's mind, to the avowal of an aggressive policy.

These two letters were sent by the President to the Senate on April 29 to be considered in connection with the treaty. They were supplementary materials voluntarily offered to cast light on the documents sent earlier with the treaty.

On May 10 the Senate Committee on Foreign Relations, which had received the treaty seventeen days before, reported it back "without amendment." Its Whig majority seemed to consider the instrument beyond repair and fit only for the fire. The reception of the treaty by the public at the time of the Tappan betrayal had perhaps suggested that kind of report.[41]

On May 13 Benton opened a campaign to breach the wall of

[39] Pakenham to Calhoun, April 19, 1844, *British and Foreign State Papers 1844–1845,* XXIII, 240–2.

[40] Calhoun to Pakenham, April 27, 1844, *Sen. Doc.,* 28 Cong., 1 sess. (ser. 435), no. 341, 65–7.

[41] *Journal of the Executive Proceedings of the Senate, 1789–* (Government Printing Office, Washington, D.C., 1828–   ), VI, 271 (hereafter cited as *Jour. Exec. Proc.*).

secrecy behind which the Administration had barricaded itself in obtaining the treaty. He introduced a series of resolutions, half of inquiry, the others declaratory, all designed to undermine its ratification. One was directed against the mission of Duff Green to London in the summer of 1843 and the resulting "private letter" to Upshur. It ran:

> *Resolved,* That the author of the "private letter" (believed to be Duff Green) from London, in the summer of 1843, and addressed to the then American Secretary of State (Mr. Upshur), and giving him information of the supposed slavery designs of Great Britain in Texas, and which information was the basis and moving cause of the American Secretary's leading dispatch to the American chargé in Texas to procure the annexation of Texas to the United States, be summoned to appear at the bar of the Senate to be examined on oath in relation to the subject matter of his said communication from London; and also to be examined by the Senate on all points that they shall think proper in relation to his knowledge of the origin, progress, and conclusion of the Texas treaty, and all the objects thereof, and of all influences and interests which may have operated in setting on foot and carrying on the negotiations for the conclusion and ratification of said treaty.
>
> *Resolved, also,* That the Senate will examine, either at its bar or by a committee, any other persons that it shall have reason to believe can give information on all or any one of the foregoing points of inquiry.[42]

On May 16, three days after the presentation of the resolutions, Benton launched a tremendous speech explaining them, which ran on for three days. It dealt with the issues in all his resolutions, but was especially revealing regarding that of Duff Green's letter and the use to which it was at once put by Upshur in opening annexation discussions with the Texan government. Citing Upshur's letter

---

[42] *Jour. Exec. Proc.,* VI, 276–7. The Senate approved a similar resolution on May 28. It also approved two requests to the President for information as to a temporary armistice between Mexico and Texas and as to a messenger sent to Mexico with a view to obtaining consent to an annexation treaty. It also listened with approval to three declaratory resolutions submitted by Benton: first, that ratification of the treaty would be tantamount to adopting the Mexican-Texan war, the conduct and conclusion of which would devolve upon the United States; second, that the treaty-making power does not extend to making war, which Congress alone can authorize; and third, that the area that the treaty of 1819 surrendered ought not to be reunited to the Union until it can be done with the consent of the majority of the people of the United States and Texas, and when Mexico either consents or ceases to make war.

of August 8, 1843, to the American chargé in Texas, and his letter four months later to Edward Everett in London, Benton went on:

> Thus commenced the plan for the immediate annexation of Texas to the United States, as the only means of saving that country from British domination, and from the anti-slavery schemes attributed to her by Mr. Duff Green. Unfortunately it was not deemed necessary to inquire into the truth of this gentleman's information; and it was not until four months afterwards, and until after the most extraordinary efforts to secure annexation had been made by our government, that it was discovered that the information given by Mr. Green was entirely mistaken and unfounded! The British minister (the Earl of Aberdeen) and the Texian chargé in London (Mr. Ashbel Smith), both of whom were referred to by Mr. Green, being informed in the month of November of the use which had been made of their names, availed themselves of the first [opportunity] to contradict the whole story to our minister, Mr. Everett.[43]

Publication of these words of Benton seemed important to Senate opponents of the treaty. The public already was aware of the treaty and the documents submitted with it, thanks to Tappan, but the veil of Senate secrecy still embarrassed those of the opposition who wished to analyze the documents for the benefit of the nation. To remove the remaining shreds of the veil had been the goal from the outset of Clay's successor in the Senate, John J. Crittenden. On May 15, the day before the opening of Benton's great speech, he obtained Senate approval, in amended form, of a resolution he had earlier proposed. The preamble was a stiff blow to the policy followed by the Administration in obtaining the treaty:

> *Resolved,* That whereas the annexation of the Republic of Texas to the United States is a subject of great importance, on which the will of the people of this Union ought to be consulted; and whereas the treaty for that annexation, now before the Senate, is of great moment, and there is nothing in said treaty, or the documents accompanying it, which requires the further observance of secrecy, and, resting as it does upon its own peculiar circumstances, cannot be drawn into precedent for different cases in time to come: Therefore, the injunction of secrecy be, and the same is hereby, removed from said treaty, and all documents and papers in relation thereto, now before the Senate.[44]

[43] *Congressional Globe,* 28 Cong., 1 sess., App., 480 ff.
[44] *Jour. Exec. Proc.,* VI, 283.

The resolution was easily passed. But something more was desired by the opponents of the treaty. They wished the day-to-day speeches and proceedings to become public. Exposure of the origins of the treaty, and of its salient documents, to Jacksonian Democrats would be most telling if done by an orator of Benton's standing in the party. Benton himself shared this view. On the day after the second installment of his speech, he asked for the removal of the injunction of secrecy on it. His Whig colleagues were happy to meet his wishes, and they joined forces to free not only his speech and resolutions, "but all other speeches on the same subject, as soon as delivered." [45] The "will of the people of this Union" was thus consulted.

Benton was impatient for word from the President concerning Duff Green. His May 13 resolution seems to have been lost in the bombardment of the President with other resolutions of inquiry. On May 28 he induced the Senate to request of the President a copy of the whole of the "private letter" from London, with its date, quoted by Upshur in his letter to the American chargé in Texas; to give the name of the writer, information as to whether he had been employed by the government, and if so, what funds had been used to pay him, what instructions he had carried, and what other letters relative to the annexation of Texas he had written.[46]

The reply of the President on June 3 took the form of a letter from Calhoun, in which the undersigned had the honor to report to the President that

> After diligent inquiry, no letter of the character referred to can be found on the files of this department, nor any evidence that such has ever been placed on them. He is unable to ascertain the name of the writer in question, from any documents in possession of the department, and presumes that the letter referred to in the resolution of the Senate, being "private," is amongst the private papers of the late Mr. Upshur.[47]

The Senate was still unsatisfied. It asked the President on June 7 whether Duff Green had been employed by the executive in

[45] *Ibid.*, p. 290.
[46] *Ibid.*, p. 294.
[47] Calhoun to Tyler, June 3, 1844, in *Sen. Doc.*, 28 Cong., 1 sess. (ser. 436), no. 351.

Europe in 1843 and requested copies of all correspondence relative to the annexation of Texas that Green might have sent.[48] Calhoun's reply was that there was "no communication whatever, either to or from Mr. Green, in relation to the annexation of Texas, to be found on the files of this department." [49]

In these repeated suave replies to the Senate, Calhoun and the President were, strictly speaking, not falsifying. No communications whatever, either to or from Mr. Green, in relation to the annexation of Texas were "to be found on the files of this department." Neither did his name appear anywhere in the documents that had gone to the Senate. Yet Green was serving the President in 1843 as executive agent in London. He had been provided a personal letter of introduction from the President to Everett for his mission, he had received pay from the secret fund of the President, his activities in London had been the subject of embarrassed report from Everett to Upshur, and he had written numerous personal letters in just this period to the President, Upshur, and Calhoun on the Texas issue.

What is still more remarkable is that Green had already publicly admitted that he was the author of the crucial "private letter" received by Upshur which had induced Upshur and Tyler to seek immediate annexation of Texas. He told of this in a communication to the *Madisonian,* published on May 8, 1844, in reply to an editorial in the Washington *Daily Globe* of May 4, attacking him, which he suspected Benton had written.[50] He stressed that he had reported only what he had heard from the lips of Ashbel Smith, and he offered additional evidence concerning the British plot from statements of abolitionists in London. But he did not linger long on that subject. He passed quickly to the statement Aberdeen had made in Parliament in the exchange with Brougham. This was just the tactic Upshur and Calhoun had employed. In the meantime, the discrepancy between Green's letter to the *Madisonian* and Calhoun's replies to the Senate's inquiries must have widened the cred-

[48] *Jour. Exec. Proc.,* VI, 310.
[49] *House Doc.,* 28 Cong., 1 sess. (ser. 444), no. 271, 101.
[50] *Madisonian,* May 8, 1844. The Washington *Daily Globe,* under the editorship of Francis P. Blair, was a supporter of Benton and an opponent of the treaty of annexation. The letter of Green appears under its date in the Documents.

ibility gap in the minds of senators already suspicious of the Administration and its treaty.[51]

The three-day speech of Benton in May against the treaty had been directed primarily to opening such a gap. One of his themes in the speech had been the conflict between the assurances Aberdeen had tried to convey to the Administration regarding British policy in Texas and Calhoun's twisted interpretation of them. He quoted Everett's dispatches on the issue at length and read the entire Aberdeen dispatch to Pakenham of December 26, 1843, denying any British intent to interfere with slavery in Texas or in the United States, or any covert designs on Texas. He listed the repeated denials Aberdeen had made of such a policy. He declared that the Administration's charges were just another pretext for dragging the British government into the fight over annexation after the Duff Green charge had been discredited. He sarcastically dismissed Calhoun's letter to Pakenham regarding the Aberdeen dispatch as an "afterthought." [52]

This defense of the British by a Western senator, who himself had a reputation as a twister of the lion's tail, impressed Clay Whigs and Van Buren Democrats in the Senate. But Andrew Jackson, on learning of it, could explain it only on the ground that Benton had become deranged.[53]

IN THE SENATE PROBE into the treaty negotiation, a focal point was the risk, taken by the Administration, of a war with Mexico in the effort to acquire Texas. A respected Whig, John J. Crittenden of Kentucky, proposed to the Senate on May 10 a resolution adopted three days later, asking the President to inform it whether any military preparation had been ordered since the opening of the

[51] Another harassing question, sent to the President on June 12 at the instance of Benton, was whether Green had been at any time subsequent to March 4, 1841, paid for foreign services out of the contingent fund, how much, and whether he still had claims outstanding. The President's reply contained an admonition as to such queries but admitted that Green had been employed to gather information from private and other sources for a negotiation which had been contemplated but abandoned, that he had been paid $1,000 and had afterward submitted an additional claim which had not been allowed. *Jour. Exec. Proc.*, VI, 319, 352.

[52] *Congressional Globe*, 28 Cong., 1 sess., App., 474–86 (May 16, 18, 20, 1844).

[53] Bassett, *Correspondence*, VI, 299.

annexation negotiation in anticipation of war, and with whom such war was apprehended.[54]

The President informed the Senate in a message of May 15 that owing to Mexican threats of war in case of an annexation treaty, he had felt it necessary to concentrate a large part of the home squadron in the Gulf of Mexico and to assemble at the borders of Texas as large a military force as was available. At the same time the President declared that having "acquired a title to Texas, which requires only the action of the Senate to perfect, no other power could be permitted to invade and by force of arms to possess itself of any portion of the territory of Texas, pending your deliberations upon the treaty, without placing itself in an hostile attitude . . . and justifying the employment of any military means at our disposal to drive back the invasion." [55]

With this message the President submitted copies of the march and sailing orders sent to portions of the army and the navy. These made evident the degree to which the Administration was prepared to use its military forces to shield Texas against a Mexican invasion. Not confided to the Senate was whether copies of those instructions had been sent to the government of Texas.

The Senate continued to be curious. On May 22 it raised the question, on Benton's motion, whether an actual agreement had been concluded with the President of Texas regarding naval or military aid in the event of signing a treaty of annexation, and asked specifically for copies of any orders given the military to communicate with President Houston on the issue.[56]

In reply the President sent a message on May 31 in which he referred, in a tone of slight exasperation, to the message on the subject he had already sent a week earlier. He repeated what he had then said: that General Taylor had been ordered to communicate with Houston and that Captain Connor had been ordered to communicate with Murphy if a Mexican invasion impended.[57] With this message he submitted a Calhoun letter enclosing, among others, the letter of Van Zandt to Upshur of January 17, and his own April

[54] *Jour. Exec. Proc.*, VI, 274.
[55] *Ibid.*, pp. 279–80.
[56] *Ibid.*, p. 291.
[57] *Ibid.*, p. 301, and *Sen. Doc.*, 28 Cong., 1 sess. (ser. 435), no. 349, 1.

11 letter to Van Zandt and Henderson with assurances of military aid in case of an attack.[58]

Another problem worrying the Senate, especially Benton, was the absence from the treaty of a defined boundary between Texas and Mexico. The words of the treaty were merely, cession by Texas of "all its territories" to the United States. What that meant was well understood by Texans. An act of the Texan Congress, passed on December 19, 1836, had specified that the boundary was the Rio Grande from its mouth to its source, and thence a line due north to the boundary of the United States at the forty-second parallel. The Senate requested of the President, on the day it received the treaty, copies of any communications, papers, or maps in his possession that would clarify this problem. The answer sent was printed copies of a *Memoir* written by Lieutenant W. H. Emory of the Bureau of Topographical Engineers, and copies of a map he had drawn of Texas and adjacent countries. The *Memoir* described the Rio Grande as "the only strong natural boundary between the United States and Mexico." The river formed, in connection with the mountainous desert, a first-class military obstacle. It extended 1,200 miles northward to the region of perpetual snow, where it came within about 100 miles of South Pass, and "rolls down with swiftness a vast volume of turbid waters." [59]

The map, dated 1844, bore the suggestive citation that it had been prepared for the State Department by the War Department. It was a clear cartographic representation of the Texas Act of 1836. It depicted upper California as one of the "adjacent countries" of Texas at the north. Further south it showed California separated from Texas by a mere sliver of territory labeled "New Mexico." South Pass, the gateway to California and the Oregon Country, lay only a short distance west of the panhandle of Texas; and the trading community of Santa Fé lay safely within the grasp of Texas. The map had clearly been drawn to please the State Department.[60]

---

[58] *Sen. Doc.,* 28 Cong., 1 sess. (ser. 435), no. 349, 2–12. See also editorial in the *National Intelligencer* of June 3, 1844, in the Documents under this date.

[59] For the *Memoir* see *Sen. Doc.,* 28 Cong., 1 sess. (ser. 435), no. 341, 55–63.

[60] The map is listed in Philip P. Phillips, *List of Maps of America in the Library of Congress* (Washington: Government Printing Office, 1901), and is widely found in American libraries. Five thousand copies were printed on motion of C. J. Ingersoll of Pennsylvania, an expansionist and chairman of the House Committee on Foreign Affairs.

During the debate on the annexation treaty, the President sent the Senate a message (May 16) that served chiefly as a vehicle for added voluntary offerings.[61] The offerings were copies of letters —some from illustrious figures such as Andrew Jackson and Sam Houston, others from anonymous patriots—upholding the view the President himself had set forth in the treaty message: that the opportunity to annex Texas, if lost now, would probably be lost forever. If the treaty were not approved, Texas would make treaties of alliance with Great Britain, offensive and defensive. The letter of Jackson, written on March 11, 1844, and published in excerpt in the *Madisonian* on April 3, was especially graphic on this point:

> The present golden moment to obtain Texas must not be lost, or Texas must, from necessity, be thrown into the arms of England, and be forever lost to the United States. Need I call your attention to the situation of the United States—England in possession of Texas, or in strict alliance, offensive and defensive, and contending for California. How easy would it be for Great Britain to interpose a force sufficient to prevent emigration to California from the United States, and supply her garrison from Texas! Every *real American,* when they view this, with the danger to New Orleans from British arms from Texas, must unite, heart and hand, in the annexation of Texas to the United States. It will be a strong iron hoop around our Union, and a bulwark against all foreign invasion or aggression. I say again, let not this opportunity slip to regain Texas, or it may elude our grasp forever, or cost us oceans of blood and millions of money to free us from the evils that may be brought upon us. I hope and trust there will be as many *patriots* in the Senate as will ratify the treaty, which I have no doubt will be promptly entered into.[62]

Appeals by Jackson for ratification, of even greater warmth, appeared in the press while the treaty was before the Senate. One had been sent on May 3, 1844, to Major William B. Lewis, an old friend, of which the salient paragraphs were published in the Baltimore *Republican,* a Tyler organ, and thence spread widely. The paragraph ran:

---

[61] For the message see *Jour. Exec. Proc.,* VI, 286–7. For the letters accompanying the message see *House Doc.,* 28 Cong., 1 sess. (ser. 444), no. 271, 101–10.

[62] The letter was originally published in the *Richmond Enquirer* and then in the *Madisonian,* April 3, 1844. It had been shown, at Jackson's wish, to Robert J. Walker. See Bassett, *Correspondence of Andrew Jackson,* VI, 264–5.

Now when we can obtain that country which once belonged to us, so essential to the security of Neworleans, and the whole western portion of our Union, can there be an American, or a patriot who will not unite, and rejoice in this annexation, so essential to our security, and growing greatness, in every way that the subject can be viewed. I am sure there cannot be, and the Senator who votes against the ratification of the Treaty, must be a traitor to the best interest of our beloved country, whatever pretext he may attempt to shield himself under.

The treaty must and will be ratified. These Eastern Senators dare not vote against it. Should I be mistaken in this I trust some of our members will have energy enough to present a bill and have it passed thro Congress accepting of the tender, and annexing Texas to this Union. This will be both legal and constitutional, but as the Treaty is before the Senate, I would prefer to have it ratified. Please, with my respects to Senator Walker, to give him my ideas, should the Senate fail to ratify the treaty, of having a law passed by Congress, accepting of the annexation of Texas.[63]

The debate in the Senate on the treaty ran from May 16 to June 8. It was featured by ten speeches important enough to appear in full later in the *Congressional Globe,* interspersed with briefer remarks and resolutions.[64] Seven of the speeches were by Democrats. Of these Benton's, the longest and most vehement, was against ratification. It ran from May 16 to May 18. As already indicated, it assailed the initiation of the treaty negotiation, with special reference to the Duff Green letter to Upshur. It scoffed at the thesis that the British had forced annexation on the United States and that the treaty constituted self-defense against British designs on slavery in Texas and in the Southern states. It contained sarcastic comments on Calhoun's ex post facto dispatch to Benjamin Green in Mexico. In particular, it assailed the line of 1836 claimed by Texas, which would mean the transfer to the United States of a major part of four Mexican states with a native population of thirty thousand people. It would give the United States Santa Fé, the capital city of New Mexico. If the Senate were to ratify the treaty, it would be

[63] The manuscript of the letter is among the Ford MSS, Manuscript Division, New York Public Library. Portions were published in the Baltimore *Republican,* the *National Intelligencer,* and in *Niles' Register,* 66, 241 (June 15, 1844). The entire letter appears in Bassett, *Correspondence of Andrew Jackson,* VI, 282.

[64] These speeches may be found in the *Congressional Globe,* 28 Cong., 1 sess., App. (1843–4), with page references to them in the Index.

annexing a boundary dispute two thousand miles in length. It would in any case annex a war with Mexico. Benton ridiculed the notion that the boundary had been left without specification in the treaty in order to permit a later fair and full discussion with Mexico. He asked, "Would we take 2000 miles of the Canadas in the same way? I presume not. And why not? Because Great Britain is powerful and Mexico weak." [65]

The other major Democratic speakers all favored ratifying the treaty. They were evenly divided geographically between North and South. The Northern speakers were Levi Woodbury of New Hampshire, James Buchanan of Pennsylvania, and Sidney Breese of Illinois; the Southerners were George McDuffie of South Carolina, Robert J. Walker of Mississippi, and A. H. Sevier of Arkansas. Taken as a whole, they repeated the arguments which had been broadcast before the fact was known that a treaty was under way: the natural advantages to the North that would flow from annexation, the hardships that would fall on the South, compensated only by the greater security to be gained for its institution (which in any case was under constitutional protection), the military safety from British attack that annexation would provide, and the broad national interest that would be better safeguarded against European interferences in North American affairs.

Woodbury's arguments were outstandingly legalistic and expansionistic, and he was later appointed by Polk to the United States Supreme Court. Buchanan heavily emphasized military security, and he thought the Rio Grande was prescribed by nature as the line between the Anglo-Saxon and Mexican races. He was among those who contrasted the material advantages that an acquired Texas would bring the North, with the material damage it would bring the South. He relied, as did McDuffie, on the safety-valve function of Texas for solving the slavery issue. Breese stressed the security from a British attack that an acquired Texas would bring, and pointed out the fact that Texas extended northward to within a few miles of the gateway to Oregon. Sevier demonstrated that Texas had always extended to the Rio Grande and that it still did. He restated Duff Green's economic thesis to account for British interference with slavery in Texas. He denied a charge made on the

[65] *Ibid.,* p. 482.

floor of the Senate that the treaty, fathered by the Administration, was a "bantling of political ambition."[66]

Walker's speech was as dramatic and almost as long as Benton's. Its approach was historical, with its history bent to the requirements of the case as consistently as his famous *Letter* had been. Its hostility to the British was marked. Its peroration was a call to the senators to defeat the foe as thoroughly as he had been defeated by American patriots earlier:

> I wish to see British intrigues and British influence forever expelled from the republic of Texas, and the ever glorious ensign of my beloved country unfolded throughout its borders. Such a result would indeed be great and glorious; it would be hailed with rejoicing from the St. Croix to the Del Norte; the swelling heart of every unprejudiced and true American would beat with joy, and England would feel as she did when her armies surrendered at Yorktown, and the forces of Pakenham retired discomfited from the plains of Orleans. But should it be otherwise—should the treaty fail, and Texas be lost to the Union—great will be the joy of England; for it will be a British triumph, achieved in the American Capitol, and by the votes of American senators.[67]

Three of the ten major speeches were by Whigs: Archer of Virginia, J. M. Berrien of Georgia, and Spencer Jarnagin of Tennessee. All were hostile to the treaty. A notable Whig, John J. Crittenden of Kentucky, refrained from speech-making but registered his views by offering and pressing resolutions hostile to ratification. Archer brought the debate to a close in a powerful speech attacking more particularly the manner in which the negotiation had been opened, the details of which he described as "revolting." He had in mind Duff Green's activity, exposed by Benton, and the exploitation afterwards of Aberdeen's dispatch to Pakenham. He thought they revealed a "fixed purpose that the English government was not to be allowed to shake off the imputation of dangerous practices or purposes in regard to slavery in Texas which had been fastened upon its forehead." He noted that the treaty, "so far from having been sought on the part of Texas, had been repelled, then presented again with circumstances of false statements, cajolery, menace, and the surrender of a military and naval force, without

[66] *Ibid.*, pp. 557–60.
[67] *Ibid.*, pp. 548–57.

color of constitutional authority, to the peremptory requisition of the Texian authorities."

In closing, Archer took up the argument "Now or Never." "If, then, this was decided to be the election presented to us—annexation in the circumstances of this treaty—by this treaty now, or annexation never—if this were truly the real question—now or never, was there room for hesitation? No! The loud exclamation! Let it go out from this hall—resound through this land—reverberate from Texas—Never! oh, never!" [68]

Immediately following the speech, on June 8, the vote was taken. It was an overwhelming rejection of the treaty: thirty-five negative votes to sixteen affirmative. Of the negative votes twenty-seven were from Whigs. Every Whig in the Senate but one—John Henderson of Mississippi—voted against the treaty. Eight Democrats joined the Whigs. Seven of these were Northerners; the eighth was Benton of Missouri. The hostile Democrats were disciples of Van Buren and critics of the Administration's tactics. The size of the adverse vote is a commentary on the assurance given by the Administration to Van Zandt six months before, that a "clear constitutional majority of two-thirds are in favor of the measure." [69]

Through the weeks of Senate deliberation on the treaty, the Whig majority, aided by Benton, had been countering the propaganda tactics of the President; its tactic was to extract embarrassing documentary materials from the President and at once turn them over to the public. Thus it extracted the Calhoun assurance that no "private letter" from Duff Green regarding the British conspiracy in Texas was in the State Department files, which looked queer, and let the public have it. It got documentary evidence of the assurances given the Texans regarding armed help in case of invasion during the pendency of the treaty, and also of the directions given by the Administration to the armed forces, and released these to the public. It undertook thus to demonstrate the underhandedness, the deceptiveness, and the divisiveness of the Administration's drive

---

[68] *Ibid.,* pp. 693–6.

[69] The vote is recorded in *Jour. Exec. Proc.,* VI, 312. The Democrats voting against ratification were Benton (Missouri), Niles (Connecticut), Allen (Ohio), Tappan (Ohio), Atherton (New Hampshire), Fairfield (Maine), and Wright (New York). They have been characterized by William N. Chambers, *Old Bullion Benton* (Boston: Little, Brown & Co., 1956), p. 277, as "old-school agrarian radicals."

for annexation. The method was to promptly remove the injunction of secrecy from these executive materials and to order large printings for the benefit of the public.[70] Few tears were wept over Tappan's betrayal of the treaty and its documents to the press. A show of discipline was maintained by administering to Tappan a slap on the wrist.[71]

But they refused to release to the public the propaganda the President was sending them. They voted not to remove the injunction of secrecy from his May 16 message and its enclosures: the "golden moment" letter of Andrew Jackson, the Houston letter, and four anonymous Texan letters which prophesied that, unless the treaty were ratified, the British would establish themselves in Texas, break down slavery there, and interfere with it in the South in general. They refused on May 17 to print those materials even for Senate use,[72] and on June 8 renewed their vote not to release them, though releasing other proceedings concerning annexation not earlier released.[73] The explanation of this behavior doubtless is that the President's message and enclosures were thought by the Senate to be propaganda in the presidential election campaign of 1844, in which the Texas issue was expected to be central, and that canvass was already under way.

[70] The injunction of secrecy was formally removed on May 15 from the treaty and documents relating to it. *Jour. Exec. Proc.*, VI, 281, 283. On May 20, on motion of Archer, the injunction of secrecy was removed from all proceedings on the treaty up to that time, which included Benton's three-day speech, and the vote was later extended to all future speeches, as soon as given. *Ibid.*, 285, 290. Printings of the President's executive messages were promptly ordered. On June 1 printing was ordered, to the extent of 20,000 copies, of the message of May 31, which revealed the promises made to Texas concerning protection. *Ibid.*, p. 302. On June 3, on motion of Benton, the Senate ordered the printing of 20,000 copies of the President's message, with Calhoun's letter, reporting the inability of the State Department to locate the "private letter" of the citizen of Maryland. *Ibid.*, 305.

[71] *Ibid.*, 273.

[72] *Ibid.*, 287.

[73] *Ibid.*, 312.

CHAPTER IV

Pendency of the Issue:
The Election of 1844

I<small>N THIS BATTLE</small> with the Senate the President replied by a counterattack. On June 10, two days after the Senate's rejection of the treaty, he sent the House a message asking it to take over the Texas issue. He pointed out in the message that Congress was as competent under the Constitution to annex territory as was the Senate. He had thought the treaty mode the most suitable, but should Congress prefer some other, he was prepared to yield his prompt and active cooperation.[1]

He took this occasion to send the House the documents he had earlier sent the Senate, including those from which the Senate had not yet removed the injunction of secrecy. He made the following pointed reference to the treatment given by the Senate to the documents he had submitted to it on May 16:

> I feel it to be my duty to communicate for your consideration, the rejected treaty, together with all the correspondence and documents which have heretofore been submitted to the Senate in its executive sessions. The papers communicated embrace not only the series already made public by orders of the Senate, but others from which the veil of secrecy has not been removed by that body, but which I deem to be essential to a just appreciation of the entire question.

The message containing these words was immediately printed in the *Congressional Globe,* and on June 11, the House voted to

[1] James D. Richardson, *Messages and Papers of the Presidents,* 10 vols. (Washington, 1896–8) IV, 323–5.

print all the documents sent by the President, including those withheld by the Senate.[2] Thus the President succeeded in placing before the public the persuasive words of Andrew Jackson with regard to the annexation of Texas. The President had outflanked the obstructionists in the Senate and had scored a major propaganda victory in the campaign of 1844.

In this message, as in the one of April 22 to the Senate, the President emphasized the national character of the interests which annexation would benefit, observing how very fortunate it was that "the question involved was in no way sectional or local, but addressed itself to the interests of every part of the country and made its appeal to the glory of the American name." He showed that annexation would be especially beneficial to the North by "making an addition to the carrying trade to an amount almost incalculable and giving a new impulse of immense importance to the commercial, manufacturing, agricultural and shipping interests of the Union, and at the same time affording protection to an exposed frontier and placing the whole country in a condition of security and repose."

He reviewed some of the objections raised in the Senate to the treaty, among them the indefinite boundary. He had thought that this question needed to be raised only after Texas had been annexed—that to have raised it sooner would have proved not merely abortive but offensive to Mexico and insulting to Texas. He was prepared to negotiate fairly and frankly with Mexico and to make the fullest and most ample recompense to her for any loss she might convince us she had sustained.

He introduced into the message a subject on which all sections of the Union would be agreed: resistance to European interference. He observed, "The Government and people of the United States have never evinced nor do they feel any desire to interfere in public questions not affecting the relations existing between States of the American continent. We leave the European powers exclusive control over matters affecting their continent and the relations of their different states; the United States claim a similar exemption from such interference on their part."

[2] *House Journal*, 28 Cong., 1 sess. (ser. 438), 1070. A motion to print 15,000 extra copies of the message and documents was defeated. The documents accompanying the message are in *House Doc.*, 28 Cong., 1 sess. (ser. 444), no. 271, 1–110.

While the Senate was wrestling with the treaty of annexation, Calhoun had a breathing spell during which he was able to turn to the irritating issue of those census statistics. He had on his desk Adams's unanswered resolution concerning the gross errors alleged to exist in those statistics. The resolution had been copied and sent to the State Department on February 26. In the copying a mistake had crept into it, apparently in the office of the Clerk of the House, whereby the date "1841" specified in the resolution had become "1843." Calhoun could have raised the question whether the transcription of the House resolution had not produced an error. Instead, he wrote the Speaker a letter on May 4, 1844, making full use of the error:

> The Secretary of State, in obedience to a resolution of the House of Representatives of the 26th of February, 1844, directing him to inform the House whether any gross errors have been discovered in the printed "sixth census, or enumeration of the inhabitants of the United States, as corrected at the Department of State in 1843," has the honor to report: That there was not any work bearing that title, corrected at the Department of State in the year 1843. The corrections of the returns of the census, made at the department, were previous to the printing, in 1841, of the work, for the use of Congress. They were confined, principally, to clerical errors in relation to the additions and making of the aggregates. Such errors as were discovered in the printed copy previous to its delivery to Congress, are noted in errata on the last page of the work.
>
> The duties imposed upon the Secretary of State in relation to the census having been performed by the delivery, to the printers to Congress, of the copy of the corrected returns, there has been no subsequent examination made, nor have any gross or material errors been discovered in the printed copy.[3]

This letter was not read to the House in full. The Speaker merely summarized it, dwelling on its closing sentence, which alone was entered on the *House Journal*. The letter was then laid on the table, and the House adjourned.[4]

At the next meeting Adams promptly gained the floor and moved to amend the entry on the *Journal*. He had seen the letter, which

---

[3] Calhoun's letter is published in *House Doc., 28* Cong., 1 sess. (ser. 443), no. 245. The "errata," mentioned by Calhoun as found previous to printing, were inconsequential.

[4] *House Journal,* 28 Cong., 1 sess. (ser. 438), 876–7 (May 4).

he pronounced "the most extraordinary communication ever made from the State Department." In the ensuing discussion, objection was made to amending the *Journal.* This led an Ohio Whig, R. C. Schenck, to move that the entire letter of Calhoun be printed in the *Journal,* but the motion was soundly defeated.[5]

The maneuvers of the Speaker, and even more, the Calhoun letter, curdled the little equanimity of spirit possessed by Adams, and he arranged a confrontation with Calhoun at the State Department. After some preliminary discussion of two other matters, he raised, as a third, the question of the errors in the printed census of 1840. He recorded afterwards in his diary that Calhoun

> answered like a true slavemonger on the third. He writhed like a trodden rattlesnake on the exposure of his false report to the House that no material errors have been discovered in the printed census of 1840, and finally said that where there were so many errors they balanced one another, and led to the same conclusion as if they were all correct.[6]

The use to which those statistics had been put by Calhoun in writing Pakenham a month before was known to Adams, who had seen the letter among the betrayed Senate documents, and this doubtless accounts for the wrath of his entry in his diary. Calhoun had written Pakenham that it would be neither wise nor humane to change the relation between the races that had existed in the Southern states from their first settlement:

> The census and other authentic sources of information establish the fact, that the condition of the African race throughout all the States where the ancient relation between the two has been retained, enjoys a degree of health and comfort which may well compare with that of the labouring population of any country in Christendom;

[5] *Congressional Globe,* 28 Cong., 1 sess., 577.

[6] Charles F. Adams, ed., *Memoirs of John Quincy Adams,* 12 vols. (Philadelphia, 1874–7) XII, 29 (May 18, 1844). A week after this episode Dr. Jarvis commented bitterly to Dorothea Dix concerning the Texas treaty documents, which had just appeared in the press: "I little thought, when I wrote my pamphlet last fall, that so soon would the second officer of our nation make such use of the falsehoods of the census and produce such an atrocious piece of sophistry as Mr. Calhoun has in regard to slavery & Texas." Edward Jarvis to Dorothea Dix, May 25, 1844, Dorothea Dix Papers, Houghton Library. See also Norman Dain, *Concepts of Insanity in the United States, 1789–1865* (New Brunswick: Rutgers University Press, 1964), pp. 104–7.

and, it may be added, that in no other condition, or in any other age or country, has the Negro race ever attained so high an elevation in morals, intelligence, or civilization.[7]

In this letter Calhoun also extensively cited the census statistics to demonstrate the deplorable condition of free Negroes in New England and especially in Massachusetts, and pointed out that the Northern Negroes "have been invariably sunk into vice and pauperism, accompanied by the bodily and mental inflictions incident thereto—deafness, blindness, insanity, and idiocy, to a degree without example."

Earlier reliance had been placed on these statistics by Upshur in pressing Everett to action in 1843, and by Walker in pressing a different thesis in his *Letter Relative to the Annexation of Texas*. In one way or another the theme implicit in those statistics powered the Southern drive for annexation, and the tenacity with which Calhoun clung to them was testimony to their usefulness. It testified also to the grip that slavery had on the group advising Tyler.

But Calhoun's use of those statistics disgusted many Northern Democrats as well as Whigs. It disgusted George Bancroft, a supporter of Van Buren, though not of Van Buren's views on Texas. He had learned of Calhoun's exchange with Pakenham as a result of the Tappan betrayal of the treaty and its documents to the public. He wrote Van Buren on May 2, 1844, "What can be more sad than for a man to serve under John Tyler? What: unless it be to found an argument in defense of slavery on fictitious statistics, and address it to a British minister!"[8] Like views were held by many in the Van Buren wing of the Democratic party.

Several days before his confrontation with Calhoun, Adams had received from Boston the Memorial of the American Statistical Association describing the gross errors of the census. It had been sent to him by J. Wingate Thornton, an associate of Jarvis in writing it.[9] Adams undertook at once to get it presented on the floor of Con-

[7] Calhoun to Pakenham, April 18, 1844, in *Sen. Doc.*, 28 Cong., 1 sess. (ser. 435), no. 341, 50–3.
[8] George Bancroft to Van Buren, May 2, 1844, in *Massachusetts Historical Society Proceedings*, 42 (1908–9), 425–6. The letter related to a campaign biography of Van Buren that Bancroft was writing in anticipation of Van Buren's nomination for the presidency on the Democratic ticket.
[9] Thornton was a well-known Boston historian and genealogist, founder of the New England Historic Genealogical Society. His letter to Adams enclosing the

gress, but he did not succeed. His memorials and petitions had been too numerous over the years and too likely to be of the sort banned from the floor under the operation of the gag rules. The Speaker, backed by the Democratic majority in the House, blocked its acceptance. Adams had to be content with submitting it quietly to the Clerk of the House. It was then referred to a select committee, safely Democratic, which had been established to consider the creation of a bureau of statistics.

The chairman of that committee was Zadock Pratt, a New York Democrat, who could be trusted to dispose of petitions without fireworks. He was an industrialist of large wealth—the owner of one of the greatest tanneries in the United States. He had constructed the tannery as a young man at Schoharie Kill in southeastern New York on the upper waters of the Schoharie River. His site was ideal. It gave access to unlimited sources of hemlock bark, hides, and water. The tannery prospered exceedingly. Pratt built a hundred dwellings there for his workmen, and the city was eventually renamed Prattville in his honor. He was successful in winning election to the Twenty-fifth and Twenty-eighth Congresses. In the Twenty-eighth Congress one of his prime interests was to obtain the creation of a bureau of statistics and commerce in the Treasury Department. In deference to his importance to the Administration, a committee was established, of which he was made chairman. This accounts for his having received petitions and memorials relating to the statistics of the census.[10]

Among the petitions referred to his committee were two relating especially to the census. One was sponsored by Thomas Earle and twenty-four Pennsylvanians; the other was that of the American Statistical Association. Thomas Earle was a native of Massachusetts who had moved to Philadelphia and had won standing there as a writer and reformer. He had been named by moderate antislavery elements as the candidate for the vice-presidency on the Liberty party ticket in 1840, but he had been thought too conservative by

Memorial is found in The Adams Papers, Microfilm 529, Letters Received and Other Loose Papers, April–July, 1844, under date May 14, 1844. Courtesy of the Adams Family Trust.

[10] An illuminating autobiographical account of the rise of this self-made man is Hon. Zadock Pratt, *Chronological Biography* (New York, 1868). Its publisher was the Shoe and Leather Reporter Press. The select committee on statistics, of which he became chairman, was established on January 29, 1844. *Congressional Globe,* 28 Cong., 1 sess., 204.

abolitionists, and his name had been withdrawn.[11] His petition to the House reflected moderate Whig opinion. It declared:

> that your petitioners have reason to believe that the returns of the last census of the United States, in reference to the proportion of deaf, dumb, blind, insane, and idiots among the colored people of the northern States, are materially incorrect; that your petitioners understand that reference has been made to these returns, and to the alleged state of morals of the free colored people, as affording arguments favorable to slavery, and to the admission of Texas into this Union. Your petitioners, therefore, pray that you will cause an inquiry to be made as to the accuracy of the last census, and also as to the state of morality of the emancipated population of Antigua and Bermuda, in comparison with that of the free and slave population of the southern states of the Union.[12]

The Pratt committee on June 17 made a cautious report on the Earle petition. It was primarily interested in the petition as evidence of the need for a new statistical bureau. Pratt wrote that the truth of the charges in the petition could not be ascertained without examining the original census returns, and such an investigation would in any case be futile. The committee begged leave, therefore, to be discharged from all further consideration of the petition. However, Pratt observed, if the census returns were found to be defective and in need of correction, this would be an additional reason for the creation of a statistical bureau under the direction of the secretary of the treasury, which the committee recommended. To drive that argument home, Pratt submitted a further twenty-six-page plea for a bureau of statistics, supporting his case largely by a statistical survey, borrowed mostly from the book *Progress of the United States,* a statistical compilation prepared by Professor George Tucker of the University of Virginia.[13]

Pratt's second report, also submitted on June 17—the crowded last day of the session—was devoted to the Memorial of the American Statistical Association. At the outset it candidly admitted that the committee, having compared the Memorial with the printed census, had found its charges correct. Pratt felt that the Memorial's

---

[11] For a sketch of Thomas Earle see Allen Johnson and Dumas Malone, eds., *Dictionary of American Biography* (New York: Charles Scribner's Sons, 1928–44).

[12] For the petition see *House Doc.,* 28 Cong., 1 sess. (ser. 447), no. 579, 2.

[13] The report of the committee is in *ibid.* See also *House Journal,* 28 Cong., 1 sess. (ser. 438), 941.

findings had destroyed the utility of the census, "so far as the subjects referred to it are concerned, and render completely nugatory any conclusions which may be based upon them. It will be very desirable that some mode of collecting the materials for the next and subsequent censuses should be adopted, which may prevent the recurrence of error so far as is possible. The committee know of no mode of doing this so easy and practicable as by the establishment of a bureau of statistics, agreeably to the plan which they have recommended." This was followed by a reprinting, in abbreviated form, of the Jarvis Memorial.[14]

An interpolation is needed here as to the politics of Pratt and his fellow committeemen. Pratt was a Democrat loyal to the Administration, the kind the Whigs irreverently described as "doughface," which meant a Northern man with Southern principles. His committee of five was composed of four Southerners and himself. The Southerners were three Democrats and one Whig. Except for the Whig, all the members later voted for the Joint Resolution to annex Texas. In the report on the Earle petition the committee made a warm plea for congressional measures that would induce harmony between the Northern and Southern sections of the Union. This seemed of basic importance. One measure specifically recommended was the annexation of Texas by Congress. This would induce harmony by eliminating from sectional relations the heated issue of slavery. Texas, if annexed, would draw off the slaves of the South to its virgin soils. Then, after the soils had lost their virginity, the slaves would have to be emancipated by their masters, and would cross happily from the United States into Mexico and Latin America. That was the thesis—the safety-valve thesis—of Senator Walker, to whom acknowledgment was dutifully made. Thus the famous *Letter,* which had won wide Northern circulation since its publication in the preceding February, got a further puff in the Pratt reports, which doubtless accounts for the fact that the reports were published in the House documents, though the question of doing so was never brought before the House. Those reports were part of the propaganda quietly subsidized in the Tyler Administration by the exponents of annexation.

[14] *House Doc.,* 28 Cong., 1 sess. (ser. 447), no. 580. See also *House Journal,* 28 Cong., 1 sess. (ser. 438), 1170.

One statistical study sent to the Senate in 1844 never attained the status of publication in a committee report. It was a memorial sent by a committee, headed by a Negro doctor of distinction, James McCune Smith. The committee had been appointed at a mass meeting of free Negroes of New York City on April 29, 1844, to consider the "calumnies against free people of color uttered by John C. Calhoun" in his letter to Richard Pakenham. Smith was a son of a former New York slave freed under the Manumission Act of 1785. He had exhibited unusual promise as a student in New York City schools and had been sent to complete a medical education at the University of Glasgow. At the age of thirty-one he had already won recognition as a medical writer [15] and physician. On February 1, 1844, the New York *Tribune* had opened its columns to him for a notable article on the census statistics. The article carried a challenging preamble: "Figures cannot be charged with fanaticism. Like the everlasting hills, they give cold, silent evidence, unmoved by the clouds and shadows of whatever present may surround them. Let us see what they say of the vital statistics of the slaves of the South and of the Free Blacks of the North." From that prelude Smith moved on to examine the effects of "the shadows of the South" on the census statistics. He cited the *Southern Literary Messenger* and its "pretty theory" regarding the prevalence of insanity among Northern free Negroes. He also cited Dr. Jarvis and his tables of statistics, which made Maine "a very madhouse, with six towns containing a total of one colored inhabitant and yet credited by the census with 19 insane blacks." He went on to say, "To make 19 crazy men out of one man, is pretty fair calculation even for 'down east.' " [16]

Early in May the committee, appointed by the Negro mass meeting of April 29, headed by James McCune Smith, was ready to report. At a large assembly Smith read a memorial on the "calumnies" of Calhoun with respect to Negroes. The memorial followed the pattern of the Jarvis study in the *American Journal of the Med-*

---

[15] James McCune Smith won an award from the Boylston Medical Committee of Harvard University in April, 1845, for an essay on "Influence of Climate on Longevity." The essay was published in two installments in *Hunt's Merchants Magazine*, 14 (April and May, 1846), 319–20, 403–18.

[16] New York *Tribune*, February 1, 1844. See also an article by the same author on intellectual and religious statistics in the *Tribune*, February 28, 1844.

ical Sciences (January, 1844), exhibiting disparities between the total population of free Negroes in towns of the Northern states and numbers of the colored insane in those states. But it also dealt with statistics of pauperism and vice among free Negroes to meet Calhoun's charges. Smith used the records of almshouses in New York and in Philadelphia, where more than a sixth of the entire Negro population of the free states lived, to show that the proportion of colored paupers there was about the same as that of the whites. Regarding vice, he came to such conclusions as he could from religious statistics. The whole number of African churches in the free states was 114, serving a colored population of 170,718. The number in the slave states, serving a larger colored population of freemen, was 24.[17]

The memorial was addressed, at the wish of the Negro mass meeting, to the Massachusetts senator, Rufus Choate, for presentation to the Senate. It was actually presented by the New York senator, N. P. Tallmadge, on May 27, 1844. It was referred in the Senate to the Committee on the Judiciary, and this was the last heard of it.[18] Negro memorials on the deficiencies of the census received less publicity than those offered by more vocal whites.

In the turbulent days preceding the adjournment of Congress a personal altercation occurred over the annexation issue between two very vocal whites, Senator McDuffie of South Carolina, a disciple of Calhoun, and Senator Benton, a bitter foe of both Calhoun and the Administration. It occurred on June 15, with an assault by McDuffie on a speech of Benton delivered two days before in defending his bill of June 10 for a new negotiation with Texas, including Mexico. Benton had made provision in the bill for an adjustment of the boundary separating the two states, and thereafter, the annexation of Texas to the Union. This would have been a reversal of the order of procedure regarding the boundary that Calhoun and Tyler had followed in their secret treaty negotiation.[19] McDuffie's attack on it was more than normally personal. He intimated that Benton was a Brutus who had struck down Caesar; he charged his colleague with being schoolmasterish in his relations with the Senate and with lack-

[17] New York *Tribune,* May 8, 1844.
[18] *Congressional Globe,* 28 Cong., 1 sess., 625 (May 27, 1844).
[19] *Ibid.,* App., 568–76 (June 12–13, 1844).

ing common sense. He suggested that Benton had read himself out of the Democratic party in his attacks on the Administration.[20]

The instantaneous reply of Benton was in the same temper. For two hours he berated and ridiculed the South Carolinian. At one stage he advanced to the desk where his opponent sat and banged it with his fist. Witnesses of the drama were apprehensive that it would be followed by a duel.

In denouncing the secret tactics and the falsehoods of the Administration, Benton added his own view of the purposes that had fueled the annexation drive. He believed it was disunion, a duplication of the earlier South Carolina nullification episode by the extremists surrounding Tyler. He observed:

I have often intimated it before, but now proclaim it. Disunion is at the bottom of this long-concealed Texas machination. Intrigue and speculation cooperate; but disunion is at the bottom; and I denounce it to the American people. Under the pretext of getting Texas into the Union, the scheme is to get the South out of it. A separate confederacy, stretching from the Atlantic to California, (and hence the secret of the Rio Grande del Norte frontier), is the cherished vision of disappointed ambition; and for this consummation every circumstance has been carefully and artfully controlled. A secret and intriguing negotiation, concealed from Congress and the people: an abolition quarrel picked with Great Britain to father an abolition quarrel at home: a slavery correspondence to outrage the North: war with Mexico: the clandestine concentration of troops and ships in the southwest: the secret compact with the President of Texas, and the subjection of American forces to his command: the flagrant seizure of the purse and the sword: the contradictory and preposterous reasons on which the detected military and naval movement was defended: all these announce the prepared catastrophe; and the inside view of the treaty betrays its design. The whole annexed country is to be admitted as one territory, with a treaty promise to be admitted as States; when we all know that Congress alone can admit new States, and that the treaty promise, without a law of Congress to back it, is void. The whole to be slave States, (and with the boundary to the Rio Grande there may be a great many;) and the correspondence, which is the key to the treaty, and shows the design of its framers, wholly directed to the extension of slavery and the exasperation of the North. What else could be done to get up Missouri controversies, and make sure

[20] *Ibid.*, 588–90 (June 15, 1844).

of the non-admission of these States? Then the plot is consummated; and Texas without the Union, sooner than the Union without Texas (already the premonitory chorus of so many resolves) receives its practical application in the secession of the South, and its adhesion to the rejected Texas.[21]

This withering review of the rejected annexation treaty and its negotiation was a national sensation. The author was a ranking leader of the Democratic party, a devoted follower of Van Buren who had steadily resisted injecting the Texas issue into the nation's politics, yet had a record of championing annexation whenever it could be achieved without a disruption of the Union. His charges had behind them the driving force of fiery eloquence, and also the unquestioned furtiveness of the Administration's proceedings. The conclusion easily derived from the furtiveness was that the Administration was committed to a program of disunion, and this conclusion was adopted by major leaders of the party, among them Francis P. Blair of the Washington *Globe,* and William Cullen Bryant of the New York *Evening Post.*[22] Needless to say, the Whig press agreed with that conclusion.

On May 26, ten days after the first Benton assault on the annexation treaty in the Senate, the Democratic national nominating convention had assembled in Baltimore. It had been rigged against Van Buren by the Texas annexationists in the party. Van Buren had once commanded a majority of the delegate votes. Against him the two-thirds rule was called into play; and in the mêlée which followed, the slaveholder and expansionist James K. Polk, who stood pledged to the immediate annexation of Texas and the reoccupation of Oregon, won the nomination.

[21] *Ibid.,* 607–11 (June 15, 1844).

[22] As early as May 2, 1844, Blair believed that Calhoun's scheme was "dissolution of the Union, and a Southern confederacy." On July 7 he wrote Jackson, "I sincerely believe that Calhoun and his old Junto of conspirators are more than ever anxious to separate the South from the north. They want Texas only as a bone of contention." John S. Bassett, ed., *Correspondence of Andrew Jackson,* 7 vols. (Washington: Carnegie Institution, 1926–35), VI, 281–30. The New York *Evening Post,* in an editorial on the Texas issue on July 25, 1844, observed, "But for our shame and misfortune the matter fell into the hands of a few fanatics as crazy on the subject of the 'domestic institutions,' as the maddest abolitionists in the Union—men who believe or affect to believe that the *summum bonum* of Republican freedom lies in the possessing of a few hundred slaves; and by these slaveholding fanatics was the question of Texas, a great question of extension of empire, dwarfed into one of enlarging the influence of that pernicious institution which defaces and disgraces our otherwise glorious country."

A Tyler convention, meeting at the same time in Baltimore, unanimously named the President as its candidate. Its delegates were to a considerable degree officeholders, and they believed his services in the foreign field, especially his resurrection of the Texas issue, had won him the favor of the electorate. The Whigs had met in early May, just after the appearance of Clay's letter opposing the annexation of Texas. The letter had not destroyed his availability. Indeed, he was unanimously named the candidate of the party.

The central issue in the ensuing campaign was expansionism. As phrased in the Democratic platform, it was "the re-occupation of Oregon and the re-annexation of Texas at the earliest practical period." [23] The "earliest practical period," in both cases, was considered to be at once, as nearly as possible. The Oregon and Texas planks were intended to balance each other—the one attractive especially to the Northwest, the other, to the South. The prefix in each case was meaningful. According to the Democrats, a perfect title to all Oregon had once been held by the United States. But two Whigs, John Quincy Adams and Henry Clay, had compromised the title in the early negotiations by agreeing to a joint occupation with the British. An end must be put to this by "notice" to the British, followed by re-establishment of American sovereignty over all the area. In the case of Texas, American ownership to the Rio Grande had once been indisputable, since Texas was part of the Louisiana Purchase. In 1819, however, it had been ceded by Adams to Spain in an unconstitutional and lamentable treaty. The region had passed later into the hands of American pioneers, who were offering to restore it, with its old boundaries, to the land of their birth. The Democratic platform reflected a new spirit spreading in expansionist circles—the spirit of "Manifest Destiny." [24]

Whigs were less land-hungry than Democrats. Their leaders, including Clay and Webster, would have been content to have sisterly republics surrounding the United States. Clay would have been willing to see both Canada and Texas independent nations, and Webster would have included Oregon among them. In his "Raleigh Letter," published with Van Buren's on April 27, Clay expressed

[23] Edward Stanwood, *A History of the Presidency from 1788 to 1897* (Boston, 1898), pp. 215–16.

[24] Frederick Merk, *Manifest Destiny and Mission in American History* (New York: Alfred A. Knopf, 1963), *passim*.

95

actual opposition to annexing Texas. He thought any talk of resuming an old title, relinquished in 1819 to Spain, was perfectly ridiculous and dishonorable. An annexation of Texas, in view of the aid Americans had given to its separation from Mexico in 1836, would open us to the charge of selfish designs. Annexation, moreover, would be followed by war with Mexico, and would in any case imperil the Union.[25]

But Clay altered his position in the course of the campaign in response to pressure from Southern Whigs. On July 27, 1844, in the second of his "Alabama Letters," he wrote:

> I have, however, no hesitation in saying, that, far from having any personal objection to the annexation of Texas, I should be glad to see it, without dishonor—without war, with the common consent of the Union, and upon just and fair terms. I do not think that the subject of slavery ought to affect the question, one way or the other. Whether Texas be independent, or incorporated in the United States, I do not believe it will prolong or shorten the duration of that institution. It is destined to become extinct, at some distant day, in my opinion, by the operation of the inevitable laws of population. It would be unwise to refuse a permanent acquisition, which will exist as long as the globe remains, on account of a temporary institution.[26]

This retreat by the leader of the party from the party stand seemed to Northern Whigs a betrayal. The letter was described in a New Haven journal as a "poisoned chalice" to Whiggery in Connecticut, and in the crucial state of New York it led to party disaster.

Retreat from the party standards was a phenomenon also in the Democratic party. Polk set a significant example early in the campaign. The party was pledged to the principle of a low tariff. The issue was the most important, next to expansionism, in the party's platform. Yet it was clear that the party would lose votes, especially in Pennsylvania and Louisiana, if it adhered too rigidly to its principles. The electoral vote of those states was important to win, and the controlling interests there were addicted to protectionism. Soon after Polk won his nomination, he sent a Pennsylvania adherent, J. K. Kane, a letter calling attention to his unvarying record of support for low-tariff measures in Congress. He added, however, that it "was the duty of the government to extend, so far as practical by its

[25] *Niles' Register,* 66 (May 4, 1844), 152–5.
[26] *Ibid.,* 66 (August 31, 1844), 439; citing the *North Alabamian,* August 16, 1844.

revenue laws and all other means within its power, fair and just protection to all the great interests of the whole Union, embracing agriculture, manufacturing, the mechanic arts, commerce and navigation." [27] The list included all the great interests of the Union. It could be used to assure Pennsylvanians and others that the Democratic party was the special champion of the tariff of 1842. Indeed it was freely used to picture Clay as a dangerous enemy to the protective system wherever this was necessary.

The *National Intelligencer,* which earnestly believed in the principle of the protective tariff, had this sardonic comment to make on July 8, 1844, on the tariff tactics of Polk's supporters:

> The Whigs, poor fellows, are so hard run that they have but *one set of principles* for the North and South, East and West. Not so with their opponents. They have *principles* for all sorts of people and every neighborhood. At the South, Mr. Polk is held up as being deadly opposed to the "Black Whig tariff" and the very *beau ideal of free trade* candidates. At the North, however, and especially in Pennsylvania and New Jersey, the tune is pitched upon another key. At Morristown, in the latter State, in the neighborhood of which *factories abound,* they have a club of Polkites calling themselves "Young Hickories," and here is the light in which they regard Mr. Polk's *principles:* Citing the Democratic *Augusta* [Georgia] *Chronicle:* Resolved, That the story of Mr. Polk being a *free trade man,* so industriously circulated by the Whigs, *must be told to other ears* than those of the Democrats of Morristown, in order to gain credence; *we do not believe a word of it, and shall not,* until we have some better proof than the bare assertions of Whig office-holders and office seekers. *Resolved,* That believing a permanent tariff of some kind to be of great consequence to the manufacturer, we, *like our candidates* for President and Vice President, are opposed to disturbing the present tariff law.

The conclusion of the editorial by the *National Intelligencer* was, "What a break-down *crash* we should have were the friends of the *Tennessee Accidency* from the North and the South to meet in general conclave and each advocate their peculiar doctrines!" [28]

[27] For the Kane letter, see Carl Schurz, *Henry Clay,* 2 vols. (Boston, 1899), II, 257–8. See also Malcolm R. Eiselen, *Rise of Pennsylvania Protectionism* (Philadelphia: University of Pennsylvania Press, 1932), chap. 8.

[28] *National Intelligencer,* July 8, 1844. The reference to the "Tennessee Accidency" was a jibe at Polk, but also at Tyler, who was dubbed "His Accidency" on succeeding Harrison to the presidency. Polk was the "Accidency" because of succeeding the real leader of the Democracy, Van Buren, knifed at the nominating convention.

The tariff tactics of Polk and his followers in the campaign have been characterized by Carl Schurz as "one of the most audacious political frauds in our history," [29] and they were important in turning Pennsylvania's large electoral vote to Young Hickory in November.

Walker contributed a comparable service to his party. While his *Letter Relative to the Annexation of Texas* was circulating through the North, designed to prove that slavery would be put on the road to extinction throughout the Union if annexation occurred, another pamphlet from his pen, entitled *The South in Danger,* was broadcast through the South. It demonstrated that Clay was allied to Northern abolitionists, intent on destroying slavery, and that, to save slavery, Texas must be annexed at once, which required voting for Polk. The authorship of the pamphlet was discovered and exposed by a Whig member of Congress from Kentucky, whereupon Whig campaign committees hurriedly printed three large editions of it, for distribution to Northern readers, which contained appropriate forewords revealing the contradictions and hollowness of both the Walker pamphlets.[30]

The canvass of 1844, despite these aberrations, was not as objectionable a form of politics as had been the preceding maneuvers for the treaty of annexation. At least it was in the open. In an open campaign the distortions of fact and of language that had been so profitable during the treaty negotiation could be more quickly detected and denounced. Also, less use could be made of the Administration's thesis that the federal government had an obligation under the Constitution to annex Texas as the only sure means of defending slavery against the machinations of European powers. It was also a relief that Tyler, who had permitted himself to become the leader of the slavery extremists of the South in the quest for Texas, withdrew from the contest for election. On August 20, in a letter tinged with bitterness, he gave up a hopeless candidacy, with solace only in the thought that his sacrifice might help to defeat the Whigs.[31]

[29] Carl Schurz, *Henry Clay,* II, 258.
[30] Thomas W. Streeter, *Bibliography of Texas, 1795–1845,* 5 vols. (Cambridge: Harvard University Press, 1955–60), Pt. 3, vol. 2, 450–2.
[31] Lyon G. Tyler, *Letters and Times of the Tylers,* 3 vols. (Richmond, 1884–96), II, 342–9.

In the campaign the charge of European interference in the affairs of the New World was stressed. It was leveled principally at the British, though the French were also implicated in it. Actually the so-called interference antedated the Peel-Aberdeen era. In November, 1840, Lord Palmerston, foreign secretary in the Melbourne ministry, received a suggestion from the British minister in Mexico, Richard Pakenham, that an Anglo-French mediation be offered in the war between Mexico and Texas. The United States was to be included in the plan. But Palmerston leaned to the view "that it would be better on all accounts that each party should act separately, but similarly in point of time and argument, in urging the Mexican Government to reconsider the subject dispassionately and impartially, and to lose no time in coming to an accommodation with Texas, on the basis of a recognition of her independence." [32] The French government adopted this suggestion and sent instructions of this tenor to its minister in Mexico. [33]

The Mexican minister of foreign affairs, Juan de D. Cañedo, accepted Palmerston's suggestion and recommended it to the Council of State. One of the committees of the Council also approved it. But M. E. Gorostiza, a former minister of foreign affairs, opposed it, and Cañedo abandoned it rather than risk carrying it to the Chamber of Deputies of his proud nation. The prospect of peace broke down. [34]

In the Peel ministry Aberdeen returned to the plan of mediation with the addition of an offer of an Anglo-French guarantee of independence to Texas and of a negotiated boundary. In the framing of that plan the Mexican minister in London, Tomás Murphy, was consulted, and gave his approval. Approval was also given by the Texan minister in London, Ashbel Smith, with the understanding that Spain would be induced to open Cuban markets to Texan trade. [35]

[32] *British and Foreign State Papers,* XXIX, 1840–41, 84–5; Smith to Van Zandt, January 25, 1843, A.H.A. *Report,* 1908, II (2), 1103–7; Van Zandt to Webster, January 24, 1843, in *House Doc.,* 28 Cong., 1 sess., (ser. 444), no. 271, 70–1.

[33] E. D. Adams, *British Interests and Activities in Texas, 1838–1848* (Baltimore: Johns Hopkins Press, 1910), chap. 2.

[34] *Ibid.*

[35] Justin Smith, *The Annexation of Texas* (New York: Baker and Taylor Co., 1911), pp. 382–91. A "corrected edition" was published in 1941. The pagination is identical in both editions.

After the Senate had rejected Tyler's annexation treaty, the Aberdeen plan was enlarged into a projected "diplomatic act." In this the United States was to be a partner. The plan was to consist of a joint guarantee of the independence of Texas and of a boundary that Texas and Mexico would agree to draw.[36] This seemed to Ashbel Smith less desirable than the earlier plan, since it betokened formal recognition of European interference in inter-American affairs. However, Smith did assure Aberdeen that Texas wanted to retain her independence. The King of France and his first minister, Guizot, approved the plan, and so did Houston on behalf of Texas. Houston directed his secretary of state, Anson Jones, in writing, to inform the British government of his approval.[37] But Jones, who was soon to succeed Houston, deferred acting, since he opposed both the idea and its timing, and the approval was not sent. Jones was unwilling, especially in collaboration with European states, to renounce annexation, and he feared future armed clashes if the American government should insist on an annexation and on the Rio Grande boundary or even something beyond.[38]

A copy of the "act" was sent by Aberdeen to Pakenham (then in Washington) with a request for a report on it after consultation with the French minister in Washington, Alphonse Pageot. The requested report was sent by Pakenham on June 27. It was an emphatic warning that the "act," if it became known, would have the effect of ensuring the election of Polk in the pending campaign. The French minister sent his government a like report. The warning had a sobering influence. The British government, and subsequently the French government, abandoned all thought of concluding the "diplomatic act."[39]

[36] A good survey of the evolution of the "diplomatic act" and of its later abandonment is Adams, *British Interests and Activities,* pp. 167–96. The account in Smith, *Annexation of Texas,* pp. 391–5, attributes more belligerency to Aberdeen in developing the "act" than does Adams.

[37] Houston's letter of direction to Jones is published in an undated communication from Jones to the editor of the *Western Texian,* which was republished in *Niles' Register,* 74 (December 27, 1848), 413.

[38] Jones to the editor of the *Western Texian,* October 19, 1848, republished in *Niles' Register,* 74 (December 27, 1848), 413. But see Adams, *British Interests and Activities,* p. 195.

[39] Smith, *Annexation of Texas,* pp. 395–6.

CHAPTER V

A Plan to Outflank the Senate

I N THE UNITED STATES, in the November balloting, the electorate registered no clear mandate for annexation. The vote was scattered among three candidates: Polk, Clay, and James G. Birney, an avowed abolitionist. Had the Birney vote stayed Whig, Clay would have had a popular majority by a margin of 24,119, in a total vote of 2,698,605. More significantly, he would have carried New York and Michigan, and would have won in the electoral college by a margin of 146 to 129. As it was, Polk won an electoral majority of 170 to 105, on the basis of a mere plurality in the popular vote. The fact was that 24,119 more popular votes were cast *against* him than the total *for* him.[1] The propagandists of annexation, however, ignoring the popular vote, pointed with pride to the electoral majority and cited it as evidence of the wishes of the American people. Such was the line President Tyler took in his annual message to Congress of December 3, 1844. He observed:

> The decision of the people and the States on this great and interesting subject has been decisively manifested. The question of annexation has been presented nakedly to their consideration. By the treaty itself all collateral and incidental issues which were calculated to divide and distract the public councils were carefully avoided. These were left to the wisdom of the future to determine. It presented, I repeat, the isolated question of annexation, and in that form it has been submitted to the ordeal of public sentiment. A controlling majority of the people and a large majority of the

[1] Edward Stanwood, *History of the Presidency from 1788 to 1897* (Boston, 1898), p. 223.

States have declared in favor of immediate annexation. Instructions have thus come up to both branches of Congress from their respective constituents in terms the most emphatic. It is the will of both the people and the States that Texas shall be annexed to the Union promptly and immediately. It may be hoped that in carrying into execution the public will, thus declared, all collateral issues may be avoided.[2]

In this paragraph the President dexterously combined two themes. One was that the annexation treaty had carefully avoided what he referred to as the "collateral and incidental issue" of slavery. This was the truth as regards the treaty itself, in which the slavery issue had been studiously omitted. But it was certainly not the truth as regards the documents accompanying the treaty. In them there had been a persistent intertwining of slavery and annexation. With regard to the second theme—the election—the assertions of the President that the decision of the people had been "decisively manifested," and that instructions had "thus come up to both branches of Congress from their respective constituents in terms the most emphatic," were patently false. By combining a number of half-truths in a single paragraph, the President hoped to manufacture one that was whole, but actually he produced only a deception.

The President also defended, in the message, the boundary provision of the defeated treaty. He ascribed its vagueness to consideration for the feelings of Mexico and Texas. He offered assurances that if an agreement were concluded with Texas, a most liberal settlement would follow with Mexico. He made no reference to the dimension of the territory in dispute. It was a major portion of four Mexican provinces with a native population of 30,000 Mexican citizens. A promise of liberal treatment, if Texas were to become a part of the United States, was unlikely to be reassuring to the Mexicans or to Northerners concerned about the extension of slavery.

The issue of military aid to be given to Texas in case of an invasion by Mexico was also discussed by the President. He was most

---

[2] James Richardson, *Messages and Papers of the Presidents,* 10 vols. (Washington, 1896–8), IV, 344. The comment of the New York *Evening Post* on the message on December 4, 1844 was: "Never was algebraist more expert than Mr. Tyler in cancelling impractical quantities. Mr. Benton, we wot, will be a little surprised on reaching Washington, to be told that in giving his vote at the polls he has been voting for Mr. Tyler's treaty."

happy to inform Congress that no invasion had yet occurred. He made clear that his promises of military aid to Texas during the pendency of the treaty had lapsed because the treaty had been rejected. But he added that it was "the imperative duty of the Executive to inform Mexico that the question of annexation was still before the American people, and that until their decision was pronounced any serious invasion of Texas would be regarded as an attempt to forestall [an American] judgment and could not be looked upon with indifference." This indicated that the President was prepared to give Texas the same degree of military protection for the indefinite period of "pendency" ahead, as for the briefer period while the treaty was before the Senate. From a constitutional point of view this was ominous.

The President used the occasion of the message to describe at length and in enraptured terms the advantages of the American confederate system of government, which left each state supreme as to its local interests while confiding to the Union the protection of the general interests. He emphasized the importance of cherishing a love of Union in all the states and of frowning upon efforts to alienate states and their people from each other. He pointed out that the confederate system was destined to be felt as beneficially on the distant shores of the Pacific as it had been on the shores of the Atlantic in consequence of improvements made in transportation and communication. He alluded, however, to one of the weaknesses of confederacies:

> One of the strongest objections which has been urged against confederacies, by writers on government, is the liability of the members to be tampered with by foreign governments, or the people of foreign States, either in their local affairs, or in such as affected the peace of others, or endangered the safety of the whole confederacy. We cannot hope to be entirely exempt from such attempts on our peace and safety. . . . It therefore may, in the progress of time, occur that opinions entirely abstract in the States in which they prevail [slavery at the North], and in no degree affecting their domestic institutions, may be artfully, but secretly, encouraged with a view to undermine the Union. Such opinions may become the foundation of political parties, until at last the conflict of opinion, producing an alienation of friendly feeling among the people of the different States, may involve in one general destruction the happy

institutions under which we live. It should ever be borne in mind, that what is true in regard to individuals, is equally so in regard to States. An interference of one in the affairs of another is the fruitful source of family dissensions and neighborhood disputes; and the same cause affects the peace, happiness, and prosperity of States. It may be most devoutly hoped that the good sense of the American people will ever be ready to repel all such attempts should they ever be made.[3]

This warning by the President of dangerous tampering by hostile foreign governments and deluded Americans with the internal affairs of the United States was a throwback to the interference in the slavery concerns of the Southern states by British and Northern abolitionists that had so alarmed Duff Green in 1843. But also it had reference to attempts by the Mexican government to produce dissension in the Union by appeals to Northern abolitionists on the issue of the annexation of Texas, the evidence of which was offered in the documents accompanying the message.

Those documents, selected and arranged by Calhoun, were a formidable body. Their extent is indicated by the fact that they formed in print ninety-one pages in the congressional documents.[4] One of them, dated June 20, 1844, was an instruction from Calhoun to Wilson Shannon, newly appointed minister to Mexico. It covered such provocative issues as the defaults by Mexico in payments under an agreement concerning damage claims of American citizens against Mexico, authorizations to governors of Mexican states to expel foreigners who were obnoxious, and prohibitions against foreigners engaging in retail Mexican trade; above all, problems arising from the unsettled issue of the annexation of Texas. That issue, Calhoun wrote, had brought "menaces and offensive language," from the Mexican government.[5]

This dispatch was followed by another from Calhoun to Shannon, of September 10, relating to a threatened Mexican invasion of Texas. Its information was derived from correspondence received from the Texan government that showed that Santa Anna was seeking funds from the Mexican Congress to finance an army of 30,000, which was to strike Texas.[6] A decree of Santa Anna and an order

[3] *Ibid.*, 336–7.
[4] *House Doc.*, 28 Cong., 2 sess. (ser. 463), no. 2, 1–90.
[5] *Ibid.*, 24.
[6] *Ibid.*, 29–34.

to General Woll, commander of the Northern army of Mexico, were reproduced by Calhoun to prove that the war on Texas was to be one of utter extirpation.[7] To emphasize the atrocities lying ahead, Calhoun adverted to the recent execution of a filibusterer, General Sentmanat, and party at Tabasco, and to an earlier decree by Santa Anna in 1835 at the outset of the Texan revolution, under which "the cold blooded butchery of Fannin and his party, and other prisoners was ordered."[8] As Calhoun put it, "All that breathe are to be destroyed or driven out, and Texas left a desolate waste; and so proclaimed to the world by Mexico, in advance of his projected invasion."

One reason only, Calhoun wrote in the dispatch, could be given for the atrocious war ahead, and that was defeat of the projected annexation of Texas. The American people would be blind not to see that the war was intended either to subject Texas to Mexican power or to force her into some foreign and unnatural alliance that would produce lasting hostility between her and the United States to the permanent injury and perhaps the ruin of both. Shannon was instructed to protest against such a war, and the manner of conducting it, "in strong language, accompanied by declarations that the President cannot regard them with indifference, but as highly offensive to the U. States."[9] Calhoun's dispatches were written in the midst of the American canvass for the presidency and were intended to be read by Congress and the public after the election during the deliberations on the Joint Resolution of Annexation.

Shannon was not loathe to carry out the instruction to use strong language with the Mexican government. In a letter to Rejón, the Mexican minister of foreign relations, written on October 14, he closely copied the choice of topics and tone of Calhoun's instruc-

---

[7] *Ibid.*, 34–6.

[8] *Ibid.*, 30. In the reference to Sentmanat Calhoun was using information received from the United States consul in Tabasco in a letter of August 20, 1844. The letter related to a party of Spanish and French adventurers, accompanied by a few Americans, under the leadership of a Cuban who had been governor of Tabasco—Francisco Sentmanat. The party had been driven ashore in Tabasco and had been captured. Thirty-eight had been summarily shot, including Sentmanat, whose head had been severed, boiled in oil, and exhibited to view in a public square. The remainder of the party, including the Americans, had been imprisoned. See W. R. Manning, ed., *Diplomatic Correspondence of the United States: Inter-American Affairs 1831–1860*, 12 vols. (Washington: Carnegie Endowment, 1932–9), VIII, 639–40. The reference to Fannin and his party is to the execution of a Texan force taken prisoner during the war by the Mexicans at Goliad.

[9] *House Doc.*, 28 Cong., 2 sess. (ser. 463), no. 2, 34.

tions. He repeated Calhoun's view that the nature of the war about to be fought in Texas was to be inferred from the fate of the strangers who had landed with Sentmanat, as well as from the fate of Fannin and his party, and he drew, in conclusion, a moving picture of the Texan people whom the Mexicans were proposing to annihilate:

> It is such a people, living under such institutions, successfully resisting all attacks from the period of their separation nine years ago, and who have been recognized and admitted into the family of nations, that Mexico has undertaken to regard as a lawless banditti, and against whom, as such, she has proclaimed a war of extermination; forgetful of their exalted and generous humanity in refusing to exercise the just right of retaliation when, in a former invasion, victory placed in their hands the most ample means of doing so.[10] The government of Mexico may delude itself by its fictions, but it cannot delude the rest of the world. It will be held responsible, not by what it may choose to regard as facts, but what are in reality such, and acknowledged so to be by all, save itself.
>
> Such are the views entertained by the President of the United States in regard to the proposed invasion while the question of annexation is pending, and of the barbarous and bloody manner in which it is proclaimed it will be conducted; and, in conformity to his instructions, the undersigned solemnly protests against both, as highly injurious and offensive to the United States.[11]

The Calhoun instruction of September 10, and a copy of Shannon's October 14 letter to Rejón in compliance with it, were available in Washington for inclusion in the documents sent to Congress on December 3.[12] The fiery reply of Rejón of October 31 was still to come. He charged in the reply that the American government had sent its citizens to Texas, then had stimulated them to revolt, and now was undertaking to annex the province. Mocking Shannon, Rejón wrote "that the North American government may thus far deceive itself by its fictions; but it will not be able to deceive the world."[13]

---

[10] Shannon to M. C. Rejón, October 14, 1844, in *ibid.,* 46–50. The refusal "to exercise the just right of retaliation" is a reference to the fact that Santa Anna was not executed by Texans when captured at the Battle of San Jacinto.

[11] *Ibid.,* 49–50.

[12] *Congressional Globe,* 28 Cong., 2 sess., App. 1–8.

[13] Rejón to Shannon, October 31, 1844, in *ibid.,* 29; also in *House Doc.,* 28 Cong., 2 sess. (ser. 463), no. 19, 8–16.

Shocked by this letter, Shannon replied to it on November 4 that it was grossly offensive, that it charged the people of the United States with falsehood, artifice, intrigue, and designs of a dishonorable character, and with barefaced usurpation. He demanded that it be withdrawn and indicated an intention to send it by special courier to his government. He declared that future relations between the United States and Mexico might depend on the representations he would make in his dispatch. He called for an immediate reply.[14]

Nothing daunted, Rejón replied on November 6, that the government of the United States was seeking to provoke a rupture. He could have returned insult for insult, he wrote, by using the same uncourteous language the American minister had been using. However, he had limited himself to what was absolutely indispensable to render his case clear. He had shown every consideration due "to the majority of the American people, from whose representatives he hoped for amends for the excesses committed on this point by the actual President of that republic, whose Senate, composed of honorable and respectable men, such as Adams and Clay, has given to Mexico proofs of the justice of its character." In conclusion, he declared, he had orders from his government to recapitulate what he had said in every point, and also, in case relations of amity should be broken, Mexico "will accept the hard conditions which are forced upon it and will repel the unjust aggression committed against it." Then, having uttered this defiance, Rejón sent his notes to the press in Mexico City.[15]

Shannon felt obliged, on November 8, to have another word before the departure of his special courier. It was an extended defense of the honor of his country, of former President Jackson, and of Texas. It pointed out that in its intercourse with all nations the American government during its sixty-nine years of successful operation had been open, frank, and undisguised, "demanding nothing but what is right and submitting to nothing that is wrong." It had commanded the confidence and respect of the civilized world. "If the government of Mexico constitutes an exception to this truth the

[14] Shannon to Rejón, November 4, 1844, in *Congressional Globe*, 28 Cong., 2 sess., App. 30; also in *House Doc.*, 28 Cong., 2 sess. (ser. 463), no. 19, 16–17.
[15] Rejón to Shannon, November 6, 1844, in *Congressional Globe*, 28 Cong., 2 sess., App. 30; also in *House Doc.*, 28 Cong., 2 sess. (ser. 463), no. 19, 17–19.

government of the United States, to whom the undersigned will refer the notes of his excellency Mr. Rejón, knowing what is due to its character, can and will correct the erroneous opinion . . . by means more efficient than any written refutation by the undersigned of the calumnies made and reiterated in the notes of Mr. Rejón would be." This was followed by an extended historical refutation of the calumnies, by a justification of the Texan revolt, and by a demonstration of the disinterestedness of American action regarding annexation.[16]

As has been noted, only Shannon's first letter to Rejón was included among the documents published with the President's message of December 3. The remainder of the exchange reached the public through the enterprise of the *National Intelligencer*. On December 6 it received, by way of its normal Mexican newspaper exchanges, the correspondence following Shannon's letter of October 14. It speedily translated the whole and gave American readers everything down to the conclusion of Shannon's menaces on November 8, which was a real journalistic scoop.[17]

The publication called forth not only Whig, but Democratic, denunciations of the tone and quality of Shannon's letters. On December 14 the *Intelligencer* published a preliminary list of American journals taking this stand. The Whig journals were the Boston *Daily Advertiser,* the New York *Courier and Enquirer,* the Philadelphia *United States Gazette,* and the Cincinnati *Gazette.* Among the Democratic journals the New York *Evening Post* was listed and, surprisingly enough, the expansionist New York *Morning News.*

The New York *Morning News* was especially critical of the Shannon letters. It observed:

> It adds further confirmation to the truth, already before universally admitted, of that gentleman's want of qualification for his place. Even where its argument is most sound, it is clumsily and feebly put; while it is so grossly disfigured with personal abuse of the individual addressed—the *lie direct* being repeated over and over again with ingenious variety of insult—as to reflect certainly much more discredit on its author than on its object. It is a thousand pities that, at this juncture, we should have happened to be repre-

[16] Shannon to Rejón, November 8, 1844, *Congressional Globe,* 28 Cong., 2 sess., App. 31; also in *House Doc.,* 28 Cong., 2 sess. (ser. 463), no. 19, 19–27.
[17] *National Intelligencer,* December 7, 13, 14, 17, 1844.

sented in Mexico by a Minister who [has], superadded to ignorance of the language, a total want of experience in diplomatic affairs.

There is one passage in it calculated to arrest particular attention. Mr. Shannon does not content himself with having laid before the Mexican Government a virtual copy of Mr. Calhoun's despatch of instructions to him, the character of which ought to have made it especially manifest to him that it could not have been intended for such use. He now, when it is of no use, and when his official intercourse with the Mexican Government has reached a point at which it is impossible for him to hold any further communications with it, opens another fold in the portfolio of his instructions and lets Senor Rejón know all about *how he was empowered* to offer to Mexico to buy her off [18] on terms so liberal that she will probably have reason to repent Senor Rejón's "notes of the 31st ultimo and the 6th instant. . . . Was there ever before heard of such blundering in the execution of instructions?" [19]

Among the documents sent by Tyler to Congress on December 3 one was a Calhoun dispatch to William R. King, minister to France. It had been sent on August 12. King was an Alabama Democrat, deeply devoted to slavery, to the annexation of Texas, and to Calhoun. His appointment in the preceding May had fitted well into the master plan of Calhoun sketched out to Upshur, one specification of which had been that at the French court there must always be a trusted defender of Southern institutions.[20] This seemed especially in point after the failure of the annexation treaty in the Senate. By that time Anglo-French policy regarding Texas had matured into a definite plan. It was designed to reduce the attractiveness of annexation in the minds of Texans by arranging and guaranteeing peace between Texas and Mexico. Part of the plan

[18] This could be a reference to a proposal, alleged to have been made by Calhoun, to buy off Mexican opposition to the annexation treaty (April–May, 1844), by an offer of payment for a favorable Texan boundary and a cession of California. The proposal is said to have been carried by Waddy Thompson to Mexico. Its nature and reception by Santa Anna are shadowy and controversial subjects, with which Justin Smith has dealt at some length in *The Annexation of Texas* (New York: Baker and Taylor Co., 1911), pp. 288–95. See also Van Zandt to Jones, June 18, 1844, A.H.A. *Report*, 1908, II (1), 287–8; B. E. Green to Calhoun, May 30, 1844, A.H.A. *Report*, 1899, II, 960–1; and *National Intelligencer*, August 12, 1844.

[19] Reprinted in the *National Intelligencer*, December 20, 1844. On this date the paper reprinted the entire Shannon-Rejón exchange.

[20] The identity of views of King and Calhoun on the Texas issue appears in King to Calhoun, December 28, 1844, in A.H.A. *Report*, 1899, II, 1013–15. For the master plan see above, pp. 20–2.

had been that Mexico be induced to recognize the independence of Texas, and that a negotiation between the two states should follow, to draw up the terms of their separation and especially to fix the boundary line between them.

In Paris an initial meeting between the American minister and the French monarch occurred at a welcoming dinner held (with a view to recalling old times) on July 4, 1844. The dinner was followed by a cordial conversation during which Louis Philippe pleasantly referred to the American war for independence from England, in which France had been so helpful to the Americans. This led to a discussion of independence versus annexation in Texas. The monarch wished to know why annexation had failed in the Senate. The minister replied that the issue was far from settled and added that in this case there existed wide differences between French and British interests. French interests were commercial, while those of the British were political. This drew from the monarch an admission that there were wide differences between French and British interests in North America.[21]

Louis Philippe could have had in mind that France was no longer a colonial power on the continent of North America and so had less reason to be unsettled by American ambitions of continental expansion. Also, France still permitted slavery in her West Indies islands, and was therefore less troubled than the British over the matter of slavery in Texas. Again, the increased monopoly the United States would have in cotton production, if Texas were annexed, would not disturb the French as much as it did the English. Finally, French cooperation with the British in any policy at variance with the wishes of the United States was traditionally unpopular in France.

This feeling had come to the surface in 1841–2, in the controversy over the Quintuple Treaty for the suppression of the slave trade. Guizot had agreed to that treaty but had encountered repugnance to it in the Chamber of Deputies, and the treaty had gone down to a resounding defeat. One of its most strident critics had been Adolphe Jollivet, who was a deputy in the Chamber representing the sugar interests (based on slavery) in Martinique. He was an

[21] King to Calhoun, July 13, 1844. Dispatches from United States Ministers to France, vol. XXX, National Archives. See also Frederick Merk, *The Monroe Doctrine and American Expansionism, 1843–1849* (New York: Alfred A. Knopf, 1966), pp. 40–56.

intense Negrophobe and had made known his views not only in Paris, but in a stream of pamphlets addressed to the French public. He was convinced of the hypocrisy of the British crusade against the slave trade and slavery, with views strikingly like those of Duff Green, and it is likely the two men had been in touch with each other in Paris in 1842. He was a great admirer of Calhoun and his views.[22] Yet in France there were many humanitarians touched by the growing sentiment against slavery and the slave trade and warm supporters of the Guizot ministry.

Louis Philippe did not spell out for the American minister just what the differences on the Texas question were between British and French interests. But he amiably gave the American to understand "that in any event no steps would be taken by his government in the slightest degree hostile, or which could give the United States just cause of complaint." This seemed to King important as coming from a monarch who was no mere figurehead in the government, and he reported it in triumph to Calhoun.

Calhoun was dubious of the assurance. It did not accord with information he had of an Anglo-French collaboration to maintain the independence of Texas. However, it was a declaration that could be used to produce a rift in the collaboration and even to break it up. He consulted Tyler, who encouraged him to develop the idea. Accordingly, on August 12, Calhoun sent a carefully phrased dispatch to King. He expressed the President's gratification with the French monarch's assurance, which was all the greater "because our previous information was calculated to make the impression that the government of France was prepared to unite with Great Britain in a joint protest against the annexation of Texas, and a joint effort to induce her government to withdraw the proposition to annex, on condition that Mexico should be made to acknowledge her independence. He is happy to infer from your despatch that the information, so far as it relates to France, is, in all probability, without foundation."

Calhoun then went on in the dispatch to point out that a leading

---

[22] For a biographical sketch of Jollivet, see Pierre Larousse, *Grand Dictionnaire Universel du XIXᵉ siècle*, 17 vols. (Paris, 1866–90), IX, 1006. The Jollivet pamphlets are listed, with descriptions, in Thomas W. Streeter, *Bibliography of Texas, 1795–1845*, 5 vols. (Cambridge: Harvard University Press, 1955–60), pt. 3, vol. 2, 541–2. See especially one listed as A. Jollivet, *Documents américains, annexion du Texas, Émancipation des Noirs* (Paris, 1845).

objective of British diplomacy was to produce the abolition of slavery not only in Texas, but in the United States and throughout the North American continent. The British government was acting in this under the incitation of abolitionists in England and in the United States cooperating with each other. Great Britain had devoted to this end $250,000,000, counting the costs of emancipation under the Act of 1833, of subsidies given since, in the form of tariff preferences to sugar imported from those islands, and of expenses incurred in the suppression of the slave trade. This vast expenditure of capital and effort had brought only a disastrous failure —a failure imperiling the entire British investment in empire production of colonial staples. The government was unable to reverse its course, owing to the strength of British public opinion. It had decided therefore to destroy slavery everywhere else in the world in order to reduce, to the low British level, the effectiveness of competitors. The argument was an amplification of Duff Green's thesis. In clarity of statement, wealth of statistics, and breadth of outlook it surpassed any of the Maryland citizen's writings.

The audience Calhoun was addressing in this dispatch was the public in France—especially two groups in it. One was the opposition in the Chambers, which was denouncing the Guizot ministry for subservience to the British government. The other was the French West Indies planter interest, which was fearful that France might be brought in the near future to follow the British example of emancipation of slaves in its colonies. It was to these groups that Calhoun addressed the following section of his dispatch:

> Can it be possible that governments so enlightened and sagacious as those of France and the other great continental powers can be so blinded by the plea of philanthropy as not to see what must inevitably follow, be her motive what it may, should she [Britain] succeed in her object? It is little short of mockery to talk of philanthropy, with the examples before us of the effects of abolishing negro slavery in her own colonies, in St. Domingo, and the Northern States of our Union, where statistical facts, not to be shaken, prove that the freed negro, after the experience of sixty years, is in a far worse condition than in the other States, where he has been left in his former condition. No: the effect of what is called abolition, where the number is few, is not to raise the inferior race to the condition of the freemen, but to deprive the negro of the guardian

care of his owner, subject to all the depression and oppression belonging to his inferior condition. But on the other hand, where the number is great, and bears a large proportion to the whole population, it would be still worse. It would be to substitute for the existing relation a deadly strife between the two races, to end in the subjection, expulsion, or extirpation of one or the other: and such would be the case over the greater part of this continent where negro slavery exists. It would not end there; but would in all probability extend, by its example, the war of races over all South America, including Mexico, and extending to the Indian as well as to the African races, and make the whole one scene of blood and devastation.[23]

The inclusion of this dispatch—without comment—in the documents sent to Congress by Tyler on December 3 is a problem for the historian. The dispatch was out of line with the President's assurance to Congress in the accompanying message that the "collateral and incidental" issue of slavery had played no part in the treaty, nor did it implement his hope that the issue be "avoided by Congress." [24] Neither did it reveal any of the regret later expressed by him concerning Calhoun's emphasis on the protection of slavery in the diplomatic exchanges.

Two further observations may be ventured regarding the dispatch and its publication. One is that Calhoun's reference in it to "statistical facts not to be shaken" concerning the deleterious effects of freedom on the Negro made clear a determination on his part and that of the Administration not to be shaken by the storm that had been raised in and out of Congress regarding the truth of those "facts." And the broadcasting to the world of a pleasantry the French monarch had made to the American minister at a social gathering was a gross impropriety that discredited American diplomacy.

The broadcasting came with the newspaper publication of the President's documents—first in the American press, then, at the end of December, in the British. The effect produced in Europe was everything the President and Calhoun could have desired. In London and in Paris Calhoun's dispatch to King produced a sensation.

[23] Calhoun to King, August 12, 1844, in *House Doc.,* 28 Cong., 2 sess. (ser. 463), no. 2, 38–45. Also in *Congressional Globe,* 28 Cong., 2 sess., App. 5–7.
[24] Richardson, *Messages and Papers,* IV, 334–53, esp. p. 344.

In the British press it called forth denunciations of French duplicity in the collaboration regarding Texas. The London *Times* was especially vigorous. It wrote:

> Admitting that one of the main objects of British policy in this question is to check the progress and ascendancy of slave institutions, he [Calhoun] contends that "France can have no interest in the consummation of this grand scheme, but that her interests, and those of all the continental Powers of Europe, are directly opposed to it." In other words, he argues explicitly that the interest of European Powers demands that they should not only tolerate, but encourage and promote slavery in America. . . . This is the question stripped by its own advocates of all disguise; and the odious motives in which this abominable scheme has originated—namely the aggrandizement of the United States for the express purpose of perpetuating the servile condition of the negro race—are laid bare to the wonder and execration of mankind. On these grounds Mr. Calhoun appeals to civilized France and civilized Europe for encouragement and support. . . . It is by a laboured defence of slavery and slave interests that Mr. Calhoun courts the sympathy of the French government.[25]

The reverberations of Calhoun's dispatch were heard in Europe for a year after the explosion. Guizot made a harried effort to pacify Aberdeen. At the same time he assured the American minister that the French government was committed to the policy mentioned by the monarch and confirmed this in a confidential letter, which King at once sent to a London newspaper for publication, with the result of a renewal of charges and countercharges. Meanwhile, in the Chamber of Deputies, the opposition taunted the ministry with subservience to the British, with the result that all thought of resurrecting the Anglo-French collaboration in Texas vanished.[26]

As a result of the astuteness of Calhoun, not only the rough waters of Anglo-French relations were made stormier, but also those of French party politics. In France the rift between parties eventuated in a revolution early in 1848, in which Louis Philippe was forced to abdicate his throne, Guizot was driven to England as an exile, and slavery in the French West Indies was abolished by the revolutionary government. In the turmoil of the revolution,

---

[25] London *Times*, January 2, 1845.
[26] Merk, *Monroe Doctrine and American Expansionism*, pp. 45–7.

Jollivet, the apostle of slavery, who had published translations of Calhoun's stirring dispatch to King in several pamphlets, met death at the barricades in Paris.

In the United States, in the meantime, Tyler met and outmaneuvered the opposition in another sector of foreign relations—the Mexican-American—on the issues of slavery and Texas annexation. A prominent Whig critic of annexation, Senator William C. Rives of Virginia, had read in the *National Intelligencer* of December 7, 1844, the translated Shannon-Rejón correspondence. Troubled by the provocative tone of Shannon's letters, he induced the Senate on December 9 to request of the President copies of the recent Mexican-American correspondence not included in the message of December 3.[27]

With that request the President readily complied. On December 18 he sent the Shannon-Rejón correspondence—October 31 through November 11—to both houses of Congress, accompanied by a special message of his own. He called attention to "the extraordinary and highly offensive language which the Mexican government has thought proper to employ" in responding to a remonstrance from the American minister against a renewal of the war in Texas and the manner in which it was to be conducted. He thought Mexico

has no right to violate at pleasure the principles which an enlightened civilization has laid down for the conduct of nationals at war, and thereby retrograde to a period of barbarism, which, happily for the world, has long since passed away. All nations are interested in enforcing an observance of those principles; and the United States, the oldest of the American republics, and the nearest of the civilized powers to the theatre on which these enormities were proposed to be enacted, could not quietly content themselves to witness such a state of things. They had . . . remonstrated against outrages similar, but even less inhuman than those which by her new edicts and decrees, she has threatened to perpetrate, and of which the late inhuman massacre at Tabasco was but the precursor.

The bloody and inhuman murder of Fannin and his companions, equalled only in savage barbarity by the usages of the untutored Indian tribes, proved how little confidence could be placed on the most solemn stipulations of her generals; while the fate of others who became her captives in war—many of whom, no longer able to sustain the fatigues and privations of long journeys, were shot

[27] *Sen. Journal,* 28 Cong., 2 sess., (ser. 448), 25 (December 9, 1844).

down by the way side, while their companions who survived were subjected to sufferings even more painful than death—had left an indelible stain on the page of civilization. The [American] executive, with the evidence of an intention on the part of Mexico to renew scenes so revolting to humanity, could do no less than renew remonstrances formerly urged.[28]

The President took occasion also to return to a theme noticed in his message of December 3—the dangerous efforts of foreign governments to produce dissension in the Union over the Texas issue. He dwelt especially on Mexican efforts of that sort and found evidence in the replies made by Rejón to the remonstrances of Shannon. Rejón had maintained that the Texan revolution had been abetted and aided by the government of the United States with a view to later annexation of the revolted state. He had contended that the annexation drive had been a conspiracy to extend the area of slavery and had contrasted the behavior of the Southern states with that of the Northern "on whose honor Mexico relies, doing to it the justice which it merits." He had even cited Northern individuals, notably John Quincy Adams, and had contrasted his behavior with that of Andrew Jackson. To Tyler this seemed intolerable. In his message he wrote:

> Nor will it escape the observation of Congress that in conducting a correspondence with a minister of the United States, who can not and does not know any distinction between the geographical sections of the Union, charges wholly unfounded are made against particular States, and an appeal to others for aid and protection against supposed wrongs. In this same connection, sectional prejudices are attempted to be excited and the hazardous and unpardonable effort is made to foment divisions amongst the States of the Union and thereby imbitter their peace. Mexico has still to learn that however freely we may indulge in discussion among ourselves, the American people will tolerate no interference in their domestic affairs by any foreign government, and in all that concerns the constitutional guaranties and the national honor the people of the United States have but one mind and one heart.[29]

Not all Whig members of Congress who listened to this message were of one mind and one heart with the President "in all that con-

---

[28] *House Doc.,* 28 Cong., 2 sess. (ser. 463), no. 19, 1–4.
[29] *Ibid.,* 27.

cerns the constitutional guaranties and the national honor." One dissenter was John Quincy Adams, who entered this comment in his diary on the day of the message:

> A message was received from the President, with the brawling correspondence between Calhoun, Shannon, and the Mexican Minister of Foreign Affairs, Manuel Crescencio Rejón. The message rails at the Mexican Government with the temper of a common scold, and concludes by saying that, although we should be fully justified in declaring war against them, he will not recommend that; but only that we should take Texas, and then, if Mexico makes war upon us, all the responsibility of it shall rest upon her.

On the next day Adams had this further comment to make:

> I read this morning the whole correspondence communicated yesterday with the message of the President, and see the subjugation of the Union to the double slave-representation with the deplorable certainty of proof. John C. Calhoun and South Carolina are in the ascendant, and an internal convulsion in Mexico happens this moment, as if by interposition of the evil principle, to help him to consummate his abominable purpose. The prospect is death-like.[30]

To Calhoun and to Tyler publication of the "brawling correspondence" seemed not abominable at all. It seemed humane and protective. It gave timely warning of atrocities ahead in Texas unless that state were soon admitted to the safety of the Union. At the same time it warned of foreign designs, some even in the Western hemisphere—in Mexico—to produce dissension in the Union over annexation.

IN THIS CRITICAL PERIOD an eruption occurred again in Congress over the problem of those census returns. It was set off when the American Statistical Association resubmitted its Memorial, as soon as Congress met. The Memorial was addressed to John Quincy Adams in the House and to J. W. Huntington, a Connecticut Whig, in the Senate. On December 10 Adams offered his copy to the House and moved that it be referred to a select committee and also that it be printed. These motions had to be seriously considered, for

[30] Charles F. Adams, ed., *Memoirs of John Quincy Adams,* 12 vols. (Philadelphia, 1874–7), XII, 127–8 (December 19, 1844).

the gag rules had been rescinded. It was necessary to use a new technique for dealing with such fractious matters. The Speaker himself therefore put to a vote the question of the creation of a select committee, and even before the voting had been completed, announced that the motion had been carried. Then the motion to print was put. A demand for a reading of the Memorial was raised, rather ineptly, by a Georgia Democrat, but was withdrawn after some reading by the Clerk of the House. A vote was taken on the motion to print, and the motion was handily defeated. Three days later the names of a select committee of nine to consider the Memorial were announced by the Speaker. The majority of the committee was safely Democratic and also safe, as shown later, on the issue of annexing Texas.[31]

Adams was named chairman of the committee and promptly informed his fellow members of the day and hour of the first meeting. An ill-attended meeting, which had to be adjourned almost as soon as it opened, was held on January 29. At the next meeting the chairman and another Whig were present, but none of the other seven of the committee showed up. Actually the committee never really got together.[32] The majority had no interest whatever in exposing the errors of the sixth census. Adams was able only to perform the melancholy rite of announcing the demise of the committee on March 3, 1845, the day of the adjournment of Congress, when he asked as a routine matter that the committee be discharged.[33]

In the Senate the Memorial of the Statistical Association fared better. The Senate was under Whig control, and the Memorial was referred on December 10 to a joint library committee of the two houses, the names of whose members were announced soon after. They were Choate of Massachusetts and James A. Pearce of Maryland, both Whigs, plus Tappan of Ohio, the antislavery Democrat, and Edmund Burke of the House, a loyal Democrat from New Hampshire.[34] The committee's report, which Burke wrote, contained the view that even a cursory examination of the Memorial demonstrated the validity of the criticisms in it and destroyed con-

---

[31] *Congressional Globe,* 28 Cong., 2 sess., 17, 27.

[32] Adams, *Memoirs,* XII, 156 (January 29, 1845), 165 (February 12, 1845).

[33] *Ibid.,* p. 176 (March 3, 1845).

[34] Burke eventually voted for the Joint Resolution of Annexation and was appointed Commissioner of Patents early in the Polk Administration.

fidence in the accuracy of the census. The committee did not think it useful formally to withdraw the sanction of Congress from the census: "Yet, in view of the manifest and palpable, not to say, gross errors of the late census, the committee feel bound to suggest . . . the necessity of some legislation, with a view to prevent similar errors and inaccuracies in the census to be taken in 1850." [35] This report would probably have satisfied Jarvis and the American Statistical Association.

In his autobiography Jarvis recorded a conversation he had had with Senator Berrien, the Georgia Whig, regarding the census statistics. Those statistics were in error, Berrien believed, but he added that they were "too good a thing for *our* [Southern] politicians to give up, and many of them have prepared speeches based on this, which they cannot afford to lose." The argument of the speeches was that slaves in the Eastern states had increased in number beyond the means of keeping them occupied. If they were to be emancipated and set adrift, they would become subject to mental disorders—a calamity worse than slavery. "Humanity then demands that Texas be added to our nation, and opened to the occupation of our surplus slaves to save them from mental death." [36]

The crusade of Jarvis for truth in the census had a less immediate than future impact. It did not in the least deter Upshur, Walker, Calhoun, or any of the proslavery extremists surrounding Tyler from exploiting the statistics in support of the annexation of Texas. Neither did it influence Polk, the successor to Tyler, who used the territorial gains of annexation to get yet more territory from Mexico in the Mexican War. But it did impress open-minded Democrats such as Edmund Burke and Zadock Pratt, both of whom became enlisted in the cause of census reform. As for Whigs, they were no sooner restored to control of the federal government in 1849 than they moved energetically to reform the census. They summoned Jarvis and his mentor, Lemuel Shattuck, as consultants to prepare the way for the census of 1850, and that census made greater advances in gathering and analyzing social statistics than any of its

[35] The report of the committee appears in *Sen. Doc.*, 28 Cong., 2 sess. (ser. 457), no. 146.

[36] Edward Jarvis [Autobiography], p. 136. Manuscript in Houghton Library, Harvard University.

predecessors.[37] As for Jarvis, he was chosen president of the American Statistical Association in 1852, and remained its president for the remainder of his active career.

The silences maintained by Tyler and his associates in their zeal to acquire Texas were as eloquent as the din of their propaganda. The silence they maintained concerning Jarvis and his crusade for truth as to the census statistics is especially striking and significant to the historian. No mention was made by them of his name or of the cause he represented either in public or in their private correspondence, though the issue was for years before Congress and in the Whig press. And this silence has continued in biographies of the Tyler junto. In none of the biographies of Upshur, Walker, Calhoun, or Tyler is the name of Jarvis found. Equally surprising is the fact that in the detailed account of *The Annexation of Texas* by Justin Smith, the issue of those census statistics and the use made of them by the Administration finds only incidental mention.[38]

[37] For an excellent account of the evolution of the census and especially of the improvements made in the census of 1850, see Carroll D. Wright, *The History and Growth of the United States Census* (Washington: Government Printing Office, 1900). This work is printed as a government document in *Sen. Doc.*, 56 Cong., 1 sess. (ser. 3856), no. 194.

[38] Justin Smith, *Annexation of Texas,* p. 202.

CHAPTER VI

Joint Resolutions in Congress: Constitutional Issues

I N THE ANNUAL MESSAGE to Congress of December 3, 1844, President Tyler renewed with added emphasis his recommendation of the preceding spring that a joint resolution annexing Texas be enacted. An abundant affirmative response to the recommendation came from both houses. Seven resolutions of the kind came from the Senate, ten from the House. Most of the resolutions were offered by Democrats. Only two resolutions were offered by Whigs, one in each house, and the Whigs were both from the state of Tennessee. This heavy Democratic preponderance of proposals would seem to indicate that the President's appeal for a national rather than a party response to an urgent need had not created a consensus.

A Senate resolution of December 10, 1844, was the first to appear. Its author was McDuffie of South Carolina, a colleague of Calhoun while the latter still was in the Senate. It loyally supported what Calhoun had accomplished as secretary of state and proposed merely to resurrect, by the process of a joint resolution, the defunct treaty of annexation.[1]

Benton was the author of the second Senate resolution, that of December 11. It registered disagreement with Calhoun's treaty.

---

[1] *Congressional Globe,* 28 Cong., 2 sess., 16–17 (December 10, 1844). A useful guide through the maze of resolutions is Sarah E. Lewis, "Digest of Congressional Action on the Annexation of Texas, December 1844 to March 1845," *Southwestern Historical Quarterly,* 50 (1946–7), 251–67.

It proposed new negotiations with Mexico and with Texas, though the one with Mexico could be dispensed with if Congress should come to consider Mexican assent to a treaty unnecessary. The boundary to be sought in the Mexican negotiation should start where the line of the "Old Texas" had started—in the desert prairie west of the Nueces. It should proceed inland along the highlands separating the waters of the Rio Grande from those of the Mississippi to the northern latitude of forty-two degrees. In the negotiation with Texas, a state and an adjoining territory should be the result. The state—to be called "The State of Texas"—should have an extent not exceeding the largest state of the Union, but its boundaries should be left to itself to draw, and it should be admitted to the Union on an equal footing with the original states. This meant it would have the freedom to determine for itself the question of slavery.

The territory coming with it into the Union should be called the "Southwest Territory," and should be held and disposed of by the United States as one of its territories. The existence of slavery in the territory should be forever prohibited west of the one-hundredth degree of longitude, "so as to divide, as equally as may be, the whole of the annexed country between slaveholding and non-slaveholding States." The sovereigns of Texas, the people, were to express their assent to annexation, "by a legislative act, or by any authentic act which shows the will of the majority." [2] There were ambiguities and inconsistencies in the measure, an indication, perhaps, that the author was not sure, at this stage, of his own views.

Four weeks later, on January 7, 1845, Senator John M. Niles, a Connecticut Democrat, offered a joint resolution that resembled Benton's in some respects. It proposed the annexation of a state and a residual territory, with slavery prohibited in the territory to correspond with the terms of the Missouri Compromise. It proposed further that the boundary with Mexico be left to the United States to negotiate.[3]

On January 14 a bill was offered by Senator W. H. Haywood of North Carolina which proposed that Texas be annexed as two territories divided by the thirty-fourth parallel. Each territory could

[2] *Congressional Globe,* 28 Cong., 2 sess., 19 (December 11, 1844).
[3] *Ibid.,* 99 (January 7, 1845).

be divided into at least two territories which would eventually become states. The principle of the Missouri Compromise of 1820, that slavery be forever prohibited north of the line of 36° 30', was to be applied. The public lands and public debt of Texas were to be taken over by the United States. All boundary disputes with foreign powers were to be left to the United States to settle.[4]

On February 5 a new annexation proposal was offered by Benton as a substitute for his first. It canceled much of the detail of the first. It provided merely for the admission of the present republic of Texas as a state with suitable extent and boundaries as soon as the terms of admission, "and the cession of the remaining Texian territory to the United States shall be agreed upon by the government of Texas and the United States." Texas was to be admitted on an equal footing with the existing states, which meant that it would be free to choose slavery or otherwise as it wished. The sum of $100,000 was to be appropriated to defray the expenses of missions and negotiations to agree upon the terms of admission and cession, either by treaty to be submitted to the Senate, or by articles to be submitted to the two houses of Congress, as the President would direct.[5] In part, the bill was a response to voices that had reached the Senator from his Missouri constituents; in part, it was a response to action that had been taken by the House of Representatives, which will be later described.

On February 13 Senator Chester Ashley of Arkansas introduced into the Senate yet another proposal for annexation. It provided that Texas be admitted as a state on the same footing as the original states in all respects whatever, and that the United States be authorized to settle all questions of boundary that might arise with other governments. The constitution of Texas was to be amended to provide that its territory might be divided into new states not exceeding five in number, all to be eligible for admission as states upon the same footing as the original states. The public lands of Texas were to be transferred to the United States in trust to be sold on the same terms as other federal lands. The proceeds were to be used to pay the public debt of Texas to an amount not exceeding the sum of $500,000. After the liquidation of these debts,

[4] *Ibid.*, 184–5 (January 14, 1845).
[5] *Ibid.*, 244 (February 5, 1845).

the proceeds were to be paid annually to Texas and to the states formed from her domain. Thus the measure made sure that the bondholders of Texas would be properly taken care of.[6]

The one Whig measure coming to the Senate was that of E. H. Foster of Tennessee. It was offered shortly after that of Niles. It proposed that the territory "properly included within and rightfully belonging to, the republic of Texas be erected into a new State," subject to adjustment by the United States of all questions of boundary that might arise with other governments. Other states might, with the consent of Texas, be formed from its territory. Any new states so formed south of the line of 36°30′ were to be admitted to the Union with or without slavery as the people seeking admission might desire. All mines, harbors, and means of defense were to be ceded to the United States, but all public lands and public debts were to be retained by the state. The lands were to be used to extinguish the debts.[7]

House resolutions for annexing Texas were not basically different from those appearing in the Senate. They contained the same items, though differing in their combinations. One new feature, appearing in some, was the conception that Texas had always been part of the Louisiana Purchase and that annexation would really be re-annexation. That idea had been stressed by Walker in his *Letter Relative to the Annexation of Texas,* and its appearance in Northern as well as in Southern proposals for a joint resolution, signified what was constantly urged by Tyler: the national character of the movement for the annexation of Texas. The emphasis on this idea in the House, rather than in the Senate, was doubtless a reflection of the more popular character of the House. Conversely, its absence from the Senate resolutions may reflect loyalty to Senate-ratified treaties, such as that with Spain in 1819, which fixed the Sabine River as the boundary line of the Louisiana Purchase in the Southwest.

In the list of House resolutions the first was that of C. J. Ingersoll of Pennsylvania, who was chairman of the Committee on Foreign Affairs. It was offered on December 12, 1844, and copied the pattern of the McDuffie resolution in the Senate. It proposed simply copying the terms of the abortive treaty of the preceding

[6] *Ibid.,* 278 (February 13, 1845).
[7] *Ibid.,* 127–8 (January 13, 1845).

April.[8] Its chief use proved to be that it became the base for a later proposal by Milton Brown of Tennessee to strike out everything except its enacting clause and substitute another proposal, as will appear.[9]

A second resolution came from J. B. Weller of Ohio on December 19. It also proposed to annex Texas on the basis of the Treaty. It was a duplicate in briefer form of Ingersoll's proposal.[10]

A resolution by Stephen A. Douglas of Illinois, introduced four days later, was marked by the concept, already mentioned, of re-annexing Texas.[11] This was repeated in resolutions offered by J. W. Tibbatts of Kentucky on January 3, 1845, and by J. J. McDowell of Ohio on January 7.

A resolution by J. E. Belser of Alabama, submitted on January 2, contained an idea that had been absent from Senate resolutions: that during the pendency of the annexation proposition, if "any attempt shall be made by any foreign power to occupy by military force, or to invade any part of the said republic of Texas, or to harass or destroy her commerce, the President of the United States is hereby authorized and directed to afford protection to the same; and for that end may employ such parts of the military and naval power of the United States as may be necessary." [12] This would have legitimized the protective arrangements the President had made on his own authority with Texas. The same protective authority was proposed in the resolution offered by Tibbatts.

On January 13 Milton Brown of Tennessee submitted his Whig proposal, which the House accepted as an amendment to that of Ingersoll. It authorized admitting Texas as a state, with all questions of boundary to be settled by the United States. It also authorized the creation of new states of convenient size from the territory of Texas with her consent, with the provision that those lying south of 36°30′ were in the future to be admitted to the Union with or without slavery as their people should desire. Texas was to retain her public lands, and the proceeds of the lands were to be applied as long as necessary to extinguish the public debts.[13]

[8] *Ibid.*, 26–8 (December 12, 1844).
[9] *Ibid.*, 129–30, 193 (January 13, 25, 1845).
[10] *Ibid.*, 49 (December 19, 1844).
[11] *Ibid.*, 65–6 (December 23, 1844).
[12] *Ibid.*, 81 (January 2, 1845).
[13] *Ibid.*, 129–30 (January 13, 1845).

Other proposals were brought to the House by G. C. Dromgoole of Virginia, by Edmund Burke of New Hampshire, and by Orville Robinson of New York, which added few new ideas to those already before the House but demonstrated a disposition to please constituents who were expansionists.

Speeches defining and defending these proposals kept the post-election Congress busy. They left little time for other business. They once again subjected the public to annexation propaganda that had been spread first by Administration spokesmen under cover, then by expansionists after the betrayal of the treaty, and again on the hustings. In equal volume came answers from embattled Whigs and antislavery Democrats.

Two constitutional issues, not clearly visible before, rose to the surface to increase the complexities imbedded in the joint resolutions. One concerned a provision in Article I, Section 2, of the Constitution, that in determining a state's population for apportionment of representatives in Congress, three-fifths of the slaves, in addition to all free persons, should be counted. The other was the two-faceted constitutional issue: whether it was constitutional to annex a fully organized foreign state, and, if so, whether any means besides a treaty would conform with the Constitution. The first had been discerned at a distance by William Ellery Channing, the New England clergyman, as early as 1837, in his famous letter on the Texas issue. He had written that the three-fifths clause was a circumlocution employed shamefacedly in a Constitution drawn for a free people by framers who could not bring themselves to pronounce the word "slave" in an instrument for the government of a free people. He observed further:

> Were slavery to be wholly abolished . . . no change would be needed in the Constitution . . . except [omitting] an obscure clause, which, in apportioning the representatives, provides that there shall be added to the whole number of free persons three fifths of all other persons. . . . How little did our forefathers suppose that it [slavery] was to become a leading interest of the Government, to which our peace at home and abroad was to be made a sacrifice! [14]

[14] William Ellery Channing, *Works,* 6 vols. (Boston, 1866), II, 256–7. The three-fifths clause is found in Article I, Section 2, paragraph 3, of the Constitution. "Representation and direct taxes shall be apportioned among the several states . . . according to their respective Numbers, which shall be determined by adding to the

With the reopening of the Texas issue, after Gilmer's letter of January 10, 1843, the evil potentialities of the three-fifths provision became apparent to the North. If Texas were annexed with the understanding that it could be divided into an indefinite number of new states as soon as population warranted, not only would Southern power in the Senate multiply but also, by virtue of the three-fifths provision, in the House and the electoral college. The policy of balancing the admission of slave and free states would likewise break down. The whole program of balance of power between the sections would disintegrate. Tyler's promise that the annexation of Texas would "put an end to faction and unify the nation" was not at all realistic in view of these Northern apprehensions.

On March 3, 1843, the Massachusetts legislature adopted a resolution urging in strong terms the elimination of the three-fifths provision by amendment of the Constitution. It ordered that copies of the resolution be sent to the Massachusetts representatives in Congress, to the President, and to the governors of all the states. This augured ill for the harmony desired by the President.[15]

On December 21, 1843, the resolution was offered to the House by Adams. It could not be conveniently brushed under the rug of the twenty-fifth rule of the House, since it was a legislative request for an amendment to the Constitution. Adams moved at once that it be referred to a select committee of nine, and his motion prevailed after a debate of two days, described by him in his diary as the most memorable ever held in the House.[16] The select committee

---

whole Number of free persons, including those bound to service for a term of years, and excluding Indians not taxed, three-fifths of all other persons."

[15] *Massachusetts Acts and Resolves 1843, 1844, 1845* (Boston, 1845), p. 79. The resolution was drafted for the legislature by Charles Francis Adams, the son of John Quincy Adams. Charles F. Adams, ed., *Memoirs of John Quincy Adams,* 12 vols. (Philadelphia, 1874–7), XI, 455.

[16] *Congressional Globe,* 28 Cong., 1 sess., 60, 63–6; Adams, *Memoirs,* XI, 455–8 (December 21, 22, 1843). In the Senate a motion to print the resolutions called out a fiery denunciation of Massachusetts from two Alabama senators. One of these was William R. King, who pronounced the resolutions "the Hartford convention amendment" and declared that the federal government would not "last twenty-four hours after it was made." He charged Massachusetts with believing "there was contamination [of] the Union which existed between the two sections of the country." Senator Bagby objected to circulating resolutions "which were seditious and incendiary." By a vote of 14 to 26 the Senate refused to print the resolutions. An excellent discussion is Herman V. Ames, *Proposed Amendments to the Constitution,* A.H.A. *Report,* 1896, II, 46–9. See also *Congressional Globe,* 28 Cong., 1 sess., 175–6.

was named by the Speaker several days later, with Adams prescriptively its chairman, but surrounded by colleagues who could be depended on to keep radicalism within bounds.[17]

In the meantime, further petitions from Northern groups desiring removal of the three-fifths clause flowed into Congress. Ten, numerously signed, came from Ohio; eight from New York; and one each from Indiana and Massachusetts. They came in the months of January and February, 1844—evidence of a grass-roots uprising against the annexation of Texas even before it became evident that annexation was the pet project of the Administration.[18]

The select committee, to which the Massachusetts resolution and the others were assigned, submitted six reports rather than just one. The first to be written was that of Thomas Gilmer, close friend of the President and author of the significant letter of January 10, 1843, on the Texas question. His report was ready for his colleagues by February 16, 1844. It bore the signature also of Armistead Burt of South Carolina, who had been appointed to the committee after R. B. Rhett of that state had refused to take any part in discussing so reprehensible a proposal as that of Massachusetts.

The Gilmer report was a history-based argument. It pronounced the Massachusetts proposal destructive of the compact between the states and aimed at the dissolution of the Union. The force pressing the dissolution was a "wild fanaticism which demands the sacrifice of the constitution to propitiate a foreign power." According to Gilmer, a proposition precisely like it was made in 1814 by the notorious Hartford Convention, acting in concert with the same foreign foe. The proposal, if agreed to, would convert the Union into a consolidated despotism of numbers. The slaveholding states were already under-represented in Congress. Their decline in power in Congress was to be measured in successive censuses. To restore equality, the slaves should be counted for representation on the basis of five-fifths, not three-fifths, of their numbers. As for the right of petition, the House should restrict the abuse of it, not the right itself. Concerning blacks, "the livery of nature proclaims them, whether bond or free, the inferiors of the white man."

[17] *Congressional Globe*, 28 Cong., 1 sess., 64–7, 73.
[18] *House Doc.*, 28 Cong., 1 sess. (ser. 446), no. 404, 120–1.

It is not the voice of the negro which urges this injustice [the amendment]. That voice cries aloud against the cruelty which would be perpetrated [by abolitionists] in the name of benevolence and equality. It pleads for protection against the hypocrisy or delusion of its friends and benefactors. It cites the happiness and comfort of the slave, in contrast with the misery and want [offered by] some of his pretended benefactors. It begs these philanthropists to remember the more cruel and hopeless bondage of Africa, from which the negro of America has escaped, and entreats them to forbear, from pity to the black, if they will not, from justice to the white man.[19]

To Adams the views of Gilmer were anathema. He believed the theory underlying the Constitution's three-fifths provision was indefensible. Though he was not yet ready to join the legislature of his state in pressing an immediate amendment on the issue, he considered the provision "repugnant to the first and vital principles of republican popular representation; to the self-evident truths proclaimed in the Declaration of Independence . . . to the liberties of the whole people of all the free States, and of all that portion of the people of the States where domestic slavery is established, other than the feudal owners of the slaves themselves." He went on:

If the fundamental principles proclaimed in the Declaration of Independence as self-evident truths, are real truths, the existence of slavery, in any form, is a wrong. No subterfuge of evasion, no ingenuity of sophism, can escape the conclusion, that if *all* men are created equal, and endowed with the unalienable rights enumerated in the Declaration, to hold men, guilty of no offence themselves, in perpetual and hereditary bondage, is a transgression of the laws of Nature and of Nature's God.[20]

The practical operation of this provision of the Constitution has been as evil as its theory:

The first consequence has been a secret, imperceptible, combined and never-ceasing struggle, to engross all the offices and depositories of power to themselves. . . . At this day the President of the United States, the President of the Senate, the Speaker of the House of Representatives, and five, out of nine, of the Judges of the supreme judicial courts of the United States, are not only citizens of the slaveholding States, but individual slaveholders

[19] *Ibid.,* 25–44.
[20] *Ibid.,* 1–3.

themselves. So are, and constantly have been, with scarcely an exception, all the members of both Houses of Congress from the slaveholding States; and so are, in immensely disproportionate numbers, the commanding officers of the army and navy; the officers of the customs; the registers and receivers of the land offices, and the post-masters throughout the slaveholding States. The Biennial Register indicates the birthplace of all the officers employed in the government of the Union. If it were required to designate the owners of this species of property among them, it would be little more than a catalogue of slaveholders.

Among the offices thus monopolized by the silent but uniform operation of the slave representation, is that of Speaker of the House of Representatives. The members of the House from the free States, having no common centre of attraction to rally their forces upon any one of their own number, are reduced to the condition of mere auxiliaries to the rival candidates of the South; and though the choice is consummated by the votes of the Northern men with Southern principles, they are never admitted even to propose a candidate of their own, but are magnanimously permitted to choose between the slaveholders him whom they believe will prove to them the most complacent master.

The people of the free States have little conception of the power of influence exercised by the Speaker of the House of Representatives. First, by the appointment of all the committees, vested in him alone; and secondly, by the arbitrary power of deciding all questions of order. All the important business of the House is prepared or matured by the standing or select committees. By the recent practice of the House, the Speaker is always selected as a determined, uncompromising party-man. All the important committees are organized to fortify the ascendency of the slaveholding party. All questions of order are decided by the Speaker's arbitrary will; and, being decided on party grounds, are always sure of being sustained by a party majority in the House. A captious quibbling spirit of chicanery draws into the vortex of order, questions of vital interest to the whole Union. A single member of the ruling party can arrest and defeat any inquiry instituted, or any resolution offered by a member of the minority; while any leading member of the majority can carry any measure, if objected to, by the suspension of the rules.[21]

One question of vital interest to the whole Union that Adams had in mind was the right of petition. It was a right, named in the Bill of Rights of the Constitution and more remotely among the

[21] *Ibid.*, 1–21.

rights of Englishmen, to petition government for the redress of grievances. It was especially relied on in the antislavery North during the excitement produced by the annexation issue. Adams had been indefatigable in this period in presenting on the floor of Congress petitions from antislavery groups against the interstate traffic in slaves, the marketing of slaves in the District of Columbia, slave representation in Congress, and slavery itself. He had won veneration thereby in Northern antislavery circles; detestation, as a firebrand, in the South. In his report he cited Jefferson as believing that error can be safely tolerated while reason is left free to combat it. Yet the current spirit of slaveholders tolerates no discussion. It deprecates free debate. It trembles at agitation of the question of its despotism. This fear of examination into the rightfulness of slavery is a full confession that it will not bear examination. It is the key also to the gag rules—the suppression of the right of petition, one of the unalienable rights of man.

Adams turned, at this point, to an historical account of encroachment on the right of petition in the United States. From 1789 to 1834 petitions for the abolition of slavery had been received, referred to committees, and acted on like all others. A petition for the abolition of slavery in the District of Columbia had been received, referred to the committee on the District, and favorably reported on by its chairman, who was from the state of Virginia. Not until the emergence of the Texas issue in 1836, when abolition memorials and petitions came in great numbers to the House, did the system of refusal to receive them begin, which developed into the twenty-fifth rule of the House.

> The 25th rule of the House is not only a violation of the Constitution, by the arbitrary suppression of the right of petition; it is the suppression of the freedom of debate in the House; a curtailment of the powers of the House itself, delegated by the Constitution. It deprives the House of the power of deliberating upon subjects of vital importance to the whole Union, delegated to them by the people. It refuses to consider the memorials, remonstrances, and solemn resolutions of State Legislatures, and interdicts to every member of the House the exercise of the powers delegated to him by his constituents, and the discharge of the duties prescribed to him by the Constitution. It is a perpetual denial to the House of the power to deliberate on the means of ameliorating

the condition of the people; of mitigating the sufferings of the oppressed; even of regulating that traffic in slaves which the laws of Congress itself have declared piracy, punishable with death.

To Adams the immediate object of these encroachments on the liberties of the people was the project, secretly conceived by the Administration and now openly avowed, to annex Texas on behalf of the slave oligarchy of the South. It was to dismember the republic of Mexico by fraud or by force under the infamous banner of a re-instituted slavery. The use of force would be consistent with the urgent recommendation of the President in the last annual message to enlarge the army and navy by the expenditure of at least fifty million dollars a year. This was designed to provoke a war with Mexico, and as an inevitable consequence, war with Great Britain for the extension of the scepter of slavery over the whole of the North American continent. The report was signed by another representative of the New England conscience, Joshua Giddings of Ohio, as well as by Adams.

Another report sponsored by two on the committee was that of J. R. Ingersoll of Pennsylvania and Garrett Davis of Kentucky, both Whigs. It contained a survey of the conditions which had led the framers of the Constitution to adopt the three-fifths compromise. The conclusion of the report was that this compromise, having once been essential to the formation of the Union, was now necessary to its preservation, and that it should be left, upon the basis "selected for it by those whose example it is wise to emulate, and whose counsels it is virtuous to obey." [22]

Of the three reports signed individually, one came from an Indiana Whig, S. C. Sample. His conclusion, after anxious deliberation, was that the proposal of Massachusetts was a matter of expediency, and that to go forward with it was inexpedient. [23] Another report was by a Northern man with Southern principles, Edmund Burke of New Hampshire. Its conclusion was blunt: that the proposal of the legislature of Massachusetts, "divested of its extraneous mantle of plausibility, is no more nor less than a plain and naked proposition: TO SUBVERT THE CONSTITUTION AND TO DIS-

---

[22] *Ibid.*, 45–79. The compromise consisted in balancing direct taxation with representation. See n. 14.

[23] *Ibid.*, 98–104.

SOLVE THE UNION." [24] The final individual report was that of F. H. Morse, a Maine Whig. It showed sympathy with the Massachusetts resolution, without actually favoring it. It concurred with Adams's that one of the great evils of slave representation in the House was abridgment of the right of petition.[25]

The six reports of the committee were adventures in divergence. They registered all temperatures of heat and cold on the subject of slavery and its expansion. However, the majority of the committee did manage to agree that the Massachusetts resolves not be recommended, that the House be requested to accept a journal of proceedings they had kept, and that they be discharged from further service.[26] Even Adams was content to recommend that further action on the Massachusetts resolves be deferred until the next session of Congress.[27] Those recommendations may have registered the hopes of both Whigs and Democrats that the election campaign of 1844 would bring victory to their side. For the historian, the reports of the committee are full of significance. They epitomize the problems the drive for Texas created and the fragmentation it was to produce in parties and in sections.

Awkward incidents marred the presentation of the work of the committee to Congress. One was the arrival, before the committee had completed its labors, of a new set of resolves from Massachusetts. The new set was like the old, except that it had been signed by the governor, which made it more authoritative. Adams sought to present it to the House on several occasions but failed. The House knew of its nature, and the Speaker felt that one of its kind was enough.[28] It did, however, stimulate a new flow of such petitions from other parts of the North, which Adams tried dutifully to present.

Another awkward development was Gilmer's appointment as secretary of the navy to replace Upshur, who had become secretary of state. Gilmer wished to present his report before he left Congress. This induced Adams, as chairman, hastily to complete his

[24] *Ibid.*, 79–95.

[25] *Ibid.*, 105–14.

[26] *Congressional Globe*, 28 Cong., 1 sess., 476. A journal that the committee kept is printed with the report, *House Doc.*, 28 Cong., 1 sess. (ser. 446), no. 404, 115–21.

[27] *Ibid.*, 21.

[28] *Congressional Globe*, 28 Cong., 1 sess., 205, 229.

own. On successive days in mid-February he and Gilmer, in that order, read their reports to the committee. Adams bemoaned the defects of his as excessively hurried and "consequently feeble and indigested," a judgment present-day readers would consider too self-critical. He stigmatized Gilmer's report as "the quintessence of slavery." [29] The committee voted to permit no report to be submitted to the House until every member had presented his views to the committee. This delayed proceedings to April 2.

On April 3, the assembled reports were submitted and acted upon by the House. The three motions offered by the committee—that the Massachusetts amendment be not approved, that the committee's journal be part of the report, and that the committee be discharged—were cheerfully accepted. Also, the House agreed readily to laying the report on the table, and on the following day, to printing the report.[30] The proposals, state and local, for eliminating the three-fifths clause from the Constitution seemed to have been laid at rest.

However, they remained, indirectly, much alive. They had revealed to the antislavery elements in the North the evil connection of the clause with the drive of slavery elements for Texas and with their ability to secure gag rules to throttle opposition to slavery. On December 3, 1844, on the reassembling of Congress, Adams moved to implement Northern anger over the gag rules, by the following resolution:

> Resolved, That the twenty-fifth standing rule for conducting business in this House, in the following words, "No petition, memorial, resolution, or other paper praying the abolition of slavery in the District of Columbia, or any State or Territory; or the slave-trade between the States or Territories in which it now exists, shall be received by this House, or entertained in any way whatever," be, and the same is hereby rescinded.

A hostile motion to lay the resolution on the table failed, whereupon Adams called for the ayes and nays. The resulting vote, as he recorded in his diary in ecstasy, was favorable—"one hundred and eight to eighty. Blessed forever blessed, be the name of God!" [31]

---

[29] *House Doc.,* 28 Cong., 1 sess. (ser. 446), no. 404, 117–19; Adams, *Memoirs,* XI, 511, 512 (February 15, 16, 1844).

[30] *Congressional Globe,* 28 Cong., 1 sess., 476, 481. The vote not to recommend the amendment was 156–163.

[31] Adams, *Memoirs,* XII, 115–16. For Adams's resolution of December 3, 1844, on the twenty-fifth rule, see *Congressional Globe,* 28 Cong., 2 sess., 7.

During the session of Congress, moreover, the dangers that had been revealed in the three-fifths clause became more clear. A number of the proposed joint resolutions to annex Texas would authorize its division into four or more other states as soon as their population permitted. All the evils attributed to the three-fifths clause would materialize if such developments should occur. On January 17, 1845, the General Assembly of Ohio adopted a resolution echoing that of Massachusetts. It listed four major objections to the annexation of Texas and added a fifth:

> an union between the United States and Texas, with the guaranty, or understanding, that the whole or any part of the territory of Texas shall be formed into a state or states where slaves shall be counted in determining the relative weight of such states in the councils of the Federal Union, would still farther extend the undue advantage which the citizens of the slaveholding states have over those of the states in which slavery is not permitted.[32]

More divisive even than the challenge to the three-fifths provision was the other constitutional issue already referred to. It was whether the federal government had, under the Constitution, the power to add a vast foreign state to the national domain. This was an awkward issue for Administration spokesmen to pronounce upon. In the Constitution no specific power can be found authorizing the addition of foreign territory to the union. In Article II, Section 2, is a general power to conclude treaties with foreign governments—treaties to which the Senate must give consent. Whether that power would authorize acquiring an area so vast that it would upset all the balances of the Constitution, was the question. The question tormented Jefferson when the Louisiana Purchase Treaty was dropped in his lap. He doubted that the Constitution authorized accepting the world beyond the Mississippi. He toyed with the idea of obtaining a constitutional amendment that would authorize accepting the treaty. But his colleagues warned him that Napoleon might change his mind about the cession, and since the treaty quieted an emergency situation at the mouth of the Mississippi, he agreed with reluctance to its ratification.

This precedent was relied on sixteen years later to obtain the ratification of the Florida Treaty. Precedents are easily upgraded

---

[32] *Acts of the General Assembly of Ohio*, XLIII, 437.

into policy in cases of territorial expansion. By 1843 the issue of acquiring dependent territory of foreign states by treaty was established to a degree that would have permitted the Supreme Court to confirm it on the legal ground of *stare decisis,* which means: Don't disturb settled matters. Legal experts such as Gilmer, Crittenden, Webster, Gallatin, and Levi Woodbury, certainly took that stand.

But when the issue of annexing Texas arose in 1837, a distinction was drawn by those disliking slavery between incorporating a Louisiana by treaty, and annexing a Texas—between admitting an inchoate territory that had neither dominion over itself nor a numerous population, and annexing a nation invested with sovereignty and supporting a large population. As William Ellery Channing had put it in the summer of 1837, in voicing his protests against annexing Texas:

> We shall not purchase a territory, as in the case of Louisiana, but shall admit an independent community, invested with sovereignty, into the confederation; and can the treaty-making power do this? Can it receive foreign nations, however vast, to the Union? Does not the question carry its own answer? By the assumption of such a right, would not the old compact be at once considered as dissolved? [33]

John Quincy Adams put the question more bluntly. As chairman of the Committee on Foreign Affairs of the House, he submitted the following resolutions on February 28, 1843:

> Resolved, That by the constitution of the United States no power is delegated to their congress, or to any department or departments of their government, to affix to this union any foreign state, or the people thereof. Resolved, That any attempt of the government of the United States, by an act of congress or by treaty, to annex to this union the republic of Texas, or the people thereof, would be a violation of the constitution of the United States, null and void, and to which the free states of this union and their people ought not to submit.[34]

These resolutions, which seemed too radical to the majority of Adams's committee, were not approved.

[33] Channing, *Works* (1866), II, 237.
[34] Adams, *Memoirs,* XI, 330 (February 28, 1843); *Niles' Register,* 64 (May 13, 1843), 174.

Daniel Webster, one of the outstanding Northern interpreters of the Constitution, held similar views. In a letter written to the citizens of Worcester County, Massachusetts, on January 23, 1844, which was published, he cited with approval a communication John Forsythe, Van Buren's secretary of state, had sent Memucan Hunt, Texan minister to the United States, on August 25, 1837, in which a distinction had been drawn between annexing unorganized foreign territories such as the Louisiana region or Florida, and annexing a sovereign state such as Texas. Forsythe had defended the decision of Jefferson to use the treaty-making power in the Louisiana case, but had thought it could not be used to cover the case of Texas. Webster took the same stand. He wrote: "If there were insuperable objections, even to entertaining any negotiations on the subject of [Texan] annexation, seven years ago, it seems to me that time and events have served only to strengthen such objections." [35]

An alternative to the treaty mode of admitting Texas into the Union was advanced during the debate on the treaty. It was advanced by those who were becoming fearful that the treaty mode could not be relied on, that the treaty might be rejected by the Senate. The alternative lay in Article IV, Section 3, of the Constitution, which reads: "New States may be admitted by the Congress into this Union." Surely Texas was a "New State" and could therefore be admitted into "this Union" by legislation. Legislation would, in one respect, be a superior mode of admission. It would be safer, for it required only a majority of the votes of the two houses, whereas the treaty mode set the high requirement of a two-thirds vote in the Senate. Ideas of that sort had long been in the President's mind.

As early as June 10, following the rejection of the treaty by the Senate, the President had declared in his message to the House:

> While the treaty was pending before the Senate I did not consider it compatible with the just rights of that body or consistent with the respect entertained for it to bring this important subject before you. The power of Congress is, however, fully competent in some other form of proceeding to accomplish everything that a formal ratification of the treaty could have accomplished, and I therefore feel that I should but imperfectly discharge my duty to yourselves

[35] Daniel Webster, *Writings and Speeches,* 18 vols. (Boston: Little, Brown, 1903), XVI, 420.

137

or the country if I failed to lay before you everything in the possession of the Executive which would enable you to act with full light on the subject if you should deem it proper to take any action upon it.

The President continued with a fervent account of the advantages to the United States of annexation and the weakness of the objections raised against it, and concluded:

> So much have I considered it proper for me to say; and it becomes me only to add that while I have regarded the annexation to be accomplished by treaty as the most suitable form in which it could be effected, should Congress deem it proper to resort to any other expedient compatible with the Constitution and likely to accomplish the object I stand prepared to yield my most prompt and active cooperation.[36]

The President's message had been most conciliatory, even though it called for a reversal of the Senate's action on the treaty. In fact, it constituted a reversal of his own basic views. It offered to give up the principle of strict construction of the Constitution, on which he had been adamant in domestic policy. He was saying to Congress that on an issue in foreign policy involving the extension of slavery he was prepared to go as far in stretching the Constitution as Congress might think was compatible with the language. He had earlier exhibited, in his preparations for the Northeastern boundary negotiation, an equal inclination to yield his principles regarding strict construction of the Constitution, in that case with regard to states' rights.[37]

On December 3, 1844, the President inched closer to the surrender of principles of strict construction in his annual message to Congress. He pointed out that a controlling majority of the people and a large majority of the states had declared in favor of immediate annexation, that the American and Texan governments had agreed to the terms of annexation, and that therefore a joint resolution of Congress should be passed, which would be binding when adopted by both governments. He was clearly suggesting use of the

[36] James Richardson, *Messages and Papers of the Presidents,* 10 vols. (Washington, 1896–8), IV, 323–7.

[37] Frederick Merk, *Fruits of Propaganda in the Tyler Administration* (Cambridge: Harvard University Press, 1971), pp. 1–16.

provision of the Constitution that "New States may be admitted by the Congress into this Union." [38]

That provision had never before been relied on for bringing a foreign state into this Union. It had been employed only to authorize the forming of states from territory already part of the national domain. Could it be used for adding foreign nations from whose territory new states would be brought into the Union? That was the issue. Using the provision for such a purpose required twisting, indeed wrenching, the language of the Constitution. It required reliance on a broad construction of the Constitution that had seemed poisonous to Tyler and to Calhoun. Objection to broad constructionism had caused Tyler to split the Whig party on coming into the presidency, and had caused Calhoun, years before, to take refuge in the doctrine of nullification.

One of the elder statesmen of the country who was troubled about the new doctrine of a legislative annexation of Texas was Albert Gallatin. He was the bearer of the Jeffersonian tradition in American politics. He had served as Jefferson's secretary of the treasury and knew well the views of the framers of the Constitution. Soon after a joint resolution of annexation appeared in Congress, he was asked by another antislavery Democrat—David D. Field, himself an eminent interpreter of the Constitution—to write a statement regarding the constitutionality of such a measure. The reply of Gallatin, written on December 17, was published at once in the New York *Evening Post*:

> I have received your note of yesterday asking my opinion respecting the constitutional character of the resolution annexing Texas by a legislative act, now before Congress.[39] Had not that resolution been proposed, I should not have thought that there could be a difference of opinion on that subject.
>
> A doubt has been suggested, whether the general government has the right, by its sole authority, to add a foreign independent state to the Union; and I have ever been of opinion that conditions might occur in a treaty ratified by the President and Senate, such as any binding the United States to pay a sum of money, which would require the free assent of Congress before such conditions

[38] Richardson, *Messages and Papers,* IV, 344.

[39] Gallatin is referring to the McDuffie resolution, *Congressional Globe,* 28 Cong., 2 sess., 16–17.

could be carried into effect. But it is unnecessary on this occasion to discuss those questions. That now at issue is simply this. In whom is the power of *making* treaties vested by the constitution? The United States have recognized the independence of Texas; and every compact between independent nations is a treaty.

The Constitution . . . declares that "the President shall have the power, by and with the advice and consent of the Senate to *make* treaties, provided two-thirds of the Senators concur." This power is not given to Congress by any clause of the constitution.

The intended joint resolution proposes that the treaty of annexation . . . signed on the 12th of April, 1844 (which treaty is recited verbatim in the resolution) shall, by the Senate and House of Representatives . . . , be declared to be the fundamental law of union between the said United States and Texas, so soon as the supreme authority of the said Republic of Texas shall agree to the same.

The Senate had refused to give its consent to the treaty, and the resolution declares that it shall nevertheless be made by Congress a fundamental law binding the United States. It transfers to a majority of both Houses of Congress, with the approbation of the President . . . the power of *making* treaties, which, by the constitution was expressly and exclusively vested in the President with the consent of two-thirds of the Senate. It substitutes for a written constitution, which distributes and defines powers, the supremacy, or, as it is called, the omnipotence of the British Parliament. The resolution is evidently a direct, and, in its present shape, an undisguised usurpation of power and violation of the constitution.

It would not be difficult to show that it is not less at war with the spirit . . . of that sacred document; and that the provision which requires the consent of two-thirds of the Senate, was intended as a guarantee of the states' rights, and to protect the weaker against the abuse of the treaty-making power, if vested in a bare majority.[40]

That opinion was held widely by Northern antislavery Democrats. It was held even more widely by Northern and Southern Whigs. One Northern Whig, Rufus Choate of Massachusetts, expressed it with particular vigor on February 18, 1845. He was the holder of Webster's seat in the Senate and was an influential figure on the Committee on Foreign Relations. More radical than Webster on the unconstitutionality of acquiring Texas, he believed that no power existed in any branch of the federal government to add a

[40] New York *Evening Post*, December 19, 1844.

foreign nation to the Union. Such a power would have to be created by an amendment of the Constitution. As for a legislative annexation of Texas, he forthrightly declared:

> Until it was found [that] the treaty of last session had no chance of passing the Senate, no human being, save one—no man, woman, or child in this Union, or out of this Union, wise or foolish, drunk or sober, was ever heard to breathe one syllable about this power in the constitution of admitting new States [Article IV, Section 3] being applicable to the admission of foreign nations, governments, or states. With one exception, till ten months ago, no such doctrine was ever heard of, or even entertained.[41] The exception to which he alluded was the letter of Mr. Macon to Mr. Jefferson, which Mr. Jefferson so promptly rebuked that the insinuation was never again repeated till it was found necessary ten months ago by some one—he would not say with Texas scrip in his pocket—but certainly with Texas annexation very much at heart, brought it forward into new life, and urged it as the only proper mode of exercising an express grant of the constitution.[42]

Whigs of the South were even more eloquent in denying the applicability of Article IV, Section 3, to the annexation of Texas. This was true especially of two Whigs in the Senate from the President's own state, both members of the Foreign Relations Committee: William C. Rives and William S. Archer. Rives, on February 15, 1845, delivered a speech on the issue unrivaled for lucidity and force. He opened by putting the issue in its proper setting:

> Everything that might be deemed by us expedient is not, therefore, lawful and justifiable. What would it profit us should we gain Texas, if thereby we lost our regard for that sacred instrument which was the bond of our national union, the pledge and palladium of our liberty and happiness? The mode in which Texas was to be acquired, in its aspect upon the principles of our political compact, was, with him, a vital and a paramount consideration. . . .
> The legislative department in other governments arrogated to itself supreme power, the *jura summa imperii,* but, thank God! such legislative supremacy was unknown in ours. The legislative as well as other departments of government in our system, were

[41] Choate's thesis was overdrawn. The constitutionality of congressional annexation was assented to by Van Buren in his famous letter to W. H. Hammett of April 20, 1844, and certainly he had no Texan scrip in his pocket. His opposition to immediate annexation was based on grounds of expediency.

[42] *Congressional Globe,* 28 Cong., 2 sess., 303–5 (February 18, 1845).

in the impressive language of Mr. Jefferson "chained down" by the limitations of delegated authority. "An elective despotism," as he had so well said, "was not the government we fought for." In our system the powers were so balanced between the several bodies of magistracy that neither could transcend its own limits without being immediately checked by the others. This was the fundamental conception of American constitutional liberty, as understood by the enlightened founders of this republic, and it had been faithfully carried out in the constitution of the United States. In that instrument all the legislative powers of the government were specifically enumerated and vested in the two Houses of Congress; the executive power was defined and intrusted to the hands of the President; while the judicial authority was confided to the Supreme Court, and to such other subordinate courts as should be established . . . by Congress. This organization embraced all the great internal interests of the country.

But there remained other interests to be provided for, which had respect to the relations of this country with foreign powers. . . . All these interests, whether of peace or war, of alliances, of succors, of commerce, of territory, of boundaries, were regulated by treaty. It became therefore, . . . a matter of primary importance to determine where this great power should be lodged. In all the modern governments of Europe, it was an appendage to the executive, but in ours it was different. . . . When the convention met to frame the new constitution, it was an . . . important inquiry, where this power should be deposited. The first idea suggested was to place it in the Senate exclusively; then it was suggested that the President should be associated with the Senate; and when this was resolved on, there arose the question whether the President and a mere majority of the Senate should exercise the power, or whether more than a majority should be required. In this question great interests were involved. The northern States entertained great jealousy in regard to the interests of the fisheries, and feared lest, . . . these might come to be ceded by treaty; while the southern States were equally jealous respecting the navigation of the Mississippi and the question of their western boundaries, both which points were then in controversy with Spain. Both North and South, therefore, united in demanding that more than a simple majority of the Senate should be requisite for the ratification of a treaty, and the proportion of two-thirds was finally agreed on. . . .

Soon after the new government went into operation, an important discussion arose in Congress as to the extent of this very power [discussion as to House appropriations to implement the Jay treaty]. The House called on the President for the instructions under which the treaty had been made, and Gen. Washington sent them an answer in which, with the highest authority which had ever accompanied any merely human words, he gave his testimony as to the true intent and meaning of this part of the constitution. His words were these:

"Having been a member of the General Convention, and knowing the principles on which the Constitution was formed, I have ever entertained but one opinion on this subject; . . . that the power of making treaties is exclusively vested in the President, by and with the advice of the Senate . . . and that every treaty, so made and promulgated, thenceforward became the law of the land. . . .

"It is a fact . . . that the Constitution of the United States was the result of a spirit of amity and mutual concession. And it is well known, that under this influence the smaller States were admitted to an equal representation in the Senate with the larger States; and this branch of the government was invested with great powers: for on the equal participation of those powers, the sovereignty and political safety of the smaller States were deemed essentially to depend." [43]

Having seen where the constitution has deposited the power of making treaties, the next question which presented itself was this: What is a treaty?—for on that question depended the rightful decision on the measure now proposed. . . . A treaty, according to the highest authority, was simply an international compact. [Rives cites *The Federalist,* no. 75, p. 322.]

Now, with the lights derived from this authoritative definition of treaties and the treaty-making power, Mr. R. turned to the joint resolution which had been received from the House of Representatives; and he would inquire whether it was not, to all intents and purposes, in every practical sense, a treaty, and nothing but a treaty? . . . He put it to gentlemen to say whether this joint resolution was not in substance a "contract with a foreign power?" Was it not a treaty in the language of the Federalist, just as much as Mr. Tyler's treaty, which had been submitted to the last session? . . .

Mr. R. said this much in relation to the treaty-making power, because he considered it an indisputable preliminary to another question. If the general power of making conventional arrangements with foreign nations was delegated by the constitution to the President and two-thirds of the Senate . . . then he held that

[43] For Washington's letter to the House of Representatives (March 30, 1796), from which this excerpt is taken, see John F. Fitzpatrick, ed., *Writings of George Washington,* 39 vols. (Washington: Government Printing Office, 1931–44), XXXV, 2–5.

no other clause in the same instrument could be so interpreted as to nullify that grant. . . . Under the power of Congress to admit new States into the Union it was contended that a mere majority of the two Houses of Congress could enter into stipulations and agreements with foreign States for their incorporation into our political system, although the power of treating with foreign States had been expressly restricted to the President and two-thirds of the States, as represented in this body. Would it not be most extraordinary, indeed, that the wise and sagacious men who framed the constitution should have placed so strong a check on the most unimportant transactions of this government with foreign powers, such as the payment of a sum of money, the surrender of criminals, the fixing of some small and unimportant boundary line, by requiring the assent of two-thirds of the States, and yet should have abandoned to a simple majority of the House the vast, formidable, transcendent power of treating with a foreign nation for its incorporation into our Union? The mere statement of the proposition was sufficient. It could not bear a moment's consideration. . . .

And in what part of the constitution was this vast, imperial power, capable of subverting all its well adjusted balances, to be found?—this lever of Archimedes, with which to [pry] up from its stable foundations the whole system of our constitutional government? Where, he asked, was it to be found? In the forefront of the constitution? In the same phalanx of enumerated powers with the power to make war, the power to coin money, the power to raise armies, to build navies, to levy taxes? No sir. At the very foot of the instrument, amid the odds and ends of miscellaneous provisions. It was relegated to an obscure corner; it was pushed off into a dark hiding place, where it lay concealed, like some Guy Fawkes, beneath the Senate House, prepared to blow up and involve in one common ruin the constitution and the Union of the country. Surely if this provision had the colossal magnitude which the honorable senator [Buchanan] supposed, it would not have been thus sneaked off (to use the memorable expression of a former distinguished member of this body, now no more) into a corner. . . .

Rives held out a "piece of history" of 1786 as a lesson to the South: the blocking of the Jay-Gardoqui agreement, which would have surrendered to Spain American navigation rights on the lower Mississippi for twenty-five years in return for commercial concessions elsewhere. Under the Articles of Confederation the vote of nine states had been required to ratify treaties—the precedent for

the two-thirds provision of the Constitution—and this had enabled
the Southern states to protect their interests. Basing his words on
this precedent, Rives continued:

> They were the weaker party. They should be the very last to give
> up the conservative features of the constitution. If they were now
> so blind as to recognize the dispensing power of a mere majority,
> the time might come when the peculiar interests of the South,
> involving their rights of property, their domestic peace, the security
> of their firesides, would be placed at the mercy of such a majority.
> Let the present measure be consummated; and the principle it
> involved be sanctioned, and Southern gentlemen might expect
> soon to see, by way of reprisal, a majority in both Houses under-
> taking to abolish slavery in the District of Columbia; and the next
> thing would be, under the clause to regulate commerce, an act pro-
> hibiting the removal . . . of slaves from State to State; but, more
> than all, and beyond all, he would ask Southern gentlemen how
> they would then stand in regard to that great fundamental act,
> which constituted the sole security of the South as to their reten-
> tion of their Slave property? . . .
>
> On a great occasion in the history of his country . . . a renowned
> Irish patriot and statesman used these memorable words: "If any
> body of men should think the Irish constitution incompatible with
> the union of the British empire—a doctrine he abjured as sedition
> against both—he would answer, "Perish the empire, live the con-
> stitution!" In the spirit of that noble declaration he would now
> say here . . . as a senator of Virginia, that if the sacred provisions
> of the constitution of his country could not be reconciled with a
> further enlargement of its territory—a doctrine he rejected as
> utterly contradicted by the history of the past, for under that con-
> stitution, and by a faithful compliance with its forms, we had
> already added to our limits an empire greater far than the whole
> territory of the United States at the time of its adoption—but were
> it so, and the issue now presented was to give up hope of acquir-
> ing Texas or to break through all the barriers of the constitution
> to accomplish it, he would say with the immortal Grattan . . .
> "Perish all thought of illegitimate acquisition: live forever our
> free and glorious constitution—the sole pledge of our peace, of our
> safety, of our honor, of our blessed and happy Union." [44]

The views of Rives were supported by other eloquent Southern
Whigs, notably by Berrien of Georgia and Archer of Virginia.
Archer spoke last in the debate, before a vote was taken and es-

[44] *Congressional Globe,* 28 Cong., 2 sess., App. 378–82 (February 15, 1845).

pecially emphasized the Rives thesis that the framers of the Constitution could not have intended to upset all the checks and balances of their covenant and its government arrangements by conferring on Congress a power of overturning them by a mere majority vote of the two houses.[45] Southern Whigs, especially Virginia Whigs, who contested the President's doctrine of congressional power to annex Texas by joint resolution, were indeed "profiles in courage."

Two House members, one a Whig and the other an antislavery Democrat, took satisfaction in taunting two South Carolinians who had abandoned strict construction to support a congressional annexation of Texas. Robert C. Winthrop was one of them. On January 6, 1845, in discussing the constitutional issue, he quoted a speech that Calhoun, as a member of the House, made on January 9, 1816.[46] Calhoun was resisting on constitutional grounds the adoption of a bill which would conflict with an Anglo-American commercial treaty concluded the preceding year. The treaty-making power, he declared,

> has for its object, contracts with foreign nations; as the powers of Congress have for their object whatever may be done in relation to the powers delegated to it. . . . Each, in its proper sphere, operates with general influence; but when they become erratic, then they are portentous and dangerous. A treaty never can legitimately do that which can be done by law; and the converse is also true.[47]

Yet Calhoun did undoubtedly approve the thesis of Tyler that Congress could legitimately annex Texas by joint resolution.[48]

G. O. Rathbun, a Northern antislavery Democrat who objected to the new constitutional concepts of the President and of his secretary of state, also expressed his objections on the floor of the House:

[45] *Ibid.,* 326–30 (February 28, 1845).

[46] *Ibid.,* 394–7 (January 6, 1845). See also a speech by George O. Rathbun of New York (*ibid.,* 131–4, January 22, 1845). Both Winthrop and Rathbun quoted Calhoun to show that his position in 1816 on the authority of the House in foreign affairs was antithetical to his position in 1844–5.

[47] Richard K. Crallé, ed., *Works of Calhoun,* 6 vols. (New York, 1853), II, 134; *Annals of Congress,* 14 Cong., 1 sess. (1815–16), 532.

[48] Calhoun formulated for Tyler on March 1, 1845, a statement that any new treaty negotiation would be fruitless and that reliance must be placed on a congressional joint resolution. See Lyon G. Tyler, *Letters and Times of the Tylers,* 3 vols. (Richmond, 1884–96), II, 364–5; Tyler to Calhoun, January 2, 1849, in A.H.A. *Report,* 1899, II, 1187–8.

But it appears not a little surprising that a gentleman from South Carolina, considered as the standard-bearer of strict construction, who is distinguished above all his compeers in contending for the sacredness of State sovereignty, and for the necessity of the two-thirds vote, instead of a mere majority—a gentleman who claims, *par excellence,* to be the oracle of State-rights doctrine—a gentleman who could not hear of an appropriation for opening a harbor, improving a river, constructing a railroad, cutting a canal, or chartering a bank, because the power to perform these things is not specifically granted in the constitution—that a gentleman thus transcendental should come here, and, throwing to the winds all these features of the true democratic creed which he had preached, and the whole South has also preached to the North until we believed them, should plant himself on powers not to be found in the constitution, and should advocate a position which would enable this government at pleasure to trample on all the rights of all the States—this, indeed, is a political phenomenon such as the history of party has rarely been able to exhibit. . . . We, of the North, love the sound doctrine of strict construction. We love the Democratic creed, and we mean to abide by it.[49]

One other issue produced opposition to annexation. It was speculation in the public debt of Texas. The debt was of undetermined size, but was estimated to amount to ten million dollars. A part of it had been incurred during the revolution, but the bulk of it was an accumulation of eight years of defense against Mexican threats and Indian raids. It consisted of bonds, exchequer notes, and other forms of liability, but chiefly of land scrip. Land scrip entitled the holder to parcels of public land wherever such existed in Texas, free of pre-existing claims. It had been issued to soldiers, merchants, and others as payment for services. Many of the original recipients did not wish to be settlers, and since they were in need and the scrip was negotiable, it quickly passed into the hands of speculators at a minor fraction of its face value.

A part of the problem was the question how extensive the remaining public lands of Texas were. Great unoccupied areas had already passed into private control. They had been granted administratively and otherwise during the Mexican era; some had been

[49] *Congressional Globe,* 28 Cong., 2 sess., App. 132 (January 22, 1845). Rathbun's speech was a reply to R. Barnwell Rhett of South Carolina, who, the day before, had urged annexation by joint resolution. Its jibes were aimed also at McDuffie and Calhoun.

granted by the joint state of Coahuila-Texas; others, under the laws of Texas after the revolution. The more extensive grants had normally been made for colonization purposes under the so-called *empresario* system.[50]

In the unsuccessful annexation treaty the debt and the public land problems were dealt with together by transferring both to the United States. The expectation was that the debt would be extinguished from receipts of the sale of the public lands. This had raised the issue whether speculators with scrip acquired at starkly depreciated rates should be permitted to make a killing at the expense of the American government. The issue had been further complicated by uncertainty as to the quantity of unencumbered land remaining in Texas to redeem the scrip. The problem was comparable to that of the bonds and certificates of indebtedness of the old Continental Congress, which had passed from their original holders into the hands of speculators who had reaped immense profits under the refunding program of Alexander Hamilton in the Washington Administration.[51]

Another element animating the drive for annexation from the beginning was the activity of land speculators, Texan and American. They were ubiquitous in Texan affairs. Some of them—Thomas W. Gilmer, for example—had valid titles to land, obtained by purchase. Others—John Woodward, for example—had claims chiefly dating from the Mexican era, and of uncertain validity. In the treaty of annexation both types were protected. A section of Article III provided, "All titles and claims to real estate, which are valid under the laws of Texas, shall be held to be so by the United States." A great rush of emigration into Texas was expected to follow annexation, and this would hoist land values.

The several categories of speculators—owners of land, claimants of land, and speculators in the Texan public debt—were organized before and after the failure of the treaty into a pressure group in Washington. They were an aggressive, if not too conspicuous, lobby

[50] The disposal of the public domain of Texas is well described in Oliver C. Hartley, *A Digest of the Laws of Texas* (Philadelphia, 1850). See pp. 38–40, 539–709.

[51] For a spirited, if not always accurate, account of the Texas speculation and its projection into the Compromise of 1850 and the congressional act of 1855, see Elgin Williams, *The Animating Pursuits of Speculation: Land Traffic in the Annexation of Texas* (New York: Columbia University Press, 1949), chaps. 3–6.

operating in the shadows of the Capitol. They maintained a "Texas fund" from which the expenses were paid of distributing proannexation propaganda addressed to the Northern public—propaganda of the kind found in Walker's *Letter Relative to the Annexation of Texas*.[52]

Exposure of the activities of this lobby was one of the services of Benton to realism after the treaty had been defeated and the annexation issue had become part of the campaign of 1844. In a speech delivered at Boonville, Indiana, on July 17 and 18, he devoted a major part of his remarks to it. He said:

He had in various speeches . . . not shown the part which land speculation and stock-jobbing acted in concocting the treaty, and pressing its ratification. He had not noticed this part; but it was a conspicuous one, and was seen by everybody at Washington. The city was a buzzard roost; the Presidential mansion and Department of State were buzzard roosts! defiled and polluted by the foul and voracious birds in the shape of land speculators and stock-jobbers who saw their prey in the treaty, and spared no effort to secure it. Their own work was to support the treaty and its friends—to assail its opponents—to abuse the Senators who were against it—to villify them and lie upon them in speech and in writing—and to establish a committee, still sitting at Washington, to promote and protect their interest. The treaty assumed ten millions of debt and confirmed all the land claims under the law of Texas.[53]

The treaty correspondence claimed two hundred millions of acres of land in Texas, of which two-thirds were represented as vacant and claimed as a fund out of which the debt assumed was to be paid.[54] Vain and impotent attempt at deception! Open and fraudulent attempt to assume a bubble debt for the benefit of stock jobbers without any adequate consideration either to Texas or the United States. Texas in all its proper extent—in its whole length and breadth from the Sabine to the west of the Nueces, and from the Gulf of Mexico to the Red River—contains but 135,000 square miles, equal to 84 millions of acres, and to get the remainder of the quantity of 200 millions of acres, they have to count the wild country under the dominion of Comanche In-

[52] The "Texas fund" is noted in Merk, *Fruits of Propaganda*, p. 123. For Gilmer, see Documents under date March 18, 1837; for Woodward, see n. 57.

[53] The treaty provisions relating to the public debt and lands of Texas are found in Articles 3–6. See *Sen. Doc.*, 28 Cong., 1 sess. (ser. 435), no. 341, 11–12.

[54] Cf. Van Zandt and Henderson to Calhoun, April 15, 1844, in *ibid.*, pp. 13–15.

dians and the left bank of the Rio Grande from head to mouth, all of which is under Mexican dominion, and the great part of which has been settled and granted above two hundred years.

It is nonsense to talk of Texas possessing vacant land. If there is anything vacant, it is because it is not worth having. Texas itself has been settled at San Antonio, Nacogdoches, and other places above one hundred years, and has been under the dominion of three different governments, each of which has been granting away its lands, and that not by forty acre and eighty acre tracts, but by leagues and parallels of latitude and longitude, and by hundreds of thousands and millions of acres at a time. The King's Government made grants there from 1720 to 1820, then the States of Coahuila and Texas, united as one State, made grants from 1820 to 1835, when the Texan revolution broke out; and since that Texas has been granting by wholesale and retail, having a General Land Office at the seat of Government, and a local one in every county, all employed in granting land, and that to the Anglo-Saxon race, whose avidity for land is insatiable.

After all this, what vacant land can there be in Texas? Not an acre worth having; so that the assumption of her debt by the treaty was gratuitous and without consideration. And what a debt! created upon scrip and certificates at every imaginable depreciation and now held by jobbers, most of whom have purchased at two cents, and five cents, and seven cents in the dollar, and would have seen their scrip, where it bore six per cent, worth upwards of one hundred cents to the dollar the day the treaty was ratified; and where it bore ten per cent interest, as three millions of it did, would have been worth upwards of two hundred cents in the dollar. . . .

These scrip-holders were among the most furious men at Washington, and cannot bear the idea of having their scrip scaled, as the continental bills of the American revolution . . . were scaled,[55] so as to give them back their outlay and interest; but they want them funded, as the soldiers' certificates were in the year 1791, not for the benefit of soldiers, but for the benefit of jobbers and members of Congress. . . . The Yazoo land speculations and the soldiers' certificate speculation, were grains of mustard to the mountain compared to the Texas land and scrip speculation which the rejection of the treaty balked. Under the bill [56] justice will be done. . . .

[55] The continental bills, which were in the hands of the people, were redeemed ultimately at the rate of about one cent on the dollar.

[56] Benton is referring to a bill he had introduced into the Senate on June 10, 1844 (*Congressional Globe,* 28 Cong., 1 sess., 653–7), which called for a new negotiation with Mexico and Texas for the adjustment of boundaries, for annexation of a "state of Texas" with an annexed territory to the United States, and for

To show the extent of these land grants, and to expose the fraudulent statements in the treaty correspondence that only sixty-seven millions of acres had been granted, Mr. B. produced and exhibited to all present a large pamphlet with a map attached to it, containing the claims of a single individual, all of which were asserted to be valid under the treaty. They were grants derived from the second of the governments which had granted lands in Texas, to wit: the States of Coahuila and Texas when united as one State, which was their condition from 1820, . . . to 1835. . . . The grants were made to a Mr. John Charles Beales, an Englishman married to a Mexican woman, or to Mexicans and purchased by him; and all obtained for little or no consideration—some in reward for introducing manufactures—some on condition of settling families—some on condition of introducing cattle—and some unconditionally. They are now all transferred to a citizen of the United States, a Mr. John Woodward, of New York, and amount to far more than the whole quantity which the treaty correspondence admits to have been granted by all the Governments which ever held Texas.[57]

This speech of Benton was widely circulated in the press by Whigs and by Northern anti-Administration Democrats. It was distributed also in pamphlet form.[58] It brought to public attention factual information damaging to annexationists by raising awkward questions as to the private interests of some of them in the cause. It necessitated a reshaping of congressional proposals of annexation.

---

compromise on the issue of slavery in the annexed territory. He sought, in a resolution submitted to the Senate on December 17, 1844, to shield the United States from "speculating operations" in Texas land or scrip. *Congressional Globe,* 28 Cong., 2 sess., 39.

[57] For the Beales grant and its transfer to John Woodward, see Streeter, *Bibliography of Texas, 1795–1845,* 5 vols. (Cambridge: Harvard University Press, 1955–1960), Pt. III, vol. 2, pp. 401–4.

[58] The speech was initially published in the St. Louis *Republican.* It was republished in the New York *Evening Post,* August 16, 1844, and was elsewhere circulated. For a discerning account of the projection of the Texas scrip and bond issue into the crisis of 1850, and the succeeding compromise, which casts reflected light on the speculators of 1843–5, see Holman Hamilton, *Prologue to Conflict: The Crisis and Compromise of 1850* (Lexington: University of Kentucky Press, 1964), chap. 7.

CHAPTER VII

Maneuvering a Joint Resolution to Success

As THE CONGRESSIONAL DEBATE wore on in the winter of 1844–5, the alignments of section and party, formed in the battle over the treaty, gave signs of shifting. They had been, on the one side, the Southern slavocracy, reinforced by Northern expansionists; on the other, antislavery elements of both parties in the North, allied with Southern Whigs, who were disgusted with Tyler and loyal to Clay and the Union. Expressed in terms of party chiefs, the alignment had been Tyler, Calhoun, Walker, Buchanan, and Douglas, on one side; Adams, Clay, Van Buren, and Benton, on the other. Overwhelming defeat had come to the slavocracy and the expansionists in the confrontation over the treaty. To convert defeat into victory required new tactics—tactics of dividing their successful opponents.

The mode of doing so was suggested in the joint resolution that a Southern Whig, Milton Brown of Tennessee, proposed to the House on January 13, 1845.[1] It made concessions, or the appearance of concessions, on two major issues. One was speculation, against which Benton had thundered—the unloading on the nation of the Texan debt, for which the security was to have been the Texan public lands. Brown proposed that both be left in the possession of Texas. The other was slavery extension, which had embittered Adams. Brown proposed what seemed a slavery limitation in the area to be acquired from Texas. The Missouri Compromise

[1] *Congressional Globe,* 28 Cong., 2 sess., 129–30 (January 13, 1845).

152

line was to be extended across Texas; by implication there was to be no slavery north of that line. South of the line, any states carved in the future from Texan territory were to have a choice between becoming free or slave states. This was local self-determination, traditionally popular in the West. Some doubt existed as to whether any legitimate claim to territory north of the Missouri Compromise line was held by Texas, but the impression created by the resolution was one of compromise.

Another controversial issue, on which an appearance of concession was made, was the boundary between Texas and Mexico. The resolution called for the annexation of "territory properly included within and rightfully belonging to the republic of Texas." A further specification was that the new Texas state be "subject to the adjustment by this government [United States] of any questions of boundary that may arise with other governments." This left the boundary issue in a convenient state of vagueness.

Finally, the controversial issue of constitutionality—the issue whether annexation must be effected by a treaty which the Senate would ratify, or could be effected by congressional action—was dealt with soothingly, by silence. The resolution simply took for granted the constitutionality of a congressional annexation.

The Brown resolution had the usefulness of a decoy. Coming from a Southern Whig, it might well attract other Southern Whigs who were hesitating, and likewise Northern Democrats who were on the fence. It might do this in the House, and more important, in the closely divided Senate.

A transplant was therefore effected. The moribund joint resolution of C. J. Ingersoll, the Northern Democrat from Pennsylvania, which had merely given the dead treaty a legislative title, was decapitated, and the title was grafted onto a renewed Brown resolution.[2] This was passed by a comfortable margin on January 25, 1845, which promised success for a like strategy in the Senate.[3]

[2] *Ibid.*, 193 (January 25, 1845). The original Brown resolution was renewed on this date to clear it of an amendment that had been attached to it.

[3] Silas Wright, a power in the Northern Democracy, who as a senator had voted against the annexation treaty, but had become reunited with the party as successful candidate for the governorship of New York and had supported Polk's candidacy, wrote his senatorial successor, John A. Dix, on February 15, 1845, "Upon one point I feel great certainty, and that is, that if any resolutions do pass the House, they will be such as the whigs shall give shape to and vote for." Wright was too

A reminder should be here interpolated: that the Congress in both houses was a holdover body, the one elected in November, 1844, not being due to arrive in Washington until December, 1845. The Senate, which had overwhelmingly rejected the annexation treaty eight months before, was still under Whig control, and whether it could be induced to accept annexation by a new mode was the great issue.

The Senate's reception of the Brown resolution was initially far from cordial. The measure was referred to the Foreign Relations Committee, headed by Archer of Virginia. He retained it until February 4, and then submitted a lengthy report on it. The report was devoted to the issue of the constitutionality of a legislative annexation of Texas, which the Brown resolution, in the spirit of avoiding controversy, had ignored. Archer's analysis of the issue was thoughtful, though it was less pungently expressed than that of Rives in the speech to be delivered on behalf of the same committee ten days later, the speech already fully covered here. The conclusion of Archer's report was "that the joint resolution from the House of Representatives, for the annexation of Texas, be rejected." [4] This was a conclusion Henry Clay would have approved.

To get this hostile recommendation reversed required conversion of at least Benton and his Democratic followers. His single vote might prove to be the swing vote. He had seemed utterly opposed to an immediate annexation. He had been borne to great heights in the minds of antislavery voters by the flow of his oratory. Yet that eminence was far from secure. After all, his constituents in

honest to mislead a friend, however, regarding the slavery provision of the Brown resolution. He wrote: "I do not believe the democracy of the State would sustain us in the annexation without some fair compromise as to the slave question, and hence I do not believe you would be sustained in voting for the proposition which passed the House [January 25]. I look upon that proposition as more unfortunate than if it had proposed no line, because all our people know that the line it marks does not touch one inch of the territory which Texas owns, or over which Texas has ever practically exercised jurisdiction and government. It is therefore no compromise in fact, while it is one in form, and almost every man you meet calls it a cheat and a fraud." Ransom H. Gillet, *Life and Times of Silas Wright*, 2 vols. (Albany, 1874), II, 1623–7. The New York *Tribune* observed on January 25, "We are disgusted by the loathsome iniquity of pretending to *compromise* the slavery question by stipulating that slavery shall not be legalized above 36½ degrees of North latitude [the line of the Missouri Compromise]. There is *no* Texas above this line, and the pretext that any exists is an impudent knavery."

[4] *Congressional Globe*, 28 Cong., 2 sess., 193–4 (January 25, 1845).

Missouri did want Texas, and he had heard from them directly in a message of instructions from the Missouri legislature adopted on January 3, 1845.[5] He had heard indirectly also from Andrew Jackson, the heart and soul of the Democracy. The indirect messages had come via Jackson's nephew, Andrew Jackson Donelson, chargé in Texas; William H. Lewis, Jackson's close friend; Francis P. Blair, whose annexation views had changed; and others.[6] If Benton had allowed himself to be carried by the rush of his oratory to the heights of antislavery approbation, he ought not to ignore the opinion of these friends. Some descent was prudent, and especially if the path down could be smoothed, so that he could return "erect" to the Democracy, as Andrew Jackson put it. The path did become helpfully smoothed.

The upward and downward paths of the senator are easily traced in his own Senate resolutions. The upward one was made on June 10, and was afterwards repeated in the resolution of December 11, 1844.[7] This proposed the opening of new negotiations with Mexico and Texas for adjusting the boundary and actually pointed out the boundary line for the negotiators as lying in the desert prairie west of the Nueces and along the watershed dividing the waters of the upper Rio Grande from those of the Mississippi to the forty-second parallel. The resolution also proposed that Texas be admitted as a state with an appended territory, and that slavery be forever prohibited in the northern and northwestern parts of said territory. A kind of afterthought followed: that the assent of Mexico could be dispensed with when the Congress of the United States deemed it unnecessary.

The downward movement of Benton began on February 5, 1845, after the arrival in Washington of the January 3 instructions from the Missouri legislature. It took the form of a resolution greatly simplified. The resolution provided that Texas be annexed, with "suitable extent and boundaries," as soon as the terms could be agreed on by Texas and the United States. A sum of $100,000

[5] *Local Laws and Private Acts of the State of Missouri Passed at the First Session of the 13th General Assembly, 1844–1845* (Jefferson, 1845), pp. 403–4.

[6] For the correspondence referred to here, see John S. Bassett, ed., *Correspondence of Andrew Jackson,* 7 vols. (Washington: Carnegie Institution, 1926–35), VI, 352–79.

[7] *Congressional Globe,* 28 Cong., 1 sess., 657 (June 10, 1844); 28 Cong., 2 sess., 19 (December 11, 1844).

was to be appropriated to defray the expenses incurred in agreeing on terms of admission of Texas, either by a new treaty or by articles to be submitted to Congress as the President might direct.[8] The President whom Benton had in mind was James K. Polk. Andrew Jackson was immensely cheered by this resolution. He saw in it evidence that the senator was headed right.[9]

The final steps taken by Benton on the way down came on February 27, 1845, when the Senate gave consideration to Brown's proposal, adopted by the House on January 25—the one which freed the annexation question of the ugly issues of the public debts and lands of Texas that had troubled Benton so much. If adopted by the Senate, this would put to flight the buzzards befouling the White House, the State Department, and the lobbies of Congress. Senators would be able to take their stand on the annexation issue with a clean conscience.

To Robert J. Walker, the Brown measure and its House acceptance suggested the final maneuver in the Senate. On February 27 he proposed, as an amendment to it, a set of resolutions strikingly like those Benton had proposed to the Senate on February 5. The amendment empowered the President (Polk was in Walker's mind also) to offer Texas the choice of the joint resolution of annexation or a new treaty of annexation, and authorized an appropriation of $100,000 for the negotiation, all in the exact language of Benton. The Walker amendment was in reality the Benton resolution.[10]

To head off this amendment, Archer proposed another. He proposed simply to substitute the negative report of his committee for the House measure. Had this succeeded, it would have scotched the annexation proceedings for the session.[11] The challenge failed. The Archer amendment was rejected and that of Walker upheld. The vote upholding it was an omen—it was twenty-seven to twenty-five.[12]

A New Jersey Whig, Jacob W. Miller, now moved yet another amendment to the House measure. He proposed to strike out everything in it after the word "resolved" and to replace it by Benton's

[8] *Ibid.,* 244 (February 5, 1845).
[9] Bassett, *Correspondence,* VI, 352, 366, 379.
[10] *Congressional Globe,* 28 Cong., 2 sess., 359 (February 27, 1845).
[11] *Ibid.,* 360 (February 27, 1845).
[12] *Ibid.,* 362 (February 27, 1845).

earlier proposal in the Senate, that of June 10 and December 11. He explained in offering his motion that the speech delivered by the honorable senator from Missouri in introducing that proposal "had made a strong impression upon him, and he hoped the Senator would not destroy his own child." To which Benton made the laconic reply, "I'll kill it stone dead." Cheers rang through the chamber, which could only with difficulty be suppressed. For the Senator had announced in these few words his return to the fold, with head "erect," and this gave assurance that the joint resolution would pass. When the final vote on the Walker amendment was taken, immediately afterward, it was again upheld, twenty-seven ayes to twenty-five nays.[13] The amended House measure had now to go back for approval to the House. It was approved there by a bigger margin than before. "Thus," the *Congressional Globe* recorded, "the joint resolution for annexing Texas to the United States is finally passed, and awaits only the signature of the President to become law." [14]

The triumph of the Joint Resolution in the Senate was thus the outcome of effective maneuvering to close party ranks. The egregious errors of the Tyler junto had been recognized and corrected. Every Democrat in the Senate, including those who had joined the Whigs in rejecting the treaty nine months before, toed the party line on February 27.[15]

Outside the Senate the same process was at work. Francis P. Blair of the Washington *Globe,* who had savagely assailed the treaty, warmly supported the Joint Resolution. So did William Cullen Bryant of the New York *Evening Post* and other Democratic editors of lesser prominence. They were attracted to annexation by the same allurements that had moved Benton. They wanted Texas. They represented the spirit of Manifest Destiny. They had no deep aversion to the expansion of slavery and may have been

---

[13] *Ibid.*

[14] *Ibid.,* 372 (February 28, 1845).

[15] Six of the Northern Democrats in the Senate who had registered opposition to the treaty voted "aye" on the Joint Resolution. They were Atherton of New Hampshire, Fairfield of Maine, Niles of Connecticut, Tappan and Allen of Ohio, and Benton of Missouri. Tallmadge and Wright of New York, who had voted "nay" on the treaty, were in 1845 no longer in the Senate, but their replacements, Dickinson and Dix, voted "aye" on the Joint Resolution. This shift of votes is a striking illustration of the success of the tactics employed by the Democrats. *Jour. Exec. Proc.*, VI, 312; *Congressional Globe,* 28 Cong., 2 sess., 362.

drugged by Walker into believing that an annexed Texas would some day produce the end of slavery and the race issue. They had no affection for free Negroes, certainly not for those residing in the North. They hated Tyler and Calhoun, but had hope and respect for Polk. He was, it was true, a major slaveholder, but he was sound on the tariff and on strict construction of the Constitution. He could be trusted to choose wisely between the alternatives of proposing to Texas annexation by joint resolution or by a new negotiation. For all these reasons it was desirable to join their strength with that of the slave oligarchy.

The Joint Resolution, signed by Tyler on March 1, was a cluster of provisions to attract a coalition. Each provision had its special function. One function was to exclude issues that had proved divisive. This was done in Article II, Part 2, which relegated to Texas the problem of speculation in the debts and public lands that had troubled Benton. Another provision had the function of obfuscating those who had scruples about slavery. This was Article II, Part 3, which, in applying the Missouri Compromise line to Texas, stipulated expressly what Brown's original resolution merely implied—that slavery would not be permitted in any state carved out of its territory north of that line—while repeating Brown's declaration that in states carved out of territory south of that line, slavery might be permitted if the people there wanted it. Two articles effectively dodged the issue of the boundary. Article I provided that "territory properly included within, and rightfully belonging to the Republic of Texas" could be admitted into the Union as a state. But the issue was left dangling in Article II, Part 1, by the provision that the annexation would be subject to the "adjustment by this government [United States] of all questions of boundary that may arise with other governments." The difficult issue of constitutionality was also dodged. Article III left it to the chief executive (which one, incoming or outgoing, was not disclosed) to decide whether annexation should be by acceptance of the act of Congress or negotiation of a new treaty.

The effectiveness of Democratic tactics in closing ranks on the Joint Resolution is highlighted by the divisions opened in the ranks of the Whigs. In the vote in the Senate on the Joint Resolution, a crucial trio of Southern Whigs cast their votes with the Democrats, two of whom had voted against the Tyler treaty of annexation.[16] It was a rupture of solidarity symptomatic of what was happening to Whigs. They were increasingly torn by the conflict between the sections over slavery which had already led Clay astray in the presidential campaign of 1844. Even as to expansion they were not of one mind. Adams was still an expansionist, except where expansion involved slave territory. Webster had yearnings for California. Other Whigs were attracted by the dollars an annexed Texas would bring. Whig divisions were deep and more enduring than those of the opposing party, as was to become evident in the disintegration of the party in the not-distant future.

The triumph of the Joint Resolution was acclaimed by Democrats and lamented by Whigs. John Quincy Adams, who felt numbed by what had happened, wrote in his diary on February 28:

> The day passes, and leaves scarcely a distinct trace upon the memory of anything, and precisely because, among numberless other objects of comparative insignificance, the heaviest calamity that ever befell myself and my country was this day consummated.[17]

The New York *Tribune,* in an editorial on "Annexation and its Consequences," mixed flagellation with prediction of war to come with Mexico:

> Call it by what specious names we may, the lust of Dominion, the lust of Power, the lust of Avarice, the lust of holding our fellow men in Bondage, are the real incitements of all this zeal for Annexation. To grasp more and more of the face of the earth, has ever been a besetting sin of individuals and nations. Few men are satisfied with as much land as they can well cultivate, few Nations have been satisfied to improve to the utmost their own, but must covet and seize what is justly their neighbor's. At length we have rushed upon this downhill road, and our course may henceforth be like theirs. The few are aggrandized, the many degraded and made wretched,

---

[16] Senator John Henderson of Mississippi, who had voted for the treaty, was joined in the final vote on the Joint Resolution by W. D. Merrick of Maryland and Henry Johnson of Louisiana. *Jour. Exec. Proc.,* VI, 312; *Congressional Globe,* 28 Cong., 2 sess., 362. In the House vote on the Brown Resolution in January, eight Whigs, all from the South, had voted "aye," showing their willingness to break party solidarity. However, when Brown's resolution, modified by Walker's amendment, came back to the House, some refused to go along. *Congressional Globe,* 28 Cong., 2 sess., 194, 372.

[17] Charles F. Adams, ed., *Memoirs of John Quincy Adams,* 12 vols. (Philadelphia, 1874–7), XII, 173.

by every act of injustice and aggression. There never was a truly successful war except a strictly necessary and defensive one, and no nation was ever strengthened by conquering another. But when did rapacity ever heed the lessons of history or of conscience? [18]

The Joint Resolution, in the form in which it emerged from Congress, gave the President the choice between immediately inviting Texas into the Union or permitting the incoming President to decide between that and a new negotiation. What the strategists who had maneuvered the measure through Congress wanted was that the decision should be left to the new President. Deference to the incoming President might have suggested restraint to Tyler. But he dearly wanted the credit for the work he had initiated. He believed that present and future generations should confer on him the accolade of triumph for his Texas policy.

Tyler consulted Calhoun, who also preferred action to deferment. He had no desire to leave to bitter enemies the fruits of his work. He believed speed was necessary to prevent a crisis. If a new negotiation were to be opened, the British would at once get into it, and the great end would be defeated. The decision of the President was "now or never," and a courier was dispatched, just before Polk became President, with the invitation to Texas to come into the Union.

Later, on learning of Polk's message to Congress of December 2, 1845, Tyler was filled with indignation. He wrote to his son Robert:

> I was most struck at that portion of the message relating to Texas. In speaking of my election of Brown's resolution he [Polk] says: "This election I approved and accordingly the *chargé d'affaires* was on the 10th March instructed etc." Now my instructions had already gone on the 3rd and Mr. Polk on the 10th did nothing more than confirm them. He would have told the whole [truth] if he had said "This election I approved as also the instructions to our chargé which [were] issued at the same time, and which, by instructions of 10 March, I directed him to carry out." [19]

Three years later the former President was still troubled about reports of what had happened after the vote on the Joint Resolu-

[18] New York *Tribune*, March 3, 1845.

[19] John Tyler to Robert Tyler, December 11, 1845, in Lyon G. Tyler, *Letters and Times of the Tylers*, 3 vols. (Richmond, 1884–96), II, 447–8.

tion. He sent to former members of his Cabinet a statement, formulated by Calhoun, and asked them to confirm it. It ran:

> The resolutions reached me, and received my approval, on the 1st day of March, 1845. My official term expired on the 4th. . . . After my approval had been officially given to the resolutions, Mr. Calhoun . . . called on me, and the conversation immediately turned to the subject of the resolutions. Mr. Calhoun remarked that the power to make the selection between the alternative resolutions rested with me, and that he hoped I would not hesitate to act. I replied that I entertained no doubt in the matter of selection; that I regarded the resolution which had been moved and adopted in the Senate, by way of amendment to the House resolution, as designed merely to appease the discontent of some one or two members of that body, and for no other purpose; and that my only doubt of the propriety of immediate and prompt action arose from a feeling of delicacy to my successor. We both regarded the opening of a new negotiation, as proposed by the Senate resolution, as destined to defeat annexation altogether—that Texas, in consequence of the defeat of the late treaty by the Senate, would listen reluctantly to any new proposition for negotiation; that this reluctance would be greatly increased by reason of the very small majorities in Congress by which the resolutions had passed, which might well create a doubt whether a two-thirds vote could be obtained for ratification of a treaty, and that these doubts might very wisely incline Texas to throw herself upon the good offices of Great Britain and France, with a view to obtain the recognition of her independence by Mexico, in preference to relying on the uncertainty of a new negotiation. Upon the point of delicacy to my successor, Mr. Calhoun urged strongly the necessity of immediate action, which he regarded as sufficiently great to overrule all other considerations.[20]

It was significant that in this long statement, neither of these strict constructionists found it necessary to refer to the issue of the constitutionality of the congressional annexation of Texas.

IN THE LAST MONTHS of Tyler's Administration evidence again became public of the undercover service of one of his and Calhoun's agents in the Southwest. The agent was Duff Green, whose earlier service in London had proved so useful. On September 12,

[20] *Ibid.,* 364–5. For Calhoun's part in framing the statement, see Tyler to Calhoun, January 2, 1849, in A.H.A. *Report,* 1899, II, 1187–8.

1844, he was appointed consul at Galveston, Texas, and received the ordinary printed instruction from Calhoun. His job carried no salary, consuls being expected in that day to draw their sustenance from the fees they could collect. But he was given directions, on the quiet, to proceed to Mexico City as a courier to deliver dispatches to Shannon, the American minister there. Later in life he wrote of this mission:

> At his [Calhoun's] request I went to Mexico to aid in conducting the negotiation for the acquisition of Texas, New Mexico, and California, and upon handing me his letter of instructions, he remarked: "If you succeed in this negotiation our commerce in the Pacific will, in a few years, be greatly more valuable than that in the Atlantic." [21]

During a preliminary stay at Galveston, en route to Vera Cruz, Green sent political news to Calhoun. It was that Anson Jones was rumored to have been elected president of Texas by a small majority, but this was no proof of opposition to annexation in Texas, for Jones was pledged to annexation. The most important item in the news was a conversation Green had had with General Thomas J. Green, whose hospitality he was enjoying and from whom he had obtained enticing vistas of opportunities west of the Rio Grande:

> He describes the valley of the Rio Grande west of that River as about fifty miles in width and of unexampled fertility. He thinks that nothing can prevent the occupation of that valley by the Anglo-Saxons; and that the best route to the Pacific is that indicated . . . on Tanner's Map of Mexico. If he is correct, a steamboat can leave Pittsburg, and go to Chihuahua [apparently via the Mississippi, Rio Grande, and Conchos] and [be] within three hundred miles of the navigable waters of the Gulf of California. . . . This is an important feature of the Texas question.[22]

As soon as possible Duff Green made the journey to Mexico City, where he delivered dispatches to Shannon, gave advice to the min-

[21] Duff Green, *Facts and Suggestions, Biographical, Historical, Financial, and Political* (New York, 1866), p. 85.

[22] Green to Calhoun, September 27, 1844, in MS. Special Agents, Department of State, National Archives. For a biographical sketch of General Thomas J. Green, see Elizabeth L. Jennett, *Biographical Directory of the Texan Conventions and Congress* (Austin, 1941), pp. 90–1. The Tanner map referred to may be the Henry S. Tanner *Map of Mexico* (Philadelphia, 1839), that shows a mountainous area of about 225 miles between Chihuahua on the Conchos and the Rio Hiaqui, which enters the Gulf of California. Green conceived of a future railroad spanning the two points.

ister, and busied himself writing letters to Calhoun. In a letter of October 9 he reported the likelihood of a British negotiation with Mexico for California, "under a belief that war between Mexico & the U.S. is probable and that having possession of California she may use that possession as a means of strengthening herself in the possession of Oregon." [23]

As for any hope of an American acquisition by purchase of either Texas or California, Green was very pessimistic. On October 28 he described at length the chaotic conditions prevailing in Mexico, the prejudices felt against the United States, and most alarming, a mortgage on California held by British creditors, said to contain a provision that if the loan was not repaid in 1847 the creditors were to take possession of the country.

> You will see that the war against Texas is the pretence on which both [Mexican] parties are seeking office and that the embarrassed condition of the Treasury is used as a means of enriching those who have possession of the Government. When to this you add the fact that the state of public opinion is such that any party, being in power, and selling Texas or California to the United States, would be driven from office and that the chances are as ten to one that their doing so would be used as an argument for shooting them and confiscating their property. You can then understand why I say that it [is] impossible to make any new arrangement with Mexico as to Texas or California for some time yet to come, at least.[24]

Frustrated in this principal mission, Duff Green returned to Galveston. He found his service there frustrating also—the fees were meager and the life dull. He appointed a vice-consul to his post and hastened to the Texan capital where the action was. He formed a land company for which he hoped to obtain a charter from the legislature. The company was to have rights to acquire and sell real estate, manage railroad and trust companies, and exercise a perpetual monopoly of the use of all navigable streams in Texas. At the same time Green formed the "Del Norte Company," which was to procure the "conquest and occupancy in behalf of Texas of the Californias and the Northern Provinces of Mexico" with an army

[23] Duff Green to Calhoun, October 9, 1844, in MS. Special Agents, Department of State, National Archives. An alarming item in this report was hearsay news that the British were about to make a loan of ten million dollars to Santa Anna.

[24] Duff Green to Calhoun, October 28, 1844, in A.H.A. *Report,* 1899, II, 975–80.

organized in Texas and reinforced by some sixty thousand Indian warriors that were to be brought to Texas from the United States. The plan was such a mixture of official and private enterprises as Green had carried to London in 1843.[25]

In quest of charters for his companies Green called on the Texan President, Anson Jones, on December 30, 1844. He held out to Jones an offer of stock in the land company to win his favor, a tactic sometimes effective in American state legislatures. It angered Jones, who had to check a temptation to shoot Green on the spot, as Charles Elliot, the British chargé in Texas, reported to Aberdeen, who passed the word on to Edward Everett.[26]

In this stormy exchange Green warned President Jones that a convention would be called and the Administration toppled. He added that the Administration was suspected by the public in Texas of being opposed to annexation and that this rendered its tenure insecure. Jones replied that Green's own tenure was insecure, that his consular status would be revoked. Green went to the public in reply, charging the President with being opposed to annexation and being too much under the influence of Elliot. The matter was now so unpleasant that Jones referred it to the Cabinet, and the acting secretary of state, Ebenezer Allen, wrote the American chargé, Donelson, that Green would be handed his passports and would be expelled.[27]

But expulsion was a measure that might be followed by reprisal. Green was no ordinary consul. He was a confidant of Tyler and Calhoun. He epitomized the annexation cause. Expulsion might irritate annexationists in both countries. Yet to ignore the matter was not feasible either, since the letter of Green had appeared in the press. All that was feasible was to lower the affair's crisis potential, and to this end Donelson turned all his diplomatic talents.

He wrote Allen a soothing letter in which he showed that Green had no official status whatsoever in making proposals to President Jones. He had given up even his consular status in delegating it to a deputy in Galveston. His stay in Texas had been only for the purpose of becoming a citizen of Texas. He had not intended to show

[25] For an account of the plan, see Ebenezer Allen to A. J. Donelson, January 4, 1845, A.H.A. *Report,* 1908, II(1), 332–4. Allen was acting secretary of state.
[26] Edward Everett Diary, February 15, 1845, M.H.S.
[27] Allen to Donelson, January 4, 1845, in A.H.A. *Report,* 1908, II(1), 332–4.

the slightest disrespect to the President, and the objectionable conduct imputed to him ceased to have any higher importance than
what belonged to his private character. The public letter was left
unexplained, but Green offered the explanation that it had been
written under an apprehension that the President was seeking a
quarrel. "It was but natural . . . I should yield to the suggestion that
he was in fact opposed to annexation and was acting under the advice of the British Minister. Yet you will see by reading the letter,
that I do not make the charge, but reserve my opinion subject to
his future action." Publication of the letter was the editor's fault.
He had printed prematurely.[28]

Donelson was able to restore peace. Green was permitted to remain in Texas. The only harm done was the loss of the California
opportunity and the unfavorable publicity, which was widespread.
In Texas, Charles Elliot, the British chargé, read of the episode in
the press while in Galveston, and at once wrote his friend, President Jones:

> I see by the papers that Gen. Green is singing another verse to the
> old tune of British influence. Till I read his letter I was not quite
> sure of his position here, but he has made it manifest, and there-
> fore I owe him thanks. He speaks of his expectation "to encounter
> the combined influence of the British Minister, and the President
> of Texas, acting in concert for the purpose of defeating the wishes
> of a majority of the people of Texas and the United States;" and
> again, "I am aware of the powerful odds against me, but I am not
> dismayed." It is plain, in short, that he has some official mission
> *behind* Major Donelson's chair, which I do not believe you knew
> of till this confession. I wish you could have acceded to my wish,
> and left him just where he was. If he and Mr. Calhoun do not
> blow up annexation, it is *fire-proof,* that's all.[29]

In London, to which the news had traveled, Peel wrote Aberdeen,
when it seemed that Green might be expelled, that the expulsion
might be made a "pretext with the U.S. for direct hostility against
Texas—and annexation by that means instead of by amicable arrangement."[30]

[28] Donelson to Allen, January 20, 1845, in *ibid.,* 346–8. See also John T. Tod
to Walker, December 31, 1844, Robert J. Walker Letters, III (1815–46), Library
of Congress.

[29] Anson Jones, *Memoranda and Official Correspondence Relating to the Republic of Texas* (New York, 1859), pp. 413–4.

[30] Peel to Aberdeen, February 23, 1845, Peel Manuscripts, British Museum.

But the repercussions of the Green affair were loudest in the United States, especially among Whigs. On February 4, 1845, a New Jersey Whig—Senator W. L. Dayton, a foe of annexation on slavery grounds—brought into the Senate a pointed series of questions in the form of a resolution, which was sent to Tyler:

> Resolved That the President be requested to communicate to the Senate, if in his opinion not inconsistent with the public interest, whether Mr. Duff Green does now hold, or has lately held, any diplomatic or official station near the government of Texas; and if so, what, when appointed, at what salary, and with what instructions.[31]

The President's answer came in the form of a letter from Calhoun, dated February 6:

> The Secretary of State, to whom has been referred the resolution of the Senate of the 4th instant, requesting the President "to communicate to the Senate . . . whether Mr. Duff Green does now hold, or has lately held, any diplomatic or official station near the Government of Texas; and, if so, what, when appointed, at what salary, and with what instructions?" has the honor to state, in reply thereto, that Mr. Duff Green was appointed consul of the United States at the port of Galveston, in Texas, on the 12th day of September, 1844, and received from this department his ordinary printed instructions as such, and none other; that no salary attaches to the appointment; and that he neither holds, nor has held, any diplomatic or official station near the Government of Texas.[32]

This letter was read in the Senate, referred to the Committee on Foreign Relations, and ordered to be printed. It was characteristic of Calhoun's letters, written under pressure. It contained scarcely a word of untruth, but was filled with truth of the kind that concealed the truth.

Dayton lacked the pertinacity and pugnacity of Adams. He did not press the matter further, and the exploit of Green produced no further eruptions in the Senate. But it can hardly be said to have added to the "glory of the American name," which the President had stressed so much in his message to Congress of June 10, 1844, urging a legislative annexation of Texas.[33]

[31] *Congressional Globe,* 28 Cong., 2 sess., 237 (February 4, 1845).
[32] *Sen. Doc.,* 28 Cong., 2 sess. (ser. 451), no. 83.
[33] James Richardson, *Messages and Papers of the Presidents,* 10 vols. (Washington, 1896–8), IV, 324.

CHAPTER VIII

Texas Becomes a State of the Union

TYLER'S HASTE in sending to Texas the invitation of Congress to enter the Union seemed to Polk uncalled for. The incoming President, he thought, should have had the decision between the alternative modes of annexation offered in the Joint Resolution. Polk was no less eager for Texas than his predecessor, no less a slaveholder, and no less on guard against British intervention there. Indeed, he was pledged publicly to the "re-annexation of Texas at the earliest practical period." He decided to redo what Tyler had done. He wished advice from his Cabinet, however, and the Cabinet had not yet been named. So he countermanded the message sent by Tyler to Texas and held off his own decision until the Cabinet had been formed. Then, on March 10, 1845, he accepted the Cabinet's advice, sent orders reactivating the Tyler offer of immediate entrance into the Union, and thereafter ran things as he desired.

In the Texan government the leaders—Anson Jones, President; Ashbel Smith, Secretary of State; and Ebenezer Allen, Attorney General—were aware of the terms of the Joint Resolution before the document itself arrived. They were dissatisfied with the terms, and so was Houston, who was still a power in Texas, though no longer in office.

The wish of Houston was that Texas be admitted to the Union as a territory rather than as a state, a territory divisible, as its population became sufficient, into as many states as the United States would think proper. On April 9, 1845, he wrote Donelson that he desired a negotiation with the United States to set the terms of entrance, the negotiation already authorized by Congress in the Joint Resolution. He thought the terms that had been proposed by Brown, and sanctioned by Congress, illiberal. They would take from Texas "all public edifices, fortifications, barracks, ports and harbors, navy and navy-yards, docks, magazines, arms, armaments, and all other property and means pertaining to the public defence" without compensation. This would be "a tribute, or *bonus,* to the U. States, for leave to surrender our sovereignty, and national Independence." These facilities had cost at least a million dollars, and the cost formed part of the public debt of Texas, which Brown's resolution left the state to liquidate. Texas ought to be compensated, moreover, for any public or private lands lost in a boundary settlement with Mexico, whereby territory held by her under law was abandoned. The compensation should be at the rate set by the United States as the minimum price for the public lands.

Houston also took exception to the manner of the annexation proposed by Tyler and Polk. The manner was derogatory to Texas. "The terms are dictated, and the conditions are absolute. They are of a character not to have been expected by any one who regarded annexation as a compact between two nations, where each had substantive and acknowledged sovereignty, and Independence."[1]

A response such as this by Houston (and by the other Texan leaders) to the Joint Resolution of Congress, was not surprising. It was predictable as a reaction to a joint resolution framed by scheming politicians to win a majority vote in a narrowly divided Congress. The victory achieved in Congress in converting a treaty issue into a legislative act ricocheted. There developed in Texas an opposition to annexation of sufficient extent to induce Polk to embark upon a program of interference in Texan internal affairs far more real than any charged by American expansionists to have come from the British.

An offer alternative to the American offer was suggested to the Texan leaders by the British and French chargés, Charles Elliot and Alphonse de Saligny. It was similar to the earlier plan offered

[1] Houston to A. J. Donelson, April 9, 1845, in Sam Houston, *Writings,* ed. A. W. Williams and E. C. Barker, 8 vols. (Austin, University of Texas Press, 1938–43), IV, 417. The list of terms of annexation Houston would have found acceptable on December 13, 1844, is set forth in a memorandum acquired by Donelson and confided to Calhoun. *Ibid.,* 407–8.

to Texas by their governments, but without its guarantees. It proposed a Mexican acknowledgment of the independence of Texas, an undertaking by Texas not to annex herself to the United States or to become subject to any other power, and a negotiation between Texas and Mexico regarding the terms of their separation. The boundary separating them would be one of the terms. If negotiations concerning the boundary should present differences that could not be compromised, the question should be referred to an umpire. An allowance of time was necessary to carry the proposal to Mexico City, to obtain a decision on it, and to return to Texas. An estimate of ninety days was suggested, and President Jones accordingly agreed to a corresponding date for a special meeting of the Texan legislature. A choice could then be offered the legislature, if the mission to Mexico succeeded, between peaceful independence and annexation to the United States.

The scheme was advantageous to Texas, and it cost little. If it succeeded, alternatives would be before the Texan legislature, each of which could perhaps be improved by competition between the American and Mexican bidders. If the Mexican government should remain stubbornly hostile and the American Congress ungenerous, the status quo could be retained. The cost of the venture was no more than a ninety-day delay in submitting the American offer of annexation to the Texan legislature.

To carry out the mission, speed and secrecy were essential. The answer to the American invitation could not be too long withheld. Secrecy was required so that charges could not be brought of acting under British inspiration and huckstering for terms. The messenger carrying the plan to Mexico City had to be a person of standing who could present it authoritatively to the Mexican leaders. The obvious man for the job was the intimate of President Jones, Charles Elliot. He had, on an earlier occasion, volunteered such service as a go-between. Yet he was apprehensive of the secrecy of such a mission. Were he to go incognito and be recognized, his mission would be guessed and exploited as evidence of British intrigue. He was pressed by Jones, however, to go secretly, and against his better judgment agreed to do so. He went by water to Vera Cruz and thence overland to Mexico City.

In Mexico his mission prospered. The hand of the government

had been forced by the American annexation offer to Texas. The Mexican government agreed to make peace with the understanding that Texas agree to retain her independence and that the terms of separation be worked out in a negotiation. What the Texan government wanted, it got. Yet time had been consumed in Mexico. The return to Texas took time. Elliot had the misfortune to be recognized on the way to Mexico City under cover of a big white hat. His mission was guessed. News of it was rushed to the American press. The affair of the "Man in the White Hat" became a political sensation in the United States. In the State Department it produced apprehensions as acute as those aroused by the British loan plot that Duff Green had reported. It became the subject of an excited dispatch of Secretary of State Buchanan to the American chargé in Texas and was exploited similarly in the expansionist press.[2]

On June 3, 1845, Elliot was back in the Texan capital with the eagerly awaited news of the agreement he had obtained from the Mexican government. On the next day Jones issued a proclamation informing the public that, through the good offices of the British government, he had obtained peace with Mexico and that Texas now had a free choice between a peaceful independence and annexation to the United States. But the only reward he got for his pains was the accusation that he was a British stool pigeon.

As for Elliot, his yielding to the pressure of President Jones and consenting to go on a secret mission to Mexico City had been a grievous error. Secrecy in itself was not the error. In diplomacy it was normal. It had been the staple of Tyler's negotiations with Texas. What was wrong with it was that it had been detected. Just as Tyler's treaty had been exposed by Tappan and Benton, so the mission of Elliot, detected, had backfired. As soon as word of the mission came to Aberdeen, he wrote Peel in anxiety:

> The only part of the transaction which I do not much like, is the journey of Capt. Elliot to Mexico at the request of President Jones, and his attempt at concealment. This cannot succeed, and it will make English agency appear too active, and too hostile to the United States. The Texian Government has taken a great responsibility on themselves by acting in opposition to the wishes of the people, and after all it is very doubtful if their decision will be con-

[2] *Sen. Doc.,* 29 Cong., 1 sess. (ser. 470), no. 1, 44–5.

firmed by the Congress [of Texas]. Much will depend on Mexico, and here unfortunately there is very little reason to expect anything like discretion or common sense. It is their last chance; and if they do not now secure the independence of Texas, annexation is certain.[3]

Peel agreed. He wrote Aberdeen:

Should the [Texan] Congress refuse to ratify the act of the Texas executive, and should Captain Elliot's secret mission be discovered—our failure to prevent annexation will be more marked and give more triumph to the United States than if Captain Elliot had been less active and had less of temporary success.[4]

To Elliot, Aberdeen sent a reproof in which he drew a distinction between the aims of British policy and the mode used by Elliot in attaining them. Elliot was commended for helpful cooperation with the Texan government in its effort to preserve its independence. But the trip to Mexico, Aberdeen wrote, was concealed, and that was its mischief. The program of Great Britain had been to prevent, by preserving the independence of Texas, a collision between the United States and Mexico. British aims in fostering independence for Texas had been general, not special, and she wished to pursue them openly. Elliot was warned not again to compromise his government by clandestine operations.[5]

In Texas two aspirations for the future had been in conflict. One was that of the people, which could not be denied: annexation to the United States. For the most part the people were Americans. Their flow into the rich prairie lands of Texas had been in progress for twenty years, in response to the invitations of *empresarios*. It had expanded to an actual flood in the forties, reflecting hope of annexation to the United States. These emigrants were eager for reunion with the homeland, in whose institutions and progress they took pride. They valued annexation to the United States for the security it would bring from future Mexican harassment and for the likelihood that it would raise land values. They were content with

---

[3] Aberdeen to Peel, May 11, 1845, Peel MSS, British Museum.
[4] Peel to Aberdeen, May 12, 1845, Peel MSS, British Museum.
[5] Aberdeen to Elliot, July 3, 1845, Arthur Hamilton-Gordon, comp., *Selections from the Correspondence of George Hamilton-Gordon, Fourth Earl of Aberdeen,* 13 vols. (London, 1854–[85?]), VI, 210–11.

the terms of the congressional resolution and were ready to unite their destinies with the destiny of the old homeland.

On the other hand, among the leaders of Texas were ambitious men who had visions of greatness for a Texas that would maintain its independence—a Texas that would expand before long over the provinces of northern Mexico, would reach the Pacific in California, and would become a transcontinental power of a stature rivaling that of the United States. They dreamed of acquiring even the Oregon Country. Houston, in particular, nursed such dreams.[6] After the passage of the Joint Resolution—while Elliot was on his mission— the leaders, in the hope of at least better terms from the United States, held out for the new negotiation permitted under the terms of the Joint Resolution. They chose not to consider seriously Donelson's suggestion, that improved terms would be offered by Congress in an ultimate act of incorporation if the offer of immediate annexation were accepted. They adopted the tactic of stalling with regard to summoning the Texas Congress, the tactic already adopted for awaiting the news from Mexico.[7]

From Polk in this critical period had come more than a mere offer of annexation. At his direction, visitors went to help the Texans make up their minds. Among them was Charles A. Wickliffe, former governor of Kentucky and postmaster general in the Tyler Administration. He held an appointment from Polk to proceed to Texas as executive agent "to oppose the machinations and influence of Great Britain and France." He was to use arguments on proper occasions best adapted to convince the authorities and people of Texas that reunion with the United States would promote their best interests and those of their posterity.[8] An unnamed half of this assignment was to counteract the machinations and influence of the Texan leaders. Another of the visitors was Archibald Yell, a member of Congress and former governor of Arkansas. Another was Captain

[6] Houston to Murphy, May 6, 1844, in Sam Houston, *Writings,* IV, 320–5; and Houston's Farewell Message, December 9, 1844, in Republic of Texas, *Executive Records,* Book 40, p. 385. See also William C. Binkley, *Expansionist Movement in Texas 1836–1850* (Berkeley: University of California Press, 1925), chap. 5.

[7] Justin Smith, *Annexation of Texas* (New York: Baker and Taylor Co., 1911), chap. 20.

[8] Henry M. Wriston, *Executive Agents in American Foreign Relations* (Baltimore: Johns Hopkins Press, 1929), 718–19.

Robert F. Stockton of the United States Navy, charged with guarding the Texan coast. His assignment was light, and he had time to come inland to counteract British influence. Duff Green was on the scene, active still in foiling the British. Finally, there was A. J. Donelson—the American chargé in Texas and the nephew of Jackson—who combined skill with tact and became a major force in the Texan councils.

If Ashbel Smith is to be believed, the American visitors, including Donelson, went up and down the settlements of Texas holding out promises of American aid if annexation were consummated:

> The promises were among others to clear out our rivers for navigation, to deepen the entrances of our harbors, to build light houses on our coast for commerce, to erect military works, fortifications for the defense of the coast, to execute important works of internal improvement, and to do various and sundry other good things for Texas which were beyond our means, or which they could do for us better than we of ourselves could. Under the fostering protection of the United States it was gloriously prophesied, with spread eagle magniloquence, that capital would flow into Texas in ocean streams to develop and utilize our incalculable natural resources. Employment, wealth, prosperity would reign in this land. Here in the West lay the inexhaustible Orient.[9]

According to Ebenezer Allen, the visitors instigated the calling of public meetings to whip up enthusiasm for annexation and held out the hope to Texan politicians of obtaining federal office if it took place.

For Houston a shift was necessary from positions he had held. He had become aware, already by April 15, of strong winds blowing for annexation and had decided it was best to sail before them. He was intrigued by suggestions made to him that he might someday be chosen President of the United States. In any case he was likely to become a senator soon. He was eager to please Andrew Jackson, whose earnestness for annexation was touching and who was approaching death. Houston let Donelson know of his conversion, to the latter's joy, and early in May, he arranged for a visit to the Hermitage. On May 29 he was in New Orleans awaiting passage up

---

[9] Ashbel Smith, *Reminiscences of the Texas Republic* (Galveston, 1876), p. 76.

the river. He made a significant speech there, which disclosed that inwardly he had always favored annexation. He opened with a "statement of facts." Then he concluded:

> He would leave to the public to infer whether he was opposed to, or in favor of, annexation. It was true, he said, that he had coquetted a little with G. Britain, and made the United States as jealous of that power as he possibly could; and had it not been, he said, for the eagerness of the Texan congress in passing and sending this country [in 1844] a declaration that nine-tenths of the people of Texas were in favor of the measure, he would have so operated on the fears of the American Senate . . . as to have secured the ratification of the treaty last spring.[10]

The hero of San Jacinto recovered in this way his old rapport with the people of Texas. He made evident to them that, though he had seemed at odds with their wishes for a time, it was only because he had been cleverer than they in effecting what they wanted. The speech prepared the way for his election as one of the two original Texan senators in Congress. But it left President Jones holding the bag. Jones thought the speech infamous, false, and disgraceful, though at the time he kept his peace.[11]

On June 18, during the absence of Houston from home, the Texan Congress met. It rejected out of hand the Mexican peace proposal and unanimously approved the offer of annexation to the United States. A specially summoned convention did the same on July 4 by a virtually unanimous vote. The convention remained in session to frame a state constitution for presentation to Congress. It completed its work on August 27, 1845.

The constitution contained a carefully drawn bill of rights. It created the traditional three departments of government. Its pattern regarding slavery and the status of free Negroes was wholly Southern. It prohibited any general legislation for emancipating slaves and any legislation restricting the right of immigrants to bring slaves with them into Texas. It gave the right of suffrage to all free white males, but not to untaxed Indians or to Africans, or to the descendants of Africans. It ordered a census to be taken every eight

---

[10] *Niles' Register,* 68 (1845), 230.
[11] Anson Jones, *Memoranda and Official Correspondence Relating to the Republic of Texas* (New York, 1859), p. 453.

years in which all free inhabitants were to be enumerated, but not untaxed Indians or Africans, or the descendants of Africans.[12] In October, a popular referendum accepted annexation and the new constitution.

On December 3, 1845, President Polk, in his first annual message to Congress, presented the state and its constitution in a glowing speech of welcome. He declared:

> This accession to our territory has been a bloodless achievement. No arm of force has been raised to produce the results. The sword has had no part in the victory. We have not sought to extend our territorial possessions by conquest, or our republican institutions over a reluctant people. It was the deliberate homage of each people to the great principle of our federative union. If we consider the extent of territory involved in the annexation, its prospective influence on America, the means by which it has been accomplished, springing purely from the choice of the people themselves to share the blessings of our union, the history of the world may be challenged to furnish a parallel. The jurisdiction of the United States, which at the formation of the Federal Constitution was bounded by the St. Marys on the Atlantic, has passed the capes of Florida and been peacefully extended to the Del Norte [Rio Grande]. In contemplating the grandeur of this event it is not to be forgotten that the result was achieved in despite of the diplomatic interference of European monarchies. Even France, the country which had been our ancient ally . . . most unexpectedly, and to our unfeigned regret, took part in an effort to prevent annexation and to impose on Texas, as a condition of the recognition of her independence by Mexico, that she would never join herself to the United States. We may rejoice that the tranquil and pervading influence of the American principle of self-government was sufficient to defeat the purposes of British and French interference, and that the almost unanimous voice of the people of Texas has given to that interference a peaceful and effective rebuke. From this example European Governments may learn how vain diplomatic arts and intrigues must ever prove upon this continent against that system of self-government which seems natural to our soil, and which will ever resist foreign interference.[13]

[12] *House Doc.*, 29 Cong., 1 sess. (ser. 482), no. 16. For the constitution of the Republic of Texas, including guarantees of slavery, see Hartley, *A Digest of the Laws of Texas* (Philadelphia, 1850), pp. 25–43. The ordinances of annexation and the state constitution of Texas are also to be found in Hartley.

[13] James Richardson, *Messages and Papers of the Presidents,* 10 vols. (Washington, 1896–8), IV, 387–8.

The declaration of the President that the jurisdiction of the United States had been "peacefully extended to the Del Norte" was a self-contradiction. One phrase was that the jurisdiction of the United States had been "peacefully extended"; the other was, "to the Del Norte." It was true that jurisdiction had been "peacefully extended" in the sense that no armed conflict with Mexico had yet developed. But that the extension was "to the Del Norte" meant aggression. The Texan claim to the Del Norte boundary was flimsy, and in any case an international boundary is not unilaterally established. But the emphasis on the peacefulness of the extension and the casualness of the reference to the Rio Grande had the effect desired. Not even such distrustful journals as the *National Intelligencer* and the New York *Tribune* were roused to challenge what was in fact an arrogant assertion, portentous for the peace of the future.

In Texas, on February 14, 1846, Anson Jones presided over the ceremony of the transfer of his state's sovereignty to the United States. Before an audience of legislators and citizens he delivered a brief valedictory with this peroration:

> The lone star of Texas, which ten years since arose amid clouds over fields of carnage, and obscurely shone for a while, has culminated, and, following an inscrutable destiny, has passed on and become fixed forever in that glorious constellation which all freemen and lovers of freedom in the world must reverence and adore—the American Union. . . . The final act in this great drama is now performed. The republic of Texas is no more.[14]

In the silence following the peroration the President lowered the flag of the republic. As it came down, the pole which had been carrying it broke in two. For a moment, before the banner of the Union was raised, the Lone Star flag shrouded the retiring President.[15] Thirteen years later, deeply depressed over the misunderstanding of his efforts on behalf of Texas, which had reappeared in his defeat for election to the Senate of the United States, he took his own life.[16]

A REVIEW OF THE BACKGROUND STAGES of the annexation of Texas is desirable in this closing chapter, familiar though it is to many

---

[14] Smith, *Annexation of Texas*, p. 468.

[15] Herbert Gambrell, *Anson Jones: The Last President of Texas* (Austin: University of Texas Press, 1964), p. 419.

[16] *Ibid.*, p. 439.

readers. An introductory stage was the general flow of American pioneers westward. It was a flow in search of good land and opportunity. In the 1820s the Mexican government had been won to the view that advantage could be gained from diverting some of the flow into its Texan province. It wished to convert that wilderness into a civilized society as a means of enrichment and as a protection for the adjacent provinces from marauding Texan Indians. A proposal, initially made to the Spanish authorities by two Americans, Moses and Stephen F. Austin, was adopted. It was to draw settlers into the wilderness by means of colonizing agents or *empresarios* who would offer lands to settlers from large grants reserved to them for this purpose. A colonization law of this design was adopted by the Mexican Congress in 1823, and Stephen F. Austin was awarded an early grant. *Empresarios* were to be of different nationalities—Mexican, American, and European—as a protection against predominantly American settlement. American pioneers who were to be attracted were expected to be drawn chiefly from neighboring Louisiana and to be of French and Spanish origin. However, as it proved, settlers were drawn from other parts of the United States. The attractions of the plan to Americans were rich lands, virtually free, in the prairies of Texas that would have cost, in the United States, a minimum of $1.25 an acre. A steady flow of Americans to Texas occurred from 1823 to 1830.

By 1830, however, the perils of the flow became apparent to the Mexican authorities. The Americans who were responding to the allurements of the *empresarios* were principally Anglo-Saxons from Kentucky and Tennessee—land-hungry, restive, and aggressive. Few settlers came from the Mexican provinces. Mexicans preferred to remain in the safety of their settled regions. Europeans in general preferred to settle in the United States.

In 1826 Hayden Edwards, one of the American *empresarios,* whose settlement lay near the Louisiana border, became engaged in a dispute with the provincial authorities of Coahuila-Texas, and was so aggressive that his contract was canceled, whereupon he started a revolution, proclaimed the republic of Fredonia, and sought alliance with the wild Indians of Texas. He was promptly defeated by Mexican troops with the aid of Austin, and expelled. But the revolt highlighted the dangers of Americanization. The fears of the Mexican government were intensified by the persistent efforts of the government of the United States between 1825 and 1829 to purchase Texas, and by the warnings of the British minister in Mexico City of the dangers of the course it was following.

As a result, the Mexican government sent a fact-finding commission—the Terán Commission—to Texas in 1828. This commission made a report, after a year's investigation, that was very disquieting. Not only were Americans in overwhelming majority in Texas, but they were ignoring and evading the requirements of the colonization law in regard to slavery, tariffs, and religion.[17]

In response to this report the Mexican Congress enacted a law in 1830 reversing its Texas policy. The law forbade further American settlement in Texas. It also prohibited further importation of slaves into Texas. It gave encouragement to native Mexicans to move to Texas as a counterweight to the Americans. To ensure obedience to the law, the government established garrisons of troops near the American settlements.

But the law was feebly enforced. The flow of Americans into Texas continued almost as if no new law had been adopted. Evasions of the law were tolerated. Trusted *empresarios* such as Austin were given virtual exemption from its restrictions by special interpretations. Counter colonization by native Mexicans failed. The prohibition on further importation of slaves was set at naught by bringing in Negroes as indentured servants. The tariff law was evaded by wholesale smuggling. The chief result of the law was friction between the Americans already in Texas and the Mexican government.

An old source of friction was the status of Texas in the Mexican federation. It dated back to 1824, when the Mexican constitution was adopted. Under the constitution, Texas was joined to the neighboring state of Coahuila. In the joint legislature Coahuila had nine delegates, Texas three, which accorded with their population. The legislature was ineffective, and it was also corrupt, especially in matters of land administration.

Another source of friction was religion. The Mexican government was officially Catholic; the Texans were prevailingly Protestant. The Texans were supposed to become Catholics as a condition of receiving land. They did not take this obligation seriously—not

[17] George L. Rives, *The United States and Mexico, 1821–1848*, 2 vols. (New York: Charles Scribner's Sons, 1913), I, chap. 8.

even Austin, who was otherwise law-abiding. The issue was not pressed by the government. But marriages were required to be performed by Catholic priests, and children born to marriages otherwise performed had no legal rights of inheritance.[18]

The first major uprising of the Texans occurred in 1832 when an army officer in command of the Mexican garrison at Galveston arrested several Texans. A forcible release of the arrested men was attempted, which led to a fight, and the fight became an uprising. The uprising was paralleled by another in Mexico City, one of the constantly recurring Mexican revolutions. Ostensibly the aim of the revolution, led by Santa Anna, was the restoration of the federalism of the Mexican constitution of 1824, with a return to provincial autonomy. Actually it was a bid for power by Santa Anna. The two uprisings succeeded together. Santa Anna became President. As President he threw off his mask of reform and went forward with centralism.

In the summer of 1833, Austin arrived in Mexico City in quest of reforms demanded by the Texans. These were the repeal of the prohibition on further American migration to Texas, further exemption from the tariffs of Mexico, and separation from Coahuila. The first was granted, the second was vaguely promised, the third was denied. With the mission only partly successful, Austin set out for home. On the way he was arrested. His offense was a letter written home, suggesting that separation from Coahuila should be effected even without Mexican consent—a letter that had been intercepted. He was returned to Mexico City and detained for eight months, part of the time in prison.

In the meantime an incident occurred in Galveston that set off the final revolt of 1835—an incident reflecting the turbulence of the Texan pioneers and their contempt for Mexican authority. The incident was a practical joke played on a customs officer. Under the Mexican law all exports from Mexico had to be inspected and had to pay an export tax. A practical joker, Andrew Briscoe, filled a box with sawdust and marked it for export. A crowd collected to watch the officer open the box. When he opened it and found what was in it, he was hooted. He tried to arrest Briscoe. A fight followed, and military support was called. When the news spread that the

[18] A scholarly and dispassionate survey of the Mexican backgrounds of the Texan revolution is Rives, *United States and Mexico*.

military was on the way, the revolt began. Austin, who reached home at that moment, threw his influence in favor of the uprising. By the autumn of 1835 the revolt was in full swing, and it soon became a war for independence. This was the second stage in the background of the annexation of Texas.

The explanation of the Texan revolution, that it was an uprising against Mexican tyranny, is unfounded. That explanation was propaganda, spread by the Texans in the course of the war. The Mexican administration of Texas had been weak and vacillating, the central government had been disorderly, and the provincial government of Coahuila-Texas had been corrupt. But even Texan historians are now agreed that Mexican rule had not been cruel or oppressive. The revolution was basically the outcome of admitting into the rich prairies of Texas a race of aggressive and unruly American frontiersmen, a masterful race of men, who were contemptuous of Mexico and of Mexican authority. The old Latin mistake had been repeated, of admitting Gauls into the empire. In 1837 William Ellery Channing described the situation in his public letter to Henry Clay in terms reflecting the feeling of much of New England. "The Texans must have been insane if, on entering Mexico, they looked for an administration as faultless as that under which they had lived. They might with equal reason have planted themselves in Russia, and then have unfurled the banner of independence near the throne of the Czar because denied the immunities of their native land." [19]

Channing had no wish to depict the administration of government in the United States as faultless, nor to represent that of Mexico in Texas as without fault. The view he meant to convey was that Mexican administration had not been so tyrannical as to justify a revolution.

John Quincy Adams expanded the arraignment of the Texan revolution. He charged that President Jackson was implicated in it and intended from the outset that it should end in annexation to the United States. He made this charge in an address to his constituents at Braintree on September 17, 1842, and again in an "Address to the People of the Free States" on March 3, 1843. [20] As for the

[19] William Ellery Channing, *Works,* 6 vols. (Boston, 1866), II, 194.
[20] *Address of John Quincy Adams to his Constituents at Braintree,* September 17, 1842 (Boston, 1842); also see Documents, under date March 3, 1843.

conspiracy of Tyler, it was, Adams declared, a resurrection of Jackson's, and was designed primarily for the extension of the area of slavery and the magnification of the power of the slavocracy in the councils of the nation.

The evidence to establish the charge against Tyler was the clandestine opening of the annexation negotiation, the fraudulent justification for doing so contained in the diplomatic correspondence, the unscrupulous use of census errors to prove the beneficence of the institution of slavery, the hidden and illegal pledges of armed aid to the Texans if they should be attacked by Mexico, and the shabby recourse throughout to anti-British feeling to overcome reluctance in the North to accept an extension of slavery.

Northern opponents of slavery were impressed by this evidence. They were alarmed by the recourse of the Administration to a mode of annexing territory never before employed and contrary to all the principles of interpretation of the Constitution hitherto professed by the Tyler junto. They detected deception, intrigue, and low tactics in the means employed to obtain the majorities they needed in the two houses of Congress.[21] They deplored the equivocations in the boundary provisions of the Joint Resolution, which encouraged the incoming Administration to commit further aggressions on a helpless neighbor.

To the antislavery North the triumph of such methods was traumatic. It was a national catastrophe. The lament of Adams that it was "the heaviest calamity that ever befell myself and my country" meant more than the widening of the area of slavery within the United States. It meant an example set for similar adventures in Mexico, Central America, and Cuba. The techniques and maneuvers for such adventures had been established by their success in Texas.

As the episodes of slavery expansionism followed, one after another—the war with Mexico, the pressure to acquire Cuba, the crisis of 1850 over slavery in the territories, the Kansas-Nebraska Act of 1854 repudiating the Missouri Compromise—the tension heightened until it produced the cataclysm of 1861. The roots of that tension—and of the cataclysm itself—lay deep in the soil of Texas.

[21] Smith, *Annexation of Texas,* pp. 347–8.

Documents
Arranged by Date

Thomas Walker Gilmer to Dr. James Morris

New Orleans, March 18, 1837 [1]

My dear Doctor: I arrived at this Babel of tongues and Sodom of iniquities, safe and sound on the 13th—and have been detained here, making my arrangements for Texas. I have obtained a passage on the William Bryan for Brazoria or Velasco (either) & expect to sail in a few days. It is said that some Mexican armed vessels are cruizing in the Gulf, but the news does not deter hundreds of men, women and children from embarking even in Texan merchantmen daily. I ought not therefore to quail under the Stars & Stripes (though they are not worth as much as they used to be) & especially as we may get convoy from the Balize, if it is desired. I do not think it improbable that there will be an invasion of Texas this spring or summer. The failure of Santa Anna has rendered it more probable. But I do not doubt the ultimate success of Texas. The invasion may prevent a full crop, but it can do no more, unless the Texas forces are thrown off their guard by too much confidence in their superior prowess.

Mr. Taylor's draft or letter of credit for $8000 on your account was presented here (as desired by Mr. T.) endorsed by the Bank of Virginia, and after detaining me two days for the directors to pass their sentence on it, I was informed that by paying a discount of *two per cent* I could get the money from the Bank of Louisiana, which then held funds of the Bank of Virginia. This I declined doing, regarding it as a downright imposition, and have made an arrangement with N. & J. Dick & Co. to give me the credit in Brazoria or elsewhere, by authority to draw on them. This is a vile place for impositions, but I shall probably have cut my eye teeth by the time I reach the city of Houston, which you must know is the metropolis of Texas, on Buffalo Bayou, emptying into Galveston bay. I have here seen some very intelligent people from Texas. Non residents are now prohibited from holding lands, but it seems to be generally conceded that this prohibition will be repealed by the Congress which will meet early in May. The soldiers & settlers are for the repeal & I have no doubt it will prevail. My present intentions are to buy lands of the planters, who will sell portions of their estates to enable them to improve & cultivate the remainder. I shall thus have decided advantages over those who have heretofore operated on a large scale, against whom there is already a prejudice from the soldiers & planters, with whose interests I shall on my plan become identified. I shall thus too disperse my locations & stand a better chance of hitting the nail on the head. I was offered an interest today in the celebrated Galveston Island property, the cherished site of a future New Orleans—by a Col. Menard, who is going eastward to nego-

[1] Morris Family Papers, Alderman Library, University of Virginia, Charlottesville.

tiate a loan for the Texan government. He is the most intelligent man I have seen from Texas & bears a high character here for integrity. He wants money to buy a brig here, & if his terms are not exorbitant & he will give me public & private guarantee of title, I may give him a rap for an interest in the city that is to be. I have less confidence, however, in the prospects of Texan cities—the country (as you will perceive if you have Austin's map) is too like Virginia, having many sites for towns but none for cities. I incline to think most favorably now of the upper country of Texas, on the Brazos or on Red River. But I cannot yet judge with any accuracy, as it is necessary here to believe nothing that one hears & only half he sees. I shall devote the month of April to exploration of the interior & attend the Congress at Houston in May—thence return homeward by the Red river country. There are a great many persons here on their way to Texas to buy lands. If there is no *contra temps* lands will advance by next fall 100 percent. I wish I had more funds at my disposal, as I never knew of a chance for speculation with so little ultimate risque. Great Britain, it is rumored, has sent despatches to her minister at Mexico preparatory to the recognition of Texan independence. You will see the election of Bustamente, the letter of Santa Anna etc. etc. in the papers. But these things can be estimated by you who are sufficiently acquainted with Mexican history to see to what they tend.

Our party musters 20 or 30 today & would have been 100 strong if I had not feared we should assume too military an aspect for mere seekers after a little of the soil for ourselves & our posterity.

When you go to Charlottesville you must go especially to see my wife and children and see that no harm befalls them while I am on the prairie & the blue water for you.

Remember me affectionately to all friends & believe me very truly

Yours

Every body is broke here. The failures exceed $15,000,000 it is said & the planters must have a crisis soon. The city is a very filthy place. It stinks, yet it grows rapidly. You did well to sell your land, or rather your water here—for dry land there is none. Nothing but a frog and a Frenchman can expect to live here long.

If there are any of our friends who wish to invest in Texas lands & cannot now raise the needful, I expect I can buy on credit & if they will leave their obligations with our friend Mr. Timberlake to pay the sum they wish to invest to me or my order in six or 8 months (next fall or winter) I can probably buy for them. I will charge the same as on cash investments. I must be advised however of their names & the amounts at Houston city by 1st of May next. My letters will go hence to Velasco care of Dr. Branch Archer (forwarded from this place by the Deiks) and Archer will bring them with him to the said city of Houston. Tell my wife to send her despatches too.

I believe contracts can now be made on a little time, not as favorably as for cash, but sufficiently so to realize large profits in a short time. Lands will appreciate rapidly when things are quiet in Texas. Half of Mississippi, Alabama, etc. etc. are now talking of going there. I shall make arrangements either to return to the country next fall or leave agents there in the event of my buying lands on credit.

DUFF GREEN TO JOHN TYLER
Paris, January 24, 1842 [2]

Some of your traducers have ridiculed the remark that you are born to a high destiny. I am one of those who believe that nothing in this world is the result of chance—the accidents of men are the purposes of God. My experience confirms this faith. And when we look back to the current of events which have placed you where you are at this important crisis and have prepared the great issues which are to engrave your name on the history of nations, and especially when you look to the consequences which are to flow from the part you have acted and the important bearing which your two vetoes are to have on the destiny of the world, it is not too much to suppose that he who rules the world and has accomplished so much through your agency has selected you as the instrument by which this great work is to be accomplished.

The idea is calculated to inspire a deep feeling of dependence. It is his will —not yours—you are but the agent not the principle—and yet it is a source of lofty pride—justifiable pride of gratitude to have been so chosen.

My mind is led to these reflections by the view of our relations with England presented by the correspondence between Mr. Stevenson and her Majesty's Government, by a perusal of your message and the reports from the heads of departments—especially by the able report of the Secretary of the Treasury on the Exchequer—by a careful examination of the true motives & future views of England.

I am convinced that she has resolved on war—she has taken advantage of the tenure by which the present King holds the crown of France to make France a party to the slave trade treaties—because she has determined to wage a war upon the commerce & manufactures of the world & believes that we cannot raise cotton & sugar but by slave labor—that if she can destroy the culture of these staples in the United States, Cuba & Brazil all the world will be dependent upon her East Indian Colonies for the supply of the raw material; that as she can purchase the raw materials with her manufactures and can exclude all other manufactures from her East India Colonies, all other manufacturing nations will be compelled to come to her for a supply of the raw material—the consequence will be that other nations will be compelled to manufacture such articles only as she will consent to receive at their hands. Or, in other words, if she can destroy the culture of the raw material in the United States, Brazil & Cuba, she will then be able to give employment to her surplus population because she, commanding the supply of the raw material, can command the markets of the world. It is not enough

[2] Duff Green Papers, Southern Historical Collection, University of North Carolina Library, microfilm roll no. 4.

in answer to this suggestion to say that it were folly for England to entertain such a belief. The question for you & for the world is not what England can do or what England *ought* to think—but it is what does she think?

It is admitted that her commercial necessities press so heavily upon her that her ablest statesmen are at fault, and hence they are prepared to play any game, however desperate, that gives her the remotest hope of success.

As far back as 1829 it was found that India was exhausted. England had derived 20,000,000 of dollars per annum in the shape of tribute for which England made her no return. The time was where India manufactured cotton goods & with these paid the tribute. England finds herself now under the necessity of selling cotton goods to India, and that India cannot purchase because she is impoverished.

But India would pay even greater tribute were it not that the United States, Cuba & Brazil can furnish cotton, rice & sugar cheaper than India. In this immergency England finds that all her political economists unite in saying that the only reason why Cuba & Brazil can undersell India is that Cuba & Brazil import slaves from Africa.

If England can abolish the slave trade & it be true that by doing so she will enable her East India colonies to undersell Brazil & Cuba, it follows that England can greatly increase her manufactures.

But England must see that she will even then have to encounter the manufactures & commerce of the United States so that to make all the other powers dependent on her East Indian colonies, she must destroy the culture of cotton in the United States. By doing so, or by rendering her own supply of the raw material cheaper than that furnished to our manufacturers, she gains, not all she wants, but much. And she believes she will gain this by abolishing slavery in the United States, or by rendering it so dangerous to hold slaves as to diminish its profits. Hence she has demanded of Spain that the mixed commission sitting at the Havanna shall be authorized to librate all Africans . . . (and of course their children) who have been imported since March 1820. This would revolutionize Cuba, and make it a black colony of England. The effect of this on our southern states is obvious.

I have said England has taken advantage of the precarious tenure of the french crown to commit the french government on the slave trade treaties, but there is a deep seated animosity to England in France. The party headed by Mr. Thiers has made open war on the treaty & our minister Genl. Cass has availed himself of the occasion to remonstrate with the King & Mr. Guizot. The consequence is that Mr. Guizot, in a speech in reply to Mr. Thiers said that the Americans are right in resisting the right of search, etc. Genl. Cass has prepared a pamphlet, a copy of which I send you, in which he has argued the American side of this question of the right of search, and is now having it translated into french and will not only serve each of the diplomatic corps and each of the Deputies & heads of the french Government but he will send copies to other courts & to England.[3]

[3] For this pamphlet in translated form see [Lewis Cass], *An Examination of the Question Now in Discussion, Between the American and British Governments, Concerning the Right of Search.* By an American [Privately printed, Paris, 1842].

I do him no more than justice when I tell you that I believe he & he alone, induced Mr. Guizot to make the important declaration, which if you act, as I am sure you will, may be considered as conclusive against England.

But this is not enough. I have prepared a letter for the Morning Chronicle of London, in which I take the boldest ground. I charge home upon England what I believe to be her true purpose & contrast her treatment of Ireland with our treatment of our slaves, and show that a war would be ruinous to her & of incalculable benefit to us. I have also prepared several letters on the subject for the Boston Post, intended to sustain you and to prepare our people for the war, for you may rest assured that with her it is a question of interest & that we have no hope of peace but by taking the highest and firmest ground.

You know that no one is more deeply interested in preserving peace than I am & I repeat it is my deliberate conviction that you have no hope of peace but in preparing for war.

Let the war feeling be cultivated, and every element of war put into action. Europe is deeply interested in the preservation of peace. I have satisfied my mind that the surest & best means of preserving peace is to alarm the people of England & the crowned heads of Europe by satisfying them that we are prepared for war.

In this aspect of the case I look to your financial measure as of vital importance—adhere, I say, adhere. If Mr. Clay & Mr. Calhoun are so much infatuated as to unite against you—have no fears.

I do not approve of your discount feature & it may be necessary to abandon that, but the Madisonian should speak of it as a measure for war. As a means of using the public credit which cannot be defeated by the Bankers of Europe, & permit me to say that the chief reliance of England now is a belief that we cannot borrow money. I saw Baron Rothschild and he told me that he had been applied to through his house in London by a party connected with the English government to know whether he believed the United States could borrow on the continent & he gave it as his opinion that the credit of the United States government was so much identified with the State governments that it would be impossible to borrow money. I explained to him your Exchequer bills, and that with these the Government could command the means of war, that they could immediately enter into circulation to the amount of many millions and could be converted into six percent stocks. He said that he had given it as his opinion that we could not go to war for want of money, but that if your bill was enacted you could sustain the war, especially if the states came forward and manifested a willingness to pay. He said that it did not require money; all it requires is good faith—that the interest may be converted into capital & he invited me to call on him to consult on a plan for reinstating the credit of the States. I give you these facts to be used most discreetly, because they are important and may be defeated if imprudently disclosed.

I do not believe that there is a strong party who would not hesitate to declare war if they had no other means of carrying out this purpose of substituting the cotton, rice & sugar of the East Indies for the cotton, rice &

sugar of Brazil & the United States. Yet there is a very powerful peace party in England and the Tories know that a change of administration will be attended by so great concessions to the liberal party that the aristocracy will be greatly endangered & that some of the prerogatives of Royalty itself may go. The opposition will rally on the war and such is the feeling on the subject of *cheap bread* that I do not believe the present ministry would like to go to war, if by a spirited war feeling in the United States we can animate the friends of peace in England & in Europe to come to our aid.

By the advice of Genl. Cass I have resolved to prepare an appeal to Europe on the subject and have made arrangements to have it published in the leading Review of this city. I have made myself acquainted with the state of parties here & in England & by drawing largely on Ireland I will give John Bull some trouble.

Permit me to ask your attention to the Letters I sent to the Boston Post [4] & to repeat that the hopes of the civilized world rests on you. Mr. Webster must understand his position too well to [want] war. The impression in certain quarters is that he lacks *morale* but I greatly mistake the man if he does not see & if he has not the nerve to improve the occasion before him.

A word as to your cabinet. It does my heart good to hear intelligent Americans & even strangers speak of the official documents at the commencement of the present session. Our country never had greater need of able men at the helm of state & never had she more cause to be proud of those who are there.

May he who has so long watched over our welfare guide & preserve you.

Your friend,

DUFF GREEN TO ABEL P. UPSHUR

Paris, January 24, 1842 [5]

I have read your report on the condition & organization of the Navy with great pleasure, and as the highest reward of our public servants is the approbation of their fellow citizens you must be gratified to learn that it is spoken of in terms of the highest commendation by every American & in respect by all foreigners with whom I have conversed.

Paris is the center of continental Europe, the discussions in the Chambers on the slave trade treaties & the special Mission to the United States have made the United States the subject of general conversation. It is now admitted that the President has selected an able cabinet & I but repeat the universal sentiments when I tell you that altho' there is a great desire for peace, there is a buoyant confidence on the part of the Americans that if we are to have a war, England will be humbled—deeply humbled, while no

---

[4] No letters carrying a Duff Green signature appear in the Boston *Post* from December 1, 1841, to February 1, 1842, but one communication, unsigned, headed "Foreign Correspondence of the *Post*," dated London, January 1, 1842, is found in the issue of January 25, 1842, which has all the earmarks of Green. It surveys British party politics, then describes British designs on Yucatan, and the River St. Juan commanding the Tehuantepec route across the Isthmus, and designs to control the Columbia River.

[5] Duff Green Papers, University of North Carolina Library, microfilm roll no. 4.

one is apprehensive that we are to suffer much by it. Our maritime cities may be burnt, and it may cost us some money, but it will give an impulse to the improvements of the interior, it will complete our railroads, canals, it will build up our manufactures, it will emancipate the British colonies, and must end in the abolition of protecting duties & repeal of her corn laws. When her colonies are at liberty to trade with all the world she will be compelled to cheapen the cost of producing her manufactures & this cannot be done but by low duties. But the greatest benefit to flow from this controversy with England, if it is rightly conducted at home, is that it can be demonstrated that it is a war upon the commerce & manufactures of New England through the domestic institutions of the south, & whether there be war or peace it must end in convincing all parties that the interest of the North & the South are one & that therefore we should be one in feeling, as we are, in interest.

I say unto you as I have said unto all "Be prepared for war, as the only means of preserving peace." England believes that she has no alternative but to render the continental powers of Europe dependent upon her for the raw material by increasing the cost in the United States, Brazil & Cuba above the price at which she can sell the product of the East Indies, purchased by her manufactures, or to reduce the cost of her manufactures by an abolition of the corn law & a repeal of her protecting duties.

She believes that the abolition of the slave trade will increase the cost of production in Cuba & Brazil, and ultimately end in the abolition of slavery there. Some of their statesmen take the ground that nothing but the abolition of slavery in the United States will satisfy them, and it is manifest that they persuade themselves that this must follow the abolition of slavery in Cuba, or else that the discontent will be so great as to render slave labor less productive in the United States & thus accomplish this great purpose of rendering the whole world dependant on them for cotton, rice & sugar to be furnished by them through the exchange of their manufactures.

But I beg leave to refer you to the letters which I have sent home to be published in the Boston Post, and to a letter to Mr. Calhoun with whom I hope you will confer as to the best mode of accomplishing a work which whatever may be the result of the treaty negociation I hope to make serviceable to our country. The American stocks are now so much diffused over Europe that it will be an easy matter to create an American party. Besides the continental powers are becoming largely manufacturing states & there is a growing jealousy of Great Britain as well on account of her arrogance on the ocean, which interferes with the raw material and the sale of their manufactures as on account of her being the common rival of all these states. It will soon be understood that the American side of the question is the side of these continental states & that British avarice, and not British benevolence lay at the bottom.

The consequence will be a powerful reaction must follow either the declaration of war or an adjustment satisfactory to these continental states, because I take for granted that our government will hear of no terms short of an entire abandonment of every pretension put up by England.

I have been requested to prepare a work, historical, statistical & geographical of the United States, to be printed in French, German & English, & to constitute a manual for Bankers, Emigrants, Merchants & Politicians in Europe. I have requested Mr. Calhoun to prepare me a chapter on the tariff or Nullification struggle & I would be greatly obliged to you for a brief chapter on the origin & formation of the federal constitution.[6] I must also ask you to cause to be prepared for me the statistics of your department, and like statistics of each of the other departments, to be embodied into as brief a space as possible & as far as possible in tables. The importance to us in a national point of view is so great that I hope you will concur with me in a belief that it is the duty of every American citizen to contribute whatever he can to such a work, & that your sense of public duty as well as your personal friendship will prompt you to comply with my request.

I enclose you a pamphlet written by General Cass and a letter & pamphlet from Dr. Niles [7] to me to which I beg to call your attention. Permit me to request you to call on Mr. Calhoun & confer with him freely on the subjects embraced in my letter.

HENRY WISE

Speech in the House of Representatives, April 13, 1842 [8]

Mr. WISE next addressed the chair. He said he had not expected to be called to enter into this discussion; the motion which gave rise to it was wholly unexpected by him; but as the question had been opened, he felt it a duty to his constituents and the country to take a part in it. He should, in a manner perfectly calm and dispassionate, address a few words to that class to which the gentlemen from New York (Mr. Linn) and Vermont (Mr. Slade) belonged.

The gentleman from New York had moved to strike from this bill the item for the salary of a minister to Mexico, and this just at the moment when the New Orleans papers had announced to the world his immediate departure as minister to a Government toward which we stood in the most delicate and important relations—relations to be settled by the negotiations he was

---

[6] Upshur was author of *A Brief Enquiry into the True Nature and Character of our Federal Government*. By a Virginian (Petersburg, Virginia, 1840).

[7] Refers to Dr. Nathaniel Niles of Vermont, who had been American chargé in France, 1832–3, and special agent in Austria, 1837–9.

[8] From the *National Intelligencer*, April 15, 1842. No report of the speech appeared in the *Congressional Globe*; instead, reference was made on the day it was delivered (April 13) to commotion in the House that made speakers inaudible; see 27 Cong., 2 sess., 418. Yet the speech was heard by the reporter of the *National Intelligencer* and was reported in full. Significant speeches were fully reported in the Appendix of the *Congressional Globe*, but not Wise's. He may have been advised to forego publishing it by some member of the Tyler circle. The speech was very indiscreet, and coming from one so close to the President might have done harm at this early stage in the Texas agitation. No report of the speech or reference to it appeared in the New York *Tribune*. But its significance was sensed by Adams, who discussed it on the floor of the House several days after its delivery and quoted much of it in his "Address to the People of the Free States" (March 3, 1843), which appears in the Documents.

to conduct. Yes, and whilst, for all Mr. W. knew, there might be ten or a dozen of our own native citizens in the mines of Mexico, wearing the chains of a degrading bondage, although at the very first hint from the British Minister a British citizen taken in company, side by side, with the very men of ours whom they had manacled and set to clean the streets, was promptly released. Yet the gentleman from New York would have our fellow-citizens still wear their fetters, and still endure their public degradation; and why? Because, forsooth, it had been the ulterior object of the President and of a certain party in this country to annex Texas to the Union! Our citizens had claims on that Government to the amount of twelve or thirteen millions, and yet we must not send a minister to demand the property or protect the freedom of our citizens in Mexico.

The tyrant of Mexico was now at war with Texas, and had threatened that he would invade her territory, and "never stop till he had driven slavery beyond the Sabine;" and the gentleman would let him let loose his servile horde on the citizens of Louisiana, yet send no minister to remonstrate or to threaten him.

[Mr. Slade here explained. He had not been opposed to our having a minister at the court of Mexico; but only to the individual selected to occupy that post.]

Mr. Wise said he could forgive the gentleman, because he knew not the consequences that might flow from the doctrines that he was accustomed to advance. These gentlemen would not send a minister to prevent the invasion even of the United States itself, lest by possibility it might lead to the annexation of Texas.

[Mr. Linn explained, insisting that he had not opposed the mission, but had conceded that there might be sufficient grounds for it. He had moved to withhold the salary at present, because he believed that the whole movement had originated in a design to annex Texas to the Union. Being, however, well satisfied that the committee would not consent to strike out the appropriation, he was willing to withdraw his motion.

(Loud cries of "No, no.")

Mr. Wise. No, the gentleman shall not withdraw it now.

Mr. Steenrod said he had listened attentively to the gentleman from New York, and his entire argument, from beginning to end, had been directed against the mission, and not the individual who now filled it.]

Mr. Wise resumed, and repeated what he had before said as to the possibility that the Mexican arms might drive back the slaves of Texas beyond the Sabine upon Louisiana and Arkansas. The English papers openly advanced the doctrine that it was the aim and policy of Great Britain to make what she was pleased to denominate *the insolvent nations* pay their debts to her by the cession of territory. Thus Spain must surrender Cuba, and Mexico must surrender Texas and California. He referred to the British command of the Gulf of Mexico, and the possibility of her rendering that sea a *mare clausum* to the people of the valley of the Mississippi. And it was a part of the same policy that she should keep increasing the debt of Mexico, by affording to her the means of invading Texas and the United

States, and thus ultimately force her to give up California. The gentleman had stated that it was the design of the President to accomplish the annexation of Texas, if possible. Mr. W. demanded on what proof he made that assertion?

Mr. Linn. Does the gentleman deny it?

Mr. Wise. I have no authority to deny it or to admit it.

Mr. Linn. Do you make the issue, and I will give you the proof, &c.

Mr. Wise said that though he did not know any thing of the matter, he might for the argument's sake deny it, and, if he should do so, could the gentleman produce any proof of it? What was the authority on which the House was asked to believe it? The gentleman's mere *ipse dixit*. What did *he* know of the opinions or purposes of the President of the United States? His assertion must go for nothing. But suppose the President should be desirous of such an issue, what then? Mr. W. knew no more of the fact than the gentleman, but he earnestly hoped and trusted that the President was as desirous as he was represented to be. But Mr. W. was prepared to show, and from the highest authority, not what was the opinion of a slaveholder, but of an individual now on this floor, but who occupied the Presidential chair at the time the gentleman from Vermont (Mr. Slade) was a clerk in the Department of State. He would show that the individual had offered a million of dollars for the addition of that Territory to the United States. Here Mr. W. quoted the following letter from Mr. Clay, then Secretary of State, to Mr. POINSETT, then our minister at Mexico, dated March 16, 1825. Speaking of the boundary between us and Texas, the letter said:

"Some difficulties may possibly hereafter arise between the two countries from the line thus agreed on, against which it would be difficult to guard, if practicable; and, as the Government of Mexico may be supposed not to have any disinclination to the fixation of a new line which would prevent those difficulties, the President wishes you to sound it on that subject, and to avail yourself of a favorable disposition, if you should find it, to effect that object. The line of the Sabine approaches our great Western mart nearer than could be wished. Perhaps the Mexican Government may not be unwilling to establish that of the Rio Brassos de Dios, or the Rio Colorado, or the Snow Mountains, or the Rio del Norte, in lieu of it. By the agreed line, portions of both the Red river and branches of the Arkansas are thrown on the Mexican side, and the navigation of both those rivers, as well as that of the Sabine, is made common to the respective inhabitants of the two countries," &c.

In a subsequent letter, dated March 15, 1827, the same officer opened the subject more fully to our minister in Mexico, as follows:

"The great extent and facility which appears to have attended the procurement of grants from the Government of the United Mexican States, for large tracts of country to citizens of the United States, in the province of Texas, authorize the belief that but little value is placed upon the possession of the province by that Government. These grants seem to have been made without any sort of equivalent, judging according to our opinions of the value of land. They have been made to, and apparently in contemplation of being settled by, citizens from the United States. These emigrants will carry with them our principles of law, liberty, and religion; and however much it may be hoped they might be disposed to amalgamate with the ancient inhabitants of Mexico, so far as political freedom is concerned, it would be almost too much to expect that all collisions would be avoided on other subjects. Already some of these collisions have manifested themselves, and others, in the progress of time, may be anticipated with confidence. These collisions may insensibly enlist the sympathies and feelings of the two Republics and lead to misunderstandings.

"The fixation of a line of boundary of the United States on the side of Mexico, should be such as to secure not merely certainty and apparent safety in the respective limits of the two countries, but the consciousness of freedom from all danger of attack on either side, and the removal of all motives for such attack. That of the Sabine brings Mexico nearer our great Western commercial capital than is desirable; and although we now are, and for a long time may remain, perfectly satisfied with the justice and moderation of our neighbor, still it would be better for both parties that neither should feel that he is in any condition of exposure on the remote contingency of an alteration in existing friendly sentiments.

"Impressed with these views, the President has thought the present might be an auspicious period for urging a negotiation, at Mexico, to settle the boundary between the territories of the two Republics. The success of the negotiation will probably be promoted by throwing into it other motives than those which strictly belong to the subject itself. If we could obtain such a boundary as we desire, the Government of the United States might be disposed to pay a reasonable pecuniary consideration. The boundary which we prefer is that which, beginning at the mouth of the Rio del Norte in the sea, shall ascend that river to the mouth of the Rio Puerco, thence ascending this river to its source, and from its source, by a line due north, to strike the Arkansas, thence following the course of the southern bank of the Arkansas to its source, in latitude 42 degrees north, and thence by that parallel of latitude to the South sea. The boundary thus described would, according to the United States Tanner's map, published in the United States, leave Santa Fe within the limits of Mexico, and the whole of Red river or Rio Roxo and the Arkansas, as far up as it is probably navigable, within the limits assigned to the United States. If that boundary be unattainable, we would, as the next most desirable, agree to that of the Colorado, beginning at its mouth, in the bay of Bernardo, and ascending the river to its source, and thence by a line due north to the Arkansas, and thence, as above traced, to the South sea. This latter boundary would probably also give us the whole of the Red river, would throw us somewhat further from Santa Fe, but it would strike Arkansas possibly at a navigable point. To obtain the first-described boundary, the President authorizes you to offer to the Government of Mexico a sum not exceeding one million of dollars. If you find it impracticable to procure that line, you are then authorized to offer for the above line of the Colorado, the sum of five hundred thousand dollars. If either of the above offers should be accepted, you may stipulate for the payment of the sum of money, as you may happen to agree, within any period not less than three months after the exchange at the city of Washington of the ratifications of the treaty.

"Should you be able to conclude a treaty, it will be necessary that it should contain a stipulation for the mutual right of navigation of the Rio del Norte or the Colorado, as the one or the other of them may be agreed on, and for the exercise of a common jurisdiction over the river itself. The treaty may also provide for the confirmation of all bona fide grants for lands made prior to *its date*, with the conditions of which there shall have been a compliance; and it may contain a provision similar to that in the Louisiana and Florida treaties for the incorporation of the inhabitants into the Union, as soon as it can be done consistently with the principles of the Federal Constitution, and for their enjoyment of their liberty, property, and religion.

"There should also be a provision made for the delivery of the country to the United States simultaneously, or as nearly so as practicable, with the payment of the consideration. We should be satisfied with a surrender of possession at that time, as far as the river line extends, (the Del Norte or the Colorado,) and to receive the residue as soon as the line to the Arkansas can be traced, which the treaty ought to provide should be done without unnecessary delay, and, at all events, before a future day to be specified."

Here, then, was proof that a former President of the United States not only wanted more territory added, but was willing to pay a million of dollars if it extended to the Rio del Norte, and half that sum if it went no further than the Colorado. And it showed further that he was not only for the purchase of the territory, but for admitting its inhabitants into the Union. This was authentic information, information on which the gentleman might rely with much more certainty than on any vague report about the existing Chief Magistrate. This was a line of policy which Mr. W. had approved and applauded at the time, and which he still applauded and approved, if, as was said, it was the policy of Mr. Tyler. There was now no money to be paid for the territory, and it was occupied by a sovereign power which had authority to transfer it. If the annexation had been wise and peaceable, and practicable and desirable in 1827, it was not less so in 1842. It was fair to presume that the same motives still continued to operate on those who sought the same thing.

And why should not Texas be united to this Union? What would the effect of such an event be? To extend slavery? Not at all. Slavery existed in Texas to just the same extent now as it would were Texas a part of the United States. The only difference would be to bring it under our own jurisdiction. It was now in a foreign State, where we could exert no influence over it to mitigate its severity or restrain its abuse. Was it in the spirit of philanthropy that gentlemen opposed it? In the spirit of christian missionaries? Mr. W. thought it was held among them that to benefit the heathen you must be among them. Christianity must be brought to bear upon their minds; and so, if these philanthropic gentlemen wanted to mitigate those evils of slavery over which they made such doleful lamentations, let them bring it within our reach and jurisdiction.

Could they multiply their petitions ten thousand fold, would they reach slavery in a foreign State? If the spirit of emancipation was to go forth, like an angel, from the North toward the South, striking off manacles and drying up tears, (Mr. W. now spoke as one of themselves,) why not bring the slavery of Texas also within its range? Why leave that one dark spot untouched? Did they not perceive that, as long as Texas remained in a separate state, it would be an asylum for slavery? Drive it South, as they might, here the slaveholder could set them at defiance; for, once beyond the Texian boundary line, their jurisdiction was at an end. Yet they were banded together as one man to oppose the annexation. Could any thing more strikingly show the blindness of fanaticism?

But possibly they would evade the force of this argument by looking to England to emancipate the slaves of Texas: If so, they utterly mistook the motives and the means of England. She had in the Republic of Texas a rival to the United States in the production of cotton, and as long as she wished to retain her as such, she would keep up the slave labor in Texas against the slave labor in the United States. Mr. W. scouted the idea of England being sincerely engaged in the work of emancipation, referred to the late detection of a conspiracy between British cruisers on the coast of Africa and the slave dealers, and also to her undeviating course of oppression in India, as proofs to the contrary. If gentlemen wished to keep Texas as a foreign State in juxtaposition with our Southwestern border, that she might be a mart for contraband dealers in cotton for the benefit of England, and to the injury of the Southern States—if that was their plan—then it was the surest way that could be taken to rivet upon her the chains of slavery forever. No: if they were really sincere in their professed desires to see slavery abolished, their true and only course was to annex Texas to the United States. [A laugh in certain portions of the House.]

Mr. W. now took a different view of the subject. There was an anomaly connected with Texas, which, when first stated, appeared to be a paradox, but, when duly considered, was quite intelligible and undoubtedly true. While she was, as a State, weak and almost powerless in resisting invasion, she was herself irresistible as an invading and a conquering Power. She had but a sparse population, and neither men nor money of her own to raise and equip an army for her own defense; but let her once raise the flag of foreign conquest—let her once proclaim a crusade against the rich States to the south of her, and in a moment volunteers would flock to her standard in crowds from all the States in the great valley of the Mississippi—men of enterprise and hardy valor before whom no Mexican troops could stand for an hour. They would leave their own towns, arm themselves, and travel on their own cost, and would come up in thousands to plant the lone star of the Texian banner on the proud ramparts of the Mexican capital. They would drive Santa Anna to the South, and the boundless wealth of captured towns, and rifled churches, and a lazy, vicious, and luxurious priesthood, would soon enable Texas to pay her soldiery and redeem her State debt, and push her victorious arms to the very shores of the Pacific. And would not all this extend the bounds of slavery? Yes, the result would be that before another quarter of a century the extension of slavery would not stop short of the

Western Ocean. We had but two alternatives before us; either to receive Texas into our fraternity of States, and thus make her our own; or to leave her to conquer Mexico, and become our most dangerous and formidable rival.

To talk of restraining the people of the great Valley from emigrating to join her armies was all in vain; and it was equally vain to calculate on their defeat by any Mexican forces, aided by England or not. They had gone once already; it was they that conquered Santa Anna at San Jacinto; and three fourths of them, after winning that glorious field, had peaceably returned to their homes. But once set before them the conquest of the rich Mexican provinces, and you might as well attempt to stop the wind. This Government might send its troops to the frontier to turn them back, and they would run over them like a herd of buffalo. Or did gentlemen intend to put forth the odious, exploded, detestable doctrine of "no expatriation?" The Western people would mock at such a barrier; they would come armed to the frontier, and who should stop them from crossing the line and going where they pleased? Let the work once begin, and Mr. W. did not know that this House would hold *him* very long. Let Texas give him but five millions of dollars, and he would undertake to pay every American claimant against Mexico four-fold his demand. He would fix our boundary, not where Mr. Adams had tried to fix it, at the Rio del Norte, but far, far beyond; ay, and he would soon fix California where all the power of Great Britain should never be able to reach it. Slavery should pour itself abroad without restraint, and find no limit but the Southern ocean. The Camanches should no longer hold the richest mines of Mexico; but every golden image which had received the profanation of a false worship should soon be melted down, not into Spanish milled dollars, indeed, but into good American eagles. [Laughter, mixed with some exclamations.] Yes; then should more hard money flow into the United States than any Exchequer or sub-Treasury could ever circulate. He would cause as much gold to cross the Rio del Norte as the mules of Mexico could carry; ay, and make a better use of it, too, than any lazy, bigotted priesthood under heaven. [A general laugh.]

He knew that gentlemen might hold all this as chimerical; but he told them it was already begun, and it would go on. He here referred to the story of Captain Boyle, an enterprising commander of a small craft in the Revolution, who proclaimed a blockade of all the coast of England, and actually had his proclamation printed and circulated in the streets of London. Yes; the peaceable cockneys had gone quietly to sleep in all security, and waked up in the morning and found London blockaded! [Loud laughter.] And this adventurous Capt. Boyle had threaded all the dangers of the British channel, escaped all their cruisers, and returned in safety to this country, having performed the feat of blockading Great Britain. So Texas had proclaimed a blockade against all the coast of Mexico, and though she had no fleet to enforce it, she would be able to make it good by hewing her way to the Mexican capital. Nor could all the vaunted power of England stop the chivalry of the West till they had planted the Texian star on the walls of the city of Montezuma. Nothing could keep these booted loafers from rushing on till they kicked the Spanish priests out of the temples they profaned. Gentlemen might be horror-stricken at this.

[A voice: "Oh no, sir, not at all; we are quite calm."]

Mr. W. went into a calculation to show that it would be impossible for Mexico to resist the force of Texas when recruited from the Western States: referred, in illustration, to the heroic resistance by 600 American troops under Fanning of a Mexican army 3,000 strong, causing even their cavalry to recede before men who had not a bayonet among them; and inquired with what hope of success they could withstand a regiment of flying artillery, a couple of regiments of riflemen, and a body of light infantry?

He wanted no war with Mexico: he went for sending a minister to preserve peace; but, unless she treated our citizens on an equal footing with those of England, he was for war, and cared not how soon.

It was said that this would marry us to a war with England. This had been too well answered by his friend (Mr. Cushing) already; but for his own part, if he was to choose a war with any Power, the prospect of a war with England was the very thing he should desire. If he were to pick out a war to suit his taste, it would be a war with England. Here was a "foeman worthy of our steel." He would leave Mexico to Texas and the people of the Valley: they could soon dispose of her. Let a war come; with France, the United States, and Texas, on the one side, and England and Mexico on the other; he would ask nothing better.

Mr. W. proceeded to insist that a majority of the people of the United States were in favor of the annexation: at all events, he would risk it with the democracy of the North. He would ask the men of Maine and New Hampshire, and the whalers of Nantucket, whether they were willing that England should get possession of California? He would risk all the blue lights. Our policy was peace, but our people were warlike: and to threaten them with the growl of the British lion was the very way to rouse the American eagle from her eyrie, cause her to plume her wings, and take her soaring flight to the ramparts of Mexico, and there demand a compliance with all our just demands. Nor would Mr. W. stop there: he would demand the non-invasion of Texas; he would say to Mexico, "if you strike Texas, you strike us:" and if England, standing by, should dare to intermeddle, and ask "Do you take part with Texas?" his prompt answer should be, "Yes, and against you."

Such, he would let gentlemen know, was the spirit of the whole people of the great valley of the West.

One of the best effects of this state of things would be to cause the abolition party, to which these gentlemen belonged, to hide their diminished heads. Yes; it would very quickly subject them to the law of tar and feathers. Let them utter such sentiments as they now poured forth so freely when the country was once in an actual state of war, and they would meet the fate which their friends met in the last war. They were burnt children, and they never would venture to oppose another war; if they did, they were doomed men.

Mr. W. then touched on the intimation which had been thrown out that

the President sought to involve the country in war to promote his own ambitious purposes. Did he believe John Tyler to be such a man, he would
denounce him from the Capitol to Accomac. But, on the other hand, he
would denounce him as loudly if he suffered a tittle of the national honor
to be sacrificed. He adverted to the growth of the worship of mammon
throughout our country in these piping times of peace, and said that, if the
crystal waters of peace proved insufficient to cleanse us from the accumulated
corruption, he would let the bloody streams of war perform the work. It
would sweep off drones and loafers, and men of broken fortunes and broken
reputation, many of whom would hail the first blast of the trumpet as the
renovating note of their emancipation. War was a curse, but it had its blessings too, as the destroying lightning of heaven purified the atmosphere. He
would vote for this mission as the means of peace; but if it must lead to
war, then he would vote it the more willingly.

Mr. BUTLER, of South Carolina, here obtained the floor, but yielded
it for a motion that the committee rise; which prevailing, the committee rose
accordingly.

And, after several fruitless efforts of gentlemen to get in reports, resolutions, &c., the House adjourned.

THOMAS WALKER GILMER

TO THE BALTIMORE REPUBLICAN AND ARGUS

*Letter dated January 10, 1843, introduced
by editorial comment* [9]

TEXAS AND THE UNITED STATES

The subject of the annexation of Texas to the United States, begins to
attract much attention, and many persons already appear to have made up
their minds, that sooner, or later, such union will most certainly be consummated:—Conversing with a friend, a few days ago, on the subject of Com-
modore Jones' recent *coup de main* upon California, we expressed this sentiment. Upon which, he told us he had a very interesting letter from a distinguished member of Congress, placing the policy of the annexation of Texas
to the United States in a very striking and imposing point of view; which,
if he could obtain his consent to publish, he would place in our hands. He
called on us this morning and handed us the letter from the Honorable
THOMAS W. GILMER, late Governor of Virginia, which will be found
below. We need not invite attention to this letter. The subject of which it
treats, and the source from which it comes, will ensure it that. But as it
was neither written nor published with a view to affect any political party,
we invite for it that candid and dispassionate consideration which the importance of the subject so fully entitles it to.

[9] From the Baltimore *Republican and Argus*, January 19, 1843, reprinted in *Madisonian*, January 23, 1843.

Washington, January 10th, 1843

Dear Sir:

You ask if I have expressed the opinion that Texas would be annexed to the United States? I answer, yes; and this opinion has not been adopted without reflection or without a careful observation of causes, which I believe are rapidly bringing about this result. I do not know how far these causes have made the same impression on others; but I am persuaded that the time is not distant when they will be felt in all their force. The excitement which you apprehend may arise, but it will be temporary, and in the end salutary. The excitement of prejudice or passion is to be deprecated under any government, as it only confirms error and injustice. But the excitement of the mind, the popular intelligence, is always beneficial; and it is indispensable in free governments. It leads to investigation. It establishes truth, justice, and the public good. It is the surest and safest means of guarding against the artifices of those who, afraid to trust their fellow men with the privilege of thinking, have been always willing and ready to think for them.

Without having time just now to consider this subject in the various interesting and comprehensive aspects in which it may be viewed, I do not hesitate to say that it is capable, if approached in a proper spirit, of doing more to conciliate and consolidate the conflicting interests and prejudices of our Union than any question which has arisen since the foundation of our republic. I proceed to notice, very briefly, some of the objections you anticipate.

I am, as you know, a strict constructionist of the powers of our federal government; and I do not admit the force of mere precedent to establish authority under written constitutions. The power conferred by the constitution over our foreign relations, and the repeated acquisitions of territory under it, seem to me to leave this question open, as one of expediency. As such, it cannot be considered a Southern or local question. It affects and interests every portion of the Union.

I assume what no one will deny, that, under the jurisdiction of the United States, the large and unusually fertile territory of Texas will be rapidly peopled, and that an immense accession will be made to our strength and productive energies. The settlement of Texas under these auspices, will open a market at home for the manufactures and agricultural products of all the non-slaveholding States; a market which, otherwise, can only avail them under the restrictions and disadvantages of foreign competition. The means of supply for those States will be increased in the same manner. This is true not only of the Eastern Atlantic States, but of the country extending over the fertile vallies of the Ohio, the Mississippi and the Missouri. It will be more permanently valuable to these than all the home markets which legislation can force by the artificial means of impoverishing one interest for the purpose of giving bounties to another. On the true principles of social and commercial intercourse, it will be reciprocal and mutually advantageous. The only interest in the Union which as such merely, could find a reason for opposing the measure, is the interest of the cotton and sugar planters of the Southern and Southwestern States. The annexation of Texas would foster a competition for which they could find no immediate equivalent, except in the vast acquisition of national wealth, prosperity and harmony which would result.

But you anticipate objections with regard to the subject of slavery. This is indeed a subject of extreme delicacy, but it is one on which the annexation of Texas will have the most salutary influence. Some have thought that the proposition would endanger our Union. I am of a different opinion. I believe it will strengthen the union. I believe it will bring about a better understanding of our relative rights and obligations. Slavery is one of those subjects which the people of the slave-holding States are content to leave where the constitution of our Union found it. They ask for no new concessions to their rights guaranteed by that instrument; they are prepared to make none to prejudices which they must cease to respect when under the garb of civil or religious fanaticism they become criminal. Are our countrymen of the non-slaveholding States disposed to assume that *they* will not live at peace with *us* on account of our State institutions, institutions recognized and guaranteed by positive provisions of the constitution? If this be so, the sooner it is known to all the better for all. It is obvious that the Union is already dissolved, or that its burdens are all on one side, its benefits on the other, when such a spirit is generally evinced. But I do not believe that such is the disposition of the masses of our fellow citizens of the non-slaveholding States. I believe that the security so long enjoyed under our constitution has taught them, as it has us, to regard it in its spirit and letter as indispensible to our future common welfare, and to deprecate any revolution, effected by fraud or force, which shall impair its solemn obligations. I have not been an inattentive or indifferent observer of events for the last few years. To recite them, or to animadvert on the want of American feeling, which they have sometimes disclosed, might only add to prejudices already too much exasperated. It should be the first wish of every American to allay an excitement which is fast ripening into crime. I aver my belief that there is no measure which would have a happier tendency to repudiate feelings so unworthy of countrymen, so incompatible with the duties of fellow citizens, and to reestablish the supremacy of our compact on the permanent foundation of mutual rights and mutual interests, as the annexation of Texas. The foreign dangers which threatened the infancy of our republic are forgotten in the meridian of our strength. They no longer exist in force enough to bind us together. Our present dangers are nearer home.—They can be averted only by the agency of some cause powerful enough to revive the feelings of other days, to absorb the selfishness of sections again in the more enlarged sentiments of pride and patriotism. These sentiments are already extinct in that bosom, which does not kindle at the contemplation of our country's unexampled prosperity and grandeur, as they are heralded by the dawning future. Nations, like individuals, must live up to their destiny, and we must act the part assigned us by our position on the globe. Our federative Union, in the spirit of its adoption, is capable of indefinite extension. Space and numbers will only add to its strength by multiplying its blessings. In any other spirit it would not have been long preserved, even by the Old Thirteen.

If then, I am right in supposing that our countrymen of the non-slaveholding states are not disposed to renounce their union with the slaveholding states, and if I have not erred in supposing that like ourselves and all the rest of mankind, they can and do perceive the force of that mysterious power, which binds individuals in society, and states in union, by rendering conflicts of opinion and interest the very sources of harmony, happiness and strength, I do not apprehend any evil consequences from the excitement which this subject will give rise to.

The action of no government, state or federal, on the subject of slavery, can produce any thing but mischief. Its end, like its origin, is within the compass only of those laws which man has neither the wisdom to perceive nor the power to arrest, though he is the agent in their fulfilment. When the federal constitution was adopted, slavery existed (I believe) in all the states. That it does not exist now in a large majority of the original states, is owing less to their philanthropy than their interest. Slave labor is unprofitable in grain growing countries. Instances of voluntary emancipation are as frequent in those states where slave labor is most profitable as they ever were in grain growing states. The culture of cotton and sugar in the United States has done more to withdraw slavery southward, than all the expedients which the wisdom of this or other generations could devise. It is a process which does no violence to our federal compact, none to private rights, which hazards neither our social peace nor the union.

England, whose possessions and jurisdiction extend over so large a portion of the globe, whose influence is felt every where, will either possess or control Texas, if it does not come under the jurisdiction of the United States. The prejudices of England against slavery are philosophically confined to sympathic meetings, popular harangues, & a neighbourly disposition to see us dissolve our union on account of it. If she abolishes it in her West Indies it is only to multiply it in her East Indies. It is impossible that Mexico can ever subjugate Texas. Though covering a much larger extent of territory and numbering many more people, Mexico is really in no better condition and not stronger than Texas. There is more probability of revolt in other provinces than of the reconquest of Texas. The fashions of dress are not more capacious in their changes than are the forms of Mexican government. I apprehend it is destined for some time, to continue in a state of civil chaos, giving no signs of energy, but occasional spasmodic convulsions in a body of bigoted priests and mercenary soldiers, whose victims the people have long been. Texas is recognized by our government, and by the most powerful governments of Europe, as exempt from Mexican dominion. Spain is as likely to reconquer Mexico itself, as Mexico Texas. It is true Mexico has not formally recognized Texas, as one of the nations of the earth. She still claims the right to conquer or to dispose of her. Texas then in all probability, will exist, under some form of government, independent of Mexico. Will she be independent of European influences prejudicial to us, fatal to the harmony of two rival coterminous republics?

Having acquired Louisiana and Florida, we have an interest and a frontier on the Gulf of Mexico and along our interior to the Pacific, which will not permit us to close our eyes or fold our arms with indifference to the events which a few years may disclose in that quarter. We have already had one question of boundary with Texas; other questions must soon arise under our revenue laws and on other points of necessary intercourse, which it will be difficult to adjust. The institutions of Texas and her relations with other governments are yet in that condition which inclines her people, (who are our country men) to unite their destinies with ours. This must be done soon or not at all. There are numerous tribes of Indians along both frontiers which can easily become the cause or the instruments of border wars. Our own population is pressing onward to the Pacific. No power can restrain it. The pioneer from our Atlantic sea board, will soon kindle his fires and erect his cabin beyond the Rocky mountains and on the Gulf of California. If Mohammed comes not to the mountain, the mountain will go to Mohammed. Every year adds new difficulties to our progress in that direction, a progress as natural and as inevitable as the current of the Mississippi. These difficulties will soon "like mountains interposed"—

> "Make enemies of nations
> Which *now* like kindred drops
> *Might* mingle into one."

> *Truly yours,*
> *Thomas W. Gilmer*

DUFF GREEN TO JOHN TYLER
(*confidential*)

Annapolis, February 18, 1843 [10]

Dear Sir

I once ventured to say to you that the Madisonian was doing you injury by the frequent repetition of your name—by making the great question so deeply involving the interests of the country personal as between you and the other candidates for the Presidency.—By doing so you lose the benefit of your position—It separates you from the people, who have but little personal interest in the fortunes of John Tyler—but who have a deep and controlling interest in the honest faithful and patriotic administration of the Government—Permit me to suggest that your name should be used seldom, very seldom—The people should see you *in the administration* instead of being taught to consider the administration in you,—they should be taught to support you for the sake of the country—for the sake of themselves and of their children, instead of being taught to look upon you as an individual— It is of much more importance to the people that the Govt be *well* administered than that it shall be administered by any single *individual*.

I hope my dear sir that you will understand me—I have ventured to make the same suggestion to the Editor. His personal devotion to you prevents his seeing that, by isolating you, he deprives you of the sympathy which the people would feel for you as the head of the administration—I see that he

[10] Copy in the O. P. Chitwood Papers, University of West Virginia Library.

has acted on my suggestion as to the extraordinary declaration of the Whig.[11]
I send you two articles illustrating the manner in which I would fight the
battle—Every thing depends upon the issue and the manner of making it.
This declaration of the Whig will act as much for you in the Democratic
as in the Whig ranks—If treated with skill it will be as efficient as the
"bargain intrigue & management" of 1828 & the "log cabins" of 1840 were.—
It will arouse the old feeling which carried every thing before it then, and
which can break down the strong array of "party" now. There is a cord in
the bosom of every free man which vibrates to a common sentiment and
all that we have to do, to secure a triumph over faction now, is to play
upon it—Your adversaries, in this folly, have tuned the instrument, all that
you have to do is to identify yourself with the popular sentiment which they
have outraged.

Your sincere friend,

JOHN QUINCY ADAMS AND OTHERS

*Address to the people of the free states of the Union,
Washington, March 3, 1843* [12]

We, the undersigned, in closing our duties to our constituents and our
country as members of the 27th congress, feel bound to call your attention
very briefly to the project, long entertained by a portion of the people of
these United States, still pertinaciously adhered to, and intended soon to
be consummated—THE ANNEXATION OF TEXAS TO THIS UNION. In the press of
business incident to the last days of a session of congress, we have not time,
did we deem it necessary, to enter upon a detailed statement of the reasons
which force upon our minds the conviction that this project is *by no means
abandoned;* that a large portion of the country interested in the continuance
of domestic slavery and the slave trade in these United States have solemnly
and unalterably determined *that it shall be speedily carried into execution,*
and that, by this admission of a new slave territory and slave states, *the
undue ascendency of the slaveholding power in the government shall be
secured and rivetted beyond all redemption.* That it was with these views and
intentions that settlements were effected in the province by citizens of the
United States, difficulties fomented with the Mexican government, a revolt
brought about, and an independent government declared, *cannot now admit
of a doubt;* and that, hitherto, all attempts of Mexico to reduce her revolted
province to obedience have proved unsuccessful, is to be attributed to the un-
lawful aid and assistance of designing and interested individuals in the United
States; and the direct and indirect co-operation of our own government, *with
similar views,* is not the less certain and demonstrable.

The open and repeated enlistment of troops in several states of this union
in aid of the Texian revolution; the intrusion of an American army, by order

[11] Refers probably to the Richmond *Whig.*
[12] Printed initially in the *National Intelligencer,* May 4, 1843. Reprinted in *Niles'
Register,* 64, 173–5 (May 13, 1843).

of the President, far into the territory of the Mexican Government, at a moment critical for the fate of the insurgents, under pretence of preventing Mexican soldiers from fomenting Indian disturbances, but in reality in aid of, and acting in singular concert and coincidence with, the army of the revolutionists; the entire neglect of our Government to adopt any efficient measures to prevent the most unwarrantable aggressions of bodies of our own citizens, enlisted, organized, and officered within our own borders, and marched in arms and battle array upon the territory and against the inhabitants of a friendly Government, in aid of freebooters and insurgents; and the premature recognition of the independence of Texas, by a snap vote, at the heel of a session of Congress, and that too at the very session when President Jackson had, by special message, insisted that "the measure would be contrary to the policy invariably observed by the United States in all similar cases, would be marked with great injustice to Mexico, and peculiarly liable to the darkest suspicions, *inasmuch as the Texians were almost all emigrants from the United States,* AND SOUGHT THE RECOGNITION OF THEIR INDEPENDENCE WITH THE AVOWED PURPOSE OF OBTAINING THEIR ANNEXATION TO THE UNITED STATES;" [13] these occurrences are too well known and too fresh in the memory of all to need more than a passing notice. These have become matters of history. For further evidence on all these and other important points we refer to the memorable speech of John Quincy Adams, delivered in the House of Representatives during the morning hour in June and July, 1838,[14] and to his address to his constituents, delivered at Braintree, September 17, 1842.[15]

The open avowal of the Texians themselves, the frequent and anxious negotiations of our own Government, the resolutions of various States of the Union, the numerous declarations of members of Congress, the tone of the Southern press, as well as the direct application of the Texian Government, *make it impossible for any man to doubt* that ANNEXATION and the formation of several new slaveholding States were *originally* the policy and design of the slaveholding States and the Executive of the nation.

The same references will show, very conclusively, that the *particular objects* of this new acquisition of slave territory were *the perpetuation of slavery and the continued ascendency of the slave power.*

The following extracts from the report on that subject adopted by the Legislature of Mississippi, from a mass of similar evidence which might be adduced, will show *with what views* the annexation was *then* urged:

"But we hasten to suggest the importance of the annexation of Texas to

---

[13] Jackson's special message was that of December 21, 1836. See James Richardson, *Messages and Papers of the Presidents,* 10 vols. (Washington: 1896–98), III, 265–9. Jackson had sent a special commissioner, Henry M. Morfit, to assess the situation in Texas. The essence of Morfit's report was contained in the Jackson message. The message was quoted by Adams in much stronger language than Jackson used.

[14] The speech, assembled by Adams, is published in *Speech of John Quincy Adams . . . Delivered in Fragments . . . from the 16th of June to the 7th of July, 1838* (Washington, 1838).

[15] This speech was published in the Boston *Atlas,* October 19, 1842, and also as a pamphlet, *Address of John Quincy Adams to his Constituents at Braintree,* September 17, 1842 (Boston, 1842).

this Republic, upon grounds somewhat local in their complexion, but of an import infinitely grave and interesting to the people who inhabit the southern portion of this Confederacy, where it is known that a species of domestic slavery is tolerated and protected by law, whose existence is prohibited by the legal regulations of other States of this Confederacy; which system of slavery is held by all who are familiarly acquainted with its practical effects, *to be of highly beneficial influence to the country within whose limits it is permitted to exist.*

"The committee feel authorized to say that this system is cherished by our constituents as *the very palladium of their prosperity and happiness*; and, whatever ignorant fanatics may elsewhere conjecture, the committee are fully assured, upon the most diligent observation and reflection on the subject, that *the South does not possess within her limits a blessing with which the affections of her people are so closely entwined and so completely enfibred,* and whose value is more highly appreciated, than that which we are now considering."

. . . .

"It may not be improper here to remark that, during the last session of Congress, when a Senator from Mississippi proposed the acknowledgment of Texian independence, it was found, with a few exceptions, *the members of that body were ready to take ground upon it as upon the subject of slavery itself.*

"With all these facts before us, we do not hesitate in believing that these feelings influenced the New England Senators, but one voting in favor of the measure; and indeed Mr. Webster has been bold enough, in a public speech delivered recently in New York to many thousand citizens, to declare that the reason that influenced his opposition was his abhorrence to slavery in the South, and that it might, in the event of its recognition, become a slaveholding State. He also spoke of the efforts making in favor of abolition; and that, being predicated upon and aided by the powerful influence of religious feeling, it would become irresistible and overwhelming.

"This language, coming from so distinguished an individual as Mr. Webster, so familiar with the feelings of the North, and entertaining so high a respect for public sentiment in New England, speaks so plainly the voice of the North as not to be misunderstood.

"We sincerely hope there is enough good sense and genuine love of country among our fellow countrymen of the Northern States *to secure us final justice on this subject*; yet we cannot consider it safe or expedient for the people of the South to entirely disregard the efforts of the fanatics and the opinions of such men as Webster and others who countenance such dangerous doctrines.

"*The Northern States have no interests of their own* which require any *special* safeguards for their defence, save only their domestic manufactures; and God knows they have already received protection from Government on a most liberal scale; under which encouragement they have improved and flourished beyond example. *The South has very peculiar interests to preserve* —interests already violently assailed and boldly threatened.

"Your committee are fully persuaded that this protection to her best in-terest will be afforded by the annexation of Texas; an equipoise of influence in the halls of Congress will be secured, which will furnish us a permanent guaranty of protection." [16]

The speech of Mr. Adams, exposing the whole system of duplicity and perfidy towards Mexico which had marked the conduct of our Government, and the emphatic expressions of opposition which began to come up from all parties in the free States, however, for a time nearly silenced the clamors of the South for annexation, and the people of the North have been lulled into the belief that the project is nearly if not wholly abandoned, and that at least there is now no serious danger of its consummation.

Believing this to be a *false and dangerous security,* that the project has never been abandoned a moment by its originators and abettors, but that it has been deferred for a more favorable moment for its accomplishment, we refer to a few evidences of more recent development upon which this opinion is founded.

The last election of President of the Republic of Texas is understood to have turned *mainly* upon the question of *annexation* or *no annexation,* and the candidate favorable to that measure was successful by an overwhelming majority. The sovereign States of Alabama, Tennessee, and Mississippi have *recently* adopted resolutions, some if not all of them *unanimously,* in favor of annexation, and forwarded them to Congress.

The honorable HENRY A. WISE, a member of Congress from the dis-trict in which our present Chief Magistrate resided when elected Vice Presi-dent, and who is understood to be more intimately acquainted with the views and designs of the present Administration than any other member of Con-gress, most distinctly avowed his desire for annexation at the last session of Congress. Among other things, he said, in a speech delivered January 26, 1842:

"True, if Iowa be added on the one side, Florida will be added on the other. But there the equation must stop. Let one more Northern State be admitted and the equilibrium is gone—gone forever. The *balance of inter-ests* is gone—the *safeguard* of American property—of the American Consti-tution—of the American Union, vanished into thin air. *This must be the inevitable result, unless, by a treaty with Mexico,* THE SOUTH CAN ADD MORE WEIGHT TO HER END OF THE LEVER! *Let the South stop at the Sabine,* (the eastern boundary of Texas), while the North may spread unchecked be-yond the Rocky Mountains, AND THE SOUTHERN SCALE MUST KICK THE BEAM!" [17]

Finding difficulties perhaps in the way of a cession by treaty, in another speech, delivered in April, 1842, on a motion made by Mr. Linn, of New York, to strike out the salary of the Minister to Mexico, on the ground that the design of the EXECUTIVE in making the appointment was to accomplish the annexation of Texas, Mr. Wise said, "he earnestly hoped and trusted

[16] For the report of the Mississippi legislative committee of 1837 quoted by Adams, see pp. 99–102 of his *Speech . . . delivered in Fragments,* which is cited above, n. 14.

[17] For this speech see *Congressional Globe,* 27 Cong., 2 sess., 173–6 (January 26, 1842).

that the President was as desirous [of annexation] as he was represented to be. We may well suppose the President to be in favor of it, as every wise statesman must be, who is not governed by fanaticism or local sectional prejudices." He said of Texas: [18]

Several other members of Congress, in the same debate, expressed similar views and desires, and they are still more frequently expressed in conversation.

[Adams quotes the Thomas Gilmer letter of January 10, 1843, at length. This also appears in full in the Documents. Gilmer is described as a former governor of Virginia and one of the "Guard."]

At the present session the resolutions of the State of Alabama in favor of annexation, and sundry petitions and remonstrances against it, were referred to the Committee on Foreign Relations. A majority of the committee, consisting of members from the slaveholding States, refused to consider and report upon the subject, and directed Mr. Adams, their chairman, to report a resolution asking to be discharged from the further consideration of the subject, which he did on the 28th day of February. At the same time Mr. Adams asked, as an individual member of the committee, for leave to present the following resolutions:

"*Resolved,* That by the Constitution of the United States no power is delegated to their Congress, or to any department or departments of their Government, to affix to this Union any foreign state, or the people thereof.

"*Resolved,* That any attempt of the Government of the United States, by an act of Congress or by treaty, to annex to this Union the Republic of Texas, or the people thereof, would be a violation of the Constitution of the United States, null and void, and to which the free States of this Union and their people ought not to submit." [19]

Objections being made, the resolutions were not received, the Southern members showing a disinclination to have the subject agitated in the house *at present.* Might it not be considered as savoring too much of a violation of private confidence, we could refer to various declarations of persons high in office in the National Government avowing a fixed determination to bring Texas into the Union, declaring that they had assurances of the aid of the free States to accomplish the object, and insisting that they prefer a dissolution of the Union to the rejection of Texas, expressing, however, at the same time, their confidence, that if the *annexation* could be effected the people of the free States would submit to it, and the institutions of the slave states would be secured and perpetuated. Contenting ourselves, however, with the above brief glance at some of the most prominent evidences in relation to the subject, we submit to you whether the project of annexation seems to be abandoned, and whether there be not *the most imminent danger* of its speedy accomplishment, unless *the entire mass of the people in the*

---

[18] Wise's speech, omitted here, is reproduced in Documents, under date April 13, 1842. See n. 8.

[19] These resolutions were presented by Adams to the House on February 28, but, as a result of objection by Wise, were not received. See Charles F. Adams, ed., *Memoirs of John Quincy Adams,* 12 vols. (Philadelphia, 1874–7), XI, 330.

free States become aroused to a conviction of this danger, AND SPEAK OUT AND ACT IN REFERENCE TO IT IN A MANNER AND WITH A VOICE NOT TO BE MISUNDERSTOOD EITHER BY THE PEOPLE OF THE SLAVE STATES, OR THEIR OWN PUBLIC SERVANTS AND REPRESENTATIVES.

Although perfectly aware that many important and controlling objections to annexation exist, aside from the question of slavery, we have in this address confined ourselves principally to that, because of its paramount importance, and because *the advocates of annexation distinctly place it upon that ground.* Most of the specious arguments and reasons in favor of annexation with which its advocates attempt to *gild the pill for Northern palates,* are just about as sincere and substantial as were those of Mr. Wise in the speech above referred to, in which he labored a long time to convince Northern philanthropists that they would best promote the objects they had in view by favoring annexation, that they might have slavery in Texas within the power and control of our own Government, that *they might abolish it or mitigate its evils,* he himself being an advocate of perpetual slavery, and among the very foremost to trample upon the right of petition itself!

None can be so blind *now* as not to know that the real design and object of the South is to "ADD NEW WEIGHT TO HER END OF THE LEVER." It was upon that ground that Mr. Webster placed his opposition in his speech on that subject in New York in March, 1837.[20] In that speech, after stating that he saw insurmountable objections to the annexation of Texas; that the purchase of Louisiana and Florida furnished no precedent for it; that the cases were not parallel, and that no such policy or necessity as led to that required the annexation of Texas.

[Webster's speech is quoted at length with special emphasis on his warnings of the dangers of raising the issue of slavery extension.]

We hold that there is not only "no political necessity" for it, "no advantages to be derived from it," but that there is no constitutional power delegated to any department of the National Government to authorize it: that no act of Congress or treaty for annexation can impose the least obligation upon the several States of this Union to submit to such an unwarrantable act, or to receive into their family and fraternity such *misbegotten and illegitimate progeny.*

We hesitate not to say that *annexation,* effected by any act or proceeding of the Federal Government, or any of its Departments, WOULD BE IDENTICAL WITH DISSOLUTION. It would be a violation of our national compact, its objects, designs and the great elementary principles which entered into its formation, of a character so deep and fundamental, and would be an attempt to eternize an institution and a power of nature so unjust in themselves, so injurious to the interests and abhorrent to the feelings of the people of the free States, as, in our opinion, not only inevitably to result in a dissolution of the Union, but fully to justify it; and we not only assert that the people of the free States "ought not to submit to it," but we say, with confidence, THEY WOULD NOT SUBMIT TO IT. We know their present temper

[20] Daniel Webster, *Writings and Speeches,* 18 vols. (Boston: Little, Brown, 1903), II, 204–7.

and spirit on this subject too well to believe for a moment that they would become *particeps criminis* in any such subtle contrivance for the *irremediable perpetuation* OF AN INSTITUTION which the wisest and best men who formed our Federal Constitution, as well from the slave as the free States, *regarded as an evil and a curse,* soon to become extinct under the operation of laws to be passed prohibiting the slave trade, and the progressive influence of the principles of the Revolution.

To prevent the success of this nefarious project—to preserve from such gross violation the Constitution of our country, adopted expressly *"to secure the blessings of liberty"* and not the perpetuation of slavery—and to prevent the speedy and violent dissolution of the Union, we invite you to unite, without distinction of party, in an immediate expression of your views on this subject, in such manner as you may deem best calculated to answer the end proposed.

Washington, March 3, 1843.

> John Quincy Adams,
> Seth M. Gates,
> William Slade,
> William B. Calhoun,
> Joshua R. Giddings,
> Sherlock J. Andrews,
> Nathaniel B. Borden,
> Thos. C. Chittenden,
> John Mattocks,
> Christopher Morgan,
> Joshua M. Howard,
> Victory Birdseye,
> Hiland Hall.[21]

JOHN TYLER TO EDWARD EVERETT
(confidential)

Washington, April 27, 1843 [22]

My dear Sir:

General Duff Green returns to England with a view to negociate with the Capitalists, touching certain important interests, which he has in connexion with extensive Coal tracts near Cumberland. I have a high regard for the General & will be obliged to you to assist him in furthering his objects so far as you can consistently do.

I have thought it well to avail the Government of the services of General Green in collating as far as a private citizen may, facts on which to found a negociation for a commercial treaty in connexion with that upon which

---

[21] Eight other members of Congress added their endorsement of the Adams address in a letter to the *National Intelligencer,* May 20, 1843.

[22] Edward Everett Papers, M.H.S.

we shall speedily enter for the settlement of the Oregon boundary. The adjustment of the last is rendered the more difficult from the fact of its isolation. Hence I have been extremely anxious to introduce the subject of California & Texas so that as to any concessions which might be made on the Columbia, which standing alone would involve the administration in violent denunciations, we might present a counterpoise in territory of incalculable value elsewhere acquired. The accomplishment of this seems at the moment to be hopeless and leaves me in some state of anxiety as to the Oregon Question. There is a decided feeling getting up in the Community for the immediate occupation of the country up to the 49th degree. A measure of that character was very near receiving favour from Congress at its last session. This is what I wish to avoid—I mean the adoption of any action on our part which might bring us in collision with England. Peace is my desire—Peace on fair & honorable terms. Other considerations looking to the future & connected with the highest state of public prosperity, demand of us as far as practicable, to remove any probable cause of quarrell with England. The peace of Europe may depend on the life of a single monarch & should war take place, I wish this country to be in a condition to become the carrier of the world. I fear that the Oregon Question cannot be placed in a situation standing alone, to meet the sanction of the Senate. But if a commercial treaty could be connected with it, having the feature of moderate duties upon importations here, giving reasonable encouragement to our manufacturing labour at the same time that we substituted permanency in place of extravagant duties—and as correlative concessions on the part of England, a reduction of duties on tobacco—cotton & rice, and the abolition of all duties on Indian corn—salted provisions &c & if possible a low duty exclusively in favour of American flour & wheat, then a circle of interests would be completed which embracing the whole union & every interest, would secure us peace in any contingency and give a new vigour to public prosperity. These are great objects & should you have declined the mission to China you may have a most important part to play in the great drama of politics.

Under the circumstances I have thought such a man as General Green, acting under limited countenance and known only as a private citizen, might be of great service in bringing facts to our knowledge, by holding consultations with persons possessing important interests in the trade & commerce of England. English public sentiment might thus be brought to bear upon the English Ministry. He will confer freely with you if it should be your pleasure & possess you of all the information he may acquire. You will perceive the interests involved in all this matter, & be gradually feeling your way with the British Ministry.

Be assured of my constant regard & abiding confidence.

John Tyler

Gilmer to Editor, Niles' Register, May 15, 1843

THOMAS WALKER GILMER
TO THE EDITOR, NILES' REGISTER,

Charlottesville, May 15, 1843 [23]

Having recently published a letter signed by Messrs. ADAMS, GATES, SLADE, WM. B. CALHOUN, GIDDINGS, SHERLOCK J. ANDREWS, BORDEN, CHITTENDEN, MATTOCKS, MORGAN, HOWARD, BIRDS-EYE, and HALL, members of the 27th congress, addressed "To the people of the free states of the union," in which letter these gentlemen have referred to some opinions of mine with regard to the annexation of Texas to the United States, I am sure you will not withhold from me the privilege of being heard by *the people of all the states* through the medium of your columns. In asking this, I do not propose to enter at all on the discussion of a question which certainly has not arisen, but to deprecate the improper uses to which that question has been applied in anticipation by your correspondents. The prejudices which they would excite are most unfavorable not only to the fair consideration of that question, if it should ever arise, but to the permanent harmony and best interests of the union.

In the letter which I wrote to a friend in January last, and which was published in Baltimore, I endeavored to sum up briefly a few of the reasons which I thought would recommend the annexation of Texas to the calm judgment of the people of the United States, as well as those to whom and for whom Messrs. ADAMS, &c. volunteered to speak as those whom they imagine to have a peculiar local interest in the question. I adverted to ties of mutual interest which would be strengthened and enlarged, by opening new fields of enterprise and stimulating energies, which I must be pardoned for thinking, could be better employed than in fostering unnatural and dangerous jealousies among the people of the States already in the Union. I spoke of slavery as a subject of great delicacy in all its relations, but I had reference to the attempts of a few of our own countrymen, aided by foreign emissaries, to dissolve our Union, and not, as these gentlemen have imagined, to any scheme for aggrandizing the South. I did not speak of annexation as calculated to give any ascendency to slavery in our councils, but as capable of harmonizing national discord, which some agitators, in conjunction with certain British agents at home and abroad, have long sought to inflame. I referred to the unsettled questions of jurisdiction and boundary between the United States and England along the coast of the Pacific, and to motives which might influence the British government and its friends in the United States to oppose the acquisition of Texas or California, especially since the results of British valor and diplomacy in China, results which I believe MR. ADAMS either anticipated or desired some time since.

The address which you have published is an imposing, though I think with due deference, not a very candid appeal to the people of the non-slaveholding states, not so much against the annexation of Texas as against the harmony of the Union under the present constitution.

[23] *Niles' Register,* 64, 284–5 (July 1, 1843).

Gilmer to Editor, Niles' Register, *May 15, 1843*

It will have, I do not doubt, more effect abroad than at home, in pointing out to the astute diplomacy and active intrigue of Europe the only weak points in our national position—points, which it seems to me, none but enemies can contemplate with satisfaction. The same number of your paper which contained the address of Messrs. ADAMS, &c., furnished evidence of a design on the part of Great Britain to interfere directly in the relations of Texas to that country and to this, and to disturb the question of domestic slavery on our frontier, and in a country already acknowledged by England as independent, and therefore not yet subject to British control. Is not MR. ADAMS the last man who ought to desire the establishment of British power over the country between the Sabine and the Rio Grande? Does any man know better than he that this territory ought now of right to be part and parcel of the U. States? Does any man know better why it is not? Let me remind him that posterity may be slow to ascribe to him any very patriotic motives in now attempting to invoke the prejudices of a particular section of the Union against slavery, in order to prevent the acquisition of a territory now peopled by our countrymen, and which has been improperly lost to us.

What has slavery to do with this question? Will the number of slaves in the United States be increased by the annexation of Texas? Will the number of slaveholding states be increased? It is true that the climate and soil of Texas are peculiarly adapted to the culture of cotton, sugar, &c.—crops which render slave-labor more profitable than it can be in grain-growing regions, and this may induce the slave population now in the United States to advance southward in the event of annexation. But as this population advances to the South, will it not recede from the North? Is it the object of your correspondents to confine the slave population of the United States within a compass so narrow as to multiply the hardships of the slave, and to compel the master to turn him loose upon the North and the West, nominally free, but really a burden to himself, and a scourge to *"the people of the free States!"* I ask the laboring man of the North, I ask the infatuated philanthropist of the North, if they have not already enough of the free negro? If their free colored population, which is rapidly increasing around them, is not already more injurious, more dangerous to them, than the slave population of the South is or can be to us or to any body else? Has the condition of the white or the black man been benefited by the accumulation there of free persons of color to such an extent as to suggest already the startling project of amalgamation? I ask if there be not many yet living in Northern States whose experience can testify that the relations between the negro and the white man were better even there, as master and slave, than now when there is an equality nominally recognized by law, against which every sentiment of nature and reason revolts? Let it be remembered all the slaves of the North were not emancipated. Many of them were sold at the South. Interest, then, and not philanthropy alone, aided in rendering the work of emancipation so easy at the North.

It is time however, for the men of the North as well as the South to pause and to deliberate calmly on the present dangers which surround us. They are yet within the control of that patriotic reason which founded our union, and which induced our fathers to lay aside the political, moral, and religious prejudices connected with the slavery of the black, in order to accomplish and secure the freedom of the white man. The true question is not now, any more than it was in 1787, whether there can be more territory added to the Union, or more slaveholding states admitted, but whether the territory and the states we have, can continue to be governed by a Constitution which was universally believed, until recently, to have settled forever the relative rights and obligations of the states as to slavery.

Your correspondents use the following language: "It (the acquisition by cession or annexation of Texas) would be a violation of our national compact, its objects, designs, and the great elementary principles which entered into its formation, of a character so deep and fundamental, and would be an attempt to eternize an institution and a power of nature so unjust in themselves, so injurious to the interests and abhorrent to the feelings of the people of the free states, as, in our opinion, not only inevitably to result in a dissolution of the Union, but fully to justify it; and we not only assert that the people of the free states ought not to submit to it, but we say with confidence THEY WOULD NOT SUBMIT TO IT. We know their present temper and spirit on this subject too well to believe for a moment that they would become *particeps criminis* in any such subtle contrivance for the *immediate perpetuation of an* INSTITUTION which the wisest and best men who formed our federal constitution, as well from the slave as the free states, *regarded as an evil and a curse,* soon to become extinct under the operation of laws to be passed prohibiting the slave trade, and the progressive principles of the revolution."

From the peculiar pains taken to emphasize certain passages in this portion of their letter, your correspondents leave no room to doubt that *they* contemplate the abolition of slavery in the United States by the agency of the federal government. These gentlemen cannot be ignorant of the fact that the federal constitution recognizes slavery as one of the objects entitled to its protection, and as one of the elements of the government which it created; that provision is therein made for the surrender of fugitive slaves in all the States, and that three-fifths of the slaves of the Union are to be enumerated in apportioning representation, and may thus be subjected to direct taxation. How are the "progressive principles of the revolution" to affect these provisions without subverting the Constitution? The annexation of Texas is not resisted on specific grounds of objection, but on the general ground that it would frustrate a design, at some time and in some manner to be accomplished, for the total abolition of slavery in the United States. It is your correspondents, then, and not the advocates of annexation, who meditate a dissolution of the Union by virtue of their "progressive principles of revolution." They have undertaken in advance to speak the voice of "the people of the free states," and to declare that *they will not submit to the perpetuation of an institution* which is acknowledged to be recognized by the Constitution. They have made this declaration without qualification. Its fulfillment, according to their prediction, is just as inevitable, whether Texas comes into the Union or not. They regard it only as more probable if Texas should fall under British dominion, and slavery can be there abolished by act of Parliament. Their paramount object seems to be the abolition of slavery in the United States, and not the preservation of the Constitution or the Union.

It remains to be seen whether these gentlemen speak only for themselves, or for the millions of our countrymen whom they believe to have adopted the same fatal sentiment which they have uttered. It matters little in what shape or where this question arises. The mere forms of government signify little when the spirit is gone. The paper and ink of the Constitution will avail very little when the hearts of our countrymen have become alien to the obligation of justice and the ties of blood. I have been persuaded for some years that the sooner this question of the relative rights and obligations of the States under the federal compact was presented, and in the simplest form which it could assume, the better for the harmony and security of all. If we wait till "the progressive principles of revolution" shall deny our right to a representation of three fifths of our slaves, or until it asserts authority to tax them all as property, or to make any other disposition of them which may be deemed expedient to a majority in Congress, we may not agree as speedily or harmoniously as we should now for or against the acquisition of Texas or on any other question which will permit us to discuss the interests of the whole union in the spirit of the Constitution. These "progressive principles of the revolution" were never developed in 1776. They claim a much later and less illustrious origin. When we consider the agency of the British people and the encouragement of the British government in supplying this continent with African slaves; when it is remembered that the early efforts of the colonies to abolish slavery were prevented by the "mother country," it is indeed a curious specimen of political research which your correspondents exhibit, when they announce, near the middle of the nineteenth century, that the great design of the American Revolution was to kindle the flame of civil war among the white citizens of the United States, and peril their liberties to test some scheme of mad fanaticism by experimenting on the moral, social and political capacities of the negro race. It is not the least curious part of this revelation that it comes from England, whose sympathies have rivetted the chains of the white man at home and in Ireland, while they have emancipated the negro in the West Indies. One of the gentlemen who signed the appeal which you published has been the active agent in distributing through the United States the proceedings of the World's Convention, which assembles annually at London to sympathize with the black man at the expense of the white.

I will not believe that your correspondents have spoken advisedly, or by any authority, when *they* claim to reflect the feelings of the people of the free states. Though there are thirteen of these honorable gentlemen, (and that is a revolutionary number,) I am persuaded that they will find a more practical as well as a more liberal spirit pervading the population of the non-slaveholding States. The union is as necessary now as it always was for the protection of all. It can be preserved only by preserving the Constitution which formed it, and the people of the United States will look with indignant reprobation upon any scheme for aggrandizing any one section of the country at the expense of another. They will look to the rapid march of our population towards the shores of the Pacific and along the shores of the Gulf of Mexico with no feeling of narrow jealousy as to the "length of the northern or southern end of the lever" while the fulcrum is strong. The compromises of the Constitution can be carried out so as to admit many more new states into our Union, without impairing the force of that great example by which we have already done so much to emancipate the world. Our Union has no danger to apprehend from those who believe that its genius is expansive and progressive, but from those who think that the limits of the United States are already too large and the principles of 1776 too old-fashioned for this fastidious age.

Thomas W. Gilmer

DUFF GREEN TO JOHN TYLER
London, May 31, 1843 [24]

I wrote you a hasty note by the last steamer. Since then Mr. Everett introduced me to Sir Robert Peel, who gave me an audience yesterday. I endeavoured to impress upon his mind the importance of making such a treaty with the United States as would secure to England the privilege of introducing her manufactures into our markets upon a mere revenue duty: England giving us the advantage of her markets for our agricultural products upon reciprocal terms. He gave me an attentive hearing, and, upon my leaving him, thanked me for the explanations I had given him, saying that they were interesting and satisfactorily stated, and that he was much gratified at the opportunity of renewing my personal acquaintance. I considered this declaration as a matter of course. I told him that in assuring him that it was now in his power to make a treaty with us on terms more advantageous to England than could have been made at any former period and more favorable than can hereafter be obtained, I discharged what I conceived to be my duty as a citizen of the United States, and had been induced to do so by a belief that he had a desire to promote, as far as he could, the most friendly relations between the two countries, that I was desirous on that account to strengthen his government, believing that such an arrangement with the United States would, by taking from opposition its most powerful argument, quiet agitation in England and thereby confirm power in his hands. I explained to him that, if he desired to make a treaty with the U.S., it would be indispensable that he should send a commission to Washington for that purpose, and that if done at all, it should be done before the meeting of the next Congress, and the sooner, the better, as the time had arrived when we in the United States are compelled to choose between free trade and restriction. I explained to him that such a treaty, interfering, as it would do,

[24] Duff Green Papers, University of North Carolina Library, microfilm roll no. 4.

with the taxing power, must be submitted during its next session, that so many interests will be involved as to require that all its parts should be well matured, and the negociation should therefore be conducted by a commission having the confidence of the several sections of the country, whose combined influence would thereby be secured in support of the ratification by Congress.

I endeavoured also to impress upon his mind the value of such commercial arrangements by showing that he would thereby secure a large market for the consumption of British manufactures, whereas by refusing to receive our surplus agricultural products he would necessarily force our surplus labor into manufactures, and thereby compel us to become their competitors in the markets of the world, instead of being the largest consumers of their surplus, and that the inevitable consequence of this would be to place us in such relation to the dependencies of England that it would become our interest, as it is now the interest of all the continental powers of Europe, to unite in any combination, the object of which may be to emancipate her colonies and open their markets to all the rest of the world.

I told him that I was apprehensive that he would find that so far from considering the late regulation for the admission of American wheat through Canada as a measure intended to promote trade with America, it would be considered by the Southern states as a further proof that the policy of the British Gov't. is to substitute the products of India for those of America, and that the countenance given to emancipation had for its object the abolition of slavery in America as a means of enabling them to obtain cotton, sugar & coffee from India, in exchange for manufactures cheaper than they could then be produced in America, it being now admitted that the effect of abolishing slavery in America would be to increase the cost of production; and that in case he declined to avail himself of this occasion to make a treaty securing to the two countries the benefits to accrue from a mutual and reciprocal exchange of their respective products, I for one & many others, who had entertained hopes that it would be otherwise will be reluctantly driven to the conclusion that he too had resolved to follow up this, Lord Melbourne's measure, as a means of rendering the continent dependent upon England for a supply of these articles of first necessity, and of thereby forcing back the current of trade to London as the centre of the commercial world.

I prepared and placed in his hands a brief analysis of the several great interests, showing how the labor & capital of the United States are employed, and endeavored to impress upon his mind that the question of the tariff is in fact the great question on which parties are divided; that the manufacturing interest is chiefly confined to New England, New York & Pennsylvania, that the slaveholding states are producers of cotton and tobacco, which constitute the chief items of our export; that the Northwestern states produce grain & provisions and that the effect of his refusal to send a commission to the United States and to avail himself of the present occasion to make a commercial treaty would be to alarm the slaveholding interest and by confirming their apprehensions that the British Gov't. are acting on a deliberate policy of promoting by all means in their power the abolition of slavery in the

United States, induce Southern statesmen, heretofore the advocates of free trade, to adopt measures hostile to the interests of England. I assured him that we had great confidence in him & his government, and that if he failed us we must prepare for the worst, because the time had arrived when the future relations between the two countries must be determined, that their interests must become more identified or they would necessarily become more & more adverse.

In connection with this subject I feel it my duty to enclose you a copy of a letter received here by the last steamer from Galveston. I have seen the original and have no doubt of the sincerity of the writer. You will see that he says that the attempt to amend the constitution of Texas so as to abolish slavery is about to be made, under assurances from the British Minister there that such a measure will secure for Texas the warmest support from the British Gov't. in their present struggle with Mexico, and also the means of paying for their slaves. The writer adds: "If I had time I would follow a train of reflection on this matter, as connected with our relations with the United States etc," and concludes by referring his correspondent to Captain Elliott's despatches to his Government in confirmation of what he had written.

There can be no doubt that Captain Elliott has given such assurances. How far he had the authority of his government, or how far that government will ratify what he has done, is another question. If it be true that Sir Robert Peel is endeavoring to foster abolition in the North by opening a trade to the Northern States through Canada, which he denies to the Southern States, and is stimulating rebellion and servile war in the Southern States by purchasing and emancipating the slaves of Texas, then there could be but one opinion as to what it becomes the American government to do. But I can not believe that Sir Robert Peel is governed by such motives. It may be that, acting on the state of public opinion here he has given some countenance to this movement in Texas, but I am persuaded that if he could see this matter in its true bearing on the interests of the Southern States and the manner in which it must react on the interests of England, he would disavow the assurance which Capt. Elliott has given.

The discussions in Parliament and the comment of the British will enable you to judge of the condition of things here as well as I can. It is true that I hear much speculation, and if some who profess to be well informed are to be believed, England is on the eve of a fearful revolution. But when I see so great a statesman as Sir Robert Peel predicating his measures and gravely announcing to the world as he did last year in the debate on the sugar duties:

"That it was impossible to look to the discussions in the United States of America, and especially to the conflicts between the Northern and Southern States, without seeing that slavery in that nation stood on a precarious footing." I am admonished how little reliance should be placed on the opinions predicated on partial, interested or prejudiced statements in relation to the institutions or domestic policy of other governments. If one so wise and well informed as he is, is so much misled by the monomaniacal ravings of Mr.

Adams and the fanatical representations of the abolitionists of the United States as to suppose that the institution of slavery will be abolished or that our union will be dissolved, we may well be at a loss fully to comprehend the bearing of Mr. O'Connel's repeal agitation. But it appears to me that, predicated as this movement is on a sense of civil and religious wrongs, uniting as it does, under O'Connell's lead, protestant as well as Catholic, pressed as the Government are at home by the opposition, the League, the Radicals and the Chartists, as well as the general sentiment in favor of free trade, the condition of things here is such as to incline ministers to seize upon your proposition for a treaty as the best means of confirming themselves in power by granting to commerce & manufactures all the concessions which the league should require on the one hand, & securing to agriculture all the protection which they can retain on the other, & thus by quieting agitation in England bring the united sentiment of Great Britain to bear on O'Connell's agitation in Ireland. If to this were added a judicious application of public money in aid of, or in the entire construction of railroad and other improvements, giving employment to the labor and stimulating the industry of Ireland, Sir Robert Peel would, I verily believe, become the most popular minister that ever controlled the destiny of this great nation. I am one of those who believe that God in his providence raises up men to be instruments of accomplishing his purposes, and such is my confidence in Sir Robt. Peel's wisdom, in his just appreciation of the responsibility under which he acts, and of what is due to his own fame, that I believe he will be found equal to the crisis in which he is placed.

Whatever may be the result, you will have the consolation to know that you have done your duty, and should Sir Robt. Peel fail to improve this opportunity of placing the relations of the two countries on a basis consolidating their interests and perpetuating their peace and prosperity, you will be at no loss to understand the objects which govern the policy of this Government and will be enabled to adopt such measures as this knowledge of the future will render indispensable.

I intend to furnish Sir Robert Peel with a copy of the preceding part of my letter because altho' I told him that I was acting as a private citizen, not "regularly authorized" to discuss the subject of a treaty and he therefore did not express any opinion, from which I was authorized to infer what he proposes to do, the conversation nevertheless was such as to justify him in believing that I would communicate the purpose of it to you, and it seems to me proper that he should know that I have done so, and the precise words I have used, because if he desires to act upon the suggestions I have made and wishes to be officially informed, he can communicate with you through Mr. Fox. It is proper that I should add in conclusion that this account of the interview with Sir Robert Peel is intended to explain to you the impressions which I endeavored to convey to his mind rather than to repeat the precise language. If I were permitted to advise I would authorize Mr. Everett to assure Sir Robert of your desire to make a treaty and invite him to send a commission to the United States. If this is done, you will make the treaty. If it be not done, you may fail because he is much pressed by the opposition and is not heartily sustained by the tories.

I have to thank you for your kind letter to Mr. Everett. He has already done much to serve me and I hope, through him, to accomplish the object which brought me to London.

Your sincere friend,

DUFF GREEN TO JOHN TYLER

London, July 3, 1843 [25]

My dear Sir

I enclose you herewith the London Times of the 30th of June containing Mr O'Connell's speech at Galway to which I invite your special attention, and also a copy of a letter addressed to Sir Robert Peel the reasons for my writing which I will explain.

By the last steamer I sent you a copy of my letter to Sir Robert Peel, enclosing a copy of my letter to you, the receipt of which he acknowledged in a polite note thanking me for the information but declining to intimate what he will do. In the mean time I had ascertained that the opposition, headed by Sir [Lord] John Russell, are anxious to make an issue with the present government and are prepared to denounce the ministers if they refuse or neglect to make a treaty with us, and during a conversation with Mr Gladstone I was induced to believe that Sir Robert will appoint commissioners to make the treaty as soon as Parliament is prorogued, *unless he is prevented by the new movement in Texas.*

I learn from a source entitled to the fullest credit that there is now here a Mr Andrews, deputed by the abolitionists of Texas to negociate with the British Government—That he has seen Aberdeen, and submitted his *project* for the abolition of slavery in Texas, which is that there shall be organized a company in England, who shall advance a sum sufficient to pay for the slaves now in Texas and receive in payment Texas lands, that the sum thus advanced shall be paid over as an indemnity for the abolition of slavery, and I am authorized to say to you by the Texian minister that Lord Aberdeen has agreed that the British Government will guarantee the payment of the interest on the loan upon condition that the Texian Government will abolish slavery.

The argument to be used upon Texas is that if slavery is abolished there will be a greatly increased emigration from Europe, but it is manifest that no such emigration will take place. The inducements will not be so great as are held out in South America. The consequence will be that Texas must become a depot for runaway slaves and a border war will soon commence. A part of the plan is Texas shall be placed under the protection of England & will then become the point from whence she will operate on these runaway negroes and the Indians on the Western border. The British Government is compelled to choose between your proposition to place the relation between the two countries on the most favorable basis or else the adoption of measures to impair our increasing wealth & prosperity.

[25] Copy in the O. P. Chitwood Papers, West Virginia University Library.

England gave 100,000,000$ to abolish slavery in the West Indies and is now paying 20,000,000$ in the shape of duty on sugar for the avowed purpose of abolishing slavery in Cuba and Brazil. I refer you to Sir Robert Peel's speech on the sugar duties of last year and then again to his declaration in the debate on the same question during the last week where he says that the British Government required the abolition of slavery in Brazil, and that the treaty had failed because Brazil refused to abolish it.[26] In his speech of last year he declared that he sought to abolish slavery in Brazil, as a means to abolish it in the United States. Now why should England pay 20,000,000$ per annum to abolish slavery in Brazil? Sir Robert Peel gives the answer. He tells us that an estate in Jamaica which before the emancipation gave a profit of 10,000 £ is now cultivated at a loss of more than 3,000 £ per annum. Or in other words, so long as Cuba, Brazil & the United States raise sugar coffee & cotton by slave labor they will drive the products of English East & West Indies out of the market. The abolition of slavery thus becomes the question on which depend the value of her whole colonial possessions.

With these facts and admissions before us it becomes important for us to ascertain *now* what the purposes of England are. If she refuses to make a treaty with us securing to her our market and offers to guarantee a loan to abolish slavery in Texas, we can be at no loss for her motive. If she pays 20,000,000$ per annum as one of the means of abolishing slavery in Brazil & Cuba, because she cannot compete with slave labor, then what will she not give to abolish slave labor in the United States, when she believes that the effort to do so will array the North against the South and end in the dissolution of our nation? The effect of which will be to prejudice the growing manufactures of New England as well as the agricultural interests of the South.

When we look at what the abolitionists have done & ask ourselves what will fanaticism sustained by British gold accomplish we must face the necessity of meeting the issue at once.

My letter to Sir Robert [27] was intended to demonstrate to him that it was his interest and his duty to send commissioners to the United States for the purpose of making a treaty, and that you might see that if he fails to do so it is because he believes that he better promote the interest of England by allying himself with the abolitionists in the United States & contributing to dissolve the Union through their agency. I cannot mistake the American people—I will carefully prepare the materials to demonstrate that such is the policy of this government and to enable you to take the strongest grounds in case Sir Robert fails to accede to your proposition.

If you meet this crisis as it becomes you to do you will greatly promote the interests of your country and greatly advance your own fame and popularity. I would immediately instruct Mr Everett to communicate to Lord

[26] For the Peel speeches, see *Hansard's*, 3rd ser., 63 (May–June, 1842), 1224–31; and 70 (June–July, 1843), 263–7.

[27] This letter was summarized by Green in his letter to Tyler of May 31, 1843, which is reproduced in the Documents.

Aberdeen the rumors relative to the part taken by this government to abolish slavery in Texas and demand an explanation of their purposes. I would also direct him to invite the appointment of commissioners to negociate a commercial treaty. I would then meet them in Texas by a proposition of annexation and would go before the count[r]y on that issue—be not startled. If you take the ground that annexation is the only means of preventing Texas falling into the hands of English fanatics and thus becoming a depot for smugglers & runaway slaves and your friends prove as I can prove that the object of England in all her movements in relation to slavery & the slave trade is to substitute the products of her Indian subjects for those of America and that it is as much a war on the free labor of the North as on the slave labor of the South, you will control events. Who can take ground against you? Will Mr Calhoun oppose the annexation under such circumstances? He can not. If he concurs, can Benton & Van Buren oppose you? They can not. If Calhoun Benton and Van Buren sustain you, can Clay oppose you? What can Ritchie say to such a movement? Can he prefer that Texas shall become a refuge for runaway slaves to its becoming a part of the United States? I would refer you to the Declaration of Lord Morpeth & Lord Brougham & the explanations of Lord Aberdeen on the subject of fugitive slaves. They lay down the broad principle that whatever may be necessary to his escape a slave may justifiably do!! [28] Thus they say that if murder or theft be necessary to the escape the British Government will not deliver up a runaway slave and that his being a slave will exempt him from the provisions of the late treaty for the surrender of refugees from justice. Now suppose that such a refuge for runaway negroes be established in Texas—Can we with honor exact concessions from Texas which we do not enforce as to England?

Let me entreat you to meet the crisis—Make a treaty for the annexation, put yourself before the next Congress on that issue and rely on the people. Rely on what I tell you. It is to become the question which will absorb all other questions.

If you take a bold and decided ground you will control the policy of England. The very necessities which are driving her to adopt the policy of which I complain will prevent her from pursuing it if you present to her the alternatives, I have suggested. If she finds that she cannot make Texas a refuge for runaway negroes & thus use it for abolishing slavery in the U. States she will then be glad to make a treaty securing to herself the advantages of our market. You may by a bold course secure the annexation & the treaty—but remember that *fortune favors the* BRAVE. You have the issue of peace or war in your own hands, and upon the use you make of them will depend the future welfare of your country as well as your own fame & popularity. I cannot be deceived as to the future. See what O'Connell is doing for Ireland, and see what you can do for America. *If you look on and wait for events, all the measures of England will be hostile, but if you come boldly forward and control events all the measures of England will be friendly—*

[28] The declaration of Lord Morpeth referred to here was an incidental part of an eloquent address to the British and Foreign Anti-Slavery Society at its fourth annual meeting on June 21, 1843, which is reported in *The Anti-Slavery Reporter*, 4 (1843), 115–17.

She is not in a condition now to risk an open rupture on the question of abolition, but if you wait until she shall have planted herself and her allies in Texas she will then bid you defiance. She will then endeavor to accomplish a dissolution of the Union at any cost, because she is jealous of our wealth and prosperity as a people, and will then seek a dissolution of the Union as the best means of destroying the manufactures of New England, because she cannot bear up under present burdens without her commerce, she cannot maintain her commerce without her manufactures and she now believes that she has more to fear from competition of New England than from that of all the rest of the world. It is folly to suppose that New England will not see and understand this, or that New England will not sustain you in your effort to protect her against so vile a conspiracy.

I will see the Texian Minister & if possible prevail on him so to modify his proceedings in this matter as to obtain an official declaration on the part of Lord Aberdeen of what this Government will do, & make arrangements whereby you shall be placed in possession of what transpires.

Yours sincerely

DUFF GREEN TO ABEL P. UPSHUR

London, August 3, 1843 [29]

My dear Sir:

I enclose herewith a letter to Mr. Calhoun.[30] I have not sealed it because I wish you to read it and that you should, after having submitted it to the President, seal it and send it to him at Pendleton. I have not time to make a copy.

Events here are moving with great rapidity—four weeks ago, the Whigs did not expect to reach power in less than 18 months—they now expect to supersede the present ministers in less than six months. You may rely on the facts in relation to Texas in my last letter [July 3, 1843] to the President. Mr. Smith, the Texian chargé, at my instance had an official interview [July 2, 1843] with Lord Aberdeen in which the latter told him that their government desire to prevent the annexation of Texas to the U.States, and that to accomplish that the ministry would recommend a loan for the abolition of slavery. Mr. Smith promised me to write out an official report as soon as he reached Paris & send a copy to Mr. Van Zandt to be submitted to you. Under this state of things I have seen and urged upon Lord John Russell and others in the opposition the danger of such interference and they have assured me that no such loan can be obtained. They will make an issue on that & parts of Sir Robt. Peel's American policy.

I hope to be able to bring with me letters and documents demonstrating the state of things here so plainly that the President can be at no loss as what he ought to do. If he will but reflect for a single moment on the effect which

[29] Department of State, Special Agents, National Archives.
[30] For this letter, see A.H.A. *Report*, 1899, II, 846–9. The date given it there is August 2, 1842, which is an error. The correct date is August 2, 1843.

O'Connell's abolition speech had on the repeal agitation in the U.States he will see that the strongest measure that he can now take is a treaty for the annexation of Texas upon the ground of the danger of permitting Texas to become a refuge for runaway slaves. I have obtained already a full report of the proceedings of the Anti-Slavery Convention here and there is an inexhaustible fund there, which if properly used cannot fail to excite the indignation of the non-slave holding as well as the slave holding states.

Bennet of the Herald is here. He was once my reporter and I have always treated him kindly. I have taken some pains to introduce him to the proper men and to make a right impression on his mind. I have conversed freely with Mr. Strong of New York who is a decided friend of the President and has been my room mate (not my bed fellow!!) since he came here. We have both conversed with Bennet about the course of his paper. I told Bennet that he had established the most profitable newspaper in the Country, that his fortune was now made & that what he wants is position in society and that we could give him this—that must modify the course and character of the paper and without becoming the partisan give a constant and active support to the Administration and that we would make his paper the channel of most valuable and interesting communications. He has agreed to do so and this steamer will take letters to the persons charged with the paper during his absence and his letters will be shaped to bear on the measures and policy I have explained to him.

He is making arrangements to give great power and efficiency to his paper and it can be made the most valuable auxiliary in our cause. I have not time to write to the President. Mr. Strong who has been with me will be in possession of all that I have done. He has promised to visit Washington immediately after his arrival and he will go on the packet of the 19th & will give you many personal details.

I am extremely gratified at the new organization of the Cabinet. You will find Mr. Henshaw a man of great practical good sense and by far the best selection that could have been made.

Please to remember me to Mrs. Upshur & your daughter. I have taken the liberty to enclose you a few letters.

Your friend,

DUFF GREEN TO JOHN TYLER

London, August 29, 1843 [31]

My Dear Sir

Upon the prorogation of Parliament I wrote a note to Sir Robert Peel asking him to give me a personal interview that I might submit to his consideration two letters, one from Mr. Upshur & the other from Mr Calhoun and explain to him certain proceedings in the United States which will have an important bearing on the relations between that Country and this. He

[31] Copy in the O. P. Chitwood Papers, University of West Virginia Library.

wrote to me saying that he was leaving town, and therefore could not see me himself, but that Mr Goulburn the Chancellor of the Exchequer, who had his entire confidence would see me at two oclock this day. I called in Downing street and saw Mr Goulburn. I placed in his hands the resolutions and proceedings of the Oregon Convention held at Cincinnati, and explained to him that Col. Benton had removed to St Louis in 1816. That he found a bitter opposition to Genl Clark the Governor of the Territory headed by Mr. Bates the Secretary. That the population on the frontier having suffered greatly from the Indian Allies of England were much excited against England, and especially against the N.W. fur company to whom they imputed the outrages perpetrated by the Indians—That the American fur company embracing many influential persons at St Louis were the rivals of the British Company and anxious to expel them from the American Territory. That Col. Benton, then a mere adventurer established a paper and became the partisan of the Governor and of the American fur Company—that from that day until this, the Occupation of the Oregon Region as a means of protecting our frontier from the influence of the British fur Company had been his favorite hobby. That the purpose of his opposition to the Treaty of Washington was intended to organise public opinion for the immediate occupation of the Oregon—That there is no difference of opinion in the United States as to the right of the American Government to the boundary as claimed, and that that opinion was confirmed by the declaration of Sir Robert Peel that the maps of the day in the possession of this Government recognized the N. East boundary as claimed by the U States. I told him that the people of New England, who are so largely engaged in the whale fisheries, are more directly interested in maintaining the American claim to the Oregon than the people of the West, and that hence Maine & New Hampshire had passed resolutions asserting our right. I explained that the possession of Oregon had thus become one of the questions which will enter into and probably control the next Presidential election, that the longer the adjustment is delayed the more difficult it will be. I then placed in his hands letters from Mr Calhoun & Mr Upshur in which they both express themselves favorable to an arrangement of the tariff of the two countries by treaty, and explained to him the relation which the present parties in the United States bear to the tariff. He said that they had reduced their duties and that instead of reducing ours we had increased them. I told him that the late Congress did not truly represent the public opinion of the U States, that the members were elected more in reference to the currency than the tariff—that the partisans of Mr Clay had availed themselves of an accidental majority to renew the high duties—that we had passed through a severe monetary crisis—that we had paid off our commercial and domestic debt—that the contraction in the currency had so reduced prices as to enable us to increase our exports, that the high duties had caused a very large importation of specie, that this had relieved the banks and was giving a new impulse to industry—that we had passed the crisis—that the reaction was rapidly progressing—that the advocates of protection would avail themselves of this reaction, as an argument against a reduction of duties alledging that the increasing prosperity of the Country is caused by their protective duties, and I urged the necessity of this Government availing themselves of the agitation of the subject during the next Congress to give assurances of such corresponding modifications of the British tariff as will place the commerce between the two countries on terms of reciprocity. He said that he was much indebted to me for the explanation I had given him, admitted their great importance and said that he would carefully note what I had said & submit it to his Colleagues. He told me that I must be aware that in all Governments controlled by public opinion those in power had to encounter many difficulties but without saying what this Govt would do he assured me of his earnest desire to preserve the most friendly relations and to extend as far as practicable their commerce with us. I told him that I had now been in England nearly two years, that I had been a careful observer of passing events, that I had opportunities of ascertaining public opinion, which few Americans ever had and that it did appear to me that if ministers hesitate to avail themselves of the present occasion to place the relations between England & the United States on the most favorable basis it can only be accounted for, on the supposition that they entirely misapprehend the state of public opinion in the U. States, or are resolved to pursue a course of measures which they must foresee will bring the two countries into collision. And in this view of the case I very much regretted the language used by Lord Brougham in the House of Lords & by Sir Robt. Peel & the Attorney Genl [Sir Frederick Pollock] in the House of Commons on the subject of slavery and especially the declaration of the latter, that it was the purpose of the British Government to "make every sacrifice to put down slavery where ever it existed."[32] He said that that remark had reference to the ownership of slaves by British Subjects, only, and did not contemplate an interference on the part of this Government in the question of slavery in foreign countries. I replied that I was much gratified to hear this, but that it was very unfortunate, that on the debate on the sugar duties, as well as on the American treaty Sir Robert Peel's remarks as reported had a much wider application, and that I considered it much more so that Lord Aberdeen had been reported to have given assurances to Lord Brougham in the House of Lords & to the Anti Slavery Convention that this Government would exert its influence to abolish slavery in Texas.[33]

I told him that this could not fail to alarm & greatly to excite the whole Southern Country—That the effect of abolishing slavery in Texas would be to establish a place of refuge for run away slaves, and robbers—that the inevitable consequence would be a war and the conquest of Texas by the United States, for that after the declaration by Lord Aberdeen, Lord Brougham & Lord Morpeth, that the Slave may commit murder, theft, & robbery if such offence be necessary to his escape,[34] he could not expect

---

[32] *Hansard's,* 3rd ser., 71 (July–August, 1843) 1004. Green distorts the language used by Pollock.

[33] For Peel's statement, see *ibid.,* 3rd ser., 63 (May–June, 1842), 1224. Green's rendition of it is loose. For the exchange between Brougham and Aberdeen on August 18, 1843, see 3rd ser., 71 (July–August, 1843), 915–18.

[34] Green's attribution of such a declaration to Aberdeen and Brougham is baseless. For the Morpeth statement see n. 28.

the Southern States to permit such a refuge to be established—altho it might be under the Auspices of the British Govt. I told him that after the communication I had made to him & the letters he had seen he must be sensible that it was my sincere desire not only to preserve peace between the two countries but to place their relations on the most favorable basis. He must also be aware that it would become my duty to report to my political friend whose respectability and influence he could not question, and that he must be satisfied that much would depend on that report. He said that he was sensible of this and repeated the assurance of his earnest desire to preserve the most friendly relations between the two countries but added "you know sir that war between such great nations, where there is so much diversity of interests it is always easy for parties so disposed to find cause for agitation."

I replied that I was especially anxious that he should understand the bearing of the slave question in the United States on political parties.

I told him that I had found that very few even in the best informed, in England, understood the sense in which the term democracy is applied to parties in the United States. That here it is understood to mean a government of the absolute majority—whereas in truth it means as applied to the parties in the U States precisely the reverse. I explained to him that most of the first emigrants to America, left England on account of Civil or Religious persecution—they believed that their rights as Englishmen secured to them by Magna Charta, had been violated, and hence they took with them Special Charters, pledging the Crown as a guarantee for the enjoyment of those rights, that the question on which the Colonies separated from the mother Country was a question of Chartered privilege. They denying the right of paramount legislation claimed by the Imperial parliament, that such was the jealousy of the new states that they reserved to themselves the right of voting men & money for the war of the revolution. That afterward when it became necessary to organise a central government to take charge of their intercourse with foreign nations they had not only defined the powers of that Govt by a written Constitution but that Virginia had proposed an amendment, which was adopted as part of the Constitution declaring that the powers not granted by the Constitution to the United States nor inhibited by it to the States were reserved to the States respectively or to the people. That parties had soon organised in reference to the powers of the new Government—that the federal party insisted that the Supreme Court were impowered to pass upon all questions arising under an Act of Congress while the Democratic party under the lead of Mr Jefferson, Mr Madison, & John Taylor insisted that as between a State and the federal Government there was no judge but a convention of the States themselves. That hence it was apparent that the Democratic party in the United States, (who with the exception of the late Congress & the accidental election of Mr Adams had been in power since the first election of Mr Jefferson) is that party who insist on the most rigid construction of the Constitution—binding down the Government, both state & federal to the limits prescribed by the express grants of power, and the necessary implications therefrom. That on the other hand their political opponents, insist upon an enlargement of the powers of Govt by Construction, that the question of slavery had become *political*—that it is now part of the political creed of the Democratic party that the question belongs to the States, & that no one looking to that party for political preferment will countenance the Anti Slavery movement. That he might form some opinion of the influence which this relation of that question to existing parties has in the United States, from the effect which the publications of Mr O'Connel's declaration that when he had accomplished repeal he would then devote all his energies to accomplish the abolition of slavery wherever it exists. That altho many small politicians had seized the repeal agitation as a means of creating political capital, the effect of O'Connel's speech had been to arrest the progress of agitation, even in the Northern States—I told him that if he would reflect but for a moment he would see that the effort to abolish slavery in the United States must fail and that the attempt to substitute the products of India for those of America, would react on the manufacturing interest in the United States as well as in England—That several large cotton manufactures had been established in Virginia, N Carolina, & Georgia and that it had been demonstrated that the female slaves under the administration of intelligent whites could under work the whites, that the inevitable consequences therefore of diminishing the demand for the present product of American slave labor, by high duties or the substitution of free labor produce would be to convert the American slave into rival manufacturers.

He seemed to be impressed with this view, renewed his expression of thanks and assured me of his desire to preserve the most friendly relations with us. Do you ask me what I believe this Govt will do? I hope that they will send a Commission to the U States, for the purpose of closing the Oregon question and to aid in the adjustment of the Tariff. I fear they will do nothing & my fears preponderate.

What should you do under these circumstances? My opinion is that the path before you is plain.

Lewis Tappan in a speech in the Antislavery Convention here said: "In a conversation I had with John Quincy Adams on that subject he said 'I deem it the duty of Great Britain as a Christian nation to tell the Texians that slavery must be abolished; that it shall not be planted there after all the efforts and sacrifices that have been made to abolish it all over the world. The annexation of Texas will, he said, be a leading topic next session, but I will oppose it with all the might and talent that God has given me. If slavery is abolished in Texas it must speedily fall throughout America; and when it falls in America it will expire throughout Christendom.' " [35]

Mr. Amos Phelps of Massachusetts [36] brought the subject before the convention and a committee waited upon Lord Aberdeen when his Lordship assured them that the Government would use its influence to abolish slavery in Texas, (see page 110 *Anti Slavery Reporter*). His Lordship gave the same assurance to Lord Brougham in the House of Lords.—(See *Reporter*, page

[35] For Tappan's account at the convention of a conversation with Adams, see *Anti-Slavery Reporter*, 4 (1843), 111.

[36] Amos Phelps was editor of the Boston *Emancipator*.

155). By referring to the debate on the Washington Treaty & the speeches of Sir Robert Peel on the sugar Duties and the speeches of Lord Brougham & Sir Robt Peel on Lord Brougham's bill to suppress the slave trade, you will find that they both admit that the effect of abolishing Slavery in the British Colonies has been to destroy the Value of Colonial property and that they both advocated the emancipation on the ground that having destroyed the Value of English Colonial property by emancipation, the British Govt. are therefore bound as an act of justice to the West Indian proprietors to abolish slavery elsewhere [37]—An argument of the same character as the apology given by Lord Brougham for the Conquest of Scinde to wit, that Scinde would if properly governed prove a suitably profitable source of revenue! ! and in entire accord with the principle of his bill which takes care to provide that the British subjects who are forbidden to hold slaves may *nevertheless* sell them & put the proceeds in their pockets. In my former letters I have spoken of the state of parties here, but have omitted to mention that a few intelligent wealthy young Tories under the lead of Lord John Manners, the son of the Duke of Rutland, have declared their independence of Ministers and have assumed the cognomen of "Young England" Lord J. Manners, it is said, foresees that power must soon change hands and is inclined to favor more liberal views. The leader in the Times, written before, but published the day after the prorogation of Parliament, makes favorable mention of "Young England" and is very, very severe on ministers [38]—The public mind is fast becoming more and more opposed to the discriminating duty on slave grown sugar. As this was the question on which the Tories came into power the Whigs are prepared to ridicule & denounce the hypo-critical pretense of greater sanctity & greater humanity, and one of the most striking features of the debate on the Sugar duties was the remarks of Mr [John] Bright, a quaker, who admonished Sir Robert Peel that the Anti Slavery Committees have lost their influence and do not represent public opinion (see [*Anti-Slavery*] *Reporter* page 160).

I have done what I could to stimulate the Whig party and the Whig leaders to make a bold and decided issue with Ministers on this subject, and after [a] few conversations I am to spend Thursday & Friday next in the country with Sir John Easthope, the proprietor of the Whig Chronicle who assures me of his cooperation. I expect to meet one or more influential parties there.

I have carefully refrained from taking any part in the local parties here, further than to explain to both on every proper occasion what the real state of parties in the U States is and to urge upon both that the present state of public opinion in the United States is favorable to a reciprocal arrangement of the trade between England & the U States. Those who profess to know Sir Robert Peel well say that he will do nothing. My own opinion is that much depends on the further development of public opinion, and hence after full consideration I called today on the Editor of the Times and left with him an extract from two letters, one from Mr Upshur & the other from Mr Calhoun, both, favorable to an arrangement of the duties by treaty. If the

[37] See nn. 32–4.
[38] London *Times,* August 25, 1843.

Times publishes these extracts they will elicit favorable comments and these may induce Sir Robert Peel to send a Commission to the United States.[39] If he does not, it will prepare the public opinion of this country to sustain the Whig party whose first measure, on coming into power I am assured will be to meet your wishes on all questions now open between the two countries.

I would instruct Mr. Everett to demand of Sir Robert Peel an avowal of his policy in relation to Texas, and remonstrate agt the attempt to establish in Texas a refuge for robbers & runaway slaves. If his answer on this point is satisfactory I would invite this Govt to send a commission to negociate a treaty & to adjust the question of the Oregon Territory. I would not think of surrendering anything south of Lat. 49 except it be to give the navigation of the Columbia River. I beg you to read the speeches in Parliament & the proceedings in the Antislavery Convention in relation to Texas and to run-away slaves and to take bold and decided measures on them and I assure you that you will have the party, who must soon come into power here with you. I have prepared some of the most influential of them to expect a most decided tone on your part and to second your movements.

DUFF GREEN TO THE BOSTON POST

London, September 18, 1843 [40]

[The letter opens with an account by Green of his mission of 1841–2 for Tyler, the purpose of which was to obtain from the British government an agreement to enter into a negotiation for a reciprocal lowering of Anglo-American tariffs. It describes at length the obstacles raised by the Reverend Joshua Leavitt, a New England abolitionist and editor of the *Emancipator,* who was a delegate, in 1843, to the convention in London of the British and Foreign Anti-Slavery Society. The bulk of the letter is devoted to the tariff issue, but it closes with the central theme of Green's thought: that the abolitionist societies of the United States and England are in league with each other to destroy slavery throughout the world, which is the aim also of the British government.]

I have said that I would not have noticed Mr. Leavitt's statements were he not the agent of the Abolition Society. I have obtained a mass of interesting facts and documents in connection with this subject, and I too will

---

[39] The London *Times* published in its commercial columns on September 1, 1843, extracts from the Upshur and Calhoun letters to Duff Green urging reciprocal lowering of Anglo-American tariffs.

[40] Boston *Post*, October 10, 1843. The letter was also published in the New York *Herald* (October 12, 1843), and in *Niles' Register*, 65 (October 21, 1843), 123. The sentiments of the letter are echoed in an approving editorial in the *Madisonian* of November 15, 1843.

have something to say to the American people. That there are many pious, philanthropic persons belonging to these societies, both in the United States and in England, I do not dispute, but it is now of easy demonstration, that sympathy for the black man is but a pretence for plundering and oppressing the white, and that that which is most to be apprehended from the American Abolition Society is, that acting upon public opinion in England, they may induce this government to persevere in a system of measures having for their object the substitution of the products of the labor of their East India subjects for that of the slave labor of America, until we are brought into collision, or until the war of material interests shall have progressed so far as greatly to increase the difficulties, if not to render it impracticable to place the commerce and intercourse between the two countries on that favorable basis which might otherwise be, at this time, so readily accomplished.

Sir Robert Peel folds his arms, and says, let us make no arrangement now, and why not? because, says he:

"It is impossible to look to the discussions in the United States of America, and especially to the conflicts between the northern and southern states, without seeing that slavery in that nation stood on a precarious footing. Some from humane and benevolent motives—some on account of interested fears, begin to look at the great example we have set, and also begin to look at the consequences which may result from that example nearer home." [41]

He is urged to repeal the duty on slave-grown sugar. He says no, we cannot compete with slave possessing countries, but continue to pay these duties a little longer, and then Cuba, Brazil, and even the United States, will abolish slavery—and what then? Why, as the only reason why the East Indies cannot drive Cuba, Brazil, and the United States out of the market is, that the East India planter cannot compete with slave labor, it follows, as a matter of course, that when slavery is also abolished in Cuba, Brazil, and the United States, as India has a redundant population, labor will then be cheaper in India, and that then all the world will be dependent upon England for supplies of sugar, coffee, and cotton, produced by the cheaper labor of India, and purchased in exchange of her manufactures, in consequence of her legislative control over the India market.

Who can be surprised that, Sir Robert Peel and other distinguished English statesmen entertain such opinions when we hear the speeches of Mr. Adams in Congress, and when this venerable but deluded man calls upon the British government to exert its influence to abolish slavery in Texas, with an assurance that, this being done, slavery will soon cease to exist in the United States and all over the world?

I have conceived it to be my duty to go thus into detail, because this government is in a crisis, and because I verily believe that the obstacle which now most impedes the progress of free trade in this country, is the hope that slavery will be abolished in the United States at a very early day, and that then England will again, through her monopoly of the East India market, be enabled to levy contributions on all other civilized nations. It will be seen,

[41] For the quotation from Peel see *Hansard's,* 3rd ser., 63 (May–June, 1842), 1224. Green's rendition is a loose one.

that so long as this belief prevails, we have no further concessions to expect. Am I asked, why then have the concessions already granted, been given? The answer is, that they are part of her colonial system, and are against, and not in favor, of the United States.[42]

One word more, and I have done. You will remember that I wrote to you, in advance of Lord Ashburton's mission, that the real point of contention was the north-western boundary.[43] Mr. Leavitt knows that the Oregon and right of search questions are New England questions. They are questions affecting the property and the lives of our hardy sailors, and of them almost exclusively. He knows, or he ought to know, that there is great cause to fear that England never will yield her claims, and we certainly will not relinquish our rights in the Pacific. If we are to have war with England it will be because we have first permitted her to re-establish herself in Texas—to have converted that Republic into a refuge for robbers and runaway slaves, and because she will believe that the abolitionists of the north will unite with her in a war upon the territories and property of the south, and thus accomplish her great purpose of universal dominion over the white man, under the pretence of emancipating the black.

I would call the attention of the American people to the fact that the parties in England which entertain these views are now standing with folded arms, looking at the progress of events—that no one knows what a day may bring forth; and I will add my earnest belief, that there never was a time when the condition of things in the old world so much deserved the attention of all those who wish to perpetuate the institutions and the liberty of the new.

We should remember that England is governed by her interest; that all parties here concur in the opinion that the restoration of her prosperity depends upon increasing the consumption of her manufactures. That while the Duke of Wellington and the Tory party believe that the surest and best means of doing this is to increase her colonial possessions, and monopolize their markets, the liberal and free trade party, who, disgusted with the Whigs, put the Tories into power, believe that once establish free trade, and then it will be for the interest of England that the colonies shall become independent nations, as soon as they are competent to govern themselves. That this party desire to see all other nations prosperous, because in proportion to their wealth and prosperity will be their ability to consume the products of British industry. Let us be true to ourselves—let us demonstrate that there is no foundation for Sir Robert Peel's belief, that Mr. Adams and his co-conspirators can dissolve the union or abolish slavery, and the good sense of this great people will coerce this government into making arrangements with us, that will so much identify their interests with ours as to terminate forever the intrigues which now threaten to disturb our peace. What would England care about our occupation of the Oregon, if she had free trade with us? But let her believe that we are torn by internal dissensions—that abolitionists

[42] Refers to the Canada Corn Act of 1843, which admitted American wheat (ground into Canadian flour) into British markets at a preferential tariff rate. See Frederick Merk, *The Oregon Question, Essays in Anglo-American Diplomacy and Politics* (Cambridge: Harvard University Press, 1967), p. 323.

[43] Compare *ibid.*, chap. 6.

are about to destroy the value of our slaves, and that they may soon expect to substitute the products of India for those of America, and it will be the interest of England to aid them, even by a war, in the accomplishment of that object. She has too much diplomatic tact to acknowledge her real purpose, because that might alarm the other European powers, who are to be the victims of her policy; and hence, she will keep the Oregon question open, to be used as the pretence on which hostilities are to commence. And this will be whenever their American allies, John Quincy Adams & Co., can satisfy them that their object, the abolition of American slavery, can be accomplished.

I am, respectfully,

ABEL P. UPSHUR
TO NATHANIEL BEVERLEY TUCKER

October 10, 1843 [44]

. . . I wish to talk with you about the annexation of Texas. That is *the* question of the day. In my view of it, the destinies of the country hang upon it. The union will not last ten years without it, & the preservation of peace among the nations will be impossible. I am sanguine in the belief that I can make the question so clear that even the Yankees will go for annexation. They are you know an "uncommon moral & religious people" & greatly opposed to the sin of slavery since they ceased to carry on the slave trade; but there is one point on which you may be sure of them, & that is, their *interest*. As I can show them that the annexation of Texas will be for the good of their commerce & manufactures, I shall probably have their support. If I can succeed in this matter, it will be something on which to retire to private life.

Very truly yours,

DUFF GREEN TO ABEL P. UPSHUR

London, October 17, 1843 [45]

[The letter opens with an account at considerable length of British party politics, with emphasis on the issues of free trade versus protectionism, British monopolies, the Irish problem, and the repeal of union with England.]

I know that a dictum of Washington's, suited to our infant condition, has induced our people to believe that we have no interest in progress of

[44] Tucker-Coleman Collection, Earl Gregg Swem Library, College of William and Mary, Williamsburg, Virginia.

[45] Copy in Calhoun Papers, Robert Muldrow Cooper Library, Clemson University, Clemson, South Carolina. A condensed version of the letter was written by Green to Calhoun the next day. This is published in A.H.A. *Report*, 1929, 188–90.

other nations. But we should remember that the infant of that day has grown into a powerful commercial nation, whose interests are diffused over every quarter of the globe, and that the purpose for which the federal Government was constituted was to protect those interests. You cannot look into an English newspaper that does not bear upon its face proofs that this great nation look to us as the only rivals whose competitions they have cause to fear. England feels that she depends upon her manufacturing supremacy for the maintenance of her relative position among the great nations of the world. The treaty with China opens to her new prospects, and she will be enabled to diminish the oppressive burden of her national debt if she can give activity to her manufacturing industry. A modification of the commercial systems of England and the United States which will enable them to consume the products of our agriculture & us to consume their manufactures, will identify our interests and make us deeply interested as the manufacturers of England themselves in every measure which may increase the consumption of the products of English manufacturing industry, or promote the wealth or prosperity of the mother country. When the material interests of England and the United States are thus consolidated we may confide in the friendship of British statesmen. Until this be done, we may expect them to be jealous of our growing strength and that who ever may be in power, their measures will be taken in reference to their interests. If we could have induced the Tory ministers to repeal their restrictive measures it would have been better for us first because they are now in power and we are compelled to look to them, and to them only for that measure,—and next because being the monopoly interest all concessions made by them may be considered as permanent. But failing to obtain from them such a modification of their tariff as will permit a fair exchange of the products of our labor for their manufactures, we are compelled to take our measures in reference to parties as they exist here.

This brings me to consider the bearing which the present struggle in this country necessarily has in our interest. By refering to the speeches of Mr. Baring and Mr. Pattison and the speeches of Mr. Cobden & Mr. Bright and the comment of the press on the canvass now progressing in London, you will see that the duty on Brazilian & Cuban sugar is a prominent question. I refer you to the comment of the Sunday Times in confirmation of what I have before written on the subject of the anti-slavery movement. It is now well understood that Tory sympathy for the negro is but another name for Tory oppression of the white labour of England and you may rest assured that all that is wanting to give the last blow to this humbug is for the Government of the United States to take a decided stand upon this subject. Not in favor of the slave trade, but in support of existing institutions—not in favor of slavery in the abstract—but against the impertinent interference of England in the domestic institutions of the United States, of Cuba & Brazil.

When it is palpable to all the world that under the maske of humanity to the black race she seeks to enslave the white—that under the pretence of opposition to slave labor she seeks to make all the world dependent upon her for the supply of sugar, coffee, rice, etc. I have before given you my views as to the British attempt to convert Texas into a refuge for runaway slaves and thieves. I would urge upon the Government that now is the time to make common cause with Brazil & Cuba, and that it becomes the present administration to exert themselves for the counteraction of the avowed determination of England to accomplish the abolition of slavery there. I have heard from an unquestioned source that France is about to indemnify the growers of Beetroot sugar, and that a treaty is now in progress if it is not already concluded whereby France stipulates to admit Brazilian sugars & other articles, & cotton will no doubt be included, Brazil admitting french manufactures at reduced rates of duty. I hope that you will not sleep over this question—that you will not fail to see in the position which England has assumed towards Brazil a conclusive argument why the United States & Brazil should act together against the insolent pretension of Sir Robert Peel that he is bound as the advocate of humanity to demand the emancipation of the slaves of Brazil.

I have just seen an intelligent friend who is just returned from a tour through Scotland and he tells me that all Scotland to a man are prepared to sustain *free trade*—that all parties there, Whig and Tory, demand an abrogation of the duty on sugar—that they ridicule and denounce the pretence of humanity on which Sir Robert Peel and his partisans pretend to justify it, and that if our Government act with firmness & especially if they ask Sir Robert to send Commissioners to the U.S. to adjust the boundary and confer on the subject of the Tariff, and he refuses as they believe he will, it will enable those who desire to identify the interests of the two countries, when they come into power, as come they soon must do, to arrange all matters pending between us on more favorable terms.

Not having heard from you I cannot know what you have done because for reasons which I will explain to you I have not conversed with Mr. Everett on his instructions from home,[46] but I am so deeply impressed with the importance of the measure, whether I consider it in reference to the state of parties at home or here, that I must renew my entreaty to you to instruct Mr. Everett to invite this Government to send a Commission to Washington charged with the settlement of the N. Western Boundary as well as the adjustment of the tariff. There is a time for all things and there never was a time more favorable to the United States than the present for the settlement of these questions, and to neglect to improve the occasion will be a culpable neglect of a most solemn duty.

I have much to say to you in confirmation of these views which is reserved until I see you personally which I hope will be in a few weeks after you receive this.

Your sincere friend,

[46] The reasons for Green's reticence with Everett are explained by Everett in a letter to Upshur of November 27, 1843, which appears in the Documents.

•

Adams, Address, October 21, 1843

JOHN QUINCY ADAMS

Address of the Hon. J. Q. Adams, to his Constituents
of the Eighth Congressional District, at Dedham, October 21, 1843 [47]

Friends and Fellow Citizens, of the County of Norfolk, and my Constituents of the 8th Congressional District of Massachusetts:

On the 17th of September of the last year, I had the honour of addressing, at Braintree, my then Constituents of the 12th Congressional District of Massachusetts.

It was at the close of ten years of service to them in the House of Representatives of the United States. They had passed resolutions warmly approving the whole course of my conduct as their Representative, and had invited me to meet and address them, and exchange with them mutual friendly salutations on the dissolution of the relations which, for ten years, the whole term of their political existence, had subsisted between them and me.

The occasion then called for a rapid review of the principal events which had occurred, and of the principal subjects which had been agitated in the Congress of the Union, during the period of my public service in the House, and in which I had taken a highly responsible part. Some explanation of my conduct upon certain important questions, were then seasonable; and it was especially proper that I should justify myself for the decided opposition that I had sustained against the measures of the present Administration, which had signalized the career of the individual cast, by an untoward and melancholy accident, into the Chair once occupied by George Washington, as the Chief Magistrate of this Nation. (Applause)

Shortly after this final and gratifying interview with my former Constituents was held, a new election took place of members to the popular branch of the National Legislature, under another enumeration of the People, and a new apportionment for their representation in the National Assembly of the Union. By this new apportionment, one of those *compromises,* in which the wisdom of the plantation has always succeeded in overreaching the simplicity and freedom of the farm, actually curtailed the numerical force of this Commonwealth in the National House of Representatives, to the amount of one sixth part. Instead of 12 members in a House of 242, you have now but 10 in a House of 223. How this compromise was effected, it behooves me not now to speak; but if any one of you is curious to know, I advise him to look over the lists of yeas and nays in both Houses, upon every question of the standard number, from the third day of May, 1842, when the Apportionment Bill first passed the House of Representatives, with a standard number of 50,179 persons for one Representative, to the seventeenth of June of the same year, when the House concurred in an amendment of the Senate, striking out the number 50,179, and inserting the number 70,680 in its stead, and passed the bill with this last number. Compare the two sets of yeas and nays with each other, and you will find the effect of a *compromise.* And if you will then inquire what is the effect this will have upon the

[47] From the Boston *Atlas,* October 26, 1843.

representation of the North and of the South, you will perceive how much sharper an accountant is the overseer of a plantation than his brother Jonathan of the farm. (Applause) [48]

Under this compromise, Massachusetts has lost two of her members in the House. She has now but ten—and the compromise by which this was accomplished, may serve as a sample of all the compromises between the Yankee farmer and the overseer. Under the New Apportionment, the number of constituents to each Representative was increased from 47,300 to 70,680. The District in which I resided was almost entirely changed. Only 11 towns out of the 24 composing the late 12th Congressional District, form now a part of the 8th; 19 towns are added to them, heretofore belonging to other Districts; and of my present Constituents, not more than one third have ever been represented in the House by me before.

But the inhabitants of the whole County of Norfolk are embraced in the District, the people of which have been pleased to charge me with the duty of representing them in the popular branch of the National Legislature; and a Convention of the Whigs of the County, entitled to all my respect, by the flattering resolution which has here been read, have manifested a desire that I would meet them at this time and place, and address them on subjects of National concernment, and of special interest to them. I could not hesitate for a moment to comply with their request; but the inhabitants of four towns in the County of Plymouth, and of five in the County of Middlesex, forming also a part of the District whose interests have, by their suffrages, been committed to my charge in the Representative Hall, I have desired to be honored with the presence of as many of them as might suit their convenience and their inclination, and to address them all as my Constituents, whether by their votes, or as my political adversaries—that all may know my opinions upon topics interesting to them all. . . .

The People—the *one* People of the United States—speaking in their own name, declared in the preamble to their Constitution, that it was ordained and established by themselves, "in order to form a more perfect union, establish justice, ensure domestic tranquillity, provide for the common defence, promote the general welfare, and secure the blessings of liberty to themselves and their posterity." . . .

Liberty, then, is the vital principle—the soul of the North American confederated Nation; and in so far as any portion of their Government, or of their policy, tends to impair or to entrench upon the principle of Liberty they are contrary to the nature of the North American People—self-convicting of falsehood and hypocrisy, and daring defiance to the laws of their God.

And yet they nourished in their bosom the God-defying institution of

[48] The figures given by Adams are reliable for the new apportionment of Representatives, and his view, that congressional voting on it was sectional, is substantially correct. Southern representation in the House was less affected by increases in the "standard number" than was Northern representation, because of the three-fifths compromise. The Senate, where the South had more power, desired and won a larger increase in numbers per representative than that originally proposed in the House. The Senate vote was: slaveholding states, eighteen ayes, four nays (three from border states); nonslaveholding states, twelve ayes, ten nays. *Congressional Globe,* 27 Cong., 2 sess., 472, 630, 649. See also *U.S. Statutes at Large,* V (1836–45), 491.

slavery! And yet, in this Constitution, ordained and established to secure to their posterity the blessings of Liberty, while they avoided with fastidious scruples of purity, every expression which might seem to acknowledge, even by implication, the lawfulness of Slavery, they made a compact with Lucifer, not only by the clandestine submission to slavery but by contaminating the Constitution itself, with an enormous representation of property acquired by crime, under the name of persons.

Fellow Citizens, let me not be misunderstood.

Far be it from me to charge fraud, falsehood, or hypocrisy, either upon the People of the United States, or upon any member of that Convention over which George Washington presided, and of which Benjamin Franklin was a member. The ardent aspirations of both those men for the abolition of slavery throughout the world, are attested by multiplied evidence under their own hands.

I charge no fraud or falsehood upon them or any of their associates. The African slave-trade was then, though odious, everywhere lawful.

And although more odious in this Union than in any other part of the world, yet by one of those *compromises* to which I have already alluded, for the space of twenty years from that time, that odious traffic was authorized by that very constitution. Twenty years of time was required for the slave holder to make up his mind to practice the principles of virtue and liberty. Twenty years they were to be indulged in the practice of those crimes, upon condition that at the end of that time they would turn themselves to virtue and to freedom. In this, there was no fraud. . . .

Neither was there any intention of fraud in that provision of the constitution which gives to property, and that an odious property, a representation in our National Councils, to the exclusion of all other property—an enormous representation, which controls the whole policy of the country. But yet, it was fraudulent, because under the name of a representation of *persons,* it was a representation of *property.* . . .

Now, I say, Fellow Citizens, that never was this calculated upon by your Representatives—how the effect of it is to be guarded against, I will not now undertake to say—but I call your attention to the effect of it upon you and your interests. You have ten Representatives of the persons in this Commonwealth, you have no representation of property. Your property, what you have virtuously and honestly acquired, is excluded, while the owner of the slave is not only represented, as you are, in his person, but also in the persons of his slaves. Does the slave give his vote? No. Who gives the vote? The owner of the slave. He has a vote then for himself, and three votes for every five of the slaves of which he is the owner. And, in considering this subject in its effects and consequences, we see twelve thousand millions of dollars represented by ninety members—where *you* have ten— *Slavery* has ninety members, and all these ninety are bound together by ties of such a nature, they are all the representatives of one person; they are the representatives of that property.

I ask you, Fellow Citizens, to reflect upon this; in the first place— in point of principle. If there be an objection against property being represented, how strong must be that objection, to property of such a character. If there be a *propriety* in admitting a representation of property, upon what ground is it that your house and land, your shop and merchandise, should not be represented as well as slave property in the Councils of the Nation? And experience has shown, that that representation is of the mass of those who, on every question, in which the interests of the country are concerned, vote together. And how think you it is possible in this state of things that right and justice can prevail. Out of *two hundred twenty-three members* here are *ninety* Representatives of that property, all combined together, and all going together.

I beg that it may be understood that I am not now speaking as an abolitionist. I do not put it upon the question of the propriety or justice of the abolition of slavery, but upon the ground of your equal rights, in the constitution of the United States, and in the representation of them in the legislative body.

The same inequality operates against you in the election of President and Vice President. The electoral college is founded upon the same principle. And, consequently, the chance of those who represent freemen, to be elected President of the United States, to that of those who hold slaves, is about as one to one hundred.

It is then in a political aspect, and in its aspect as connected with the original primitive principles of government, that I speak to you of this provision in the Constitution of the United States. The *first* of these consequences is that the representation of slavery in Congress refuse to hear all petitions for any change in this respect, and the consequence has shown itself now for the space of eight years. There was not this operation in the early part of the existence of the Constitution—the Congress then listened to petitions for the abolition of slavery, particularly in the District of Columbia; but when the danger of the exclusion of the representation of this species of property commenced, the jealousy of that body discovered itself; and the means of preventing was the exclusion of petitions. And how did this operate upon you? It operated so as to exclude the right of petition from the free States only, for all the petitions upon this subject came from them. . . .

All these consequences have followed, and you are now labouring under them, for should any of you be disposed to petition for the abolition of slavery, your petition would not be received. This is the first consequence of this representation of property.

In the second place, that representation constitutes an aristocracy or rather an oligarchy. Your country is no longer a democracy, it is no longer even a republic—it is a government of 2 or 300,000 holders of slaves, to the utter exclusion of the remaining part, and all the population of the other States in the Union.

And the wrong is as great upon the mass of the population of the slave-holding States themselves, as upon the free States. It has been shown that there are not more than 300,000 individuals who own slaves, in ten or twelve of the United States, and that these possess the power, which elects 90 representatives in the General Congress, and in the Electoral College, to the exclusion and wrong not only of all the people of the free States, but of a majority of the people themselves in their own States. For who has the slave property? It is of course possessed only by the rich—the poor hold none—they are hardly masters of themselves—and the proportion of the poor in numbers to that of the rich owners of slaves in the slave States, is as ten to one. In Virginia, say, there are a million of inhabitants, and out of that million there are eight hundred thousand who own no slaves. There are perhaps two hundred thousand, who own slaves; and then the consequence is that these possess a representation of property, to the utter exclusion of the property of the rest. . . .

But it is not only in suppression of the right of petition, that the representation of slave property operates in the Councils of the Nation.

[Adams passes to a long account of legislation adopted in South Carolina and other slave states forbidding entrance into their ports of free Negroes, American or foreign, under heavy penalty—legislation pronounced unconstitutional by Judge William Johnson of the Supreme Court as interference with commerce and commercial conventions, yet persisted in by these states. Adams likens this to the nullification of the federal tariff law.]

Another of the consequences of the property representation is, the project which has been conceived in the Southern States for the annexation of Texas to the Union. This is a subject which has been before you now for some years. During the Presidency of Mr. Van Buren, a formal application was made to the Government of the United States, by the Republic of Texas, for this annexation. At that time the people of the United States were not ready for the measure. They saw all the consequences which they must expect from that measure, if it should be adopted. They saw that, in connection with that principle of double representation for the slaveholders' convenience, it was such that they could not submit to it. At that time the subject occasioned so much alarm that after due consideration, Mr. Van Buren decided that the annexation could not take place; but there was a very strong disposition evinced among all the slaveholders to admit the application, and to annex the Republic of Texas to the United States. And it is now repeated, at the end of six years, and it is expected that it will be brought up the very next session. Now there is a large party at the South in favour of it. Within the last two or three days, a letter has been published from a distinguished citizen of Virginia, insisting upon the necessity of it, in order to save the institution of Slavery. I have here in my hand a letter which was published in the Boston Morning Post written by a man by the name of Duff Green (Laughter). I shall make some remarks upon it, in order to convince you that I am not such a conspirator and traitor as he represents me in this letter.

I have told you that I meant to address all my constituents here present, whether they be those who favor my opinions, or whether they be my adversaries.

I should be glad if it were in my power to address you without reference to any of the party distinctions which exist in this Commonwealth, but in the consideration which I ask of you to certain parts of this letter, it is impossible for me to forego the advertisement to you of the manner in which it was introduced in the Post. It appears to be a letter to a portion, at least, of what is called the Democracy of the Country—to at least one detachment of it. The paper in which this letter appears professes to be the representative, however, of the Democracy, and I understand the publication of it to be a recommendation of the whole substance of the letter to the consideration of the people, as if it were good counsel that was given them, and I do understand the Editor of the Post, in publishing it, to assume, on the part of the Democratic party in this portion of the country, the principles contained in that letter, and most especially that in reference to Texas. Now I had flattered myself that this was not the theory of the Democrats, in this part of the country—that they were as unwilling to have the burden of that Republic tacked to the United States, with all its slaves, and all its slavery, as the most inveterate Whigs in the country;—that they considered it as a sort of a reproach to have it intimated to them that they were in favor of this annexation; or that they were in favor of the slave interest, or the institution of slavery itself.

Under these circumstances, there are two or three passages with which I hope not to detain you too long. Mr. Leavitt, the Editor of the Emancipator, states, that Duff Green has been a sort of irregular, informal agent of our Government for the last five or six months. He is, in fact, the actual agent of the slave interest in this Country. He is in England, in a sort of official character, as the representative of the slave-holding portion of the community. How he is there, it is perhaps unnecessary to inquire; but in this letter he states, that the motive of his being there, and the manner in which he is, are known to the President of the United States, and that he had the authority of the President of the United States to do what he had done there. And what has he done? He has put himself in communication with the British Government, and has held correspondence with the ministers of her Majesty for two years; and he has endeavored to persuade them, that a part of his policy would be for the interest of their Country and of his Country; and this appears to be the purport of the letter. The material part of this letter to me, therefore, is the light in which he considers any thing and every thing which has a tendency towards the abolition of slavery. With "treason" and "conspiracy" among the rest, he has those very words—"personally I respect the man." He concludes the letter with "Let us be true to ourselves; let us demonstrate that there is no foundation for Sir Robert Peel's belief, that Mr. Adams and his *co-conspirators* can dissolve the Union, or abolish slavery."

This is an argument addressed to the people of the United States, but addressed most especially to the people of the Commonwealth of Massachusetts,—being addressed to the Editor of the Morning Post (laughter) and to him this gentleman, the representative of slavery, and the representative of Great Britain, says, "Let *us* be true to *ourselves,* (laughter); let *us* demonstrate that there is no foundation for the belief that Mr Adams and his *co-conspirators* can dissolve the Union or abolish slavery, and the good sense of this great people will coerce this government into making arrangements with us that will so much identify their interest with ours as to terminate forever the intrigues which now threaten to disturb our peace." . . .

He [Green] alludes to the Oregon question and the right of search as New England questions—as questions affecting the *property and the lives of our hardy sailors*. New England is largely engaged in commerce, and the question of the right of search might be supposed to have some bearing upon her, although it is my belief that it is altogether a humbug. But how, in God's name, the Oregon question can have anything to do with the property and the lives of our hardy sailors, and of them almost exclusively, is what Duff Green must explain for himself. Yes, he wants to make the Oregon a New England question, and to tell the people of New England, that if they abolish slavery in the South, a great party will rise up with great power in India, which will completely destroy all other interests. The argument, it seems to me, is worth reading, but I have not time to refute it.

Fellow Citizens: I did intend to say something more upon these subjects to you—to have said something about a bank, but I am compelled unwillingly to regard that "as an obsolete idea." The question about the Tariff and the Sub-Treasury will probably be very interesting at the approaching session of Congress, and then your interest will be somewhat implicated. I would say something upon these, but I have not time. But after all I wish you to understand, as my feelings, that the question of Slavery, and most particularly the question about the domination of the slave representation, which overburdens us all, is the great question on which your interests are concerned, in the government of the United States. . . .

In respect to the abolition of slavery: The principle which pervades the whole of Duff Green's letter, that any opinion favorable to the abolition of slavery is a conspiracy, has settled the slave question in Congress, and this is what you are told continually is a conspiracy, and a treason. It was upon that ground that the charge was brought against *me* of treason. This was the charge brought against me for which I was tried—treason and conspiracy— in what? Why, in entertaining the opinion that it would be well for the world if slavery were abolished. Well this is held up, and they refuse to hear any thing on the subject: That is the reason why they refuse to receive petitions. Congress will hear nothing about it.

As to the abolition of slavery, it is known that I have declared, time after time, that I would not vote in Congress for the abolition of slavery in the District of Columbia, because it has been, and is my opinion, that when the abolition takes place, it should be without doing injustice to any one,— it is, that Congress have no power to take away the slaves from those people in the District of Columbia who now hold them. You may call them property acquired by crime. But, however acquired, a sanction has been given to it by the Constitution, and I consider their protection as a part of the compact which I have sworn to fulfill. But if the abolition of slavery in the District of Columbia were a political matter, no man has a more clear and decided opinion that it should be abolished, than I have.[49]

[49] This position of Adams, clearly stated to his constituents, is well set forth by S. F. Bemis in his *John Quincy Adams and The Union* (New York: Alfred A. Knopf, 1956), pp. 351, 380–2.

I will read to you the resolutions which I offered upon the subject, in the House of Representatives, on the 21st of February, 1839:

Of course my resolutions were not received.

In these, I proposed the total abolition of slavery, from and after the fourth day of July, 1842, as an amendment to the Constitution of the United States, regularly and formally. In the second place I proposed that, on and after that day, no children should be born slaves. In doing this I copied actually from the law of the State of New Jersey—Slavery having been abolished in that State precisely after that form.

ABEL P. UPSHUR
TO NATHANIEL BEVERLEY TUCKER

October 26, 1843 [50]

I am engaged in settling the Oregon boundary question—imprudently forced upon me prematurely—& in procuring the annexation of Texas to the Union. This last is the great object of my ambition. I do not care to control any measure of policy except this; & I have reason to believe that no person but myself can control it. Perhaps I may fail, but if I retire from the cabinet no other man can succeed. *Therefore I stay.* Is it not my duty to do so? Is there any thing in my present position identified as I seek to be & probably am, only with great measures, which can involve me in the odium which awaits this administration? I hope not, & I believe not. Suppose then, that after these great objects shall have been accomplished, or shall have failed, I should choose to go to France or to England? In the present condition of our affairs Southern men ought to be at both these courts, & particularly the latter. The public interest requires it, & no man who is qualified for the station ought to refuse it. Besides, why should such a station be refused, merely because an obnoxious President confers it? I act upon the principle that public offices belong to the public a[nd] not to the functionary who bestows them. Would not this principle be violated by a refusal to accept merely because the tender was made by a particular individual? It seems to me that this would be an implied acknowledgement that the office belonged to that individual.

I confess also, that I should desire such a certificate from the *Senate,* that I had done nothing unworthy of the high stations which I had filled. I am not much afraid of being accused either of avarice or improper ambition. As to the first, I certainly should make no money by a mission either to England or France & as to the second, I already hold a higher station. I acknowledge therefore that I do not perceive that my standing before the public would be committed by the acceptance of a foreign mission; however, I think it more than probable that the alternative will never be presented to me; & most certainly I shall do nothing to invite such an offer.

Very truly yours,

[50] Tucker-Coleman Collection, College of William and Mary.

MADISONIAN

October 30, 1843 [51]

WHITE SLAVERY

It is well known that the condition of the poorer classes of the population, in any part of Europe, even the freest, is worse in every respect than that of our negro slaves. In Great Britain, where more freedom prevails, nominally at least, than elsewhere in Europe, their condition is even worse than in Russia, under the most despotic Government; and so it must necessarily be, wherever a moneyed oligarchy has sway, no matter by what name the Government be called, or how free the institutions may be in theory. It is not the phraseology of a Constitution or laws which gives liberty or equality, but the manner in which they are administered; and if wealth influences the administration of them, the poorer classes must necessarily be reduced to the condition of slaves, and the bitterness of their slavery in a country of homogeneous population, is aggravated by the reflection that they are made of the same clay, of the same feelings and faculties as their more fortunate oppressors. Nature has done nothing to reconcile them to their condition, by showing them a cause and necessity for it.

In the thickly settled parts of our non-slave holding States, the condition of the poorer class of population is fast assimilating itself to that of the servile class in Europe. Already they are but hewers of wood and drawers of water to their wealthier brethren: they are employed as menials and lacqueys, and sometimes even dressed in livery—wait behind chairs, clean boots, and polish knives. Every newspaper teems with evidences of the wretched condition of this class of the population of both sexes, in the densely peopled sections of the North. Accounts of suicide from despair, and even of death from want, are common; and of women, and delicate young girls, laboring from daybreak till midnight, for the bare means of sustenance, grudgingly afforded them as a boon by their wealthy and tyrannical employers. It is true that in the eyes of the law they are free, and on an equality with the highest: and Mr. Biddle's white *valet de chambre* or Mr. John Quincy Adams' Swiss body-guard, have as many rights, in theory, as their "bosses." So in England, the law is open to every man; but it was well replied, that it was open as the London Tavern was—to those who could pay for it.

Any man who has stood upon the levee at New Orleans and been hustled about by the brawny athletic negroes, with their merry faces and their loud deep laugh, chattering incessantly, and with as little of slavery in their mien and bearing as a Black-Foot of Saskatchawan, must have thought to himself that however lamentable their condition might be in theory, it agreed most admirably with them in practice. Finer specimens of the physical man, of the same race, could hardly be found on the plains of Bambouk, or in the forests of Sangara; and we doubt whether intercourse with the whites has diminished the mental powers of the race.

[51] Editorial in the *Madisonian*, October 30, 1843.

But one who has beheld the unhappy children of poverty who infest the wharves of a populous Northern city, haggard and spiritless, watching deferentially the countenances of nabob merchants or dandy clerks and supplicating their fellow man for "leave to toil," must have felt his cheek burn, and have thought that abolitionists might find a wide field for the exercise of practical democracy and philanthropy, without travelling to the South in search of it.

We have been led to these reflections by accidentally reading in a Northern print the following notice of a recent occurrence, which we venture to assert cannot be paralleled by any thing in the annals of Southern slavery. We think it becomes the people among whom such things can occur, to be a little more moderate in their invectives against slave-holders, and to draw a little less frequently upon their imagination for horrors in the South, when the reality can furnish them such thrilling scenes of atrocity at home.

> HORRIBLE ATROCITY.—We learn, from the Exeter (N.H.) News Letter, that on Tuesday last, 17th instant, Alfred Hill was arrested on a complaint against him for the violation and murder of a child not 9 years old, whom, but a few weeks before, he had taken from the poor house in Newmarket. He was carried before James H. Chapman, Esq., of Newmarket, for examination. It appeared in evidence that the deceased was 8 years old last March, and was in good health and in the bloom of early youth when she was taken into the family of the respondent. She soon began to fail and falter, and appeared to be treated with great severity. Hill had been seen to beat her with an ox goad, and her screams were repeatedly heard by night and by day. She died on Friday morning, the 22d ult. A post-mortem examination took place from which it was evident that the child had been brutally violated in a manner too horrible to relate, and her body most cruelly lacerated. Although there was no direct evidence against Hill, the circumstances were so strong against him that he was committed to jail to await the action of the grand jury in February next.—*Phil. Chronicle.*

A young and delicate girl, perhaps left an orphan by unfortunate but respectable parents, sent to the work-house, and taken thence to serve as a menial. A monster "had been *seen* to beat her with an ox-goad, and her screams were *repeatedly heard by night and by day*," yet not one *practical* philanthropist could be found to hurry to her rescue, or even appeal to the laws in her behalf!

If the abolitionists, with all their vigilance, could find the slightest foundation in fact upon which to charge a Southern slave-holder with the commission of such infernal cruelty, they would ring the charges upon it for a year, have prints engraved representing a child upon its knees, with its little hands uplifted, and a brute in human form about to beat out its brains with an ox-goad; and probably a session of the World's [Anti-Slavery] Convention would be called in London to take the matter into consideration: yet where white slavery prevails, such occurrences are hardly a nine day's wonder.

It is in this wretched condition, exposed to such outrages, that pretended philanthropists and lovers of freedom, would leave fellow beings of their own race, while they affect a hypocritical zeal for ameliorating the condition of negro slaves. Their philanthropy, like that of Mr. John Quincy Adams, is eager to precipitate the country into the horrors of a civil and servile war; their love of freedom would remove the negro from the place to which fate has destined him, and Nature has admirably fitted him, and compel the white man to fill the void. They will pet and pamper negroes, as they would parrots or lap dogs, while they would have white men, standing behind their chairs, to run at their beck and bidding, and shrink from their frown. They seek, in the name of Freedom, and even of Religion, to crush the spirit of Democracy, in order that they may establish and consolidate an Aristocracy.

MADISONIAN

October 31, 1843 [52]

HOW DOES THE SLAVE LABOR OF THE SOUTH
AFFECT THE FREE LABOR OF THE NORTH?

Having shown the Abolition fanatics—the self-styled philanthropists—that there was an ample field on which to exercise real benevolence—if, indeed, they have any—at home, among the poor and suffering class of their own color, we will now speak, in a political point of view, of the necessity of the non-interference of one section of the Union with the domestic arrangements of another.

It cannot be denied or concealed that there is a set of men in the country who are always attempting to create a spirit of dissatisfaction among the inhabitants of the different States, and who seem to be bent upon the accomplishment of the greatest possible mischief. One of the most fruitful themes on which they dwell, is that which stands at the head of this article. They are aware that the Constitution was designed to put at rest all disputes upon the subject of taxation and representation by settling it on the basis of what was considered a fair compromise; and knowing this, they seek to assail the whole structure, and thereby to break up the Union, by instilling unfounded and unreasonable prejudices in the minds of the People.

Mr. Adams is the acknowledged leader in this work of contemplated destruction; he raves most loudly at the representation of three-fifths of the labor of the South, while the whole labor of the North, without abatement, is represented. He talks at one moment of property being represented at the South, and in the next he delivers an episode on the rights of man, and elevates the blacks to an equality with the whites. He would not abolish slavery in the District of Columbia, because he would not break the compact between the States; and yet he does everything in his power to undermine that compact by enlisting a host of prejudices against it.

But, as we have said, the most fruitful theme of invective is to be found in the injurious effect which is ascribed to the competition between the free

---

[52] Editorial in the *Madisonian*, October 31, 1843.

labor of the North and the slave labor of the South. Now we cannot understand how this competition exists. The two classes of labor are directed to objects entirely different; and instead of coming in competition, they come in direct aid of each other. The North cannot raise sugar, cotton, rice, or, to any great extent, tobacco; these articles require for their production a fervid and glowing sun, which is given to the South and denied to the North, and in their production there can exist no rivalry or competition. The North is chiefly dependent on manufactures and their carrying trade; and while the culture of the soil continues to be profitable, we fancy the slave-holding States can have no inducement to enter into competition with the North. No farmer would think of building ships, or manning them with his negroes to navigate distant regions of the earth; and thus an absolute monopoly is given to the free States, as they are called, in the most extensive carrying trade that any other People, save those of Great Britain, ever possessed. The whole country South, as well as North, has come up to the task of protecting this great monopoly; discriminations almost endless in their character, exist in favor of American shipping, which operate exclusively to the advantage of the North. It is almost impossible to estimate the value of this great source of wealth to the North. When Holland possessed but a tithe of it in magnitude, she was the most powerful nation in the world. England has attained her formidable position by means of her shipping interest— and the carrying trade of the North has enriched a sterile soil, and caused smiling villages to spring up all over the face of the land. Where shall we go to shake hands with the millionaires—where, but to the cities of the North?

The labor of the South produces aliment for the labor of the North; the very food on which it feeds, and the source of its prosperity and power. Let a permanent blight pass over the fields of the South, and the North would feel it in every department of her industry. The labor of the South in conflict with the labor of the North! The idea is perfectly ridiculous. No; there is no conflict, no rivalry. The South raises the material which the North either exports in the raw state, or manufactures for the supply of all nations. Thus the interests of both are advanced; and those fanatics who would attempt to raise up enmities between them are traitors in disguise. The Union is necessary to both; and instead of encouraging feuds and drawing geographical lines between them, the highest duty of the patriot is to cause them to look only to the glory of their great country, and to the perpetuity of the most noble Republic the world has ever known.

MADISONIAN

November 15, 1843 [53]

NATIONAL POLICY

In Europe . . . a cession of territory is considered the last sad alternative of diplomacy. . . . With us, territory is not a matter of much importance, so far as the actual fruits of the soil are concerned; we have enough of it and

[53] Editorial in the *Madisonian,* November 15, 1843.

to spare, perhaps for ages to come; but when the question arises whether a certain tract of territory shall be occupied and peopled by us and our posterity, or by those likely to become our enemies, it is a question touching both the welfare and honor of the nation, and a surrender of our just pretensions implies a disgraceful deficiency in intelligence or spirit. . . .

The progress of Great Britain to almost universal domination has been the effect of a systematic plan of national aggrandizement, persevering, inexorably pursued. Any man who compares the acts of Great Britain with her professions; who can reckon up her possessions, and state the manner in which she acquired them; who knows the condition of the people in her Asiatic colonies, and of the great mass of her population at home, must be simple indeed to give a moment's credit to her professions of philanthropy, Christianity, or national honor, and blind not to see that her sole aim is national aggrandizement at any expense of principle whatever. If there were any truth or sincerity to her professions, her philanthropy would commence at home.

This systematic and selfish policy of Great Britain is the real and governing motive in all her intercourse with foreign nations; and in nothing will it appear more obvious to those who choose to reflect upon it than in the active part which she has taken as a nation and among nations, on the subject of negro slavery. It certainly cannot be ignorance which induces her to turn away from the imploring looks and supplications of her pauper population, at home, dying by hundreds of famine, and spend her time in contriving projects for relieving the imaginary distresses of beings of another race in remote quarters of the globe. . . . She must have a rational purpose and object; and every thing tends to show that her object is to attack the existence of our Government, and our Union, through the institution of slavery in the Southern States.

Her motive in this attack is no less obvious than the mode of it. The existence of our Union under a Republican government is no longer compatible with the safety of her Oligarchy. The constant intercourse between the two nations . . . , the effects of steam navigation in shortening the time of transit . . . has placed us in dangerous proximity with Great Britain, and she has not been slow in perceiving and taking measures to remedy the dangers of it. She has been steadily and cautiously preparing the means of attack upon our weakest point, and availing herself, among other aids, of the blind fanaticism, and want of patriotism, which she has found within our own borders.

The argument by which some endeavor to lull themselves into security . . . against the designs of the British government, that Great Britain has no inducement to provoke a war with us, as her commerce would suffer . . . is wholly fallacious. She would probably have very little reluctance in promoting dissensions or civil war among ourselves. That would, perhaps, answer her purpose far better than a war with us. But rather than renounce her purpose, a purpose . . . which she conceives necessary to the continuance . . . of her present government—she might readily undertake all the hazards, and endure all the commercial losses incident to a direct war.

MADISONIAN

November 16, 1843 [54]

GREAT BRITAIN AND TEXAS

It is urged, by those who are anxious to exculpate the British Government from the imputation of selfish or sinister designs, in its persevering and systematic agitation of the subject of negro slavery, that it is a philanthropic movement, forced on the Government by public opinion at home. This may appear credible to those who are unacquainted with the constitution of that Government; but to those who are aware of its strength, and the ease and impunity with which it may disregard or thwart any manifestation of popular opinion adverse to its designs or its settled policy, the idea is preposterous. The absurdity of it will be obvious to those who reflect how little influence the feelings and opinions of the People of Great Britain on the subject of their restrictive system—a matter of immediate and vital importance to the population—has had upon the policy of their Government.

That there is a strong, and even morbid feeling in Great Britain on the subject of negro slavery, is undeniable. It originated in the atrocious extent to which British subjects, under the active encouragement of their Government, pushed the traffic in slaves. Both in the theory and practice of slave trading, Great Britain at one time outstripped all other nations. No where has the traffic in slaves been so ably and eloquently defended, on the ground both of expediency and morality, as in the Parliament of Great Britain, by some of the most renowned statesmen which that country has produced. The traders were at one time absolute pets and favorites of the Government. Our country is indebted to them for the curse—if curse it is to prove—of negro slavery. The traffic was a most profitable source of national and individual wealth; and it has been said of one of the largest commercial cities of Great Britain, or of the world—Liverpool—that "there was not a stone in all its walls but what was cemented by the blood of Africans."

So long as the trade continued lucrative, or coincided with the policy of the Government, no difficulty was found in resisting the force of opinion among the mass of the People, and among the pious and philanthropic, though at one time quite as much excitement prevailed on the subject as has ever been displayed since. But now that the policy of the Government has changed, it willingly accepts of an auxiliary, and uses as an apology, that manifestation of public opinion which it formerly resisted with ease, and despised.

It is, indeed, a matter of little importance to us what the motive or impulse of the British Government may be, so long as it is a fact, that on this question of slavery, it has placed itself in a hostile attitude towards us. We have a right to consult our own safety, and leave that Government to adjust the matter with its philanthropists and fanatics as it best can. But the policy which it has pursued, has been marked with a far greater degree of zeal and perseverance, as well as of craft, than would have been the case, had it

[54] Editorial in the *Madisonian*, November 16, 1843.

been adopted merely to appease the cravings of a morbid philanthropy among a portion of its subjects. We shall now allude merely to one instance in proof of this.

In the year 1839, a distinguished member of the British House of Commons, conspicuous for his zeal on the subject of negro slavery, gave notice in Parliament of his intention to move to obtain "an asylum, or free State, on the North frontier of Mexico, for free persons of color." Where he considered the North frontier of Mexico to be, at that time, and why it was selected, does not appear; but certainly, whether the rights of Texas, which had declared itself independent, were to be respected or not, a location for such a colony could not have been chosen more unfavorable to our interests, or more favorable to hostile designs which the British Government might secretly cherish against us. This is the first indication which appears of the views of the British Government on Texas.

The design was no doubt abandoned in consequence of the determination of the British Government to recognise the independence of Texas; a determination which filled every one with surprise, for there was every apparent reason to believe that Great Britain, under all the circumstances, would have been one of the last of nations to acknowledge its independence.—It was a slave-holding State, and therefore the popular feeling in Great Britain, which has been represented as so powerful, would be strongly adverse to it. The commerce of Texas could be no object for many years to come; and the country was looked upon as our natural ally, likely to become identified in every way with the United States, and a part and parcel of the Southern and obnoxious division of them. But the policy of the British Government does not lie so near the surface. It was well aware that Texas, as a province of Mexico, could not subserve its purpose. It was well aware that our Government, in conformity with its well-known public declaration, would regard as a belligerent act, any attempt on the part of a European Government to acquire a new colony on our Continent, and in our vicinity, whether for the philanthropic purpose of establishing an asylum for free persons of color, or for any other purpose. Texas, therefore, as a part of Mexico, could not peaceably come into the possession, or under the controlling influence, of Great Britain; but detached from Mexico, and recognized as an independent State, her Government might be worked upon, and her population become alienated from the citizens of the United States by a show of friendship and partiality from the powerful Government of Great Britain. From a natural ally, of the Southern portion at least, of the United States, she might by an adroit policy, aided by the jealousies and disputes likely soon to arise between conterminus independent States, be converted into an enemy. Hence the determination to recognize a slaveholding province, peopled and conquered by citizens from our slave-holding States: and hence the subsequent and constant interference and show of interest by Great Britain in the affairs of Texas; until at length the object is plainly and explicitly avowed on the floor of Parliament in the declaration that, through Texas, the British Government is "to solve that great question in the history of the United States, the abolition of slavery."

DUFF GREEN TO THE EDITOR, BOSTON POST

London, November 18, 1843 [55]

The position of this country is becoming more and more interesting to the United States. As was explained in the letters written to me by Mr. Hume, and published in the Madisonian, the whigs went out of power because they had lost the confidence of the liberal and free trade party. Acted upon, however, by the movement for free trade, they proposed a fixed duty on corn and a reduction of the duty on slave grown sugar. These two propositions were opposed by Sir Robert Peel, and constituted the ostensible measures on which the whigs went out and the tories came into power. The sliding scale rallied the agricultural interest, and the proposition to admit slave grown sugar rallied the opponents of slavery and the colonial and East India interests, in favor of the tories, and gave Sir Robert Peel his great majority in the present parliament.

In the mean time the anti-corn law league was organized—they commenced and have prosecuted an agitation in favor of an entire repeal, not only of the corn laws, but a reduction of the duty on slave grown sugar to the revenue standard—their progress has equalled the anticipations of the most sanguine—they have carried their principles into the agricultural districts—they have demonstrated that the corn laws are enacted by the landlord for the purpose of keeping up rents—that it is a question between landlord and tenant—and that the working of the sliding scale is ruinous to the farmer and farm laborer. For a time, the agitation was confined to the manufacturing districts and the principal cities, and was conducted by parties of comparatively little influence. But Messrs. Cobden, Bright, Moore and others have devoted themselves to the subject for the past year with so much zeal, energy and talent that they have become a controlling political influence, and having enlarged the basis so as to embrace the general question of free trade, they now command the respect of the ablest politicians and statesmen, and constitute an important element in the new combinations which all foresee must take place. The tendency is towards a combination between the advocates of freedom in trade and freedom in religion, with the whigs. The schism in the Church of Scotland, the agitation in Ireland, the discontent of the dissenters in Wales and in England, are all political elements, and all tend to combine against the monopoly of the landlords and of the church, which seeks to ally itself with the colonial and all other monopoly interests that can be made to harmonize with theirs. . . . The whigs cannot organize a ministry but upon the principle of free trade, and the free trade party insist on a repeal of the discriminating duty on slave grown sugar, as well as an entire repeal of the duty on corn. Sir Robert Peel cannot retain power but by conciliating the church, the landlords, and the monopoly interests, of which the producers of sugar in the Indies constitute an important part, and hence he cannot recede from his position without losing place. The free

---

[55] Published in the Boston *Post*, December 9, 1843; republished in the *Madisonian*, December 30, 1843. Green's views here reflect Tyler's of April 27, 1843, introducing Green to Edward Everett, for which see Documents above.

trade party urge that a reduction of the duty on American produce will secure a reduction of our duties on British manufactures; this is denied by the opponents of free trade, and is urged again and again in the Times.

The [London] *Chronicle,* the leading opposition paper, the organ of Lord Palmerston, commenced a series of articles on the Oregon question, the manifest purpose of which is to delay, if not defeat, an adjustment of the question of boundary. The tendency of all these things to create a public opinion here very much to our prejudice, induced me to write three letters, the first and second of which were inserted in the *Times,* but the third they have suppressed, and, with characteristic want of fairness, assail with deliberate misrepresentations.

I send you these letters, and the comment of the *Times* upon them, that you may see the issue thus made up. The facts given in the suppressed letter cannot be controverted. The deductions drawn from them are demonstrations. Their bearing on our interests are manifest & have removed the flimsy veil of philanthropy and benevolence with which these people have endeavored to conceal their grasping avarice. "We stare, and are astonished as we stare," says the *Times,* in commenting on the picture of British philanthropy presented in the facts taken from the history of their legislative proceedings on the subject of Slavery. And well may they stare. Whatever may have been the motives of the few pious and benevolent persons who gave the original impulse, it is apparent that the motive of the government has been to benefit British commerce—a motive and purpose most proper for the government, if it can be accomplished without prejudice to the rights of other nations, which it is now demonstrated cannot be done.

My purpose in writing these letters was to arrest the attention of the British public, to show that there is danger of collision on the Oregon, and to point to the only motive which can induce England to go to war, and the means of preventing it. Who can believe that if England had a free trade with us she would think of a war with us for the possession of Oregon? Free trade with America would induce England to abandon her efforts to transfer the production of sugar and cotton to India by abolishing slavery, and, by rendering it her interest to preserve peace, and make peace permanent.

I send you these letters that you may publish them—(the third will be published in the [London] *Globe* of Saturday). They must carry conviction to the mind of every candid person, and the facts cannot fail to make a deep impression on the American reader—for every one must see the bearing which the progress of this country [England] will have on our interests.

There never was a time when it was more the duty of the democratic party to be united—when they were more interested in maintaining their principles—when it was more necessary that self should be forgotten in the selection of those men who are to represent us and our principles before the nations of the world. I repeat that this country [England] is in a crisis, and much, very much, will depend upon what we may do. I am for peace. If we are firm in maintaining our rights, and careful to do it in such a manner as to throw upon England the responsibility of war, England is not in condition to go to war. The condition of Greece—the objects and movements of Russia, as well as the feeling of the middle classes here—are pledges of peace; if we carefully guard against giving them justifiable cause of war. By this I do not mean that we are to waive or surrender our rights—that we are to shrink back from any cowardly apprehension of war. I mean that we should be circumspect, and throw the responsibility on England, and that, if we do this, public opinion here and on the continent will secure our rights and interests without war; but let there be union and strength, for in that consists our safety.

EDWARD EVERETT TO ABEL P. UPSHUR

London, November 27, 1843,[56] *Marked: "Not sent"*
(Private & Confidential)

My dear Sir:

I acquainted you in my last private letter of my having been obliged to authorize a contradiction of a statement contained in two of the leading papers, that General Duff Green was a diplomatic Agent of the Government of the United States & connected with this legation. This step I deemed to be imperative on me as a matter of duty, not only on general principles, but because the General was engaged in a public discussion on the subject of the American State debts. I thought it due to candor and the friendly relations subsisting between the General and myself to acquaint him that the contradiction was authorized by me, which I did by a note stating the fact. Fearful that the Editors of the papers in which the contradiction was to appear, the "Times" and the "Post," might couple it with some invidious comments, I thought it best to caution Mr. Rives to be careful not to say any thing which would countenance such comments, but to make the contradiction in the simplest terms, as a matter of fact: of which also I informed the General.

His mind being preoccupied with certain unfounded impressions, the nature of which will appear from the copy of his note which I send you, the General found matter of offence in this caution given by me to Mr. Rives, though it was given with no other design than to prevent, as far as depended on me, any offensive commentary upon the contradiction in question. I was very glad to have it in my power to satisfy the General, not merely in reference to this but to the other pre-existing grounds of complaint, that they were wholly imaginary; and I think it due to myself as well as to him, as his Agency and operations here have been of necessity a matter of frequent reference in my correspondence with the department; to transmit to you copies of the notes which passed between us on this recent occasion.

I am persuaded, however, that they will not be necessary, in order to satisfy you that I could be actuated by no feelings of personal hostility toward General Green.

From the first moment that he presented himself at my office last Spring, requesting me to "indorse him over to Sir Robert Peel," and assigning as a

---

[56] Edward Everett Letters, vol. 4, M.H.S.

motive for doing it without delay, that he hoped to derive from his conferences with Sir Robert Peel such encouragement relative to a Commercial treaty between the two Countries, as would promote the success of his private speculations with monied houses in London, I conceived that the General was disposed to embark in a very irregular and dangerous line of operations, and one to which the President's letter of introduction authorized me to give no countenance. Having subsequently so far qualified his application, as to ask of me only a private letter of introduction to Sir Robert Peel, to be accompanied with a distinct understanding on Sir Robert Peel's part that the General was not authorized by the Government to make or receive any communications, I complied (though reluctantly) with the request. I was much gratified to learn from Mr. Legaré's despatch No. 46 that I had not mistaken the President's intentions.

The General from the first seems to have attributed my unwillingness to authenticate his communications, to some difference of opinion as to the object he had more immediately in view (viz. a Commercial arrangement with England), or as it is explained in his note of the 21st instant to a general difference of political opinion.

I am confident it cannot be necessary for me to say, that no general or special difference of political opinion, if I entertained any, would ever influence me in the discharge of my duty to the Government which honors me with its confidence. I do not think it necessary to enquire very particularly whether my opinions coincide with General Green's, but that they do not differ from those intimated by the President, by yourself, and by Mr. Webster on the subject in question, I may appeal to all my correspondence public and private, for the proof.

It has given me much pain to take up so much of your time, in reference to matters in some degree personal to myself, but I think you will perceive that, under the circumstances of the case, the foregoing explanations are necessary.

I am, dear Sir,

> *with the greatest respect,*
> *faithfully Yours,*

MADISONIAN

November 27, 1843 [57]

THE EXTENSION OF SLAVERY

One of the objections against the annexation of Texas, addressed to the consciences of "the People of the free States," is, that it would extend and perpetuate the institution of slavery.

We do not see how this objection can be made out, unless upon the hypothesis that Texas, if not annexed to the United States, will become a free State, and will consent, in order to further the views of Great Britain

[57] Editorial in the *Madisonian,* November 27, 1843.

against this country, to abolish slavery within its territories. But this hypothesis would be an admission, to the fullest extent, of the sinister designs ascribed to the British Government, of the probable accomplishment of those designs, and of the absolute necessity on the part of the Southern people of insisting on the annexation of Texas. It would also be equivalent to an admission and approval of the unconstitutional designs of the abolitionists in this country.

If Texas remains as it is, slavery will be as much extended as if it were annexed to the United States. The annexation of it would add nothing to the aggregate number of slaves in both countries. Unless some change takes place in the legislation of Texas, the slave population will continue to be sent . . . in that direction, as rapidly as if the two countries were united. And we can conceive of no rational objection founded merely on the direction in which the slave population spreads itself. On the contrary, we should suppose that the People of the free States would desire to see it as far removed from them as practicable.

But in what manner is it proposed to benefit the slave population by confining it within the present limits of the Union? We take it for granted that some definite and practical good to be secured to the slave population, or evil to be averted from it, is the motive of all honest and intelligent opponents of slavery; yet we cannot imagine, and have nowhere seen stated, the precise mode in which the condition of the slave population would be bettered, immediately, at least, by restricting it within certain geographical bounds. But we can readily understand how its condition might be rendered worse by such a restriction, in impairing its value as property. As a general rule, the treatment which the slave experiences depends upon his value to his owner. If his services are profitable, he is well provided for and attended to, even from motives of interest; if otherwise, he is ill provided for, perhaps necessarily so. If he becomes an actual burden to his owner, the burden must be got rid of at any hazard.

Emancipation, from the force of necessity, must, therefore, precede any benefit likely to accrue to the slave population from confining it within geographical limits, in order, indirectly, to destroy its value. In the meantime, an infinite degree of distress must be experienced both by the slave and his owner. The one must be impoverished, and the other reduced to the verge of starvation, and the feelings of both against each other exasperated by mutual suffering.—Nothing, indeed, short of general and extreme impoverishment and distress, from which the slaves would suffer most, would induce the slave-holders, as a body, to try the experiment of a general emancipation of their slaves. And admitting that they would, at length, be coerced into that measure, there would be still a host of difficulties and troubles, to encounter and over come before the blacks could even begin to enjoy the fruits of a freedom so dearly purchased by their own sufferings. The relative civil rights of the two classes of population would have to be adjusted; and, if equalized, the utmost degree of human wisdom would be requisite to construct even frail safeguards against the collisions likely to spring from the indelible and everlasting mark of distinction which the Almighty himself has impressed upon the two races. During the process of adjustment, a civil war would probably arise, the blacks be defeated and again enslaved, and it would be necessary to commence the work *de novo*—perhaps again and again.

To the phrenzied mind all this seems easily possible. To the depraved mind, its very dangers and difficulties, and probable horrors, constitute a charm and attraction. We find an ex-President of the United States, tottering on the brink of the grave, but with all his intellectual faculties still entire, absolutely gloating over the scenes of horror which his active imagination must, time after time, have pictured to him, as the inevitable result of compulsory emancipation. In his last appeal to his abolition friends, made within a few days, he says: "That slavery will be abolished in this country and throughout the world, I firmly believe. Whether it shall be done peaceably or by blood, God only knows; but that it shall be accomplished, I have not a doubt, and, BY WHATEVER WAY, I SAY LET IT COME." Let it come even through conflagration and massacre, through the slaughter of our sons and brothers, the shrieks of violated daughters and sisters, the devastation of one half of our common country! What a sentiment to inscribe on the tomb of a fellow-countryman of Benjamin Franklin, of a successor in the Presidential chair of George Washington, of a professed follower of the meek and all-enduring Christ! He does not even profess a belief, or a wish, that the consummation for which he is laboring may be brought about peaceably; but he is willing to wade—or rather incite others to wade—through a sea of blood, in order to overthrow a Constitution which a Franklin and a Washington helped to frame and cordially approved, and which the Almighty has hitherto blessed with unexampled prosperity.

It is not, however, to frenzied or depraved minds that we are now appealing, but to the intelligent, rational and conscientious opponents of slavery. We would ask them whether they feel safe, on this question of the annexation of Texas, in following the lead of a man capable of uttering such a sentiment? Whether such sentiments can properly be supported by a sober and practical philanthropy, which cooly analyzes and weighs consequences, and hesitates to provoke the infliction of great and certain evils, in order to accomplish a remote and doubtful good? We would exhort them to acquire a clear and precise notion of the manner in which the British Government, aided by abolitionists in this country, proposed to check the extension, and accomplish the extinction, of slavery in this country, through abolition in Texas; and compare the amount of evil which they would inflict, both on the white and black population, with that which would result from an unchecked spread of the slave population to Texas.

ABEL P. UPSHUR TO JOHN C. CALHOUN

November 30, 1843 [58]

I have now the pleasure to enclose a copy of the letter from Genl Green [to Upshur, October 17, 1843] alluded to in my last to you. I submitted the letter to the President at Gen'l Green's request & he took it with him to

[58] Calhoun Papers, Robert Muldrow Cooper Library, Clemson University.

Virginia, from which place he has only recently returned. This accounts for the delay in transmitting the copy.

I thank you for your suggestions in the matter of Texas & am happy to see that they support my own views. I have reason to think that nothing more is necessary to insure success than that the South should be true to itself. I trust that no southern representative will be found so blind or so tame of spirit as not to be worthy of the present great occasion.

Very truly & resp'y yours,

DUFF GREEN TO THE EDITOR, BOSTON POST

December 14, 15, 1843 [59]

Sir—The Rev. Sydney Smith, and that degenerate American, the Rev. Mr. Leavitt,[60] are adjuncts in manufacturing public opinion for England. The one tells you that the Americans would, if they could, have long and bloody wars with England because you wear better clothes and ride in better carriages; the other tells you that he knows that the slave-holders have resolved to make war upon England for the benefit of slavery. I have explained, that if we are to have war with England, it will be for the possession of Oregon, and that that question affects more particularly the interests of the north-eastern and north-western states; but I have said that if war comes, the South will put an interpretation upon the motives of England which will excite their deepest indignation. Hence, in case of war, all sections of the country will be united, and it will be conducted with a spirit and energy hitherto unexampled.

Is there cause to apprehend collision between us, and if so can it be avoided? Is it not the interest and the duty of both governments to cultivate peace, and to establish it on the most permanent basis? That nations as well as individuals are responsible to public opinion, is admitted by Sir Robert Peel, who on more than one occasion has urged that a repeal of your discriminating duty on slave-grown sugar would be used as an argument to prove that your efforts to abolish slavery and the slave trade are not disinterested. It often happens, that in communities, where each is playing a part, persons give credit to others for sincerity which they do not themselves profess; and that hence they believe the mass to be actuated by one set of motives, when in truth they are controlled by another; and it sometimes occurs, that when the parties themselves become convinced that they have been in error, they are nevertheless impelled in the same direction, some by motives of personal interest, and others by a wish to appear consistent. This we believe to be the present condition of England. Before giving the reasons of that belief, I will dispose of the assertion of the Rev. Mr. Leavitt—which is, that "he knew that the slaveholders in the United States had long

[59] This letter, spurned by the London *Times,* to which it had been written in November, 1843, was sent to the Boston *Post,* where it appeared. For the *Times* editorial rejecting it, and a reference to it in a letter from Everett to Upshur, see *ante,* pp. 30–1.
[60] Joshua Leavitt was a Boston clergyman, editor of the Boston *Emancipator.*

since deliberately and definitely resolved to bring about a state of war between the two countries, *for the benefit of slavery."* Now, if Mr. Leavitt had said that the best informed statesmen of the South have long entertained apprehensions that England, under the hope of abolishing slavery, would seize on the first favorable pretext to make war on America, he would have told the truth; and he might have added, that in case of such a war, the south would give the most vigorous resistance. But he should have qualified his assertions by saying that the whole South are convinced that it is their interest to preserve peace, and that on all occasions the South have been favorable to peace. It is true that they see in the past measures and present policy of England cause of apprehension, but they rely on the identity of their interests with those of the great body of the people of England—on the progress of more liberal and correct views of public policy, and upon the public opinion and spirit of the age, which is for peace. In confirmation of this, and as directly contradicting Mr. Leavitt's statement, I refer you to an extract of a letter from a correspondent in New York to J. Scoble, Esq., dated 20th March, 1843, and published by the British and Foreign Anti-Slavery Society in the *Anti-Slavery Reporter* of 17th May, 1843. The writer says "You cannot but have noticed the strong desire manifested on the part of Mr. Calhoun to maintain peace with England. He doubtless feels that war would not only endanger his prospects, but the stability of the slave question."

This writer says truly, that Mr. Calhoun has manifested a strong desire to maintain peace with England, but he entirely mistakes the motive. Mr. Calhoun is governed by enlarged and liberal views of public policy, and not by sectional or personal considerations. He and his friends are advocates of peace, and will do all that is proper to be done to avoid a war; and they believe that the best, if not the only means of doing this, is so to harmonize and consolidate the interests of the two countries as to render a war impossible. But I cannot so well or so forcibly express Mr. Calhoun's opinions as he himself has done in a letter to me, dated 8th of September, 1843. . . .[61]

I may add, that the opinion of Mr. Calhoun so forcibly put, is now the opinion of a very large majority of the American people, and that a war for the Oregon, or on any other pretence, will be attributed to a desire to emancipate our slaves, because you have ascertained that neither in your colonies nor in the East Indies can you produce cotton, rice, sugar, etc. in competition with slave labor, and that therefore you cannot monopolise these great staples, but by abolishing slavery in the United States, in Cuba, and in Brazil.

In the debate on the sugar duties, in February last, Sir Robert Peel said—

"We reserved sugar from the operation of the tariff, partly because we wished to use it as an instrument to obtain a reduction of duty upon our own produce in other countries, but more upon this distinct ground—that we did not think it right to give the free and unlimited admission of sugar without reference to the consideration of its being the produce of free or

[61] For this letter, see A.H.A. *Report,* 1899, II, 545–7.

slave labor. I maintained that principle in opposition—I maintained it last year in government—I still adhere to it; that is, I think you ought, if you possibly can, to make some stipulation, *not only in favor of the abolition of slavery,* the prevention of the slave trade, but of the mitigation of slavery itself; you ought to try to get some conditions with respect to slavery before you grant an indiscriminate admission of sugar. I retain the opinion on which I acted in opposition, and which I expressed last year; and I think that considering the discussions in which this country has been lately involved—*considering the doctrines it has maintained with regard to the United States,* the principles it has avowed with regard to France—never was there a period when it was more important that this country should declare to the world that she did not relax, for any pecuniary advantage, the same principles which she has maintained with respect to slavery. There is a great disposition to charge this country with having been influenced in the zeal we have shown for the suppression of the slave trade by mercantile and pecuniary considerations. I certainly think it would very much abate the moral influence we have attained with regard to that question, if it could be supposed, or if there were any appearance which might fairly lead to the supposition, that, for the sake of obtaining free trade in sugar, we did anything that could be instrumental in continuing the slave-trade or lending it our sanction." [62]

You will here see that Sir Robert Peel places his refusal to repeal the discriminating duty on slave grown sugar on the ground that it will aid you [British] in abolishing slavery, and is necessary to protect you from the imputation of being influenced by mercantile and pecuniary considerations; whilst Mr. Calhoun (and, I may add, such will soon be the opinion of the continental powers of Europe) looks to the manner in which that question is treated by your government, as conclusive proof that your persevering efforts to abolish slavery in Cuba and Brazil are attributable, not to any benevolent desire to ameliorate the condition of the blacks, but to a conviction that your scheme of emancipation has entirely failed, and that the abolition of slavery elsewhere is indispensable to the prosperity of your colonies. Permit me to submit a few facts in confirmation of this.

One of your correspondents, under date of Kingston, Jamaica, September 20th, says—

"Few of your innumerable readers in any part of the globe require to be informed, that emancipation in every useful point of view is a total failure, and will wind up with the total ruin of this colony at least, and convincing the world at large that the abstract principle of justice on which that measure was founded, *is incompatible with the well-being of the mass for whose benefit it was intended.*"

In the debate last year, Lord Stanley said that on 62 sugar estates there had been a clear loss of $983,000, on an outlay of $1,250,000; [63] . . . and

---

[62] This statement by Peel in Parliament [February 14, 1843] is reported in the *Anti-Slavery Reporter,* 4 (1843), 30.

[63] *Hansard's,* 3rd ser., 60 (February–March, 1842), 330. Only six West Indian estates, not sixty-two, were described by Lord Stanley as having had net losses.

Lord Brougham, in his speech on his bill *"entitled* an act for the more effectual suppression of the slave trade," said—

"He was bound to state his clear and decided opinion, that not withstanding the decided enormity of the sacrifice made on our part, the planters, as a body, had suffered very greatly in their pecuniary interests. . . . He did not wish to name names—it would be invidious to do so—but some most valued friends of his, both in that house and in the other, not to go beyond the precincts of parliament, had been losers to a great extent by the act of emancipation. He knew persons who had once counted their returns by thousands, but they had now sunk to hundreds! He knew others who had drawn hundreds, but who had now scarcely any West India property at all. The question then at once suggested itself, and this brought him to the leading feature of the present bill. When parliament inflicted emancipation on the West India body, did they mean that the planters should suffer for the gain of *foreign colonies,* not for that of their own fellow subjects? . . . Did parliament tell them (the West Indians), we have taken your slave property from you in order to endow others with it, that they may gain what you have lost—*that they may become your competitors in the markets of the world for the supply of produce which we no longer allow you to reap as you heretofore have done? Quite the contrary.*[64]

And Sir Robert Peel, when the same bill was under consideration in the house of commons, said—

"What would be, he asked, the condition of the West India planters, if this bill were not passed? They were prevented from employing British capital, but they would be subject to the competition of that capital employed in foreign commerce. Never was there a grosser act of injustice than would be committed on the West Indies proprietors if that were allowed. He admitted that the West India planters had received a compensation for their direct losses, but none should be given for their indirect losses. They should not give the planters further compensation, but they might *relieve them from the competition of British capital employed in foreign countries.* They would suffer a most serious injury if the first clause of the bill were not agreed to. Suppose the legislature were to allow the colonial produce of Cuba and Brazils to be imported according to the views of some gentlemen, would it be tolerated that British capital should be employed in those countries in raising colonial produce by means of slaves to be imported hither? *Would not that cause the total ruin of our colonies?"* [65]

And again, in the debate of 22 June, Sir Robert Peel said: "I was anxious to make some inquiry upon that subject, and instead of any vague and general calculations I obtained the particulars of the estates of one individual proprietor. These estates, when slavery was permitted, on an average of years, produced about £10,000 per annum. During the apprenticeship system they produced an average of £6400 per annum, after payment of all

[64] *Ibid.,* 3rd ser., 70 (June–July, 1843), 737–8. Brougham gave a moving account of the horrors of the African slave trade in this speech.

[65] The speech of Peel (August 18, 1843) is reported in the *Anti-Slavery Reporter,* 4 (1843), 159.

expenses. I received an account, on the accuracy of which I can rely. It appears that from the 1st of January to the 31st of December, 1840, the payments altogether for labor, wages, the island taxes, repairs of buildings, and supplies of various kinds, such as machines, implements, etc., amounted to £10,861—the actual receipts were £7,028. In 1841 the payments were £9889, and the receipts £7,042; and in the last year 1842, when it has been said there has been a sufficient interval for breathing time, the payments were £9795, and the receipts, £7230. So that these estates, which produced during the existence of slavery and slave labor, £10,000 a year net income, have, since the abolition of slave labor, sustained an annual average loss of £3,081." [66]

These extracts show conclusively that you [English] are now convinced that free labor cannot compete with slave labor in the cultivation of sugar and cotton; and that your prominent statesmen believed that the abolition of slavery in Cuba, Brazil, and the United States, would affect their prosperity, as that measure has affected the prosperity of your West India colonies.

This brings up the question of how far the abolition of slavery would affect the competition between Cuba, Brazil, the United States, and your East India possessions.

We have seen that the effect of emancipation has been such that an estate which gave £10,000 per annum profit is now cultivated at a loss of £3081 per annum, notwithstanding the discriminating duty on sugar, which it is said gives them a bounty of near £5,000,000 per annum. Its effect would be much the same in Cuba, Brazil, and the United States. It would necessarily diminish the supply and greatly increase the price of sugar, cotton, etc. . . .

You [British] paid the West India proprietors £20,000,000 as an indemnity for emancipating their slaves; but to avoid the claim for an indemnity you did not declare the East India slave to be a free man, but you forbade your civil tribunals to enforce the rights of the master! Why this difference? Does justice or humanity act so inconsistently?

But am I told that the act of emancipation is nevertheless an act of disinterested benevolence? I refer you to the memorial presented by the committee of the British and Foreign Anti-Slavery Society to Lord Melbourne, and dated 26th March 1841, in which they insist that the increased consumption of your manufactured goods depends upon the increase of population and the general distribution of wealth among the community—a thing which they declare "can never take place where the great mass of the laboring population are slaves." [67]

But perhaps there is nothing in your legislation which illustrates so forcibly the difference between your profession and your practice as the amendments made in the House to Lord Brougham's bill [suppression of the slave trade]. It was objected to by Mr. Mildmay, upon the ground that "no man could enter into trade with any country between Virginia and Brazils, who did not

---

[66] *Hansard's*, 3rd ser., 70 (June–July, 1843), 266–7. Green's quotation of the speech is exceedingly loose.

[67] The memorial is published in *Anti-Slavery Reporter*, 2 (1841), 66–7.

run the risk of falling under the penalties of the bill, or seeing the Spaniards, Frenchmen, and others getting securities for their debts, and payments for their advances, which the bill would withhold from the English merchant." The bill was referred: it underwent an entire remodification, and after so reciting the act [Geo. IV, c. 113] [68] as to reconcile that act with the purpose intended, the following words were added as a fifth section:

"Provided always, and be it enacted, that in all cases in which the *holding or taking* of slaves shall not be prohibited by this or any other act of parliament, it shall be lawful to sell or transfer such slaves, anything in any other act contained notwithstanding."

The 6th section was also so amended as to authorize any British subject "to *sell* any slave or slaves which were lawfully in his possession at the time of the passing of the act, or which such person shall or may have become possessed of or entitled unto, *bona fide,* prior to such sale, by inheritance, devise, bequest, marriage, *or otherwise by operation of law.*" [69] When these amendments came before the house, Mr. Hawes inquired their effect, and the Attorney General said, "the object was to guard against any indirect encouragement of the slave trade; *but at the same time to enable British subjects in slave dealing countries to recover debts due them by the administration of the law.*" [70] Thus legalizing the taking, holding, purchase, and sale of slaves! !

If there be any one feature in the system of slavery more odious than all the rest, it is that which enables a remorseless creditor to seize upon the husband and wife, the parent and the child, and by exposing them to sale in open market, break asunder those ties which relieve the distress and console the afflictions of man, whatever may be his condition. This bill, thus enacted under the pretense of suppressing slavery and the slave trade, adopts *slave dealing,* in its most odious form, because it is for the advantage of British commerce! !

You preach a crusade against slavery, in the name of religion and humanity; but you instinctively protect British interests. You denounce the system as sinful and cruel, but you take care to profit by it as far as is consistent with your purpose of substituting another system, which you believe will still more promote your interests. Thus, while you exclude slave-grown sugar from your home consumption, that you may thereby promote emancipation, and, under pretense of discouraging the slave trade, you encourage the dealing in this same slave-grown sugar for consumption on the continent, by permitting it to be entered for re-exportation, free of duty. Now does not all the world see that the purchase of slave-grown sugar for continental consumption encourages slavery and the slave-trade just as much as if it were consumed in England? The principle and the effect is precisely the same; why, then, is the one permitted, while the other is denounced? Is it not because both the permission and prohibition are, as you believe, for the benefit of British commerce? By permitting the import and re-exportation,

[68] *Statutes at Large, United Kingdom,* IX, 914–27.
[69] *Ibid.,* XVI, 936.
[70] *Hansard's,* 3rd ser., 71 (July–August, 1843), 983.

free of duty, of slave grown sugar, you retain a market for the sale of a large amount of British manufactures, and secure a profit to British merchants, which would otherwise enrich your manufacturing and commercial competitors. By forbidding the consumption of slave-grown sugar in England, you seek to abolish slavery elsewhere, and to protect your colonial and East India interests until, by doing so, you destroy that system of cheap labor which now prevents your monopoly of sugar, cotton, etc.

I admit that there are many pious and humane persons who believe that they are doing God service, and are actuated by purely disinterested benevolence. But such has been the case with fanaticism in all ages—the same spirit gave birth to the Crusades, to the massacre of the Saints, to the witchcraft delusion, and to every atrocity perpetrated in the name of religion. What do these fanatics know of the condition of our slaves, or by what right do they interfere in our domestic institutions? Have they no suffering poor—no sins to rebuke—no grievances to redress at home, that they send their sympathies on a voyage of discovery to us?

We require no union workhouses to keep our slaves from starvation—we require no armed police to keep them in subjection; nor do we require a single battalion, much less an army of 40,000 men, to prevent a servile insurrection. That, whether slavery be or be not an evil—whether it should or should not be abolished, are questions for us, and for us alone, and about which you have no right whatsoever to interfere, is a proposition which few, even in England, will venture to controvert.

When, therefore, we see your government, by means so inconsistent, using such strenuous efforts to accomplish a measure fraught with so much injury to us, and tending, if it could be accomplished to establish the manufacturing and commercial supremacy of England by inflicting emancipation (to use the words of Lord Brougham) upon us, you must expect us to feel a very deep interest in the progress of these efforts, and that our measures will be taken in reference to them. We see that if the system of free trade prevails, those efforts will cease—because it will no longer be your interest to continue them—and the question which will be presented to the next American congress will be whether a reduction of our duties will promote or retard the free-trade movement in England. I am for free trade. I believe that the tendency of public opinion here and elsewhere, is in that direction, and that a repeal of our duties will be followed by a modification of yours, and hence I will urge it, with what influence I may have, as a means of preserving peace, and promoting the prosperity of both countries. It may be that no reduction in our tariff will be made. If so, it will be because the failure to adjust the Oregon and other questions, will be attributed to a desire, on the part of your government, to keep those questions open; because, much as you have done to enlist the prejudice of the world against the institution of slavery, and deeply interested as you may believe yourselves to be in abolishing it, we do not believe that England will consent to a war with us for the avowed purpose of accomplishing it.

Tucker to Gilmer, January 6, 1844

HENRY ST. GEORGE TUCKER TO THOMAS WALKER GILMER

January 6, 1844 [71]

. . . From my poor pen you could look for nothing but the natural ebullitions of my spleen against that firebrand of the day, John Quincy Adams. He seems to aspire to the bad eminence of that Grecian who set fire to the temple that his own name might be transmitted to all future time; for it would seem clear that his success would pull down about our ears the glorious temple of liberty we have erected, and raise up a state of discord and confusion that may not end for a century. He is attacking that clause of the Constitution which was most peculiarly matter of compromise; without which compromise there is a moral certainty the instrument never would have been ratified. If the east had insisted on taxing the whole of the Southern slaves as *property,* & had refused to consider them as of any weight in the ratio of representation, the South never would have ratified the Constitution. It would have been as absurd as for the South who held them as *property,* to claim for them full representation as persons. They thereupon adopted a middle term, making three fifths of the slaves taxable and giving three fifths of them weight in the representation. What honourable mind can now ask a change of this fundamental principle of compromise by the voice of three fourths of the states, when no one state could have been compelled to enter the Union, though all the rest had concurred in voting for the opposite proposition? What should we think of a proposition at this day to amend the Constitution by taking from Rhode Island and Delaware that equal vote in the Senate which is assured to them by the Constitution? If political knavery indeed, were to take the place of political honesty, we might raise a vote of three fourths of the states to bring down Delaware & Rhode Island by an amendment to a single senator each. But every one must see and feel, that notwithstanding the provision for amendments, it would be a gross breach of good faith towards those states if an amendment were now made reducing their weight in the Senate to a single vote. Where provisions were the result of great compromises of antagonizing interests, we cannot but be conscious that they should be regarded as sacred, and he is worthy of all abhorrence who would violate its sanctity. Such is the case of the right of representation of the small states, and such is not less the case as to the representation of three fifths of the slaves. Contemporaneous writers have assured us that this article above all others was a matter of adjustment and compromise between conflicting interests, in which the contending parties (to use a common phrase) agreed to *give and take,* to settle the otherwise unreconcilable difference between them. If this be so, then it must be clear, until might makes right, that the free states should not, if they could, commit so gross a violation of the essential agreement of the confederated republics.

[71] John Tyler Papers, Library of Congress, Presidential Series on Microfilm, reel 2, ser. 2. The writer, a relative of N. Beverley Tucker, was a professor of law at the University of Virginia. He was responding to a request from Gilmer for his views on the three-fifths issue.

Thanks be to God, they *could* not if they *would*. They must have twenty states at least to carry their proposition unless they indulge the hope that those who hold no slaves in the South are strong enough, and willing too, to bring down the weight of their parental state, by throwing themselves into the arms of their northern abolition brethren. Such, I am satisfied, is not the case. The Southern states will meet, with undivided front, those faithless invaders of their stipulated rights; and twelve of them will secure us, I hope forever, against any amendment of the Constitution which shall take from them the representation of three fifths of their slaves. If they are true to themselves there must be at least *thirty six* abolition states to carry their unrighteous project. And when will that be? *Never!!!*

There is nothing in Mr. Adams' proposed amendment which strikes one more forcibly than its impudence and inconsistency. That men who are open-mouthed about universal emancipation, who are perpetually bawling about the violation of human right in holding slaves, and who contend that the slaves should have the same privileges as their masters, that such men should contend they should have no weight in the ratio of representation, is altogether surprising. If they are *men* & to be considered entitled to the privileges of free men, ought they not *all* to be represented? Upon the abolition principle ought not the *whole* of the slaves to be represented instead of three-fifths? Is it any objection to their being represented that they would not have the right of suffrage? Surely not; for women and children are taken into the estimate, in determining the ratio, though *they* enjoy no right of suffrage; and in like manner, slaves, as men, should be estimated although the privilege of voting is denied them. What would Mr. Adams say if you were to propose that the *whole* & not three fifths should be estimated, upon the principle that they are not property but men? Such a proposition, I think may be fairly offered as an amendment to his, and this would bring forward distinctly the inconsistency of his pretentions with his notion of Universal Emancipation.

As to Mr. Adams' threat of disunion if this amendment is not adopted, I cannot fear it. He distinctly avows his attachment to the Union, and his desire for its continuance, though he admits that in his lifetime & for a long time afterwards, slavery will continue in the Southern States. He is not then for a forcible dissolution of the Union if the States do not promptly unite in a general emancipation. Why then can he suppose the great body of the free states, or even a part of them, or even his own state, will break up the union unless there be a general emancipation to the South. It cannot be. Still less can it be that the free states will break up this Union in which they are above all so deeply interested unless we will abolish slavery. They ought to know we cannot abolish it. They ought to know that a general emancipation would produce in the slave-holding states the most dangerous & disastrous consequences. They ought to know, too, that the emancipation of 400,000 slaves in Virginia (for instance) would at the average value of $50 per slave, operate as a tax upon the state, of twenty millions, and so in the other states in proportion. Moreover, this tax would only fall upon the slave holder, so that a man who has one hundred slaves worth $100 each would be taxed $10,000!! Would those who are so zealous for human liberty agree that this heavy burden should be thrown, in proportion to representation, upon the free states? Would *they* agree to it? Slavery, if it be a crime, is not our crime. It was the crime of G.B. in admitting the introduction of slaves, and the burden therefore, should not fall on us alone. Our brethren of the North, before they require us to emancipate, should consent to bear in proportion, the expense of emancipation. Will their philanthropy go this far? *Credat Judaeus Apella! Non ego.* If then they would not consent for the great public good of universal emancipation to pay a part of the expense of it, why should they expect the sacrifice from us of bearing the whole? Nothing can be more unreasonable! We cannot if we wished it, and we would not if we could, commit the suicidal act of General Emancipation. Time alone can produce a gradual abolition, if even time can do it. I sanguinely hope that time & the wants of states still farther south than Virginia, will gradually produce it. But we must *bide our time.* It is a case in which the maxim *fastina lente* most emphatically applies.

If then the Southern states cannot emancipate, what will they do if the Northern states should (which they cannot, thanks be to God) succeed in procuring an amendment providing for universal emancipation? They must separate, and if they separate, or if, as you say Mr. Adams suggests, the North will separate if the proposed amendment *cannot* pass, then will come "the hardest send off." The union must be dissolved. And what will succeed to brotherhood? *Unconquerable hatred.* A barrier must be drawn around the Southern states for the exclusion from their boundaries of Northern emissaries and abolitionists, of wretches who will come with fair faces & base hearts, to sow the seeds of insurrection among the Southern slaves. A general exclusion, except under special permits must be the consequence. Nay more—if Mr. Adams & his constituents take to their *bosoms* our slaves, *women* & all, they must & will throw us into the arms of England. So far from tariffs to protect Northern manufacturers, English goods will be admitted on the most favourable terms, and Northern goods totally excluded. Will this bring about war with those who are now our brethren? If so, & we should prove a match for them, we shall breast the storm manfully. If we should find ourselves too weak, what will be the natural consequence? I shudder to look forward to it. England—the only party who will have gained by the feud, will be *our* ally, or *theirs;* and thus these fatal measures must inevitably lead to unnatural quarrels between brethren, and a scarcely less hateful union with our former foes!

But I must have done. The subject is too grand a burden for *my* shoulders. Mrs. Tucker is writing some views which will be worthy of your attention & which I enclose.

Ticknor, Reminiscence, March, 1844

A REMINISCENCE BY GEORGE TICKNOR

March, 1844 [72]

"In May, 1843, Mr. Webster, as will be remembered, resigned his place in President Tyler's Cabinet. His position there had, for some time, been an uncomfortable one. On the dissolution of General Harrison's Cabinet, in consequence of his death, in April, 1841, and the troubles that followed, he alone had remained in office. This circumstance dissatisfied many persons at the North. The *Atlas* newspaper assailed him for it. But he maintained himself with firmness, and negotiated with Lord Ashburton the treaty which was ratified the 9th of August, 1842. Many persons of influence thought he should have resigned at that time.

"From the time of his resignation, until the 4th of March, 1845, Mr. Webster held no political office, but was looked upon with distrust by many persons of his own party at the North, who favored Mr. Clay's pretensions to the presidency, and who were displeased that Mr. Webster had not followed Mr. Clay's opinions and party in the summer of 1841.

"But, though not in office, Mr. Webster was in Washington attending the Supreme Court of the United States, during a part of the winter of 1843–44. While he was there rumors reached Boston, and articles appeared in the *National Intelligencer,* intimating that a project was on foot for the annexation of Texas. Mr. Webster's opposition to every thing of the sort had been known to the country from the date of his speech at New York in 1837, and I suppose that my conversations with him had led me to hold similar opinions. At any rate, when I read the articles in the *Intelligencer,* I became alarmed. A few days afterward, meeting Mr. Webster in State Street, and knowing that he was fresh from Washington—for, until I saw him, I supposed him to be still there—I asked him, as we walked along together, whether there was any foundation for the report we had received on the subject of Texas? I felt his arm press mine spasmodically, as he said in a low tone, but with great emphasis, 'That is not a matter to be talked about in the street; come to me this evening at Mr. Paige's, and I will tell you all about it.'

"I went at the time appointed. He was in his chamber alone. He looked concerned and troubled. He said, at once, 'It is a long story. I must make a speech to you about it, as bad as a Congressional speech.' And he began abruptly, by saying, that he and Mr. Upshur, notwithstanding the difference of their political opinions, had always been good friends, and that one day when he was sitting with that gentleman, who was then Secretary of State in Mr. Webster's place, he told him that he thought Mr. Tyler was going on unwisely. Mr. Upshur replied, that he was of the same mind, and that he was so little satisfied with the condition of affairs, that 'he would not continue in office a fortnight if he had not a particular object to accomplish.' Mr. Webster said that he conjectured in a moment what this object must be. His phrase was, 'I felt Texas go through me.' He said, however, nothing further

[72] George Ticknor Curtis, *Life of Daniel Webster,* 2 vols. (New York, 1870), II, 230–5.

268

to Mr. Upshur upon the matter; but, in two days, he said, that he knew all about it. He went on earnestly, telling me that he was astounded at the boldness of the Government. They had absolutely been negotiating with Mr. Van Zandt about Texas, which then anxiously desired the protection of the United States against a threatened invasion from Mexico, and had persuaded our Government to agree to give such protection, so far as was possible, by the United States vessels then in the Gulf of Mexico, if that invasion should take place. We might, therefore, Mr. Webster said, be in a war with Mexico at any time, with or without the authority of Congress; and he did not doubt the Administration would be willing to have such a war. Indeed, he said that he felt sure war would be the inevitable consequence of any annexation of Texas without the consent of Mexico. He then went on and described the troubles that would follow any great enlargement of our territory in the Southern direction. He thought it would endanger the Union. He became very much excited. He walked up and down the room fast and uneasily. He said he had not been able to sleep at night, and that he could think of little else in the day. He had written two of the editorial articles which I had read in the *Intelligencer,* and with great difficulty, after long conversations with Mr. Gales, had persuaded him to insert them and to take full ground against any annexation of Texas. At his earnest request also, Mr. Winthrop had introduced a resolution on the subject in the House of Representatives,[73] and as he passed through New York he (Mr. Webster) had engaged Mr. Charles King to take the same ground and had left with him more than one article to be published in the newspaper of which Mr. King was the editor.[74] His object, he said, was to rouse the whole North upon the subject. Up to that time there had been little difference between the political parties in New England and New York on the whole matter. Their Legislatures, particularly that of Massachusetts, in 1843, with hardly a dissenting voice, had pronounced the annexation of Texas unconstitutional and unjustifiable. The Legislature of 1844 was of the same mind, and had passed similar resolutions. Not a single newspaper in the country, Mr. Webster believed, had then come out in its favor, and few had failed to denounce it. This state of feeling, which he well understood and explained to me, he was urgently desirous to continue and to strengthen. An election was about to take place in Connecticut, and he alluded to it. He said that, if it was in his power, he would make the Texas question an element in its decision. 'If I had the means,' he said, 'I would send men to Connecticut who should run through the State from side to side, with their arms stretched out, crying, Texas, Texas;' and he suited the action to the word in the most fervent and impressive manner.

"But what Mr. Webster told me he had received almost entirely from private and confidential sources, and nothing but his own convictions on the subject, without their grounds and proofs, could be communicated to the

[73] The Winthrop speech of March 14, 1844, reported in the *National Intelligencer,* on the following day, is reproduced under date of its delivery in the Documents. It was not reported in the *Congressional Globe,* which is a mystery.

[74] Charles King was editor and proprietor of the New York *American,* one of the earliest of Whig newspapers to expose Tyler's secret Texas negotiation. He was a man of scholarly tastes who in 1849 became president of Columbia College.

public. He could say he was himself alarmed, but not why he was alarmed. At his request, however, I went the same evening to see Mr. Brimmer, then Mayor of Boston, in order to communicate to him these anxieties and apprehensions, and to say that Mr. Webster wished to converse with him upon the subject. Mr. Brimmer was not at home; but so earnest had been Mr. Webster's expressions to me, and so much had he alarmed me upon the great ultimate danger that would result from the annexation of Texas, that I followed Mr. Brimmer to Mr. T. G. Cary's, where he was passing the evening, and communicated to him as much as I was permitted to repeat of what Mr. Webster had told me. Mr. Brimmer saw Mr. Webster the next day, and was much impressed with the urgency of the case, so far as Mr. Webster felt at liberty to make it known. Mr. Webster's object was to get up public meetings in Boston and elsewhere, and, if possible, to have a convention of all Massachusetts to protest against the annexation of Texas.

"Mr. Brimmer endeavored to promote this with all his power. Mr. C. G. Loring, and a few other persons, he told me, assisted him, but persons of mark and note in the Whig party, with the *Atlas* newspaper for their organ, he said, earnestly opposed it. They believed that there was no real danger of the annexation of Texas. Mr. Mangum, of North Carolina, then a leading Whig member of the Senate, assured them that there was none; besides which, they feared any movement of the sort would operate unfavorably upon the prospects for the presidency of Mr. Clay, who, as they supposed, would be the next candidate, and whose nomination, they feared, Mr. Webster might be too anxious to defeat. They were mistaken in both. If I ever saw the working of strong and sincere feelings in any man, I witnessed, at that time, in Mr. Webster, a great patriotism over-leaping all the bounds of party. He foresaw clearly the dangers of the course that was pursued by so many of the Whigs of this part of New England, and was deeply distressed at the prospect for his country. He seemed to have no other feeling.

"About this time, that is, I think, the beginning of April 1844, I dined in company with him at the hospitable table of Colonel Thomas H. Perkins. Mr. N. Appleton, Mr. Edmund Dwight, and several other of the principal Whigs of Boston, were there. They expressed the opinion that Texas would never be annexed to the United States. They knew nothing of the secret history of the negotiations that had been going on at Washington, and Mr. Webster had no right to make them public, or to speak of them in such a circle, which would have been the same thing. He expressed his own opinion, however, very strongly, that Texas would be annexed, if a great effort were not made at the North to prevent it, and suggested a public meeting in Boston, and a convention of the State, as the needful and readiest means to accomplish that object.

" 'Mind,' said he, striking his hand on the table, and a little excited because some one had expressed a strong opinion to the contrary, 'Mind, I do not say that Texas will be annexed within a year, but I do say that I think I see how it can be done, and I have no reason to suppose that the Administration sees less clearly into the matter than I do.' A slight laugh followed, expressing an incredulity not quite respectful, and then the conversation was changed. Mr. Webster soon went away, and, after he was gone, one of the gentlemen said, 'He ought to come out for Clay.' No reply was made, and the party soon broke up.

"On the 1st of March following, not a year from that time, Texas was substantially annexed to the United States; and, on the 22d of December following, Mr. Webster, being then again in the Senate of the United States, pronounced there that short, but solemn protest against it, which will not be forgotten."

ROBERT C. WINTHROP

*Speech of March 14, 1844, in the House of Representatives,
on the annexation of Texas* [75]

MR. WINTHROP (to whom the attention of the reporter was not at the moment directed) rose chiefly to reply to one remark which had fallen from the gentleman from South Carolina (Mr. Holmes). The remark seemed to have been made, partly in jest, partly in earnest; yet there were some subjects that were too solemn in their character, and too momentous in the consequences they involved, to be even thus adverted to without eliciting the most serious feeling. He alluded to the idea thrown out by the gentleman, that this institution [West Point] ought to be sustained because the annexation of Texas was the settled policy of this Government. Who settled it? Not, he would undertake here to say, not the people or the Representatives of the people. *They* knew nothing about it, though he believed there were others who *did* know. He feared that there was something serious in this matter. He was almost afraid that the gentleman from South Carolina intended to try the temper of the House and the country by throwing out the idea, as he (Mr. W.) had said, half in jest, half in earnest. And the gentleman from Ohio (Mr. Weller) had commented upon it, not exactly in the terms which he (Mr. W.) would like to have heard from a Representative of that State. He believed that there was no little danger that the people of the country were about to be taken by surprise on this subject of the annexation of Texas; he believed that the momentous project, which, in his judgment, would endanger the stability of the Union, and which was utterly abhorrent to the feelings of the people in his section of the country, was at this moment in a train of secret and stealthy negotiation. He hoped that a call would be made upon the Executive for information.

A TREATY OF ANNEXATION, CONCLUDED BETWEEN THE UNITED STATES OF AMERICA AND THE REPUBLIC OF TEXAS, AT WASHINGTON, THE 12TH DAY OF APRIL, 1844 [76]

The people of Texas having, at the time of adopting their Constitution, expressed, by an almost unanimous vote, their desire to be incorporated

[75] *National Intelligencer,* March 15, 1844. The *Intelligencer* for March 16 again made reference to Winthrop's speech.

[76] *Sen. Doc.,* 28 Cong., 1 sess. (ser. 435), no. 341, 10–13.

into the Union of the United States, and being still desirous of the same with equal unanimity, in order to provide more effectually for their security and prosperity; and the United States, actuated solely by the desire to add to their own security and prosperity, and to meet the wishes of the Government and people of Texas, have determined to accomplish, by treaty, objects so important to their mutual and permanent welfare.

For that purpose, the President of the United States has given full powers to John C. Calhoun, Secretary of State of the said United States, and the President of the Republic of Texas has appointed, with like powers, Isaac Van Zandt and J. Pinckney Henderson, citizens of the said Republic; and the said plenipotentiaries, after exchanging their full powers, have agreed on and concluded the following articles:

ARTICLE I.

The Republic of Texas, acting in conformity with the wishes of the people and every department of its Government, cedes to the United States all its territories, to be held by them in full property and sovereignty, and to be annexed to the said United States as one of their Territories, subject to the same constitutional provisions with their other Territories. This cession includes all public lots and squares, vacant lands, mines, minerals, salt lakes and springs, public edifices, fortifications, barracks, ports and harbors, navy and navy yards, docks, magazines, arms, armaments, and accoutrements, archives and public documents, public funds, debts, taxes and dues unpaid at the time of the exchange of the ratifications of this treaty.

ARTICLE II.

The citizens of Texas shall be incorporated into the Union of the United States, maintained and protected in the free enjoyment of their liberty and property, and admitted, as soon as may be consistent with the principles of the Federal Constitution, to the enjoyment of all the rights, privileges, and immunities, of citizens of the United States.

ARTICLE III.

All titles and claims to real estate, which are valid under the laws of Texas, shall be held to be so by the United States; and measures shall be adopted for the speedy adjudication of all unsettled claims to land, and patents shall be granted to those found to be valid.

ARTICLE IV.

The public lands hereby ceded shall be subject to the laws regulating the public lands in the other Territories of the United States, as far as they may be applicable; subject, however, to such alterations and changes as Congress may from time to time think proper to make. It is understood between the parties, that, if in consequence of the mode in which lands have been surveyed in Texas, or from previous grants or locations, the sixteenth section cannot be applied to the purpose of education, Congress shall make equal provision by grant of land elsewhere. And it is also further understood, that, hereafter, the books, papers, and documents of the General Land Office of Texas shall be deposited and kept at such place in Texas as the Congress of the United States shall direct.

ARTICLE V.

The United States assume and agree to pay the public debts and liabilities of Texas, however created, for which the faith or credit of her Government may be bound at the time of the exchange of the ratifications of this treaty; which debts and liabilities are estimated not to exceed, in the whole, ten millions of dollars, to be ascertained and paid in the manner hereinafter stated.

The payment of the sum of three hundred and fifty thousand dollars shall be made at the Treasury of the United States, within ninety days after the exchange of the ratifications of this treaty, as follows: Two hundred and fifty thousand dollars to Frederick Dawson, of Baltimore, or his executors, on the delivery of that amount of ten per cent. bonds of Texas; one hundred thousand dollars, if so much be required, in the redemption of the exchequer bills which may be in circulation at the time of the exchange of the ratifications of this treaty. For the payment of the remainder of the debts and liabilities of Texas, which, together with the amount already specified, shall not exceed ten millions of dollars, the public lands herein ceded, and the nett revenue from the same, are hereby pledged.

ARTICLE VI.

In order to ascertain the full amount of the debts and liabilities herein assumed, and the legality and validity thereof, four commissioners shall be appointed by the President of the United States, by and with the advice and consent of the Senate, who shall meet at Washington, Texas, within the period of six months after the exchange of the ratifications of this treaty, and may continue in session not exceeding twelve months, unless the Congress of the United States should prolong the time. They shall take an oath for the faithful discharge of their duties, and that they are not directly or indirectly interested in said claims at the time, and will not be during their continuance in office; and the said oath shall be recorded with their proceedings. In case of the death, sickness, or resignation of any of the commissioners, his or their place or places may be supplied by the appointment as aforesaid, or by the President of the United States during the recess of the Senate. They, or a majority of them, shall be authorized, under such regulations as the Congress of the United States may prescribe, to hear, examine, and decide on all questions touching the legality and validity of said claims, and shall, when a claim is allowed, issue a certificate to the claimant, stating the amount, distinguishing principal from interest. The certificates so issued shall be numbered, and entry made of the number, the name of the person to whom issued, and the amount, in a book to be kept for that purpose. They shall transmit the records of their proceedings and the book in which the certificates are entered, with the vouchers and documents produced before them, relative to the claims allowed or rejected, to the Treasury Department of the United States, to be deposited therein; and the Secretary of the Treasury shall, as soon as practicable after the receipt of the same, ascertain the aggregate amount of the debts and liabilities allowed; and if the same, when added to the amount to be paid to Frederick Dawson, and the sum which may be paid in the redemption of the exchequer bills, shall not exceed the estimated sum of ten millions of dollars, he shall, on the presentation of a certificate of the commissioners, issue, at the option of the holder, a new certificate for the amount, distinguishing principal from interest, and payable to him or order, out of the nett proceeds of the public lands hereby ceded, or stock of the United States, for the amount allowed, including principal and interest, and bearing an interest of three per cent. per annum from the date thereof; which stock, in addition to being made payable out of the nett proceeds of the public lands hereby ceded, shall also be receivable in payment for the same. In case the amount of the debts and liabilities allowed, with the sums aforesaid to be paid to Frederick Dawson, and which may be paid in the redemption of the exchequer bills, shall exceed the said sum of ten millions of dollars, the said Secretary, before issuing a new certificate, or stock, as the case may be, shall make in each case such proportionable and ratable reduction on its amount as to reduce the aggregate to the said sum of ten millions of dollars; and he shall have power to make all needful rules and regulations necessary to carry into effect the powers hereby vested in him.

ARTICLE VII.

Until further provision shall be made, the laws of Texas, as now existing, shall remain in force, and all executive and judicial officers of Texas, except the President, Vice President, and heads of departments, shall retain their offices, with all power and authority appertaining thereto; and the courts of justice shall remain in all respects as now established and organized.

ARTICLE VIII.

Immediately after the exchange of the ratifications of this treaty, the President of the United States, by and with the advice and consent of the Senate, shall appoint a commissioner, who shall proceed to Texas and receive the transfer of the territory thereof, and all the archives and public property, and other things herein conveyed, in the name of the United States. He shall exercise all executive authority in said Territory necessary to the proper execution of the laws, until otherwise provided.

ARTICLE IX.

The present treaty shall be ratified by the contracting parties, and the ratifications exchanged at the city of Washington, in six months from the date hereof, or sooner if possible.

In witness whereof, we, the undersigned, plenipotentiaries of the United States of America and of the Republic of Texas, have signed, by virtue of our powers, the present treaty of annexation, and have hereunto affixed our seals, respectively.

Done at Washington, the twelfth day of April, eighteen hundred and forty-four.

J. C. CALHOUN.   [SEAL.]

ISAAC VAN ZANDT.   [SEAL.]

J. PINCKNEY HENDERSON.   [SEAL.]

DUFF GREEN TO WILLIE P. MANGUM

May 8, 1844 [77]

The [Washington] Globe of Saturday says: "We find that Lord Aberdeen and the British Minister here utterly deny the Duff Green story sent here from London in August [July] last, of the design of England upon Texas, which is made the foundation of the whole proceeding. We believe it can easily be proved that the whole scheme of getting up the Texas question, precisely as that question now is, existed long before Duff Green furnished that pretext, and that all this story of British interference now put forth as the pretext for the movement *has been invented since the movement was organized.*"

The articles in the Globe on the subject of Texas bear internal evidence that they are written by Col. Benton. The issues presented are so important that no personal consideration should enter the discussion; but as Mr. Benton drags *my name* into it, and charges that I have attempted to mislead the public judgment by inventing a false charge against the British Government, it is proper that I should disprove his accusation. This I will do by the printed documents. The extract from my letter to which he refers, is in these words:

"I learn from a source entitled to the fullest confidence, that there is now here a Mr. Andrews, deputed by the abolitionists of Texas to negotiate with the British Government. That he has seen Lord Aberdeen, and submitted his project for the abolition of slavery in Texas, which is, that there shall be organized a company in England, who shall advance a sufficient sum to pay for slaves now in Texas and receive in payment Texas lands; that the sum thus advanced shall be paid over as an indemnity for the abolition of slavery, and I am authorized by the Texan Minister to say to you that Lord Aberdeen has agreed that the British Government will guarantee the payment of interest on this loan, upon condition that the Texan Government will abolish slavery."

The fact communicated by me was, that Mr. Andrews was in London as the agent of Abolitionists in Texas; that he had made propositions to the British Government, and that the Texan Minister in London had authorized me to say that Lord Aberdeen has agreed that the British Government will guarantee the payment of the interest on the proposed loan upon condition that the Texan Government will abolish slavery. Colonel Benton says that the British Minister and Mr. Packenham have denied this and that therefore he

[77] From the *Madisonian,* May 8, 1844. Willie P. Mangum, to whom the letter was addressed, was president pro tempore of the Whig Senate, which doubtless explains the salutation.

275

believes it can be proved that it was invented as the pretext for the movement of Annexation. It will strike every one who has read what Colonel Benton has said and the Globe has published in relation to British diplomacy that there is something very extraordinary in the position which they now assume. Why is it that they are so much against England on the Northeast Boundary and Oregon questions, and so much for England on the Texan question? Why is England so much to be feared and denounced when she approaches us from the North, and so much to be courted when she approaches us in the South? Why was Col. Benton so much against England then and so much for England now? But this is not a question of what Lord Aberdeen said to me. The question is, what did Mr. Smith, the Texan Minister authorize me to say? and the published documents verify what I did say. Mr. Everett, in his letter of the 16th November to Mr. Upshur says:

"Mr. Smith informs me that he was present at the interview which took place last June between Lord Aberdeen and several persons, British subjects and others, a committee of the General Anti-Slavery Convention, who waited on him for the purpose of engaging the co-operation of the British Government to effect the abolition of slavery in Texas. On this occasion Lord Aberdeen assured the committee that her Majesty's Government would employ all legitimate means in their power to attain so great and desirable an object. One of the members of the committee afterwards informed Mr. Smith, at his lodgings, that in their interview with Lord Aberdeen, his Lordship made observations which warranted them in saying that the British Government would guaranty, if necessary, the interest of a loan which should be raised and applied to the abolition of slavery in Texas, but not of a Texan loan for any other purpose whatever." [78]

This extract fully establishes the truth of my statement; and Mr. Everett adds further that he had an interview with Lord Aberdeen on the subject; that he had submitted his memorandum of their conversation to Lord Aberdeen, and adds:

"In returning my memorandum of the conversation, with his corrections, Lord Aberdeen recapitulated, in order to the perfect understanding of the case, that there had been no communication on the part of England, with Texas, in reference to the abolition of slavery, and that no proposition whatever had been made to her by England on that subject; the loan proposed by General Hamilton on behalf of the Government of Texas, had no connexion with abolition; the proposal of a loan to promote that object last summer was the suggestion of a deputation of private individuals, and was at once rejected by him.

"Although England has made no proposition to Texas, and has no intention of making abolition the subject of any treaty stipulation with her, they had certainly recommended to Mexico to promote the abolition of slavery by the acknowledgment of the independence of Texas. But Lord Aberdeen added that he could not say that this recommendation had been listened to with any degree of favor, and nothing further was said on the subject. In all this there was no reference whatever to the United States." [79]

[78] This letter is published in *Sen. Doc.*, 28 Cong., 1 sess. (ser. 435), no. 341, 40–2.
[79] Compare *ibid.*, 38–40.

I repeat that it is a striking feature in this case that Col. Benton, a Senator from Missouri, so ferocious in denouncing England, so jealous of her measures and policy, should array himself on the side of England, and upon such evidence, assume that the avowed purpose of abolishing slavery in Texas had "no reference whatever to the United States, and he should denounce my letter as an invention, a pretext to cover the movement for annexation; and the correspondence in relation to it, a conspiracy on the part of Mr. Calhoun to dissolve the Union.—Now, sir, I will call your attention to the following striking facts in connexion with this question. My letter was written from London in July. I had just read in the Anti-Slavery Reporter, of the 28 June, the proceedings of the World's Convention. The following is an extract:

"The Rev. W. Brock, of Norwich, said the following is the proposition which I have to submit to your adoption:

"That whilst this meeting would deprecate as one of the greatest calamities that could befal the human race, the annexation of Texas to the United States, inasmuch as it would not only strengthen the system of slavery and lead to its indefinite extension on the American continent, but increase to an equal degree the internal slave trade, they have learned with satisfaction that a feeling in favor of the abolition of slavery in Texas has recently sprung up, which they trust will be encouraged and strengthened by the due exertion of the influence of the Government and people of this country (England), with a view to its complete extinction in that Republic."[80]

This resolution was seconded by Mr. Lewis Tappan, of New York, who said:

"We have been taught that there is nobility in nature as well as in birth, and it is to that nobility that I appeal when I invoke *the British nation to aid in the emancipation of slaves on the American continent!*

"It was stated in this Convention yesterday that a deputation of gentlemen had had an interview with Lord Aberdeen on this subject. He received the deputation with great kindness, and assured them that although the treaty entered into with Texas would be respected as much as a treaty with Spain, *yet so far as this nation [England] was concerned, no effort would be spared to effectuate the emancipation of the slaves.* In the view of these facts, I will state what it is that we want. Your Lordship [Lord Morpeth], in your opening address, put it to the American delegates to say, how long the United States would allow this state of things to exist in that nation. My reply is, till *Great Britain* shall step forward and use her moral influence in putting down slavery in Texas, *in the United States,* and throughout the world. May I not say in conclusion, that the brilliant reign of Elizabeth will be eclipsed by the still brighter and more brilliant reign of that youthful monarch who now sways the destinies of this empire."

Mr. Tappan further said that Mr. J. Q. Adams told him that it was the duty of the British Government to exert their influence to abolishing slavery in Texas, as a means of abolishing it in the United States, and speaking of the Annexation, said:

"The last hope of the slave will be extinguished if this union be effected. If, however, Texas is made a free State—and I do not believe it can be done

[80] *Anti-Slavery Reporter,* 4 (June 28, 1843), 120.

without the interposition of this [the English] nation—an everlasting barrier will be erected to the extension of this system. *Slavery will die out* and then we will come to London, or invite you to come to America to hold another World's Convention to celebrate the jubilee." [81]

These extracts show that the purpose of the abolitionists was to enlist the British Government in the effort to abolish slavery in Texas as a means of abolishing it in the United States; that Lord Aberdeen did promise to aid them and with that view. He says that the means by which he endeavored to accomplish it was those recommended by Mr. Tappan, to wit: to recommend to Mexico to make the abolition of slavery a condition on which Mexico is to acknowledge the independence of Texas.

But Mr. Benton says that Lord Aberdeen has disavowed the purpose attributed to the British Government, and that, therefore, the idea of British influence in Texas is a *pretext,* an invention, to give color to the movement for Annexation. The following is Lord Aberdeen's formal declaration delivered by Mr. Packenham to Mr. Calhoun:

"We are convinced that the recognition of Texas by Mexico must conduce to the benefit of both these countries, and as we take an interest in the well-being of both, and in their steady advance in power and wealth, we have put ourselves forward in pressing the Government of Mexico to acknowledge Texas as independent. But in thus acting we have no occult design, either with reference to any peculiar interest which we might seek to establish in Mexico or in Texas, or even with reference to the slavery which now exists, and which we desire to see abolished in Texas.

"With regard to the latter point, it must be and is well known both to the United States and to the whole world, that Great Britain desires, and is constantly exerting herself to procure, *the general abolition of slavery throughout the world*. But the means which she has adopted, and will continue to adopt, for this humane and virtuous purpose, are open and undisguised. She will do nothing secretly or underhanded. She desires that her motives may be generally understood, and her acts seen by all.

"With regard to Texas, we avow that we wish to see slavery abolished there, as elsewhere, and we would rejoice if the recognition of that country by the Mexican Government should be accompanied by an engagement on the part of Texas to abolish slavery eventually, and under proper conditions, throughout the Republic. But although we earnestly desire and feel it to be our duty to promote such a consummation, we shall not interfere unduly, or with an improper assumption of authority, with either party, in order to insure the adoption of such a course. We shall counsel, but we shall not seek to compel, or unduly control, either party. So far as Great Britain is concerned, provided other States act with equal forbearance, those governments will be fully at liberty to make their own unfettered arrangements with each other, both in regard to the abolition of slavery and in all other points.

"Great Britain, moreover, does not desire to establish in Texas, whether partially dependent on Mexico or entirely independent (which latter alterna-

---

[81] *Ibid.,* 120–1. Adams was skeptical of any overt British interference with slavery in Texas. See S. F. Bemis, *John Quincy Adams and the Union* (New York: Alfred A. Knopf, 1956), 464–71.

tive we consider in every respect preferable,) any dominant influence. She only desires to share her influence equally with all other nations. *Her objects are purely commercial,* and she has no thought or intention of seeking to act, directly or indirectly, in a political sense, on the United States through Texas." [82]

Here is the declaration of the purpose of interference, that the object is to abolish slavery, not only in Texas, but *throughout the world,* and that her objects are purely *commercial.* Now, by turning to the speeches of Sir Robert Peel, in the House of Commons, it will be seen that he says—"He must say that he had his doubts, if a colony in which slavery had been abolished by law could at present enter into successful competition with a district in which the system continues to exist"; and that he opposed a repeal of the discriminating duty on Brazilian sugar, on the ground that it was indispensable to the preservation of the British colonies, and as a means of abolishing slavery in the United States. His words on this latter point are so striking that I quote them. Speaking of the effort to induce Brazil to abolish slavery, he said—"Make the attempt—try to get concessions from those from whom you get your supply. Those countries themselves are in a peculiar position. They might depend on it that there was a growing conviction among the people of those countries that slavery was not unaccompanied by great dangers. In Cuba, in the United States, in the Brazils, there was a ferment on the subject of slavery which was spreading and would spread. Some from humane and benevolent motives—some on account of interested fears, began to look at the great example we had set, and had begun to look at the consequences that might result from that example nearer home. (Hear, hear) It was impossible to look to the discussions in the United States of America, and especially to the conflicts between Northern and Southern states, without seeing that slavery in that nation stood on a precarious footing." [83]

Yes, Sir, such was the motive assigned by the British Minister, for a measure which it was admitted on all hands, levied a tax of twenty-four millions of dollars per annum on the British public, not for the benefit of the British Treasury, but for the benefit of the West Indian negroes and proprietors, and why? Because, as Lord Aberdeen says, the objects of England are "purely commercial." She desires to abolish slavery throughout the world, as a means of extending her commerce, because she has ascertained that free labor cannot compete with slave labor in the cultivation of sugar, cotton and rice, and because, if she can abolish slavery in Cuba, Brazil, the United States and Texas, then she can produce these great staples in India cheaper than they can be raised elsewhere, and thus she will have accomplished her commercial supremacy, because, having achieved a monopoly of these articles of indispensable necessity, she can levy such contributions on all other nations, who must then depend on her for a supply, as her interests or her avarice may impose.

The question of abolishing slavery thus becomes truly, purely a commercial measure, and the most important commercial measure that ever agitated the public attention. The eyes of England and of the world will be

[82] Compare *British and Foreign State Papers, 1844–1845,* XXXIII, 232–3.
[83] *Hansard's,* 3rd ser., 63 (May–June, 1842), 1229.

arrested by it, and if the Congress of the United States, under Colonel Benton, shall on this occasion array themselves on the side of England, against the interests of their constituents, it will greatly encourage the British Government to persevere in her efforts, and prove they are so much engaged in the game of making Presidents, as to disregard every other consideration of public duty.

NATIONAL INTELLIGENCER

June 3, 1844 [84]

This series of papers forms a new and important, if not the *most* important chapter in the history of the negotiation of the "Treaty of Annexation" now before the Senate. We shall not enter at present into an inquiry *why* these papers have been so long kept back from the Senate, though so indispensable to the comprehension of the terms of the Treaty. What we should desire of the reader to note . . . is this; that it is now officially proven, beyond the probability of denial, that, as heretofore charged in this paper, conditions were exacted on the one hand and yielded on the other, by which the Government of the United States bound itself to the Government of Texas to take up arms for the protection of Texas against any movement on the part of Mexico; and that the agreement of the United States to these conditions was a *sine qua non* to the signature of the Treaty by the Commissioners of Texas.

It is circumstantially evident from these papers that a pledge to this effect was required from the United States before the commencement of the actual negotiation of the Treaty [See the Letter of Mr. Van Zandt to Secretary Upshur of January 17, 1844]—and that the required or desired pledge was then given, or promised to be given; but was given *orally,* and was therefore not to be found upon record in the Department of State, after the decease of Mr. Upshur.[85] The Commissioners of Texas, discovering this, and instructed apparently to require the stipulation or promise to be given in writing, addressed a letter, before the signature of the Treaty, to the Secretary of State (a copy of which letter, though an essential link in the chain of history, is *not* among the papers sent to the Senate) calling his attention to the letter of Mr. Van Zandt before referred to, and demanding an answer to it. That answer was given, as the reader will perceive, in the letter of the Secretary of State of the eleventh of April, and *on the twelfth,* the Commissioners, having obtained the written obligation from the Executive, and not before, placed their signatures to the Treaty.[86]

[84] *National Intelligencer,* June 3, 1844. This is an editorial comment on Tyler's message to the Senate of May 31, 1844, transmitting documents concerning promises of military or other aid to Texas in the event of an agreement on annexation.

[85] Van Zandt to Upshur, January 17, 1844, in *Sen. Doc.,* 28 Cong., 1 sess. (ser. 435), no. 349, 3. Upshur's oral response is reported in Van Zandt to Jones, January 20, 1844, in A.H.A. *Report,* 1908, II (1), 239–43.

[86] The *Intelligencer* was misinformed as to a written request for a military pledge sent to Calhoun by Van Zandt and Henderson. No written request was sent. But Calhoun was orally reminded of the note of Van Zandt to Upshur of January 17, and this was sufficient

Calhoun to King, August 12, 1844

JOHN C. CALHOUN TO WILLIAM R. KING

August 12, 1844 [87]

SIR: I have laid your despatch No. 1 before the President, who instructs me to make known to you that he has read it with much pleasure, especially the portion which relates to your cordial reception by the King, and his assurance of friendly feelings towards the United States. The President, in particular, highly appreciates the declaration of the King, that, in no event would any steps be taken by his Government in the slightest degree hostile, or which would give to the United States just cause of complaint. It was the more gratifying from the fact, that our previous information was calculated to make the impression that the Government of France was prepared to unite with Great Britain in a joint protest against the annexation of Texas, and a joint effort to induce her Government to withdraw the proposition to annex, on condition that Mexico should be made to acknowledge her independence. He is happy to infer, from your despatch, that the information, as far as it relates to France, is, in all probability, without foundation. You did not go further than you ought, in assuring the King that the object of annexation would be pursued with unabated vigor, and in giving your opinion that a decided majority of the American people were in its favor, and that it would certainly be annexed at no distant day. I feel confident that your anticipation will be fully realized at no distant period. Every day will tend to weaken that combination of political causes which led to the opposition to the measure, and to strengthen the conviction that it was not only expedient, but just and necessary.

You were right in making the distinction between the interest of France and England, in reference to Texas, or rather, I would say, the apparent interests of the two countries. France cannot possibly have any other than commercial interest in desiring to see her preserve her separate independence; while it is certain that England looks beyond, to political interests, to which she apparently attaches much importance. But, in our opinion, the interest of both against the measure is more apparent than real, and that neither France, England, nor even Mexico herself, has any in opposition to it, when the subject is fairly viewed, and considered in its whole extent and in all its bearings. Thus viewed and considered, and assuming that peace, the extension of commerce, and security, are objects of primary policy with them, it may, as it seems to me, be readily shown, that the policy on the part of those Powers which would acquiesce in a measure so strongly desired by both the United States and Texas, for their mutual welfare and safety, as the annexation of the latter to the former, would be far more promotive of these great objects than that which would attempt to resist it.

It is impossible to cast a look at the map of the United States and Texas, and to note the long, artificial, and inconvenient line which divides them,

---

to draw from him the written pledge of April 11, 1844. See Calhoun to Van Zandt and Henderson, *Sen. Doc.*, 28 Cong., 1 sess. (ser. 435), no. 349, 11; Calhoun to Tyler, June 4, 1844, *Sen. Doc.*, 28 Cong., 1 sess. (ser. 436), no. 361.

[87] *Sen Doc.*, 28 Cong., 2 sess. (ser. 449), no. 1, 39–47.

and then to take into consideration the extraordinary increase of population and growth of the former, and the source from which the latter must derive its inhabitants, institutions, and laws, without coming to the conclusion that it is their destiny to be united, and, of course, that annexation is merely a question of *time* and *mode*. Thus regarded, the question to be decided would seem to be, whether it would not be better to permit it to be done now, with the mutual consent of both parties, and the acquiescence of these Powers, than to attempt to resist and defeat it. If the former course be adopted, the certain fruits would be, the preservation of peace, great extension of commerce by the rapid settlement and improvement of Texas, and increased security, especially to Mexico. The last, in reference to Mexico, may be doubted, but I hold it not less clear than the other two.

It would be a great mistake to suppose that this Government has any hostile feelings towards Mexico, or any disposition to aggrandize itself at her expense. The fact is the very reverse. It wishes her well, and desires to see her settle down in peace and security; and is prepared, in the event of annexation of Texas, if not forced into conflict with her, to propose to settle with her the question of boundary, and all others growing out of the annexation, on the most liberal terms. Nature herself has clearly marked the boundary between her and Texas by natural limits too strong to be mistaken. There are few countries whose limits are so distinctly marked; and it would be our desire, if Texas should be united to us, to see them firmly established, as the most certain means of establishing permanent peace between the two countries, and strengthening and cementing their friendship.

Such would be the certain consequence of permitting the annexation to take place now, with the acquiescence of Mexico; but very different would be the case, if it should be attempted to resist and defeat it, whether the attempt should be successful for the present or not. Any attempt of the kind would, not improbably, lead to a conflict between us and Mexico, and involve consequences, in reference to her and the general peace, long to be deplored on all sides, and difficult to be repaired. But should that not be the case, and the interference of another Power defeat the annexation for the present, without the interruption of peace, it would but postpone the conflict, and render it more fierce and bloody whenever it might occur. Its defeat would be attributed to enmity and ambition on the part of that Power by whose interference it was occasioned, and excite deep jealousy and resentment on the part of our people, who would be ready to seize the first favorable opportunity to effect by force what was prevented from being done peaceably by mutual consent. It is not difficult to see how greatly such a conflict, come when it might, would endanger the general peace, and how much Mexico might be the loser by it.

In the mean time, the condition of Texas would be rendered uncertain, her settlement and prosperity in consequence retarded, and her commerce crippled, while the general peace would be rendered much more insecure. It could not but greatly affect us. If the annexation of Texas should be permitted to take place peaceably now, as it would without the interference of other Powers, the energies of our people would, for a long time to come, be directed to the peaceable pursuits of redeeming, and bringing within the pale of cultivation, improvement, and civilization, that large portion of the continent lying between Mexico on one side, and the British possessions on the other, which is now with little exception a wilderness, with a sparse population, consisting for the most part of wandering Indian tribes. It is our destiny to occupy that vast region, to intersect it with roads and canals, to fill it with cities, towns, villages, and farms, to extend over it our religion, customs, Constitution, and laws, and to present it as a peaceful and splendid addition to the domains of commerce and civilization. It is our policy to increase by growing and spreading out into unoccupied regions, assimilating all we incorporate. In a word, to increase by accretion, and not through conquest, by the addition of masses held together by the cohesion of force. No system can be more unsuited to the latter process, or better adapted to the former, than our admirable Federal system. If it should not be resisted in its course, it will probably fulfil its destiny, without disturbing our neighbors or putting in jeopardy the general peace; but if it be opposed by foreign interference, a new direction would be given to our energy, much less favorable to harmony with our neighbors and to the general peace of the world. The change would be undesirable to us, and much less in accord with what I have assumed to be primary objects of policy on the part of France, England, and Mexico.

But, to descend to particulars, it is certain, that while England, like France, desires the independence of Texas, with the view to commercial connexions, it is not less so that one of the leading motives of England for desiring it is the hope that, through her diplomacy and influence, negro slavery may be abolished there, and ultimately, by consequence, in the United States and throughout the whole of this continent. That its ultimate abolition throughout the entire continent is an object ardently desired by her, we have decisive proof in the declaration of the Earl of Aberdeen, delivered to this department, and of which you will find a copy among the documents transmitted to Congress with the Texan treaty; that she desires its abolition in Texas, and has used her influence and diplomacy to effect it there, the same document, with the correspondence of this department with Mr. Pakenham, also to be found among the documents, furnishes proof not less conclusive; that one of the objects of abolishing it there is to facilitate its abolition in the United States and throughout the continent, is manifest from the declaration of the abolition party and societies, both in this country and England. In fact, there is good reason to believe that the scheme of abolishing it in Texas, with the view to its abolition in the United States and over the continent, originated with the prominent members of the party in the United States, and was first broached by them in the so-called world's convention, held in London in the year 1840, and through its agency brought to the notice of the British Government.

Now, I hold not only that France can have no interest in the consummation of this grand scheme, which England hopes to accomplish through Texas if she can defeat the annexation, but that her interests, and those of all the continental Powers of Europe, are directly and deeply opposed to it.

It is too late in the day to contend that humanity or philanthropy is the great object of the policy of England in attempting to abolish African slavery on this continent. I do not question but humanity may have been one of her leading motives for the abolition of the African slave trade, and that it may have had a considerable influence in abolishing slavery in her West India possessions, aided, indeed, by the fallacious calculation, that the labor of the negroes would be at least as profitable, if not more so, in consequence of the measure. She acted on the principle, that tropical products can be produced cheaper by free African labor and East India labor than by slave labor. She knew full well the value of such products to her commerce, navigation, navy, manufactures, revenue, and power. She was not ignorant that the support and the maintenance of her political preponderance depended on her tropical possessions, and had no intention of diminishing their productiveness, nor any anticipation that such would be the effect, when the scheme of abolishing slavery in her colonial possessions was adopted. On the contrary, she calculated to combine philanthropy with profit and power, as is not unusual with fanaticism. Experience has convinced her of the fallacy of her calculations. She has failed in all her objects. The labor of her negroes has proved far less productive, without affording the consolation of having improved their condition.

The experiment has turned out to be a costly one. She expended nearly one hundred millions of dollars in indemnifying the owners of the emancipated slaves. It is estimated that the increased price paid since by the people of Great Britain for sugar and other tropical productions, in consequence of the measure, is equal to half that sum, and that twice that amount has been expended in the suppression of the slave trade—making, together, two hundred and fifty millions of dollars as the cost of the experiment. Instead of realizing her hope, the result has been a sad disappointment. Her tropical products have fallen off to a vast amount. Instead of supplying her own wants and those of nearly all Europe with them, as formerly, she has now, in some of the most important articles, scarcely enough to supply her own. What is worse, her own colonies are actually consuming sugar, produced by slave labor, brought direct to England, or refined in bond, and exported and sold in her colonies as cheap or cheaper than they can be produced there; while the slave trade, instead of diminishing, has been in fact carried on to a greater extent than ever. So disastrous has been the result, that her fixed capital vested in tropical possessions, estimated at the value of nearly five hundred millions of dollars, is said to stand on the brink of ruin.

But this is not the worst. While this costly scheme has had such ruinous effects on the tropical productions of Great Britain, it has given a powerful stimulus, followed by a corresponding increase of products, to those countries which have had the good sense to shun her example. There has been vested, it is estimated by them, in the production of tropical products, since 1808, in fixed capital, nearly four thousand millions of dollars, wholly dependent on slave labor. In the same period, the value of their products has been estimated to have risen from about seventy-two millions of dollars annually, to nearly two hundred and twenty millions, while the whole of the fixed capital of Great Britain vested in cultivating tropical products, both in the East and West Indies, is estimated at only about eight hundred and thirty millions of dollars, and the value of the products annually at about fifty millions of dollars. To present a still more striking view: of three articles of tropical products—sugar, coffee, and cotton—the British possessions, including the West and East Indies and Mauritius, produced, in 1842, of sugar, only 3,993,771 pounds, while Cuba, Brazil, and the United States, excluding other countries having tropical possessions, produced 9,600,000 pounds; of coffee, the British possessions produced only 27,393,003, while Cuba and Brazil produced 201,595,125 pounds; and of cotton, the British possessions, including shipments to China, only 137,443,446 pounds, while the United States alone produced 790,479,275 pounds.

The above facts and estimates have all been drawn from a British periodical of high standing and authority,* and are believed to be entitled to credit. This vast increase of capital and production on the part of those nations who have continued their former policy towards the negro race, compared with that of Great Britain, indicates a corresponding relative increase of the means of commerce, navigation, manufactures, wealth, and power. It is no longer a question of doubt, that the great source of the wealth, prosperity, and power, of the more civilized nations of the temperate zone, especially Europe, where the arts have made the greatest advance, depends in a great degree on the exchange of their products with those of the tropical regions. So great has been the advance made in the arts, both chemical and mechanical, within the few last generations, that all the old civilized nations can, with but a small part of their labor and capital, supply their respective wants, which tends to limit within narrow bounds the amount of the commerce between them, and forces them all to seek for markets in the tropical regions and the more newly settled portions of the globe. Those who can best succeed in commanding those markets have the best prospect of outstripping the others in the career of commerce, navigation, manufactures, wealth, and power.

This is seen and felt by British statesmen, and has opened their eyes to the errors which they have committed. The question now with them is, how shall it be counteracted? What has been done cannot be undone. The question is, by what means can Great Britain regain and keep a superiority in tropical cultivation, commerce, and influence? Or shall that be abandoned, and other nations be suffered to acquire the supremacy, even to the extent of supplying British markets, to the destruction of the capital already vested in their production? These are the questions which now profoundly occupy the attention of her statesmen, and have the greatest influence over her councils.

In order to regain her superiority, she not only seeks to revive and increase her own capacity to produce tropical productions, but to diminish and destroy the capacity of those who have so far outstripped her in consequence of her error. In pursuit of the former, she has cast her eyes to her

---

* Blackwood's Magazine for June, 1844.

East India possessions, to Central and Eastern Africa, with the view of establishing colonies there, and even to restore, substantially, the slave trade itself, under the specious name of transporting free laborers from Africa to her West India possessions, in order, if possible, to compete successfully with those who have refused to follow her suicidal policy. But these all afford but uncertain and distant hopes of recovering her lost superiority. Her main reliance is on the other alternative, to cripple or destroy the productions of her successful rivals. There is but one way by which it can be done, and that is by abolishing African slavery throughout this continent; and that she openly avows to be the constant object of her policy and exertions. It matters not how or for what motive it may be done, whether it be by diplomacy, influence, or force—by secret or open means; and, whether the motive be humane or selfish, without regard to manner, means, or motive, the thing itself, should it be accomplished, would put down all rivalry, and give her the undisputed supremacy in supplying her own wants and those of the rest of the world, and thereby more than fully retrieve what she has lost by her errors. It would give her the monopoly of tropical productions, which I shall next proceed to show.

What would be the consequence, if this object of her unceasing solicitude and exertions should be effected by the abolition of negro slavery throughout this continent, some idea may be formed from the immense diminution of productions, as has been shown, which has followed abolition in her West India possessions. But, as great as that has been, it is nothing compared to what would be the effect, if she should succeed in abolishing slavery in the United States, Cuba, Brazil, and throughout this continent. The experiment in her own colonies was made under the most favorable circumstances. It was brought about gradually and peaceably, by the steady and firm operation of the parent country, armed with complete power to prevent or crush at once all insurrectionary movements on the part of the negroes, and able and disposed to maintain to the full the political and social ascendency of their former masters over their former slaves. It is not at all wonderful that the change of the relations of master and slave took place under such circumstances without violence and bloodshed, and that order and peace should have been since preserved. Very different would be the result of abolition, should it be effected by her influence and exertions, in the possessions of other countries on this continent, and especially in the United States, Cuba, and Brazil, the great cultivators of the principal tropical productions of America. To form a correct conception of what would be the result with them, we must look not to Jamaica, but to St. Domingo, for an example. The change would be followed by unforgiving hate between the two races, and end in a bloody and deadly struggle between them for the superiority. One or the other would have to be subjugated, extirpated, or expelled, and desolation would overspread their territories, as in St. Domingo, from which it would take centuries to recover. The end would be, that the superiority in cultivating the great tropical staples would be transferred from them to the British tropical possessions.

They are of vast extent, and those beyond the Cape of Good Hope possessed of an unlimited amount of labor, standing ready, by the aid of British capital, to supply the deficit which would be occasioned by destroying the tropical productions of the United States, Cuba, Brazil, and other countries, cultivated by slave labor on this continent, so soon as this increased price, in consequence, would yield a profit. It is the successful competition of that labor which keeps the prices of the great tropical staples so low as to prevent their cultivation with profit, in the possessions of Great Britain, by what she is pleased to call free labor. If she can destroy its competition, she would have a monopoly in those productions. She has all the means of furnishing an unlimited supply, vast and fertile possessions in both Indies, boundless command of capital and labor, and ample power to suppress disturbances and preserve order throughout her wide domains.

It is unquestionable that she regards the abolition of slavery in Texas as a most important step towards this great object of policy, so much the aim of her solicitude and exertions, and the defeat of the annexation of Texas to our Union as indispensable to the abolition of slavery there. She is too sagacious not to see what a fatal blow it would give to slavery in the United States, and how certainly its abolition with us would abolish it over the whole continent, and thereby give her a monopoly in the productions of the great tropical staples, and the command of the commerce, navigation, and manufactures of the world, with an established naval ascendency and political preponderance. To this continent the blow would be calamitous beyond description. It would destroy, in a great measure, the cultivation and production of the great tropical staples, amounting annually in value to nearly three hundred millions of dollars—the fund which stimulates and upholds almost every other branch of its industry, commerce, navigation, and manufactures. The whole, by their joint influence, are rapidly spreading population, wealth, improvement, and civilization, over the whole continent, and vivifying by their overflow the industry of Europe, thereby increasing its population, wealth, and advancement in the arts, in power, and civilization.

Such must be the result, should Great Britain succeed in accomplishing the constant object of her desire and exertions—the abolition of negro slavery over this continent— and towards the effecting of which she regards the defeat of the annexation of Texas to our Union so important. Can it be possible that Governments so enlightened and sagacious as those of France and the other great continental Powers can be so blinded by the plea of philanthropy as not to see what must inevitably follow, be her motive what it may, should she succeed in her object? It is little short of mockery to talk of philanthropy, with the examples before us of the effects of abolishing negro slavery in her own colonies, in St. Domingo, and the Northern States of our Union, where statistical facts, not to be shaken, prove that the freed negro, after the experience of sixty years, is in a far worse condition than in the other States, where he has been left in his former condition. No; the effect of what is called abolition, where the number is few, is not to raise the inferior race to the condition of freemen, but to deprive the negro of the guardian care of his owner, subject to all the depression and oppression belonging to his inferior condition. But, on the other hand, where the number is great, and bears a large proportion to the whole population, it would be still worse. It would be to substitute for the existing relation a deadly strife between the two races, to end in subjection, expulsion, or extirpation of one or the other; and such would be the case over the greater part of this continent where negro slavery exists. It would not end there, but would, in all probability, extend, by its example, the war of races over all South America, including Mexico, and extending to the Indian as well as to the African race, and make the whole one scene of blood and devastation.

Dismissing, then, the stale and unfounded plea of philanthropy, can it be that France and the other great continental Powers, seeing what must be the result of the policy for the accomplishment of which England is constantly exerting herself, and that the defeat of the annexation of Texas is so important towards its consummation, are prepared to back or countenance her in her efforts to effect either? What possible motives can they have to favor her cherished policy? Is it not better for them that they should be supplied with tropical products, in exchange for their labor, from the United States, Brazil, Cuba, and this continent generally, than to be dependent on one great monopolizing Power for their supply? Is it not better that they should receive them at the low prices which competition, cheaper means of production, and nearness of market, would furnish them by the former, than to give the high prices which monopoly, dear labor, and great distance from market, would impose? Is it not better that their labor should be exchanged with a new continent, rapidly increasing in population and the capacity for consuming, and which would furnish, in the course of a few generations, a market nearer to them, and of almost unlimited extent, for the products of their industry and arts, than with old and distant regions, whose population has long since reached its growth?

The above contains those enlarged views of policy which, it seems to me, an enlightened European statesman ought to take in making up his opinion on the subject of the annexation of Texas, and the grounds, as it may be inferred, on which England vainly opposes it. They certainly involve considerations of the deepest importance, and demanding the greatest attention. Viewed in connexion with them, the question of annexation becomes one of the first magnitude, not only to Texas and the United States, but to this continent and Europe. They are presented, that you may use them on all suitable occasions where you think they may be with effect, in your correspondence (where it can be done with propriety) or otherwise. The President relies with confidence on your sagacity, prudence, and zeal. Your mission is one of the first magnitude at all times but especially now; and he feels assured nothing will be left undone on your part to do justice to the country and the Government in reference to this great measure.

I have said nothing as to our right of treating with Texas without consulting Mexico; you so fully understand the grounds on which we rest our right, and are so familiar with all the facts necessary to maintain them, that it was not thought necessary to add any thing in reference to it.

I am, sir, very respectfully,
your obedient servant,

Joint Resolution for annexing Texas, March 1, 1845

JOINT RESOLUTION FOR ANNEXING TEXAS TO THE UNITED STATES

March 1, 1845 [88]

Resolved by the Senate and House of Representatives of the United States of America in Congress assembled, That Congress doth consent that the territory properly included within, and rightfully belonging to the Republic of Texas, may be erected into a new State, to be called the State of Texas, with a republican form of government, to be adopted by the people of said republic, by deputies in convention assembled, with the consent of the existing government, in order that the same may be admitted as one of the States of this Union.

2. *And be it further resolved,* That the foregoing consent of Congress is given upon the following conditions, and with the following guarantees, to wit: *First,* Said State to be formed, subject to the adjustment by this government of all questions of boundary that may arise with other governments; and the constitution thereof, with the proper evidence of its adoption by the people of said Republic of Texas, shall be transmitted to the President of the United States, to be laid before Congress for its final action, on or before the first day of January, one thousand eight hundred and forty-six. *Second,* Said State, when admitted into the Union, after ceding to the United States, all public edifices, fortifications, barracks, ports and harbors, navy and navy-yards, docks, magazines, arms, armaments, and all other property and means pertaining to the public defence belonging to said Republic of Texas, shall retain all the public funds, debts, taxes, and dues of every kind, which may belong to or be due and owing said republic; and shall also retain all the vacant and unappropriated lands lying within its limits, to be applied to the payment of the debts and liabilities of said Republic of Texas, and the residue of said lands, after discharging said debts and liabilities, to be disposed of as said State may direct; but in no event are said debts and liabilities to become a charge upon the Government of the United States. *Third,* New States, of convenient size, not exceeding four in number, in addition to said State of Texas, and having sufficient population, may hereafter, by the consent of said State, be formed out of the territory thereof, which shall be entitled to admission under the provisions of the federal constitution. And such States as may be formed out of that portion of said territory lying south of thirty-six degrees thirty minutes north latitude, commonly known as the Missouri compromise line, shall be admitted into the Union with or without slavery, as the people of each State asking admission may desire. And in such State or States as shall be formed out of said territory north of said Missouri compromise line, slavery, or involuntary servitude, (except for crime,) shall be prohibited.

3. *And be it further resolved,* That if the President of the United States shall in his judgment and discretion deem it most advisable, instead of proceeding to submit the foregoing resolution to the Republic of Texas, as an

---

[88] *U.S. Statutes at Large,* V (1836–45), 797–8.

overture on the part of the United States for admission, to negotiate with that Republic; then,

Be it resolved, That a State, to be formed out of the present Republic of Texas, with suitable extent and boundaries, and with two representatives in Congress, until the next apportionment of representation, shall be admitted into the Union, by virtue of this act, on an equal footing with the existing States, as soon as the terms and conditions of such admission, and the cession of the remaining Texian territory to the United States shall be agreed upon by the Governments of Texas and the United States: And that the sum of one hundred thousand dollars be, and the same is hereby, appropriated to defray the expenses of missions and negotiations, to agree upon the terms of said admission and cession, either by treaty to be submitted to the Senate, or by articles to be submitted to the two houses of Congress, as the President may direct.

Index

For private correspondence, runningheads in the "Documents" section (pages 183 ff.) are a useful supplement to this index.

Index

Index

Index

Index

Index

Index

A Note About the Author

FREDERICK MERK is Gurney Professor of American History (Emeritus) at Harvard University, where he taught for thirty-nine years. Born in Milwaukee, Wisconsin, he took his A.B. degree at the University of Wisconsin and his Ph.D. degree at Harvard in 1920. He served on the editorial staff of the Wisconsin State Historical Society for five years, and there he developed an interest in American frontier history through writing his *Economic History of Wisconsin During the Civil War Decade* (1916). This interest brought him to Harvard—to the great historian of the American frontier, Frederick Jackson Turner. He was associated with Professor Turner in revising the *List of References on the History of the West* (1922) and became his successor in teaching the Harvard course on the American westward movement.

Professor Merk's other books include *Fur Trade and Empire: George Simpson's Journal* (1931), *Albert Gallatin and the Oregon Problem* (1950), *Manifest Destiny and Mission in American History* (1963), and *The Monroe Doctrine and American Expansionism, 1843–1849* (1966). He is co-author of the *Harvard Guide to American History* (1954) and has contributed numerous articles to historical reviews, including a series on the Oregon Question. He is a former president of the Agricultural History Society and the Organization of American Historians. Holder of a Litt.D. from Harvard, he is a member of the Massachusetts Historical Society and the American Antiquarian Society and is a fellow of the American Academy of Arts and Sciences.

A Note on the Type

The text of this book was set on the Linotype in a face called Times Roman, designed by Stanley Morison for *The Times* (London) and first introduced by that newspaper in 1932.

Among typographers and designers of the twentieth century, Stanley Morison has been a strong forming influence, as typographical adviser to the English Monotype Corporation, as a director of two distinguished English publishing houses, and as a writer of sensibility, erudition, and keen practical sense.

This book was composed, printed, and bound
by The Haddon Craftsmen, Scranton, Pennsylvania.